During the first two centuries CE there was a common awareness that familial tensions were generated by conversions to the Christian faith. Yet studies of Christian origins have so far paid little attention to the impact of the Christian movement upon attitudes to family ties and natural kinship. Stephen C. Barton remedies this deficiency by means of a detailed study of the relevant passages in the Gospels of Mark and Matthew. First, however, he examines the religious traditions of Judaism and the philosophical traditions of the Greco-Roman world, and shows that the tensions apparent within the Christian movement were by no means unique. In all three areas of thought and practice there is found the conviction that familial duty may be transcended by some higher philosophical or religious obligation. Mark and Matthew saw the Jesus movement as offering a transcendent allegiance, which relativized family ties and created the possibility of a new personal identity, based on association with Jesus himself and his community of disciples.

SOCIETY FOR NEW TESTAMENT STUDIES

MONOGRAPH SERIES

General Editor: Margaret E. Thrall

80

DISCIPLESHIP AND FAMILY TIES IN MARK
AND MATTHEW

Discipleship and Family Ties in Mark and Matthew

STEPHEN C. BARTON
Lecturer in New Testament
University of Durham

 **CAMBRIDGE**
UNIVERSITY PRESS

Published by the Press Syndicate of the University of Cambridge
The Pitt Building, Trumpington Street, Cambridge CB2 1RP
40 West 20th Street, New York, NY 10011–4211, USA
10 Stamford Road, Oakleigh, Melbourne 3166, Australia

First published 1994

Printed in Great Britain at the University Press, Cambridge

A catalogue record for this book is available from the British Library

Library of Congress cataloguing in publication data

Barton, Stephen C.
   Discipleship and family ties in Mark and Matthew / Stephen C. Barton.
      p.   cm. – (Monograph series / Society for New Testament Studies:
80)
   Revision of the author's thesis (doctoral) – King's College, University of
London, 1991.
   Includes bibliographical references and indexes.
   ISBN 0 521 46530 3 (hardback)
1. Bible. N.T. Mark – Criticism, interpretation, etc.
2. Bible. N.T. Matthew – Criticism, interpretation, etc.
3. Jesus Christ – Views on the family.
4. Christian life – Biblical teaching. 5. Jesus Christ – Family.
I. Title. II. Series: Monograph series (Society for
New Testament Studies): 80.
BS2585.2.B38   1994
222'.206 – dc20   93–46383   CIP

ISBN 0 521 46530 3 hardback

CE

To Fiona
and to our children
Anna, Thomas, Joseph and Miriam

CONTENTS

PREFACE

This study is a revised version of my doctoral thesis submitted to King's College London in October 1991. It was examined by Professors Leslie Houlden and John Riches, to both of whom I am much indebted for their encouraging reception of the thesis and their helpful comments. The birth of a study such as this, especially when the period of gestation has been some twelve years, brings with it many debts of gratitude. I should like to acknowledge some of those here.

My interest in social aspects of earliest Christianity goes back to my days as an undergraduate and early postgraduate at Macquarie University in Sydney, under the instruction and supervision of Robert Banks and Edwin Judge. They introduced me especially to the world of Paul. At Lancaster University, in the Religious Studies Department, David Catchpole initiated me into the traditio-historical study of the gospels. Under his supervision I wrote a short dissertation on 'Discipleship, Family Ties and Jesus of Nazareth in the Synoptic Tradition', which became the genesis of the present work. Then at King's College London, Graham Stanton became my supervisor and mentor. With great patience, he has nurtured my work, allowed me to develop my own style, and provided unfailing encouragement. For instruction in the social sciences, especially the anthropology of religion, I am indebted to Nancy Lindisfarne of the School of Oriental and African Studies in the University of London.

Since leaving King's in 1982, I have enjoyed the support of a number of institutions and the colleagues there. First, in the Religious Studies Department of the West Sussex Institute of Higher Education and at Chichester Theological College, where I taught part-time. Then at Salisbury and Wells Theological College from 1984 to 1988, during which years I was given time (and financial support from the Sarum St Michael Trust) to continue my research using the excellent facilities of Tyndale House, Cambridge. Finally, since coming to the Theology Department of the University of Durham, I have had not only great encouragement to complete this study, but also the support and practical help of Ann Loades, who as departmental head at the time made possible my sabbatical leave in 1991, and of my colleagues in biblical studies, especially Jimmy Dunn, Sandy Wedderburn and Walter Moberly. Among other friends and colleagues who have helped and supported me over these years of research and teaching, I should like also to thank: Colin Hickling and Sophie Laws (both formerly of King's College London), Sue Martin (also of London), Bill Gray (of Chichester), Reginald Askew, Trevor Dennis and Ruth Siddals (Salisbury), Erin White and Graham English (Sydney), and Robert and Julie Banks (now of Pasadena). One of my postgraduate students, Derek Tovey, has given invaluable assistance in the preparation of the manuscript for publication.

It has not been lost on me that there is a certain irony in writing about the subordination of family ties in earliest Christianity when my own family has had to bear so much of the cost. I should like therefore to record here my deep gratitude to my father (now deceased) and mother, George and Nancy Barton. The book is dedicated to my wife, Fiona, and to our children, Anna, Thomas, Joseph and Miriam.

ABBREVIATIONS

In general, the conventions followed for the abbreviation of the titles of journals and reference works are those of the *Journal of Biblical Literature*, 107 (1988), 579–96. In addition, note the following:

KTR   *King's Theological Review*
JTSA *Journal of Theology for Southern Africa*
PIBA *Proceedings of the Irish Biblical Association*

1

INTRODUCTION

1 Religious allegiance and the subordination of family ties

And though they take our life,
Goods, honour, children, wife,
Yet is their profit small;
These things shall vanish all,
The city of God remaineth.

These words from the final verse of Luther's famous hymn[1] are a
rhetorically powerful reminder of an aspect of religious allegiance
and devotion which has been characteristic of Christian belonging
from the beginning: that loyalty to God and discipleship of Christ
are commitments of a transcendent kind which take priority over
the closest of mundane ties, even ties of natural kinship. The aim of
this study is to demonstrate and explain the importance of this
element in the teaching about discipleship of Jesus in the Gospels of
Mark and Matthew.

2 The tensions illustrated against a wider historical background

That following Jesus or conversion to the Christian way commonly
generated intra-familial tensions and competition for the allegiance
of the believer cannot be doubted. A brief survey of evidence from
the first two centuries of the Common Era will show both the
pervasiveness and the persistence of supra-familial and (what
could be seen as) even anti-familial tendencies in early Christianity.

---

[1] Martin Luther (1483–1546), 'Ein feste Burg ist unser Gott', based on Psalm 46
and written c. 1527–28; translated by Thomas Carlyle, extract from verse 4. The
hymn was sung in the Chapel of King's College London at the service for the
opening of the Easter Term, on Wednesday 28 April 1982.

Significantly, it is a matter which attracted comment from both insiders and outsiders.

The response of outsiders

a. The hostile comment of the Roman historian Tacitus on proselytes to Judaism reflects quite accurately the fears of outsiders generally about the effect of religious conversion upon family ties.[2] Tacitus states: 'Those who come over to their religion ... have this lesson first instilled into them, to despise all gods, to disown their country, and set at nought parents, children, and brethren.'[3] Noticeable here is the assumption about the strength of the bond between cult, polity and household, leading to the inevitable conclusion that transfer of allegiance to the exclusive cult of the Jews places political and domestic ties under direct threat. It comes as no surprise, therefore, that, in describing the persecution of the Christians in Rome by Nero at the time of the fire of 64 CE, Tacitus says that they were convicted, 'not so much of the crime of firing the city, as of hatred against mankind (*odio humani generis*)'.[4] This refers to the Christians' contumacious refusal to worship any god but their own, an exclusiveness described by the Greeks as 'atheism' and which was seen by the Romans as a direct threat to the *ordo pax deorum* and to their religious, civic and domestic institutions.

b. The report of Pliny the Younger to Trajan concerning the Christians he examined in the Asian province of Bithynia in the early second century reflects similar sentiments: 'I could discover nothing more than depraved and excessive superstition (*quam superstitionem pravam, immodicam*)'.[5] Although Pliny makes no explicit comment about the effect of conversion on family ties, he does express a concern at the rapid spread of the cult among persons both young and old, both men and women, among persons of varying social status, and among the rural districts as well as in the city. Such categories have an obvious household dimension; and it is

---

[2] The focus of anxiety in pagan sources has to do often with the apparent attraction to women (and therefore, wives) of cults from the East. See on this, Balch, *Wives*, ch. V; also, MacDonald, 'Women'.

[3] *History* V.5. All quotations from Tacitus are from Hadas, *Tacitus*.

[4] *Annals* XV.44.

[5] *Epistles* X.96.

clear that Pliny sees himself as a guardian of traditional loyalties in the domestic as well as in the political and cultic sphere.

c. Shortly after witnessing the self-immolation of the Cynic philosopher Peregrinus at Olympia in 165 CE, the pagan essayist Lucian wrote a satirical account of his life and death, seeking to expose him as a fraud.[6] According to Lucian, the early career of Peregrinus was spent as a Christian living among Christian circles in Palestine and being imprisoned as a result. Lucian gives, in passing, significant testimony to the life of the Palestinian Christians who provide Peregrinus with sustenance during his incarceration. Significant for our purpose is the fact that Lucian not only levels the common charge of 'atheism' against them, but he also links this with two observations about their common life which have a clear household dimension. First, he says that 'their first lawgiver persuaded them that they are all brothers of one another (ὡς ἀδελφοὶ πάντες εἶεν ἀλλήλων)'. Second, he says that they practise community of goods, some of which, of course, they share with Peregrinus.[7] This practice of brotherhood and community of goods is something which Lucian quite evidently despises and scorns.

d. Another outsider sensitive to the social implications of conversion is Celsus, writing in either Rome or Alexandria around 177–80 CE.[8] According to Celsus, the spread of Christian teaching and adherence to the new doctrine are subversive of patriarchal authority and household ties. What he is quoted as saying is worth repeating here at length:

> In private houses also we see wool-workers, cobblers, laundry-workers, and the most illiterate and bucolic yokels, who would not dare to say anything at all in front of their elders and more intelligent masters. But whenever they get hold of children in private and some stupid women with them, they let out some astounding statements as, for example, that they must not pay any attention to their father and school-teachers, but must obey them; they say

---

[6] I am using the Loeb translation of Lucian's *The Passing of Peregrinus*. I owe the reference to Smith, *Magician*, 56.

[7] *Peregrinus*, 13.

[8] See Chadwick, *Origen*, xxviii–xxix. I have used Chadwick's translation.

that these talk nonsense and have no understanding, and that in reality they neither know nor are able to do anything good, but are taken up with mere empty chatter. But they alone, they say, know the right way to live, and if the children would believe them, they would become happy and make their home happy as well. And if just as they are speaking they see one of the school-teachers coming, or some intelligent person, or even the father himself, the more cautious of them flee in all directions; but the more reckless urge the children on to rebel. They whisper to them that in the presence of their father and their schoolmasters they do not feel able to explain anything to the children, since they do not want to have anything to do with the silly and obtuse teachers who are totally corrupted and far gone in wickedness and inflict punishment on the children. But, if they like, they should leave father and their school-teachers, and go along with the women and little children who are their playfellows to the wooldresser's shop or to the cobbler's or the washerwoman's shop, that they may learn perfection. And by saying this they persuade them.[9]

The accuracy of Celsus' claim is difficult to assess, even allowing for the polemical stance of his work. But our concern is with perceptions as much as with raw facts; and it is clear that Celsus perceives adherence to Christ as a strong threat to the network of ties and obligations which constitute a household. As Harnack points out,[10] Origen's reply does not deny that the new doctrine affects family ties: Origen claims instead that the children and women attracted to it are all the better for it.[11]

The response of insiders

The conflict of loyalties to which the observers and critics of the early Christians drew attention was expressed also by the believers

[9] *Contra Celsum* III.55.
[10] Harnack, *Mission*, 396.
[11] See further, Wilken, *Christians*, esp. 117–25, where the author discusses Celsus' conservative concern about the seditious and revolutionary implications of Christian doctrine and proselytizing generally. On p. 125, Wilken concludes: 'It was, however, not simply that Christians subverted the cities by refusing to participate in civic life, but that they undermined the foundations of the societies in which they lived. By elevating the founder of their society to divine status, they set up a rival to the one high God who watched over the empire.'

themselves. The implications of conversion for kinship ties, marital arrangements and household duties is a recurring theme in the Christian sources of the first two centuries. A number of texts, in particular, give evidence of tensions between marriage partners when one partner, often the woman, converted.

a. Perhaps the earliest literary evidence comes from the letters of Paul: in particular, 1 Corinthians 7. Here, Paul addresses matters raised explicitly by (some of) the Corinthians in correspondence with him: Περὶ δὲ ὧν ἐγράψατε ... (7.1a). From what Paul says – and without going into a detailed analysis[12] – we can make the following inferences. First, Paul himself prefers the single, celibate state (7.7a, 8, 28b, 32, 38);[13] and the general upshot of what he says about marriage is that he deprecates it (7.25–31, 32–5, 36–8).[14] This position is rooted in Paul's theological convictions concerning the imminence of the End-time[15] and the transience of this-worldly orders of relationship, together with his strong sense of vocation to single-minded devotion to the Lord. Perhaps, too, he interpreted his celibacy as an aspect of his practice of the *imitatio Christi* (see 1 Cor. 11.1). Whatever the reasons, 1 Cor. 7 provides clear evidence of the eschatological relativization of marital and household ties in the thought and practice of Paul.

Second, some Corinthian converts are interpreting the doctrine of the new creation in Christ (2 Cor. 5.17) in an explicitly ascetic direction, in accord with the slogan which Paul quotes, καλὸν ἀνθρώπῳ γυναικὸς μὴ ἅπτεσθαι (1 Cor. 7.1b). Paul's concern that the consequent practice of sexual renunciation might subvert marital ties is apparent in his carefully balanced response in favour of sexual reciprocity between marriage partners. Neither the

---

[12] The literature is enormous. Chadwick's essay of 1954, '"All Things"', is seminal. I discussed this material also in my BA Hons. dissertation of 1975: Barton, 'Accommodation', 38–46. Most recently, see Yarbrough, *Gentiles*, ch. 4, and the works cited there.
[13] See Paul's claim in 1 Cor. 9.5 to travel unaccompanied by 'a sister as wife', unlike Cephas and the brothers of the Lord.
[14] Yarbrough, *Gentiles*, 101, 107, puts it succinctly: 'Four times in vv 8–40 Paul addresses the question of believers' marrying and in each instance he argues against it ... It is striking that the only reason Paul gives in favor of marriage is the danger of sexual immorality.' On the close Stoic analogies, see Balch, 'Debates'.
[15] For traditional apocalyptic warnings against marriage and child-birth in the Last Days, cf. 4 Ezra 5.8; 6.12; 1 Enoch 99.5; and Mark 13.17, cited in Yarbrough, *Gentiles*, 103.

husband nor the wife is to withdraw from sexual relations, except by
mutual consent and then only for a limited time and for a specifically religious purpose (7.2–5). Furthermore, divorce between Christian partners is ruled out, by an exceptional appeal to a command of
the Lord (7.10–11).

Third, it is evidently the case that conversion in Corinth has not
taken place always by household. Sometimes a husband only has
converted, sometimes only a wife. Once more, the threat to social –
and, in particular, domestic – stability becomes an issue, and Paul
advises the converted partner not to initiate divorce (7.12–16). If the
unbelieving partner seeks a divorce, the preservation of the marriage is not to be sought at any cost; but 'God has called you to
peace' (7.15c), the implication being that remaining with the pagan
partner may lead to his/her salvation (7.16).[16]

In general, Paul urges that his addressees 'remain in whatever
state each was called' (7.24). This socially conservative advice
clearly reflects a concern on Paul's part about the dangers of social
innovation, particularly in the sphere of marital and household ties.
The behaviour of certain converts in Corinth must have given
grounds for Paul's concern. But this behaviour may itself have been
a response to Paul's eschatological doctrine of new creation and of
freedom in the Spirit.[17]

b. The New Testament *Haustafeln* should be mentioned
next as evidence of a concern about the detrimental effects of
conversion to Christianity upon household ties. 1 Peter is a good
case in point. David Balch has argued persuasively that the domestic
code in 1 Pet. 2.18–3.7 has a primarily apologetic function and is
intended to counter the slanderous accusations of outsiders that
Christianity is socially subversive because of the threat conversion
poses to household solidarity:[18]

> Greco-Roman society suspected and criticized foreign
> religions. Many of the Christians addressed by the author
> had rejected traditional religion (1.18b), and the author
> exhorted Christians to the kind of behaviour that would
> silence the negative reactions which such conversions

16 So too, Yarbrough, *Gentiles*, 112.
17 See Meeks, 'Androgyne'.
18 Balch, *Wives*; see also his summary of recent scholarly interpretation of the
    Haustafeln, in his 'Codes', 25–50. For a different understanding of the function
    of the household code in 1 Peter, see Elliott, *Home*.

generated (2.11–12, 15). The stress on 'harmony' in the
conclusion of the code (3.8) reveals that the author was
especially concerned about divided households: many
masters and husbands were still pagans while some slaves
and wives had converted to Christianity. In these divided
houses, the harmony demanded by the Hellenistic moralists
had been disturbed, which was judged to be a negative
reflection on the new religion. The author exhorts his
readers to make a 'defense' (3.15) by reassuring the masters
and husbands, perhaps even the governor, that they are
obedient slaves and wives, just as the culture expected them
to be.[19]

c. Moving beyond the evidence of the New Testament,
Justin begins his *Second Apology* by recounting a case of marital
breakdown resulting from the conversion of one of the partners and
trying to defend the action of the woman in seeking to divorce her
husband: 'But he, continuing in the same excesses, alienated his wife
from him by his actions. For she, considering it wicked to live any
longer as a wife with a husband who sought in every way means of
indulging in pleasure contrary to the laws of nature, and in violation
of what is right, wished to be divorced from him.'[20]
The notoriety of this case is due, no doubt, to the social location
of the couple concerned. They are members of the Roman aristoc-
racy, with access to the emperor, a large household, leisure and
finances to undertake travel, and means to patronize wandering
philosophers like Ptolemaeus the Christian, by whose teaching and
example the woman is won over. Here, then, is something of a *cause
célèbre* which leads to the intervention of the city prefect Urbicus
and comes to the attention of the senate. Clearly, the marital
breakdown precipitated by the woman's conversion is perceived as
having wider social and political repercussions, a perception based
on the fundamental assumption of the time that the household is the
state in microcosm.[21]

19 Balch, *Wives*, 109.
20 *Apology* II.2 (translation from A. Roberts and J. Donaldson, eds., *The Ante-
Nicene Fathers*, vol. I, 188). I owe this reference to Yarbrough, *Gentiles*, 1.
21 A classic expression of this assumption comes in Cicero's *De Beneficiis* I.53–5
(written c. 46 BCE). At I.54, Cicero states: 'Since it is a natural feature of all
living beings that they have the desire to propagate, the first association is that
of marriage itself; the next is that with one's children; then the household unit
within which everything is shared; that is the element from which a city is made,
so to speak the seed-bed of the state.' The text and translation come from

d. The apocryphal Acts, generally attributed to the late second/early third centuries CE, but containing individual legends from a considerably earlier period,[22] confirm Justin's witness to the intra-familial tensions created by conversion. They also confirm the attractiveness of conversion to women in particular,[23] an emphasis not nearly so marked in the earlier canonical Acts, where the conversion of prominent men is the focus of attention.[24] The apocryphal Acts show too that, in the eastern provinces of the empire especially, it was to a particularly ascetic form of Christianity that women were attracted.

The *Acts of Paul and Thecla* (c. 185–95 CE) is characteristic. Paul enters the house of Onesiphorus and shares 'the word of God concerning continence and the resurrection'.[25] As the story has it, Thecla, a young virgin betrothed to Thamyris, is entranced by this emphatically ascetic version of Christianity and completely won over to a sexually continent way of life. The effect of her new stance on her family and household is portrayed graphically: 'And those who were in the house wept bitterly, Thamyris for the loss of a wife, Theocleia for the loss of a daughter, the maidservants for that of a mistress. So there was a great confusion of mourning in the house. And while this was going on (all around her) Thecla did not turn away, but gave her whole attention to Paul's word.'[26]

The imagery of death is not coincidental. Thecla has died to her family, her betrothed, her bodily desires and to material ties generally. The repeated attempts subsequently to violate and kill her – part of the common motif of the testing of the holy one – express the mortal enmity and conflict resulting from her commitment. She has become anomic, a social outsider, and must be done away with. Her

Gardner and Wiedemann, *Household*, 2. See further the texts quoted and discussed in Balch, *Wives*, 21–62.

[22] See the discussion of Schneemelcher and Schäferdiek, in Hennecke/Schneemelcher, *NT Apocrypha*, vol. II, 167ff.

[23] See MacDonald, 'Women', for further exploration of this aspect.

[24] For conversion stories in Acts of prominent men, who are often household heads also, see 4.36–7 (Barnabas); 8.9–24 (Simon); 8.26–40 (the Ethiopian official); 9.1–19 (Saul – also, 22.4–16; 26.9–18); 10.1–48 (Cornelius); 13.6–12 (Sergius Paulus); 16.25–34 (the Philippian jailer). Of women, we hear of the conversion of the widow (?) and household head, Lydia (16.12–15) and of Damaris (17.34). At 17.12, the author comments generally that at Beroea, 'not a few Greek women as well as men' were converted. Noticeable is the fact that, rather than the motif (common in the apocryphal Acts) of division within families as a result of conversion, the canonical Acts emphasizes conversion by household.

[25] *Paul and Thecla* 5.

[26] *Ibid.*, 10.

own mother cries out: 'Burn the lawless one! Burn her that is no bride in the midst of the theatre, that all the women that have been taught by this man may be afraid!'[27] Thecla's own behaviour confirms this perception. She has refused the roles of lover, wife, mother, dutiful daughter and respected matron. Instead, she leaves her home and city and follows after Paul, adopting a male fashion in clothing,[28] and intending to have her hair cut short (again, the male fashion).[29]

Ross Kraemer has shown that all of the conversion stories in the apocryphal Acts follow a standard literary pattern of the kind outlined above for Thecla.[30] Conversion, in response to the teaching of a male apostle, finds expression in ascetic renunciation. This precipitates violence towards both the woman and her apostle. In the cases of Thomas, Andrew and Peter, martyrdom is attributable directly to hostile action on the part of the aggrieved husband. The conversion of the father/husband along with his daughter/wife is exceptional.[31] The basic assumptions underlying these conversion stories come to the fore in the prayer of *Acts of Thomas* 61:

> Look upon us, because for thy sake we have left our homes and our fathers' goods, and for thy sake have gladly and willingly become strangers ... we have left our own possessions for thy sake, that we may obtain thee ... we have left those who belong to us by race, that we may be united with thy kindred. Look upon us, Lord, who have left our mothers and fathers and fosterers, that we may behold thy Father ... for thy sake we have left our bodily consorts and our earthly fruits, that we may share in that abiding and true fellowship and bring forth true fruits, whose nature is from above.

Kraemer advances an interesting sociological explanation of this phenomenon, indebted primarily to a deprivation–compensation theory of religious adherence: 'Ascetic Christianity, in fact, offered women a new measure of worth which involved a rejection of their

---

[27] *Ibid.*, 20.
[28] *Ibid.*, 40; cf. *Acts of Philip* 44.
[29] *Paul and Thecla* 25; cf. *Acts of Thomas* 114.
[30] Kraemer, 'Conversion'.
[31] Charitine's father converts (*Acts of Philip* 44), as does Drusiana's husband Andronicus (*Acts of John* 63) and Tertia's husband Misdaeus (*Acts of Thomas* 170).

traditional socio-sexual roles.'[32] He notes the extent to which a
woman's role was both prescribed by her subordination to a dominant male (father or husband) and circumscribed by essentially
private, domestic social boundaries.[33] He points out also that the
majority of women who convert in the apocryphal Acts are women
in a state of social flux or marginality: Thecla is a virgin soon to
marry, for example. Their marginality makes them especially
vulnerable to alternative ideas, attachments and sources of identity.[34] Abandonment of natural kin and domestic ties provides
opportunities for new roles, for endeavour in the public domain,
and for belonging to an alternative, voluntary society in which
spiritual ties displace physical[35] and the values of the transcendent,
heavenly realm supersede those of the world.

In so far as such an explanation draws our attention to the
sociological and psycho-social dimensions of the supra- or anti-
familial tendencies reflected in these sources, it is to be welcomed. It
is unlikely to be the whole story, however. First, the women who
convert do not express concern about personal or social deprivation. There is, for example, no evident degree of controversy over
sex roles for which conversion becomes a solution.[36] Such controversy occurs only after conversion and is consequent upon the
convert's adherence to a radically different (i.e. ascetic) lifestyle. So
Kraemer is in danger of making a consequence into a cause. Second,
the texts themselves draw our attention more to ideological per-
suasion than to social grievances as the reason for the women's
conversions: 'Thecla ... sat at a nearby window and listened night
and day to the word of the virgin life as it was spoken by Paul.'[37]
The women may indeed have been attracted by new role prospects.
But the fact that martyrdom is shown to be one of their strongest
'role prospects' puts a question-mark against Kraemer's appeal to a
theory of compensation. Rather, acceptance of martyrdom presupposes a profound commitment at the ideological level. The women

[32] Kraemer, 'Conversion', 301.
[33] A classic expression of this 'genderization' of social space comes in Philo, *Spec. Leg.* III.169ff.; see further, Barton, 'Place', esp. 229–34, and n. 32.
[34] Kraemer, 'Conversion', 304–5.
[35] The notion of divine marriage and spiritual kinship is emphasized in *Acts of Thomas* 4ff. Kraemer ('Conversion', 303–4) points to the element of erotic substitution in all the conversion stories, where devotion to father/husband is replaced by devotion to the heavenly Lord or to his apostle.
[36] See Cameron, 'Male', 64–6.
[37] *Paul and Thecla* 7.

have come to see the world in a new way where resurrection and other-worldly salvation are to be won through adherence to the apostolic word and the practice of sexual renunciation.

3 Justification of the present study

The preceding survey of pertinent pagan and early Christian sources shows that the effects of conversion on family and household ties was an issue of no small significance for both outsiders and insiders from the very beginnings of Christianity. The subject is a substantial one, and merits investigation. In justification of the present study, I would offer the following rationale.

1. So far as I can see, intensive study of the theme of discipleship and family ties in relation to the gospels has not advanced very far. Martin Hengel's authoritative *Nachfolge und Charisma*, published in 1968, put the subject firmly on the agenda and is a model of its kind.[38] However, Hengel's study is limited (but properly so) in at least the following ways. First, it is a study of the historical Jesus and of the nature of discipleship of Jesus. On the basis of a wide-ranging *religionsgeschichtlich* investigation, and appealing primarily to the criterion of dissimilarity as the most satisfactory basis for firm conclusions about the historical Jesus, Hengel argues that Jesus' radical call of disciples to abandon their families and property to follow after him is interpreted most accurately, not in terms of the rabbinic model of the teacher and his pupils, or in terms of the analogy of apocalyptic prophets and Zealot holy warriors, or in terms of the analogy of conversion to philosophy depicted in the Greco-Roman sources, but in terms of Jesus' unique, messianic vocation as proclaimer of the imminent kingdom of God.[39] This is certainly a plausible conclusion within its own frame of reference. Left unanswered, however, is the question, how does the theme of discipleship and family ties function in the respective gospels as we

---

[38] The German original was published in Berlin by Walter de Gruyter & Co. in 1968. A translation by J. C. G. Greig was published in 1981 by T. & T. Clark of Edinburgh, under the title, *The Charismatic Leader and his Followers*.

[39] Typical of Hengel's position is the clear statement in *Leader*, 69: 'Quite certainly Jesus was not a "teacher" comparable with the later rabbinical experts in the Law, and he was a great deal more than a prophet. Even within the characterization we have preferred, of an "eschatological charismatic", he remains in the last resort incommensurable, and so basically confounds every attempt to fit him into the categories suggested by the phenomenology or sociology of religion.'

have them now? What developments have taken place in the interpretation of the traditions about the subordination of family ties by
the time the gospels have reached their final form?

Second, Hengel bases his investigation on a detailed study of just
one logion, the 'hard saying' from the Q tradition (Matt. 8.21–2 par.
Luke 9.59–60), 'Let the dead bury their dead.'[40] While he alludes to
other relevant gospel traditions in the course of his investigation, a
more comprehensive analysis remains to be done of all the relevant
material in order to assess its cumulative significance, especially in
relation to the theologies and putative communities of the respective
evangelists. Hengel's primarily *religionsgeschichtlich* analysis needs
to be taken further at the redactional and compositional levels. The
present study is an attempt to fill that gap, at least with respect to the
Gospels of Mark and Matthew.[41]

More recent than Hengel's monograph, and taking a quite different approach, is the work of Gerd Theissen: in particular, two
sociological studies of the 'Jesus movement' (*Jesusbewegung*),
written in the 1970s.[42] Working within the hermeneutical framework of the sociology of literature, Theissen argues that the ethical
radicalism of the sayings of Jesus – i.e. sayings in the gospels which
speak of the abandonment of family and property and which convey
an anti-family ethos – requires the existence, in the post-Easter
period, of people who took them seriously and practised them.
Without such people, identified by Theissen as rural, 'itinerant
charismatics' (*Wandercharismatiker*), such sayings would not have
been preserved;[43] and Theissen points to the absence of this Jesus

---

40 *Ibid.*, 3–15.
41 Mention should also be made of Schroeder, *Eltern*. This, like Hengel's, is a
    study of the historical Jesus particularly in relation to the eschatological
    dimension of Jesus' message. Schroeder focusses on the sayings tradition only.
    At the level of *Traditionsgeschichte*, it is an important contribution, relevant, for
    example, to understanding Jesus' attitude to the fifth commandment.
42 See Theissen, 'Radicalism'; Theissen, *Followers*; see also his *Shadow* for a
    brilliant approach through the narrative form.
43 See Theissen, 'Radicalism', 86, for a statement of his thesis: 'The ethical
    radicalism of the sayings tradition is itinerant radicalism. It can be practiced
    and spoken only under extreme conditions of life. Only those can strictly
    practice renunciation of home, family, possessions, rights and protection who
    have separated themselves from the daily ties to the world; who have left hearth,
    spouse and child; who let the dead bury their dead; and take as their example the
    birds and the lilies. Only here can the corresponding ethical teaching be passed
    on without becoming unbelievable … Only homeless charismatics could do
    that.'

tradition from the epistolary literature of the city-based Gentile
mission as important corroboration of his claim.[44]

Theissen's work represents a significant advance on that of
Hengel. It moves us on from the historical Jesus into the period of
oral transmission and beyond, and gives good grounds for finding a
continuity, at the sociological level, between the two. By appealing
to the existence of a group of itinerant charismatics, it also helps to
explain the apparent contrast between gospel, anti-family, radicalism and epistolary, domestic-code, conservatism. Nevertheless,
important questions remain. First, Theissen shows a surprising
tendency to take the sayings of Jesus at face-value[45] and to draw
direct sociological conclusions from them in a way that may not be
justified. If, for instance, the motif of the subordination of family
ties is part of the religious and cultural tradition of Jesus and his
followers, is it legitimate to make analytical deductions about lifestyle from their use of this idiom? Second, the sociology of literature
axiom that a group will receive, preserve and transmit only those
traditions which sustain and legitimate its particular lifestyle is
dubious, as Holmberg has pointed out also.[46] Is it not possible to
envisage the conservative redactor who passes on tradition irrespec-
tive of its 'relevance'? Third, Theissen does not engage sufficiently
with the gospel texts in terms of *Traditionsgeschichte* and *Redak-
tionsgeschichte*. As Stegemann says in his incisive critical essay on
Theissen: 'Texts from the most varied stages of tradition and the
most varied origins are juxtaposed without distinction.'[47] The result
is that his appeal to the sayings tradition appears at points superficial and question-begging.[48] Finally, the main thrust of Theissen's

---

[44] See *ibid.*, 91: 'Sayings of Jesus appear only seldom in early Christian letters. This
must also have had a sociological reason. The letters primarily come out of the
urban Hellenistic congregations ... The anti-family ethos of the early Christian
itinerant radicalism had no place here, simply because it could not be practiced.
Even if people knew these sayings, they could not have lived them. But whatever
cannot be accepted by a community from its oral tradition is excluded by the
"preventive censure" of this community.'

[45] See *ibid.*, 85: 'There should be no doubt that Jesus' sayings are meant seriously
and literally. In the early church one cannot yet assume the existence of those
exegetes who reassure us that "it ain't necessarily so", who say, this is second-
ary, that is Hellenistic, the third is symbolic, the fourth paradoxical.'

[46] Holmberg, *Sociology*, 122–5, 134–44.

[47] Stegemann, 'Radicalism?', 157.

[48] One instance is the way Theissen slips from speaking of following Jesus as
involving *voluntary* renunciation of family and property – something open to
the relatively prosperous – to speaking of the disciples' 'social rootlessness' as a
result of pressing socio-economic factors. Note, for example, the following,

investigation is to reconstruct the social patterns and socio-
economic circumstances of the first followers of Jesus in so far as
they can be deduced from the early Christian texts. Work remains to
be done, therefore, on the significance of hostility to family as a
religious idea (with social consequences) for the gospel writers and
as a literary motif in the gospels themselves.[49]

2. In spite of the fact that there has been a steady stream of studies
on the theme of discipleship in the gospels,[50] relatively little work
has been done on the specific motif of the subordination of family
and household ties. Of course, there are exceptions. For example,
Ernest Best's study *Following Jesus* of 1981 is a systematic *redaktionsgeschichtlich* analysis of the theme of discipleship in the Gospel
of Mark. In the course of his exposition, Best treats helpfully
pericopae relevant to the present investigation, particularly those
which come in the important central section, 8.27–10.45. But he
does not cover all the relevant material (for example 6.1–6; 13.9–13);
and his narrowly *traditionsgeschichtlich* approach to redactional
investigation now needs supplementing by more recent approaches
of a literary-critical and sociological kind.[51]

In relation to the Gospel of Matthew, there is the recent book by
Michael H. Crosby, *House of Disciples: Church, Economics and
Justice in Matthew*, published in 1988. Drawing upon the mass of
scholarly investigation into the importance of the οἶκος/οἰκία in the
shaping of the common life of the first Christians,[52] Crosby attempts
to show that the Gospel of Matthew uses the concept 'house' as an

highly questionable, characterization of Jesus' disciples, in *Followers*, 34: 'The
texts do not wholly conceal the economic factors behind this social behaviour
[of the wandering charismatics]: those who are called to be disciples include
"the labourers and the heavy-laden" (Matt. 11.28), the beggar Bartimaeus
(Mark 10.52), Peter, who is frustrated in his calling (Luke 5.1ff.), and the sons of
Zebedee whose father was a "poor fisherman" according to the Gospel of the
Nazarenes.' It is worth adding that Theissen's depiction of Palestine as in a
constant state of political crisis in the first half of the first century CE has been
criticized by A. E. Harvey in his review of *Followers*, in *JTS*, 30 (1979), 279–82.

49 See Stegemann on Mark 10: 28–30, in 'Radicalism?', 158–9. This is the thrust
also of Harvey's recent contribution, *Commands*, esp. 127–39.

50 See, e.g., Schweizer, *Lordship*, 11–21; the essays of Schweizer and Martin, in
Mays, ed., *Gospels*; Luz, 'Disciples'; and the collection of essays in Segovia, ed.,
Discipleship.

51 Since his 1981 monograph, Best has continued his work on Mark, and has
moved quite considerably in the direction of a more literary-critical approach:
see esp. Best, *Mark*.

52 E.g., in chronological order, Filson, 'Churches'; Judge, *Pattern*, 30–9; Banks,
Community, 40–50; Klauck, *Hausgemeinde*; Meeks, *Christians*, 75–7; Barton,
'Place'.

'assumed primary metaphor', and that Matthean ecclesiology and ethics are cast in a new light when interpreted against a house-church backdrop. Unfortunately, however, the book is something of a *tour de force*. It is right to explore the possibility that aspects of Matthew's Gospel reflect a house-church *Sitz im Leben*. Ernest Best does the same, in fact, for Mark – though in a much more modest and tentative way.[53] But it is highly questionable whether 'house' has the central theological, ecclesiological and ethical role in Matthew which Crosby attributes to it. As we shall see, the considerable amount of material in Matthew hostile to family and household ties points in a different direction. 'Kingdom of heaven' and 'righteousness' – yes; 'house' – no.

Mention should also be made of studies which provide useful analogies to the kind of investigation proposed here. Since traditions about family and household ties have a definite material (i.e. property) dimension (see Mark 10.28–30), the closest analogy is provided by the significant amount of recent work on the teaching in the gospels about wealth and poverty. I would draw particular attention to Thomas Schmidt's 1987 monograph, *Hostility to Wealth in the Synoptic Gospels*, since the theme of Schmidt's book runs parallel to the theme of the present study on 'hostility' to the family.[54] In brief, Schmidt makes two main points. Over against scholars (like Theissen, Gager and Mealand)[55] who argue along sociological lines for a positive correlation between socio-economic conditions and traditions hostile to wealth and the rich, Schmidt argues that the teaching on wealth in the Synoptic Gospels is not determined by the socio-economic circumstances of the time. Conversely, his positive thesis is that *'hostility to wealth exists independently of socio-economic circumstances as a fundamental religious-ethical tenet consistently expressed in the Synoptic Gospels'.*[56] The value of Schmidt's work for the present investigation may be summed up thus. First, Schmidt describes a religious-ethical tradition, rooted deeply in ancient Near-Eastern, biblical and Jewish sources, which advocates hostility to, or devaluation of, wealth on teleological grounds. The investigation of the family-ties material to follow will be able to test whether or not a parallel teleological

---

[53] Best, *Jesus*, 226–9.
[54] Indeed, Schmidt himself brings the two themes into parallel at the very end of his discussion: see *Hostility*, 166–7.
[55] See Theissen, *Followers*; Gager, *Kingdom*; and Mealand, *Poverty*.
[56] Schmidt, *Hostility*, 164 (Schmidt's italics).

devaluation is evident. Second, Schmidt surveys all the relevant traditions in the Synoptic Gospels and shows that there is a basic consistency between them: 'Dispossession of wealth as a way of expressing *Gottvertrauen* is a means to eternal life.'[57] Again, the present, more in-depth study of Mark and Matthew will be able to test for a similar consistency in respect of the subordination of ties of natural kinship and the household. Third, Schmidt's scepticism about the way sociological theories have been used in gospel study reinforces our reservations earlier about Theissen's analysis of the Jesus movement. But Schmidt's scepticism is not outright denial, and it remains to be seen whether inferences, at least, of a sociological kind may not legitimately be made about the kind of audiences to which Mark and Matthew are directed.

3. The last two decades have witnessed a growing methodological pluralism in gospel studies. This pluralism has arisen out of an increasing awareness of the limits of the historical-critical paradigm of interpretation, on the one hand, and a turn in the direction of various methodologies within the literary-critical paradigm, on the other.[58] The crux of the matter revolves around the question, are the gospels historical *sources*, the careful ordering and sifting of which enables us to go behind them to the solid bedrock of persons and events in history, or are they *texts* of a predominantly narrative kind whose meaning lies in the creative interaction between text and reader? To put it another way, is the meaning of a gospel something extrinsic to it – to do with what the author intended, or with the degree of correspondence between what the text says and what actually happened, for example – or is it something immanent to the text as text, where what is important is not only what the author may or may not have intended, but how the text communicates with the reader, its poetics?

Norman Petersen's essay of 1970 exposed the problem well.[59] He showed that the historical-critical paradigm is based on an evolutionary model of the growth of the tradition from underlying 'event' to final gospel text, but that the analytical method of historical criticism works in the opposite direction, from the text in its final form whose layers of tradition are peeled successively away. Redaction criticism has been developed as a tool of the historical-critical

[57] *Ibid.*, 118; cf. 134, 161–2.
[58] See *inter alios*, Morgan, *Interpretation*, chs. 6, 7; Moore, *Criticism*, part 1; Meyer, 'Challenges'.
[59] See Petersen, *Criticism*, esp. ch. 1.

paradigm to deal with the 'top layer'. But the practice of redaction criticism has functioned as a kind of Trojan horse in the camp of the historical-critical paradigm, for it has led inexorably to a focus on the final form of the text, the genre of the gospel as a whole, the interests and intentions of its author, compositional techniques at work, and so on, the consequence being that it has burst the bounds of the historical-critical paradigm and forced interpreters to ask literary questions of the gospel writings. Furthermore, because redaction criticism remains an aspect of traditio-historical method generally, literary-critical methods have been required to do a task for which redaction criticism is not equipped.[60]

This growing awareness of the limits of historical criticism of the gospels springs from a variety of sources. It does not arise only out of the *cul-de-sac* in redaction criticism. Sean Freyne points, additionally, in three other directions: the impact of the philosophical hermeneutics of Paul Ricoeur, with its focus on the role of the reader in creating the text by the act of interpretation; the contribution of narrative poetics and reader response criticism, with their concerns, respectively, for the ways texts communicate and the way texts are received by readers; and, from within the biblical guild, the work of Werner Kelber on the significance of textualization in the formation of early Christian tradition – in particular, the dislocating effect of textualization on the oral message such that the language of the oral tradition becomes severely decontextualized.[61] To these developments may be added the ever more urgent recognition in certain quarters of what Culpepper calls 'the church's need for the vitality of scripture',[62] a vitality which historical criticism is seen to

---

[60] See *ibid.*, 19: 'Moreover, by basing their method on the distinction between redaction and tradition, redaction critics are forced to look *through* the text by focusing on the relations between it and its sources. For this reason they cannot look *at* the text in order to see, for example, how the units in its linear sequence are related to one another to form the whole. Having cast off the evolutionary model, they nevertheless remain bound to the genetic sequence of stages in textual formation by construing texts as *windows* opening on the preliterary history of their parts rather than as *mirrors* on whose surfaces we find self-contained worlds. Positively, redaction criticism raises the very real problem of having to determine the author's investment in each word, sentence, and unit taken over from his sources. Negatively, however, its methodological and theoretical orientation requires us to focus on something other than the text itself. Redaction criticism's concern for composition and authors thus leads to literary problems that it is not designed to deal with' (Petersen's italics).

[61] See Freyne's 1985 Presidential Address to the Irish Biblical Association: 'Preoccupation', esp. 6–13.

[62] Culpepper, 'Story', 469.

have sapped, but to which more literary approaches offer the hope of rejuvenation.[63]

The result of this sense of the limits of the historical-critical paradigm for gospels interpretation has been a burgeoning of essays and monographs on the gospels from various literary-critical perspectives. A number of these works have been of significant help in the present study of Mark and Matthew, as will become evident. It is beyond the scope of this study to describe and analyse this new field here. In any case, Stephen Moore's recent work of metacriticism does the job in an expert way.[64] My point in the foregoing has been the more limited one of tracing some of the contours of gospels study since 1970 to show that the hegemony of historical criticism has broken down and a much greater pluralism of methods of interpretation now exists.

In certain cases, the methods of historical criticism and literary criticism are incompatible. Some forms of literary structuralism are an obvious case in point.[65] There is a tendency also in some interpretations from a reader-response perspective to appear reductionist, to lose the sense that the gospels are historical testimonies, not just deeply meaningful fictions. Thus, for example, the book on Mark by Rhoads and Michie is entitled, significantly, *Mark as Story*, and it begins with the statement, 'When we enter the story world of the Gospel of Mark, we enter a world full of conflict and suspense, a world of surprising reversals and strange ironies, a world of riddles and hidden meanings. The hero of the story – perhaps the most

---

[63] Cf. Morgan, *Interpretation*, 199: 'Theology is equally interested in the critical power of historical study, as an instrument for performing its own critical task of attacking untrue expressions of religion. But theological interpretation of the Bible aims to sustain as well as correct religion. Its theological insights stem from the combination of the interpreter's religious insight and his understanding of these texts. Its most natural ally is therefore the kind of literary criticism that enhances the appropriation and enjoyment of literature. This can help the Bible function as a catalyst of Christian faith and life. Without this there is nothing for theology to reflect on and criticize.'

[64] See Moore, *Criticism*, published in 1989.

[65] Note the comment of Eagleton, *Theory*, 109: 'I have said that structuralism contained the seeds of a social and historical theory of meaning, but they were not, on the whole, able to sprout. For if the sign-systems by which individuals lived could be seen as culturally viable, the deep laws which governed the workings of these systems were not. For the "hardest" forms of structuralism they were universal, embedded in a collective mind which transcended any particular culture ... Structuralism, in a word, was hair-raisingly unhistorical: the laws of the mind it claimed to isolate – parallelisms, oppositions, inversions, and the rest – moved at a level of generality quite remote from the concrete differences of human history.'

memorable in all of literature – is most surprising of all.'[66] In terms of the literary-critical paradigm, this title and opening statement are unexceptionable. In terms of a theological perspective which sets enormous store on the significance of the historical dimension of the gospels and Christian origins, they appear to miss the point: for 'story world' somehow lacks the theological potency of (say) 'historical stage', 'riddles and hidden meanings' sounds too hermetic, and 'hero' makes the crucified Christ religiously nondescript.[67]

Nevertheless, the methods of historical criticism and literary criticism are not necessarily incompatible. On the contrary, the multi-disciplinary approach I have adopted in this study is based on the assumption that such methods may be complementary. Indeed, one of the claims of this study is that a multi-disciplinary approach to the gospel texts helps to do most justice to the nature of the texts themselves. As the products of a process of transmission from the time of Jesus on, they justify a form-critical analysis. As the products of a creative process of editing and composition at the hands of the respective evangelists, they justify redactional analysis. As narrative texts written with skill to exhort, edify and persuade a particular readership, they justify the use of literary criticism. Finally, although by no means exhaustively, as texts which spring from, and are addressed to, historical communities, the gospels have a necessarily social dimension which justifies sociological criticism.

Such a multi-faceted approach is legitimate and timely, in my opinion. It recognizes that no single method is adequate any longer to a rounded interpretation of the gospel texts which attempts to do justice to their fundamentally religious intentions and their historical and literary aspects. Second, it accepts fully the interpretative principle that the method of interpretation needs to be appropriate to the aims of the interpreter.[68] Third, it avoids the interpretative pitfall of assuming that the meaning of the text is a matter of determining the intention of the author, while at the same time recognizing that authorial intention is intrinsic to the text and an important control on the imaginative response of the reader.[69] Fourth, it builds on the exegetical traditions of interpretation which

---

[66] Rhoads and Michie, *Mark*, 1.
[67] See also, Morgan, *Interpretation*, 231–7.
[68] See *ibid.*, 212: 'Both historical and literary questions about the Bible have to be asked. The emphasis given to each will depend on what kind of knowledge or insight or enjoyment a particular interpreter wants.' See also Mark Brett's recent attempt at a taxonomy of interpretative interests: 'Texts', *passim*.
[69] See Meyer, 'Challenges', 9–11.

the gospels themselves have generated, rather than dispensing with them in an arbitrary, doctrinaire manner.

4   The aims of the study

On the basis of the preceding justification, the present study has the following aims. First, by means of an historical survey of relevant Jewish and Greco-Roman sources, I shall show that the subordination of family and household ties spoken of in the gospels is not unprecedented. On the contrary, it is likely that followers of Jesus both before and after Easter will not have been surprised to have been taught that their allegiances in discipleship and their allegiances within a household may not always be compatible. Strong precedent for the legitimate subordination of family ties existed already, both in the biblical and Jewish traditions, beginning at least with the figure of Abraham, and in discussions to do with conversion to philosophy, in the Greco-Roman traditions.

Second, I shall demonstrate, on the basis of a detailed analysis of the relevant narrative and sayings traditions, that the implications of discipleship for family ties are a major concern in the Gospels of Mark and Matthew. In particular, it will be seen that discipleship of Jesus poses a threat to family and household ties, since it involves the disciple – every disciple – in a quite fundamental transfer of primary allegiance and commitment. This is something which is recognized by the earliest evangelist, Mark, and is taken up in his all-pervasive passion christology and his vision of cross-bearing discipleship. It is something which is confirmed by the testimony of Matthew also: for Matthew not only takes over (and modifies) the Marcan material, but also expands it considerably by the incorporation of additional Jesus tradition, in such a way that the family-ties motif serves Matthew's concern to convey the primary reality of the kingdom of heaven, the authority of Jesus' call to mission, the cost of missionary discipleship, and the meaning of membership of the Christian brotherhood now that the break with the synagogue is taking place.

Third, by treating not just one gospel – a common trend in recent scholarship – but two, it will be possible to see, not only points of significant convergence in the respective evangelists' understanding of discipleship and family ties, but also points of development or divergence between Matthew and his Marcan source. Specifically, I shall show that the family-ties material provides a window onto the

ethos[70] of Marcan and Matthean Christianity, and that there are
good grounds for describing the ethos of both as counter-cultural
and subversive of normal, household-based social patterns. That is
why conflict so dominates both. On the other hand, there are subtle
points of divergence from Mark in Matthew which a comparison of
the two will reveal: a more specific and clear-sighted focus on
missionary activity and its implications for family ties, for example,
as well as a stronger sense of rift between followers of Jesus and
their compatriots in Judaism, a rift expressed not least at the level of
ties of natural kinship.

Fourth, by drawing particular attention to those traditions in
Mark and Matthew which depict the subordination or relativization
of family ties and household belonging, my intention is to qualify in
certain respects that trend in recent socio-historical study of early
Christianity generally which has emphasized too strongly the
indebtedness of early Christian social patterns to the household
model. In this respect, this study of the gospels takes further work I
have done already on Paul.[71] Undoubtedly, the household, as both
an economic, architectural and spatial centre on the one hand, and
as a primary focus of personal identity, socio-economic alliance and
religious belonging on the other, played a very significant part in
shaping the common life of the first followers of Jesus. Certainly
also, as will become evident, there is no justification in the traditions
under discussion for seeing either Mark or Matthew as hostile to
family ties *per se*. Nevertheless, there is strong justification for
claiming that there is, in the gospels, what Schmidt usefully calls a
'teleological devaluation'[72] of ties of natural kinship and household
belonging, and that this devaluation has to do specifically with
missionary discipleship of Jesus as an alternative, transcendent
focus of identity, allegiance and role.

Fifth, the following study seeks to demonstrate, and thereby
commend, a multi-disciplinary approach to gospels interpretation
which makes possible a more holistic response to the texts, and
avoids the danger of reductionist interpretation or of hermeneutical
tunnel-vision. By approaching each relevant pericope from four
angles – form-critical, redaction-critical, literary-critical and sociological – I aim to show that the breakdown of the hegemony of the

---

[70] On the study of the 'ethos' of early Christianity generally, see further, Barton,
'Ethos' and the literature cited there.
[71] See Barton, 'Place', noting especially the conclusions on pp. 242–3.
[72] Schmidt, *Hostility*, e.g. at p. 118.

historical-critical method in gospels study need not lead to interpretative anarchy. On the contrary, what began for me as an
experiment in reading the gospels has convinced me that such
traditio-historical, literary and sociological approaches are by no
means necessarily mutually exclusive. Instead, a combination of
these kinds of approaches appears to do most justice to the nature
of the gospels themselves – as historical testimony, as written texts,
and as documents shaped in a very evident way by communal
concerns.[73]

[73] On this latter aspect, see most recently my two essays, 'Communal Dimension'
and 'Sect'.

2

THE SUBORDINATION OF FAMILY TIES IN JUDAISM AND IN THE GRECO-ROMAN WORLD OF THE FIRST CENTURY

1 Introduction

The gospel traditions provide clear evidence of a demand for, and an acceptance of, the subordination of family and household ties as a consequence of becoming a follower of Jesus. The detailed discussion of the evidence of the Gospels of Mark and Matthew will constitute the third and fourth chapters of the study. The kinds of question we ask in this second chapter are questions of historical context: how familiar to potential converts would the idea of the subordination of household ties have been, and how was such an idea viewed? Was it a common idea or a novel one? Whether common or novel, on what grounds was it justified? Were members of one society and tradition more likely to advocate such an idea than members of another? The main aim of the chapter is to show that the subordination of family ties to which early Christian sources like Mark and Matthew bear witness was not unprecedented in the traditions and practices of either Judaism or of the Greco-Roman world as a whole. To show this, it is not necessary to attempt an exhaustive survey. Rather, in what follows, I have chosen to focus on a selection of pertinent Jewish and Greco-Roman sources from the pre-Christian and early Christian period. An awareness of the various forms of 'hostility' to family in such sources will render more intelligible what we find in the gospels and provide a comparative historical setting within which to interpret the nuances of the gospel material more adequately.

2 The evidence of Philo

Family ties constitute a recurrent theme of the writings of Philo of Alexandria (c. 20 BCE–50 CE). In particular, they provide a major idiom in terms of which Philo expresses his fundamental religious and philosophical preoccupations. In what follows, attention will be drawn to both how frequently family ties become an idiom of religious discourse or a focus of attention in their own right and how common is the idea of the subordination or redefinition of family ties. As far as I am aware, the family-ties motif in general, and the idea of subordination in particular, has received only limited attention so far in Philonic studies.[1]

Presuppositions

In a significant comment upon the warning against going after false prophets in Deut. 13.1–11, Philo expresses a conviction fundamental to Judaism as a whole, that the observance of the command not to go after other gods is a mandatory obligation which transcends family allegiance. It is worth quoting at length:

> And if a brother or son or daughter or wife or a housemate or a friend, however true … urges us to a like course, bidding us fraternize with the multitude, resort to their temples, and join in their libations and sacrifices, we must punish him as a public and general enemy, taking little thought for the ties which bind us to him … For we should have one tie of affinity, one accepted sign of goodwill, namely the willingness to serve God, and that our every word and deed promotes the cause of piety. But as for these kinships, as we call them, which have come down from our ancestors and are based on blood-relationship, or those derived from marriage or other similar causes, let them all be cast aside if they do not seek earnestly the same goal, namely the honour of God, which is the indissoluble bond of affection which makes us one. For those who are so minded will receive in exchange kinships of greater dignity and sanctity.[2]

Here is a transparent statement of religious absolutes in the light of which natural and social ties are relativized profoundly. First, conjugal and consanguineous ties are made subordinate to the 'one tie' of devotion to God, summed up in the word εὐσεβεία. Second,

---

[1] The principal study of relevance is Baer, *Male and Female.*
[2] *Spec. Leg.* I.316–17. All quotations of Philo, unless indicated otherwise, are taken from the Loeb Classical Library translation. The abbreviations of the Latin titles of Philo's works follow those given at the beginning of *TDNT*, vol. I.

this one tie provides the basis for a higher kinship, where kinship relations are redefined in spiritual terms.[3] So Philo goes on to describe as sons of God those 'who do "what is pleasing" to nature and what is "good"' (318); and the corollary of this spiritual kinship is to regard God as a father (318).[4] Third, whereas the Deuteronomic law is concerned primarily with the penalties to be exacted from all who transgress the commandment, Philo draws a positive implication as well, namely that just as εὐσεβεία takes precedence over ties of natural kinship, so there is a bond uniting the pious which is also superior to bonds of marriage and blood. This then becomes a basis for patterns of association and community no longer determined solely by family ties, such as the Therapeutae and the Essenes, as we shall see.

Proselytes

It is not surprising that a thoroughly hellenized Jew like Philo, an inhabitant of the large and cosmopolitan city of Alexandria, should refer frequently to what was involved for a proselyte in converting to Judaism.[5] What is significant for our study is the extent to which the transfer to Judaism is cast in terms of its effect on family ties.[6] The proselyte is one who has left his home and native land and become incorporated into a new family.[7]

Especially interesting is Philo's interpretation of the law concerning hospitality to the sojourner (LXX, προσήλυτος), in *Spec. Leg.* I.51–3 (cf. Lev. 19.33–4; Deut. 10.18–19). According to Philo, Moses is referring to the treatment to be accorded converts; and it is noteworthy that family ties are invoked, not only as representative of what the proselyte has left behind, but also as an essential aspect of what he has converted to: 'they have left, he [Moses] says, their

---

[3] See *Quaest. in Exod.* II.29, where the prophet Moses is said to come near God 'in a kind of family relation (κατὰ συγγενῆ τινα οἰκειότητος) for having given up and left behind all mortal kinds'.

[4] See *Mut. Nom.* 127, on the man 'who has had no eyes for his kinship to created being and has given himself to be the portion of Him who is ruler and father of us all'.

[5] See Cohen, 'Boundary', esp. pp. 26–7.

[6] For the rabbinic literature, mention may be made of *Numbers Rabbah* 8.3, on God's love for the proselyte, which ends: 'So too spoke the Holy One: "I owe great thanks to the stranger, in that he has left his family and his father's house, and has come to dwell among us; therefore I order in the Law: 'Love ye the stranger' (Deut. 10.19)".' The quotation comes from Barrett, *Background*, 165.

[7] See *Som.* II.273.

country, their kinsfolk and their friends for the sake of virtue and religion. Let them not be denied another citizenship or other ties of family and friendship' (52). This is not an isolated example. There are at least three others,[8] and in each case, the transfer from paganism to Judaism is expressed in terms of family ties and their corollaries – homeland, native customs and deities, ancestors and friends. Should his reader ask of him some biblical precedent, Philo holds up Abraham: 'He is the standard of nobility (εὐγενείας ἐστὶ κανών) for all proselytes, who, abandoning the ignobility of strange laws and monstrous customs . . . have come to settle in a better land, in a commonwealth full of life and vitality' (*Virt.* 219).[9]

What Philo says about proselytes and the effect of conversion on family ties is quite consistent with what we found earlier in examining his presuppositions. Clearly, Philo's commitment to family ties is not absolute. There are motives and circumstances which allow – indeed, require – their subordination. These motives are religious and philosophical.[10] Speaking of Abraham, he says: 'Perception of these truths and divine inspiration (ὧν ἔννοιαν λαβὼν καὶ ἐπιθειά-σας) induced him to leave his native country, his race and paternal home' (*Virt.* 214). What is significant for our purposes is how frequently the religious and philosophical change or conversion is depicted in relation to its social, and above all familial, corollaries. The change of belief involves a change of community as well.[11] It is important to add that such beliefs and practices do not go unnoticed from outside Judaism either. For Tacitus, for example, they exemplify the misanthropy of the Jews and the social irresponsibility of those who convert to Judaism, as we saw earlier.[12]

Model communities

Philo's account of the Therapeutae and the Essenes is very important for our investigation of attitudes to family ties in the first

[8] See *Virt.* 102f., 219; and *Spec. Leg.* IV.178.

[9] See also the treatment of Joseph, in *Fug.* 126ff.

[10] For a similar understanding in Josephus, see *Ap.* II.210: 'To all who desire to come and live under the same laws with us, he [Moses] gives a gracious welcome, holding that it is not family ties alone which constitute relationship, but agreement in the principles of conduct.'

[11] That this is a material, as well as a spiritual, concern is evident from what Philo takes for granted, in *Virt.* 104: 'I will not go on to speak of the food and drink and raiment and all the rights concerning daily life and necessary needs, which the law assigns to incomers as due from the native born.'

[12] See above, p. 2, referring to Tacitus, *History* V.5.

century. His account informs us, not only about the beliefs and practices of these two movements of withdrawal, but also of his own perception of them.[13]

　　a. In depicting the Therapeutae as philosophers devoted to the pursuit of εὐσεβεία through the life of contemplation, Philo emphasizes both the asceticism of their lifestyle and the character of their community as a spiritual family. Both of these aspects are of interest for our study.

Their asceticism is seen in many ways. First, in the abandonment of property.[14] Unlike the Essenes, who pool their resources upon entry,[15] the Therapeutae leave theirs to their heirs as an early inheritance. This shows that the Therapeutae are not antagonistic to family ties as such: only that the call to contemplation and the worship of τὸ ὄν is a higher priority, that of the spiritual over the material.

Second, and as a corollary of their renunciation of property, is their separation from family, which he describes in *Vit. Cont.* 18.[16] Sandmel has pointed out that Philo here ascribes to a group of his contemporaries behaviour which elsewhere he ascribes to an individual contemplative of the past, namely Abraham.[17] This is certainly true, for on numerous occasions Philo draws attention to Abraham's departure from homeland and native kin in obedience to the higher demand of God, piety and the things of the spirit.[18] So Philo's depiction of the Therapeutae is idealizing. They are made to exemplify the Platonic elevation of the immaterial above the material and of the soul above the body, an ideology for which Abraham

---

[13] For the present purpose, it is not necessary to distinguish 'the historical Therapeutae' or 'the historical Essenes' from Philo's interpretation of them. For a recent account showing the extent to which Philo in fact idealizes these groups, see Sandmel, *Place*, 192–6; Sandmel, *Philo*, 32–9. In contrast, the discussion in Schürer, *History*, II, 555–97, makes little of such tendencies (although note p. 596). Certainly, Philo himself, in beginning his account of the Therapeutae (*Vit. Cont.* 1), makes a strong assertion of the accuracy of his report, but this may be no more than historiographic convention.

[14] See *Vit. Cont.* 13–18.　　　[15] *Hypothetica* II.4.

[16] 'So when they have divested themselves of their possessions and have no longer aught to ensnare them they flee without a backward glance and leave their brothers, their children, their wives, their parents, the wide circle of their kinsfolk, the groups of friends around them, the fatherlands in which they were born and reared, since strong is the attraction of familiarity and very great its power to ensnare.'

[17] Sandmel, *Place*, 95.

[18] E.g. *Abr.* 60–7; *Migr. Abr.* 1ff.; *Rer. Div. Her.* 276–83, 287–8; *Leg. All.* III.83.

serves as the primary type from amongst the patriarchs. Property
and family ties serve in such discourse as a fundamental instance of
the kind of material and sensory concerns which can distract the
pious from the metaphysical quest. The abandonment of property
ties and the subordination of family ties are part of the rhetoric of
Philo's argument for the pursuit of piety through a life of contemplation.

An awareness of the rhetorical potential of our central theme is
important for understanding its occurrence in early Christian
sources dealing with discipleship of Jesus. For Philo, it makes
possible a forceful expression of a religious and philosophical commitment thoroughly indebted to a strongly hellenized form of
Judaism. In the early Christian sources, a negative attitude to
property and family ties arises out of a commitment of a rather
different kind, as subsequent discussion will show.

Although the Therapeutae live a life of ascetic renunciation,[19]
their philosophy is not anti-social. Rather, they constitute an alternative society, many in fact congregating in a community near
Alexandria on a hill above the Mareotic Lake.[20] Contemplation in
solitude and living in community are held together. Significantly,
this alternative society is depicted partly in familial terms. The
Therapeutae live in houses (οἰκίαι) either singly or in small groups
(of men or women): Philo does not specify.[21] They regard their place
of settlement 'as their fatherland' (καθάπερ εἰς πατρίδα).[22] At the
communal meal every sabbath, those who serve, says Philo, 'give
their services gladly and proudly like sons to their real fathers and
mothers, judging them to be the parents of them all in common, in a
closer affinity than that of blood, since to the right minded there is
no closer tie than noble living'.[23] Here, as elsewhere in Philo, it is
spiritual kinship which is of greatest importance, and this trans-
forms normal patterns. In consequence, the household patterns of
the wider society are turned on their head. There are no slaves to

[19] In addition to leaving property and family, their asceticism is evident in their
escape from the cities for a life of solitude (*Vit. Cont.* 19–20), the careful
segregation of the sexes (*ibid.* 32–3), their rule of celibacy (*ibid.* 68), the practice
of fasting and abstinence from meat and wine (*ibid.*, 34–5, 73–4), and the general
frugality of their dietary practices on the principle of ἐγκράτεια (*ibid.*, 34).

[20] See *ibid.*, 21–2.

[21] *Ibid.*, 24. The statement in 30 is ambiguous. Are we to understand that each
member has his own house, or does each one practise his devotion in his own
inner chamber (μοναστήριον) within a house which he shares with several
others?

[22] *Ibid.*, 22.   [23] *Ibid.*, 72.

serve at meals;[24] seniority is determined by the length of time spent in the contemplative life rather than by natural age;[25] women and men live together in community, but do so as celibates;[26] and household-based economic practices have been given up.[27]

Here, then, we have a community of religious virtuosi in which the power of household ties and sexual identity is redirected – or better, reinterpreted – to form the basis of an alternative society where the pattern of relationships is determined by training in wisdom and piety rather than property-ownership and consanguinity, and sexual differences are transcended both in the ascetic quest for virtue and in ecstatic worship.[28] The shift, in other words, is from social relations based on ascribed status to social relations based on achieved status. One effect of this transformation of household norms is worthy of note. In concluding his account, Philo says that the Therapeutae 'have lived in the soul alone, citizens of Heaven and the world (οὐρανοῦ μὲν καὶ κόσμου πολιτῶν), presented to the Father and Maker of all by their faithful sponsor Virtue'.[29] Clearly, the abandoning of family and possessions – ties parochial in scope, distracting in demand, and divisive (or at least differentiating) in practice – makes possible a universalism of appeal and equality of opportunity otherwise unavailable or severely limited. This is why adherents of both sexes gathered 'from every side (πανταχόθεν)' to a new 'fatherland'.[30] The extent to which the subordination and redefinition of household ties in early Christianity was motivated by, or affected, considerations of a universalistic kind is certain to have been very significant also. In Philo, it is a matter of philosophical ideal: in early Christianity, it is a matter of eschatological mission to Jews and Gentiles for the sake of the gospel.

b. The communalism of the Essenes is well known,[31] and Philo is one of our primary sources, describing their ethos and lifestyle in two places: *Omn. Prob. Lib.* 75–91 and *Hypothetica* II.1–18. Once more, the transformation of family ties for the sake of group membership is an all-pervasive concern. To establish and

---

[24] *Ibid.*, 70–1.   [25] *Ibid.*, 67; cf. 30.   [26] *Ibid.*, 68; cf. 32.
[27] Philo gives no indication of their pattern of subsistence. Instead, he contrasts their adoption of the contemplative life with the Essenes' excellence in 'the active life' (*Vit. Cont.* 1; cf. 13–18). See the discussion in Schürer, *History*, vol. II, 594.
[28] See *Vit. Cont.* 83–9.   [29] *Ibid.*, 90.   [30] *Ibid.*, 22.
[31] See further the useful survey in Schürer, *History*, II, 562–74.

maintain group identity, it appears that the household pattern
which is so central to mainstream social relations is shifted to the
periphery in the ideology and practice of Essene communalism. I
shall note the following points briefly.

First, membership is voluntary rather than guaranteed by birth:
'zeal for virtue and desire to promote brotherly love' are the prime
conditions.[32] Second, and consistently with the above, only mature
male adults are eligible to join.[33] Third, Philo categorically states
(but only in the *Hypothetica*) that Essenes 'eschew marriage', and
that 'no Essene takes a wife' – and this, out of a concern to maintain
their communal life (κοινωνία), to escape the guiles of women, and
to practise ἐγκράτεια.[34] The fact that Philo refers three times here
to the threat posed by marital and paternal ties to the corporate life
of the Essenes shows the extent to which he views the Essene way as
an alternative to normal, household-based community. Fourth, like
their attitude to women, their view of property is negative, at least in
so far as the possession of property involves them in economic and
social relations from which they seek release.[35] Their critique of
property is, of course, another aspect of the Essenes' rejection of
household-based patterns of social relations. Money, land and
slaves, together with wife and children, all constitute the household
ties with which membership of the Essene community is incompatible.[36]

Nevertheless, when we turn to consider the nature of the Essene
alternative, it seems clear that the household remains to some extent
a model for their communalism. This is seen, first, in the use of the
imagery of kinship to describe relations between members. For
example, part of the rationale for not owning slaves is the egalitarian doctrine that Nature 'mother-like has born and reared all men

[32] *Hypothetica* II.2.
[33] See *ibid.*, II.3: '[N]o Essene is a mere child nor even a stripling or newly bearded
... but full grown and already verging on old age.' It is worth noting the
contrast with the condition of membership of the kingdom of God, expressed in
Mark 10.13–16 and parallels, where child-likeness is essential!
[34] *Hypothetica* II.14–17.
[35] See *Omn. Prob. Lib.* 77–8: '[T]hey stand almost alone in the whole of mankind in
that they have become moneyless and landless by deliberate action ... [nor have
they] the vaguest idea of commerce either wholesale or retail or marine, but
pack the inducements of covetousness off in disgrace.' For the more customary
attitude to commercial activity, see *Migr. Abr.* 217.
[36] See esp. *Hypothetica* II.4, with the listing together of 'house or slave or estate or
cattle (οὐκ οἰκίαν, οὐκ ἀνδράποδον, οὐ χωρίον, οὐ βοσκήματα)' amongst the
property forsaken.

alike, and created them genuine brothers (ἀδελφοὺς γνησίους), not in mere name, but in very reality'.[37] Or, in describing the treatment of elderly members, Philo says: 'The old men too, even if they are childless are treated as parents of a not merely numerous but very filial family.'[38] There is a sense also, in which the household pattern is extended or expanded in Essenism. In an important statement in *Omn. Prob. Lib.* 85, Philo says: 'First of all then no-one's house is his own in the sense that it is not shared by all, for besides the fact that they dwell together in communities (κατὰ θιάσους συνοικεῖν), the door is open to visitors from elsewhere who share their convictions.' This sharing of houses and practice of hospitality is paralleled further in the pooling of resources, the sharing of the common meals, and the division of labour to provide resources for the common good.[39] In each of these instances – house ownership, hospitality, wages and property, meals, and labour – an aspect of household order has been transformed into an aspect of Essene communalism. The same point applies to authority patterns. According to Philo's portrait, the shift in authority away from individual household heads is a shift at the same time towards a paternalistic central authority balanced by an ideal of brotherly egalitarianism. On the latter, Philo asserts: 'In no other community, can we find the custom of sharing roof, life and board (τὸ ὁμωρόφιον ἢ ὁμοδίαιτον ἢ ὁμοτράπεζον) more firmly established in actual practice.'[40]

In sum, what Philo says about the Therapeutae and the Essenes gives good grounds for suggesting that the early Christians are not alone in attempting to develop patterns of sociability alternative to that of the household and those based on marital and kinship ties. Such evidence also confirms that household and kinship relations provide a powerful idiom in first-century Judaism for expressing personal dedication to transcendent religious and philosophical commitments. It seems reasonable to infer that converts to one or other of the various 'sects' within formative Judaism (including early Christianity) would be familiar with the idea of the renunciation of family and property.

Heroic individuals

In Philo's re-presentations of the patriarchs and other leaders of the people of Israel, it is significant for our purpose that their distinction

---

[37] *Omn. Prob. Lib.* 79.   [38] *Hypothetica* II.13; see also *Omn. Prob. Lib.* 87.
[39] See *Omn. Prob. Lib.* 86–7; *Hypothetica* II.4ff.   [40] *Omn. Prob. Lib.* 86.

is illustrated frequently by their willingness to subordinate family
ties to a greater cause. What Philo says of model communities recurs
in what he says of holy and heroic individuals.

   a. Abraham is an exemplary figure, not only in the biblical
and early Christian traditions, but also in the Philonic corpus. One
aspect of the Abraham story upon which Philo places great weight is
that of his departure from Ur. This is elaborated in a number of
places. Most hyperbolic is *Abr.* 67: 'And so taking no thought for
anything, either for his fellow-clansmen, or wardsmen, or school-
mates, or comrades, or blood relations on father's or mother's side,
or country, or ancestral customs, or community of nurture or home
life, all of them ties possessing a power to allure and attract which it
is hard to throw off, he followed a free and unfettered impulse and
departed with all speed.'[41] This radical separation from kinsfolk and
homeland is cited by Philo as proof of Abraham's obedience to the
divine command, and of his being a wise man.[42] At the allegorical
level, it represents a migration from a Chaldean cosmology based on
observable phenomena to a cosmology derived from consideration
of 'the intelligible and invisible'.[43] But the language of kinship is
used, not only to show what is left behind by God's true servant, but
also to convey his new allegiance. So, for instance, Abraham's status
as an exile from his homeland is complemented by the assertion that
God is a surrogate for the things lost, and that Abraham belongs
instead to a spiritual family: 'But Thou, Master, art my country, my
kinsfolk, my paternal hearth, my franchise, my free speech, my great
and glorious and inalienable wealth.'[44] In other words, the language
of kinship functions as a way of expressing fundamental allegiances
and commitments and the transfer from one set of allegiances,
beliefs and society to another.[45]
   This is reinforced in Philo's interpretation of the story of the

[41] See also *Abr.* 62–3; *Rer. Div. Her.* 276–83, 287–8; *Leg. All.* III.83.
[42] For a comparison of the way Philo interprets biblical material about travelling
   and pilgrimage with the way it is interpreted in Hebrews, see Barrett, 'Eschatology', 377ff.
[43] *Abr.* 69.
[44] *Rer. Div. Her.* 27. See the assertion of Moses' mystical kinship with God, in
   Quaest. in Exod. II.29.
[45] See *Rer. Div. Her.* 276–83, where Abraham's separation from his Chaldean kin
   and homeland is regarded as a prerequisite of membership in, and leadership of,
   a 'novel race and nation (νέον ἔθνος καὶ γένος)' (278). The symbolic structure
   in such instances does not seem at all dissimilar to that of a gospel tradition such
   as Mark 3.31–5.

sacrifice of Isaac, which is the subject of extended discussion in *Abr.*
167–207. Its main purpose is to highlight the utter devotion of the
wise man to the will of God;[46] and Philo goes to great lengths to
show how much greater Abraham's action was in comparison with
other cases of kinship sacrifice. Thus, unlike the latter, the sacrifice
of Isaac lacked the sanction of custom, its object was his only son by
Sarah, and it was an act performed by Abraham himself rather than
by a third party.[47] So the subordination of family ties represented by
the Isaac story allows Philo both to highlight the virtues of obedience and piety personified by Abraham, and to show by how much
the hero surpasses all others in exhibiting those virtues. For the
present purpose, what needs emphasizing is that Philo's discussion
presupposes that familial obligations are not absolute and may be
subordinated to higher considerations. We note also the fundamental point that the importance of kinship as a social and ideological structure renders it extremely valuable for metaphorical
discourse, especially for discourse about identity and belonging.

      b. Moses is another figure presented and interpreted in
terms of his behaviour towards his kinsfolk and his willingness to
subordinate family ties. For example, in praise of his 'nobility of
soul and magnanimity of spirit and inborn hatred of evil', Philo says
that Moses decided 'to renounce completely his expected inheritance from the kinsfolk of his adoption'.[48] Further, upon assuming
the leadership of the Israelites, he refused to advance the interests of
his own household by promoting his own sons or nephews or most
intimate friends.[49] Once again, in Philo, virtue is given precedence
over family connections: for εὐσέβεια, φιλανθρωπία, εὐγένεια
ψυχῆς, μισοπόνηρον and the like are the absolutes in his thought.

      c. Even more striking on this score, however, is the
account Philo gives of Phineas, whose zeal for the law and horror of
the pollution to the nation brought by the idolatrous contact with
the Midianites led him to execute judgment without regard to ties of
natural kinship.[50] Together with others 'zealous for continence and

[46] See *Abr.* 170: 'Mastered by his love for God, he mightily overcame all the
fascination expressed in the fond terms of family affection'; also, 192, 196, 198.
[47] *Abr.* 184–98.   [48] *Vit. Mos.* I.149.
[49] See *Vit. Mos.* I.150; II.142; *Virt.* 53–4, 55–65; see in general the characterization
of the impartial judge in *Spec. Leg.* IV.70.
[50] See *Vit. Mos.* I.300–4.

godliness (τινες ... τῶν τὴν ἐγκράτειαν καὶ θεοσέβειαν ἐζηλω-
κότων) ... [they] massacred all their friends and kinsfolk who had
taken part in the rites ... To none of their convicted blood-relations
did they show pity.'[51] There can be no doubting the emphatic
subordination of natural ties here, confirmed as it is by the divine
voice of approval and reward, according to which Phineas and his
descendants are appointed to the Levitical priesthood.[52] It is worth
noting, in addition, the way Philo heightens this theme by modifying
the version of the story in Num. 25 (LXX). In the latter, there is no
mention of the slaying of their own kin by Phineas and his supporters, since only one offending couple are singled out, cameo-style
(Num. 25.6–8, 14–18), and the death of the twenty-four thousand is
attributed to the plague. Furthermore, the LXX is quite lacking in
the strong ascetic motivation attributed to Phineas by Philo.[53]

   d. The model for Philo's presentation of Phineas and his
colleagues is undoubtedly the Levites, the priestly tribe to whose
ranks Phineas is appropriately added. Philo refers to the Levites on
at least six occasions with respect to their special eminence in
remaining 'on the Lord's side' (cf. Exod. 32.26) and free from the
pollution of worshipping the Golden Calf, a holiness finding ultimate expression in their willingness to bring the divine vengeance
upon even members of their own kin. Thus, in *Spec. Leg.* III.124ff.,
Philo says: 'They began with their nearest and dearest, for they
acknowledge no love nor kinship but God's love' (126). This motif is
repeated in *Vit. Mos.* II.171 and 273. On each occasion, what comes
to the fore is the radical subordination of the bonds of natural
affection under the influence of an all-consuming sense of obligation
to God, an obligation expressed in terms of the language of inspiration and ecstasy, and justified by reference to Platonizing notions
of virtue, holiness and the divine nature.[54]
   What, in sum, do these examples of Philo's treatment of heroic
individuals contribute to our theme? First, we note the recurrence of
the motif of the subordination of natural ties in the characterization
of the heroes. It is as if, by appearing to stand outside, above, or

---

[51] *Ibid.*, I.303.   [52] *Ibid.*, I.304.
[53] See *ibid.*, I.301, for Phineas' horror at the Israelites' surrender to bodily
    pleasure.
[54] For a classic instance, see *Rer. Div. Her.* 68–70. The three other places where
    Philo develops further (and in predominantly allegorical terms) his interpreta-
    tion of the story of the Levites are *Ebr.* 65–76; *Sacr. AC.* 128–30; and *Fug.* 88ff.

over against ties of natural kinship, they gain in holiness and in proximity to God. Separation at one level makes possible identification at another. For Abraham, this has to do with being a wise man and a model proselyte; for Moses, it has to do with being an inspired prophet *par excellence*; for the individual man of virtue, it has to do with (ascetic) devotion to piety and the love of God.

Second, Philo uses the powerful idiom of kinship ties to speak metaphorically about religious and philosophical allegiance, and in particular, to convey certain priorities: the mental over the physical, thought over sense, nature over culture, piety over lawlessness, the love of God over idolatry, and so on. The metaphorical uses of kinship convey a programme which touches on issues religious, philosophical, ethical and social and for which the heroes serve as focal instances, representing the truth in these areas to a quintessential degree. The force of the metaphor lies in the shock which comes from the identification of what is normally valued negatively with the sphere of the holy: the Levite is like the homicide, the wise man is the one who sacrifices his child, the genius of the prophet is marked by his exhortation to slay kinsfolk. It may be no coincidence, therefore, that in the gospel stories about Jesus and the disciples, stories of kinship enmity and teaching about the subordination of family ties are not infrequent. It is likely also that, as in Philo, such stories and teaching will carry a significant metaphorical load, the exploration of which will be the aim of our analysis of Mark and Matthew.

3 The evidence of Josephus

From the writings of the Alexandrian Jew Philo, we turn to the slightly later writings of the Palestinian Jew Josephus (c. 37–93 CE).[55] As in our discussion of the Philonic corpus, our concern here is to illustrate the extent to which, and the manner in which, the subordination of family and household ties features in Josephus' writings. In interpreting Josephus, our concern is less to use what Josephus writes as evidence for the historical reconstruction of the people and events he describes than it is to read the text as evidence for the perspectives of Josephus himself, in a way analogous to

---

[55] As for Philo, I am using the Loeb Classical Library edition and translation of the works of Josephus. The abbreviations of the Latin titles of his works are taken from the introductory section of *TDNT*, vol. I.

reading the gospels for an understanding of the views of the respective evangelists.

Presuppositions

Perhaps our best access to the presuppositions of Josephus about family ties is via his autobiography. *Vit.* 1–6 shows that family ties are supremely important to Josephus' sense of personal and social identity. His genealogy is adduced as proof of his nobility of birth – he comes from lineages both priestly and royal – and constitutes an argument available against character assassination.[56] His paternity, as the father of three sons, is a further mark of his prestige.[57] The chronology of Josephus' ancestry has strong social and political significance: it is not neutral information. Hence, the mention of his great-grandfather's contemporaneity with Hyrcanus and of Josephus' own birth in the year of Gaius' accession to the principate in Rome, as well as of the birth of his three sons during the principate of his patron Vespasian.[58] So Josephus is able to tie his lineage both to the Maccabean line of royal priests of Judaism and to the rulers of the Roman empire of whose ascendancy he himself is a beneficiary.

The material covering his first nineteen years is noteworthy for making no reference to marriage.[59] In fact, Josephus appears not to have married until after 67 CE, at the age of about thirty.[60] He therefore delayed marrying, and did so for reasons of education and public affairs (and the prestige accruing therefrom), upon which he elaborates in *Vit.* 7–12. His *curriculum vitae* includes the claim to have engaged in a thorough study of the three main Jewish 'sects' – the Pharisees, Sadducees and Essenes – as well as spending three years as ζηλωτής of the eremitical holy man Bannus. In relation to his period of attachment to Bannus, the strongly ascetical aspects of his lifestyle are given special emphasis. In all this, there is an implicit acceptance of the idea that delaying marriage and adopting an ascetic lifestyle for the sake of the pursuit of παιδεία is thoroughly honourable.

---

[56] See Josephus, *Vit.* 6.   [57] *Ibid.*, 5.   [58] *Ibid.*, 3, 5.

[59] See Schürer, *History*, II, 578, n. 14, which refers to the fact that the recommended age of marriage for a man is eighteen years, according to the Mishnah (*mAboth* 5.21), as against twenty years, according to the Community Rule from Qumran (*I QSa* 1.10–11).

[60] *Vit.* 414.

The circumstances of Josephus' marriages, the first some ten years after his becoming a Pharisee, illumine further our grasp of his presuppositions about family ties. In *Vit.* 414–15, he says that his first marriage was an honour bestowed on him by Vespasian: 'it was by his command that I married one of the women taken captive at Caesarea, a virgin and a native of that place'. So, as with his treatment of his lineage, marital ties are related to an all-embracing concern with prestige. The woman remains anonymous while the patron is named repeatedly.[61] She is important primarily for her gift status in the patron–client relationship[62] between Vespasian and Josephus, as well as for her reputation as a παρθένος and native Jewess, factors important to Josephus' reputation as a Pharisee. This marriage was short – apparently his wife left him – and no offspring are mentioned. Josephus' second wife, whom he married in Alexandria, bore him three children, of whom only Hyrcanus survived. Josephus then divorced her, 'being displeased at her behaviour',[63] and subsequently married a Jewess 'of distinguished parents (γονέων εὐγενεστάτων)' by whom he had two more sons.[64]

On the basis of the foregoing, Josephus' presuppositions may be summarized in two main points. First, Josephus regards genealogy, ancestral history, marriage and paternity as basic mechanisms for attaining and enhancing social prestige, by establishing connections over time and by blood or marriage to those people and institutions constitutive both of Judaism and the Roman *imperium*. In this he is entirely conventional. Second, religious zeal and educational training provide legitimate justification for subordinating kinship ties (by withdrawing into the desert) and delaying marriage, even for a substantial period of time. The same system of values applies here also. Just as conjugal and consanguineous ties can be a source of prestige, so too the subordination of these ties (if only temporarily, and for a legitimate cause) engenders respect – otherwise Josephus would lose face by including in his *Vita* accounts of his dalliance with Essenism and his ascetic life under Bannus.

---

[61] See also Bailey, *Matriarchs*, 155 and *passim* for an excellent account of Josephus' view of women, especially as shown in his portrayal of the matriarchs in Genesis.

[62] On the fundamental contribution of the patron–client relation to the Roman social order, see Garnsey and Saller, *Empire*, 148–59.

[63] *Vit.* 426.   [64] *Ibid.*, 427.

Model communities

Josephus gives two accounts of the Essenes, the most comprehensive in *Bell.* II.119–61, and an abbreviated account in *Ant.* XVIII.18–22. It is remarkable that he begins his first and longer account by commenting upon the Essenes' attitude to marriage. He says: 'Marriage they disdain, but they adopt other men's children, while yet pliable and docile, and regard them as their kin (συγγενεῖς) and mould them in accordance with their own principles. They do not, indeed, on principle, condemn wedlock and the propagation thereby of the race, but they wish to protect themselves against women's wantonness, being persuaded that none of the sex keeps her plighted troth to one man.'[65] Equally remarkable is the fact that Josephus also ends his account of the Essenes with another extended comment on their marriage customs.[66] These comments on Essene marriage customs invite a number of observations.

First, the extent of Josephus' attention to their marriage customs, together with the pivotal location of his comments whereby they effectively bracket his entire characterization of Essene beliefs and practices, illustrates the potential contribution of marriage customs to community self-definition generally.[67] It also illustrates how important to Josephus himself as author is the subject of marital relations for his representation of the Essene sect (to whom, interestingly, he gives far more attention than to either the Pharisees or the Sadducees).[68]

Second, the Essenes are represented as being distinctive by virtue of the fact that some, at least, of their number do not marry. This distinctiveness is something of which Josephus clearly approves, since it is motivated by the right reasons – above all, the quest for

[65] *Bell.* II.120–1.

[66] *Ibid.*, II.160–1. This is worth quoting also: 'There is yet another order of Essenes, which, while at one with the rest in its mode of life, differs from them in its views on marriage. They think that those who decline to marry cut off the chief function of life, the propagation of the race, and, what is more, that, were all to adopt the same view, the whole race would very quickly die out. They give their wives, however, a three years' probation, and only marry them after they have by three periods of purification given proof of fecundity. They have no intercourse with them during pregnancy, thus showing that their motive in marrying is not self-indulgence but the procreation of children. In the bath the women wear a dress, the men a loin-cloth. Such are the usages of this order.'

[67] See the apologetic use of marriage laws made by Josephus, in *Ap.* II.199–203.

[68] See confirmation of this in Moehring, 'Josephus', 124–7. Moehring even suggests (*ibid.*, 124, n. 19) that Josephus' dark comment on women's infidelity, in *Bell.* II.121, reflects Josephus' personal experience of his first marriage!

virtue and the goal of a united communal life, both reinforced by (what is regarded as) a justifiable misogyny.[69] Of the former, he says: 'They shun pleasures as a vice and regard temperance and the control of the passions (τὴν δὲ ἐγκράτειαν καὶ τὸ μὴ τοῖς πάθεσιν ὑποπίπτειν) as a special virtue.'[70] The communal motive is reflected in Josephus' claim that 'they show greater attachment to each other than do the other sects';[71] and it seems clear that marital alliances are viewed as constituting a distraction or, even worse, a source of rivalry and general 'dissension' (στάσις).[72]

Third, Essene marriage rules as depicted by Josephus are elitist in ethos. Although Josephus refers at the end to a branch of Essenes who do marry – but for the sole purpose of procreation of the race, and not at all for reasons of ἡδονή[73] – it is clear that marriage is legitimate rather for others, who thereby run the risk of moral dissipation, sexual rivalry and household strife, not to mention the pollution associated with menstruation and sexual intercourse. The process of augmenting the community by means of adopting the children of others is elitist also, since it involves a process of selection: of children who are 'yet pliable and docile'.[74] Here we have a mechanism of control which is quite of a piece with the rigorous probationary period of three year-long stages through which the initiate has to pass in order to qualify for full membership of the community.[75] The principle of control is that of merit, evident in the tests of character applied at each stage of entry, and in the Essenes' reputation generally for cultivating sanctity (σεμνότης).[76] What we have, then, is a community of religious virtuosi where membership and status are a matter, not of what is ascribed according to marital and household ties, but rather of what is achieved by means of the renunciation of marriage and family and by initiation into the Essene order itself.

Fourth, the renunciation of marriage is all of a piece, in Josephus' presentation, with other obligations laid upon members. Rights of property-ownership are surrendered, along with the associated differences of status.[77] Members' houses and possessions become

---

[69] For the explicit misogyny, perhaps legitimated for the Essenes by scriptural statements such as Prov. 25.24, see *Bell.* II.121 and *Ant.* XVIII.21.
[70] *Bell.* II.120.   [71] *Ibid.*, II.119.
[72] See *ibid.*, II.121; *Ant.* XVIII.21.
[73] *Bell.* II.160–1; cf. *Ap.* II.199.   [74] *Bell.* II.120.
[75] See *ibid.*, II.137ff.; and the discussion in Schürer, *History*, II, 564–5.
[76] *Bell.* II.119.   [77] See *Bell.* II.122; *Ant.* XVIII.20.

available for the use of other members, quite free of charge.[78] Meals
are taken with the community rather than with one's kin group.[79]
Members are forbidden explicitly to make gifts to their kinsfolk,
except by permission.[80] All members wear uniform clothing.[81] Also,
contact with outsiders, such as for the purpose of commercial
enterprise, is restricted severely. All these are forms of sacrifice
which function as proofs of loyalty and heighten members' mutual
interdependence. There is a definite sense in which the renunciation
of kinship ties and household patterns makes Essene communalism
viable and allows the members of the community to relate to each
other as 'brothers'.[82]

Josephus' account of the Essenes confirms and reinforces what we
found in Philo's accounts of the Essenes and the Therapeutae. Both
writers express high regard for these groups of religious virtuosi,
and neither finds it unusual that zeal for virtue and a unified and
holy common life should find expression – be made possible, even –
through the subordination of family and household ties. It seems
reasonable to infer that the subordination of family ties to become a
follower of Jesus was not at all unprecedented and could be justified
along similar lines.

Enemies vilified

Confirmation of what we have found in Josephus about the importance of family ties and their subordination for defining personal and
group allegiance and identity comes in negative form in the hostile
account he gives of the various groups of rebels opposed to Roman
authority in the period leading up to the outbreak of war in 66 CE.[83]
Significant for our purpose is the fact that Josephus vilifies the
enemies of Rome by highlighting their behaviour in respect of their
neighbours and kinsfolk as an indicator of their depravity and
disloyalty.

78 See *Bell*. II.124–7.   79 See *ibid*., II.129–33; *Ant*. XVIII.22.
80 See *Bell*. II.134.
81 See *ibid*., II.123, 140.
82 See *ibid*., II.122: 'the individual's possessions join the common stock and all,
like brothers (ὥσπερ ἀδελφοῖς), enjoy a single patrimony'. For a similar use of a
household metaphor, see *ibid*. II.126: 'In their dress and deportment they
resemble children under rigorous discipline (ὅμοιον τοῖς μετὰ φόβου παιδαγω-
γουμένοις παισίν).'
83 As Hayward points out, in Schürer, *History*, II, 600, Jospehus' bias against the
heirs of the 'fourth philosophy' who waged war against Rome is seen in his use
of pejorative terms like λῃσταί, στασιασταί and νεωτερίζοντες to describe them.

Thus, in describing the power struggle in Jerusalem in 67 CE between the pro- and anti-war factions, Josephus says: 'Between the enthusiasts for war and the friends of peace contention raged fiercely. Beginning in the home (καὶ πρῶτον μὲν ἐν ὀκίαις) this party rivalry first attacked those who had long been bosom friends; then the nearest relations severed their connections (ἔπειτα ἀφηνιά-ζοντες ἀλλήλων οἱ φίλτατοι) and joining those who shared their respective views ranged themselves henceforth in opposite camps.'[84] The image of household relations breaking down and dividing along political lines is a powerful rhetorical means for conveying the acute social instability which Josephus attributes to the war party.

More pertinent still is the digression depicting the extent and character of the depravity of the fomentors of rebellion against Rome, in *Bell.* VII.254–74. Of the Sicarii and their leading men, for example, Josephus asks rhetorically: 'What ties of friendship or of kindred (ποία δ᾽ αὐτοὺς φιλία, ποία δὲ συγγένεια) but rendered these men more audacious in their daily murders? For to do injury to a foreigner they considered an act of petty malice, but thought they cut a splendid figure by maltreating their nearest relations (ἐν τοῖς οἰκειοτάτοις).' Interestingly, in view of the saying attributed to Jesus in Matt. 8.22b par. Luke 9.60a, one of the most potent ways in which Josephus maligns the Zealots (to take another example) is to cite their refusal to allow the burial of the dead during the internecine struggle for control of Jerusalem prior to the siege by the advancing Roman army. He says: 'The Zealots, however, carried barbarity so far as to grant interment to none, whether slain in the city or on the roads; but as though they had covenanted to annul the laws of nature along with those of their country (τοῖς τῆς πατρίδος συγκαταλῦσαι καὶ τοὺς τῆς φύσεως νόμους) they left the dead putrefying in the sun.'[85]

The historical veracity of Josephus' hostile report need not detain us here. What is important to note, however, is the fact that, whereas in his depiction of the Essenes the subordination of family ties is given as evidence of their virtue and piety, the opposite is the case in his depiction of the Jewish revolutionaries. Their subordination of family ties is represented as a sign of their utter depravity.

---

[84] *Bell.* IV.131–2.
[85] *Ibid.*, IV.381–2; see also, IV.317, 331–2, 359–60. For the general principle of burying even enemies or malefactors, see *Ant.* IV.265 (on Deut. 21.22–3); also, *Ap.* II.205. On the elaborate mourning and burial given by David to his rebellious son Absalom, see *Ant.* VII.39ff.

Putting Josephus' perspective in terms of the metaphor of centre and periphery used by anthropologist Clifford Geertz,[86] we may say that, in the case of the Essenes, the shift of social and symbolic location to the periphery via the renunciation of marriage and household is a movement in the direction of holiness and order (of a higher kind than found in everyday life): but for the revolutionaries, the shift to the periphery via the subordination of natural ties is a movement in the direction of profanity and disorder.

Heroic individuals

Examination of Josephus' accounts of leading figures of the biblical and post-biblical periods of Israel's history shows that, as is the case with Philo, a willingness to subordinate ties of natural kinship is a recurring motif and is presented as a sign of greatness and true piety.

   a. The testing of Abraham is the classic instance, depicted at length in *Ant.* I.222–36.[87] Especially noteworthy are the points where Josephus elaborates and embroiders the much more terse biblical account (Gen. 22.1–19). First, Josephus emphasizes the obedience and full co-operation of Isaac with Abraham in the sacrifice. Isaac, we are told, is twenty-five years old (227); and he goes to the altar willingly and with joy (232). So the episode is as much the story of the testing of the mature filial piety of Isaac as it is of the obedience of Abraham. Second, Josephus makes more explicit the grounds on which God tests Abraham and on which Abraham shows himself willing to sacrifice his son. This is made plain at the beginning: 'thus would he manifest his piety towards Himself (οὕτως γὰρ ἐμφανίσειν τὴν περὶ αὐτὸν θρησκείαν), if he put the doing of God's good pleasure even above the life of his child' (224). It is elaborated in the middle, in Abraham's long farewell speech to Isaac (228–31). It recurs at the end, in the *ex post facto* justification given to Abraham by God (233–5). Third, the extent of Abraham's obedience is augmented, even to the point where Abraham conceals the task from his wife and his household lest they hinder him from performing it, 'deeming that nothing would justify disobedience to God and that in everything he must submit to His will' (225). The entire episode assumes and exemplifies the legiti-

---

[86] See Geertz, 'Centers'.
[87] For further discussion, see Feldman, 'Binding'.

macy of subordinating family ties for a purpose of transcendent religious value, summed up in the text by the term θρησκεία (222, 223, 224, 234).

b. Other cases may be mentioned more briefly. The priority of torah-observance over allegiance to kinsfolk is an ideal which Moses teaches the people prior to the transmission of the Decalogue: 'Let them [the commandments] be had by you in veneration: battle for them more zealously than for children and wives.'[88] Moses also ensures that Aaron and his two remaining sons preserve their priestly purity by refraining from mourning the deaths of the two eldest sons, Nadab and Abihu, thereby 'putting the homage due to God above any frowning over their loss'.[89]

c. The story of the willingness of Saul to kill Jonathan his son out of respect for the oath which he has sworn to God (1 Sam. 14.24–46) is recounted at some length in *Ant.* VI.122ff. What is important for our purpose is the way Josephus uses the motif of kinship ties to highlight the absolute priority to be given to single-minded commitment to God by the keeping of vows.[90] Even the sacrifice of Saul's son is justified: 'Saul thereat swore to slay him, respecting his oath more than the tender ties of fatherhood and of nature.' We are reminded immediately of the sacrifice of Isaac: even more so when Jonathan does not hesitate to submit to death,[91] as Isaac did not hesitate.[92]

d. As a final instance, mention should be made of Josephus' account of the resistance to Antiochus Epiphanes led by Mattathias.[93] His zeal for the laws and customs of the Jews, over against Antiochus' attempts at enforced hellenization, leads him to depart into the wilderness, 'leaving behind all his property (κατα-λιπὼν ἅπασαν τὴν αὐτοῦ κτῆσιν) in the village'.[94] The motivation

---

[88] *Ant.* III.87; cf. IV.309. This is an ethic which appears subsequently in Josephus' account of the Jewish War (at *Bell.* II.197), where the Jews show themselves willing to die with their wives and children rather than disobey the torah.

[89] *Ant.* III.211.

[90] Presumably, the Deuteronomic legislation on vows, in Deut. 23.21–3, lies behind Josephus' interpretation of this episode.

[91] *Ant.* VI.127.

[92] Similar also is the episode of Jephthah and his daughter, in *Ant.* V.263–6, although in this case, Josephus expresses his repugnance at the sacrifice of the girl, willing though she is.

[93] See *Ant.* XII.265–86. [94] *Ibid.*, XII.271.

for so placing at risk his family and the families of his followers, as well as giving up his household goods, is expressed quite explicitly in his rallying call: 'Whoever is zealous for our country's laws and the worship of God (εἴ τις ζηλωτής ἐστιν τῶν πατρίων ἐθῶν καὶ τῆς τοῦ θεοῦ θρησκείας), let him come with me!'

It is fair to conclude, therefore, that the way Josephus portrays the willingness of the heroic individual to subordinate his family and household ties out of devotion of a higher kind – to God and the will of God – is consistent with what we found in the positive account he gives both of his own rather ascetic παιδεία and of the common life of the Essenes of whom he claims first-hand knowledge. It is consistent also, but by contrast, with the negative account he gives of the Jewish revolutionaries whose hostility to their own kin is seen as a mark of their depravity and devotion to disorder. Overall, the evidence from Josephus' writings gives further weight to the claim that the subordination of natural ties is a by no means uncommon idea in the Jewish milieu of early Christianity, and that it is an idea well suited to serve as an idiom for expressing claims to religious devotion and allegiances of a transcendent kind.

4 The evidence from Qumran

We have seen above that Philo claims that 'no Essene takes a wife', whereas, according to Josephus, some Essenes 'disdain marriage' while others feel obligated to marry and propagate the race.[95] The evidence from the Qumran documents is equivocal likewise, but in general terms it may be said that membership of the Qumran community required the adoption, to varying degrees, of an ascetic rule of life.

The evidence about marriage points in two directions. On the one hand, the *Community Rule* makes no reference to female members. As Vermes and Goodman point out, this is 'a fact that would be inexplicable if there had been women among the sectaries. Issues concerning marriage, divorce, ritual impurity associated with sex, and the education of children, could not have been left undetermined. Hence this is not an ordinary *argumentum e silentio* and it is legitimate to conclude that absence of reference means that there

---

[95] Pliny the Elder (23/4–79 CE) likewise reports that the Essenes reject marriage, in *Hist. Nat.* V.73: text in Vermes and Goodman, *Essenes*, 32–3.

was no problem to address.'[96] Archaeological evidence appears to
point in the same direction, by virtue of the fact that the main
graveyard has thrown up male remains only, with female and child
skeletons relatively few in number and located on the periphery.[97]
Thus, even though there is no explicit injunction enjoining the
renunciation of marriage, it is legitimate to infer that the community
at Qumran was made up primarily of celibate males. For such men,
celibacy had definite connotations, among which the following are
probable. First, it was a means of preserving their ritual purity (Lev.
15) as a priestly community dedicated to a life of perpetual worship
in God's true, spiritual temple.[98] Second, it expressed their eschatological self-understanding as consecrated warriors engaged with the
'angels of light' in a holy war against the forces of darkness.[99] Third,
it was an integral aspect of their quest for esoteric knowledge and
prophetic insight through a life of sexual renunciation and the
subjugation of natural drives.[100]

On the other hand, the *Damascus Document*, the *Temple Scroll*,
the *Messianic Rule* and the *War Rule* indicate clearly that the sect
had married members with children as well.[101] A clear instance is
Damascus Document 7.6–9: 'And if they live in camps according to

[96] Vermes and Goodman, *Essenes*, 10. It is possible, of course, to put too much
store on this argument. Coppens, 'Le Célibat', 301, points out that the Community Rule has no *halachah* concerning the sabbath, either!

[97] See Schürer, *History*, II.578 at n. 13, citing de Vaux, *Archaeology and the Dead
Sea Scrolls* (1973), 128–9; also, Vermes and Goodman, *Essenes*, 10.

[98] See Vermes, *Scrolls*, 182; Steiner, 'Essener', 11–24; Thiering, 'Asceticism', 430.
Coppens, 'Le Célibat', 301–2, puts it well: 'Insistons surtout sur le fait que la
communauté de Qumrân se comprenait comme un temple spirituel où, en union
étroite avec les esprits angéliques, devait se célébrer sans interruption un culte
spirituel, et où tous les membres de la secte y établis accédaient à un statut quasi
sacerdotal. D'où ... s'est imposée la nécessité de rendre pour tous journellement
obligatoires les règles imposées aux prêtres par la Tôrah pour s'acquitter du
service cultuel: ce qui a tout naturellement abouti à la pratique d'une continence
ininterrompue.'

[99] E.g. *War Rule* 7.4–6 (Deut. 23.10–11): 'No boy or woman shall enter their
camps, from the time they leave Jerusalem and march out to war until they
return. No man who is lame, or blind, or crippled, or afflicted with a lasting
bodily blemish, or smitten with a bodily impurity, none of these shall march out
to war with them. They shall all be freely enlisted for war, perfect in spirit and
body and prepared for the Day of Vengeance. And no man shall go down with
them on the day of battle who is impure because of his "fount", for the holy
angels shall be with their hosts' (= Vermes, *DSSE*, 132–3). For more on this
holy-warrior interpretation of Qumran asceticism, see Black, *Scrolls*, 29–30;
also, Steiner, 'Essener', 24–7.

[100] See Vermes, *Jesus*, 99–102, for an excursus on 'prophetic celibacy'; Vermes,
Scrolls, 174–5, 181–2; Thiering, 'Asceticism', 434–5, 440–4.

[101] See Vermes and Goodman, *Essenes*, 9.

the rule of the earth, marrying and begetting children, they shall walk according to the Law and according to the statute concerning binding vows, according to the rule of the Law which says, "Between a man and his wife and between a father and his son" (Num. 30.17).'[102] Significant also is *Messianic Rule* 1.8–10: 'At the age of twenty years [he shall be] enrolled, that he may enter upon his allotted duties in the midst of his family (and) be joined to the holy congregation. He shall not [approach] a woman to know her by lying with her before he is fully twenty years old, when he shall know [good] and evil. And thereafter he shall be accepted when he calls to witness the judgments of the Law.'[103] What we have here is not the renunciation of marriage, but its postponement to the age of what Black calls 'full moral maturity',[104] the point also of enrolment as a member of the congregation. So, the *Damascus Document* refers unambiguously to married men with families in the community, and the *Messianic Rule* likewise assumes that the community of 'the last days' will include 'the little children and the women also'.[105]

The evidence from Qumran appears to justify the conclusion that celibacy was practised by members of the desert community in particular.[106] This was unusual in Judaism, and must have marked the desert sectaries out, in a manner reinforced by their practice of common ownership of property, for example.[107] For the *renuntiantes* themselves, it expressed important aspects of their own priestly and eschatological belief and self-understanding. But by no means all of the sect members practised celibacy. For as well as the monastic community in the desert, there were also adherents who lived with their families in the towns and villages. Vermes describes them thus:

> In the 'towns' or 'camps', as the Damascus Rule terms them ... adherents of the sect lived an urban or village life side by side, yet apart from, their fellow Jews or Gentile neighbours. Rearing children, employing servants, engaging in trade and commerce (even with Gentiles), tending cattle, growing vines and corn in the surrounding fields, discharg-

---

[102] Quoted in Vermes, *Scrolls*, 108.   [103] Vermes, *DSSE*, 119.
[104] Black, *Scrolls*, 29. Black says: 'For Judaism, this was a most irregular, if not totally unheard of, postponement of marriage. In rabbinical Judaism, marriage was based ... on physical puberty, not, as here, on considerations of full moral maturity and the reaching of an age of discretion.'
[105] Vermes, *DSSE*, 118.   [106] See Vermes, *Scrolls*, 87–109.
[107] See *Community Rule* 1.12; 5.2.

ing their duties to the Temple by way of offerings and sacrifice, they were obliged like their brothers in the desert to show absolute obedience to the Law and to observe the sect's 'appointed times'.[108]

For these adherents, the ideal for men was to postpone marriage to the age of moral responsibility.

In relation to the theme of this study, the important point is that the evidence from Qumran shows that the subordination of family and household ties is not unprecedented in early Christianity. The men of the desert community at Qumran renounced marriage and pooled their property, while the male adherents in the towns and villages postponed marriage as part of the discipline of membership of the order. It is not unlikely also that early Christianity shares with the Qumran sectaries certain elements of the eschatological holy-war tradition (cf. Matt. 10.37–8 par. Luke 14.26–7), as Otto Betz has suggested.[109] What is equally clear, however, is that discipleship of Jesus and missionary preaching are justifications for subordinating family ties quite different from the concern for the preservation of priestly holiness and cultic purity practised at Qumran.[110]

5 The Cynics

From a representative sample of Jewish sources which illustrate the motif of the subordination of family and household ties, we turn to Greco-Roman sources to do with conversion to philosophy and its social implications.[111] The outstanding examples of the socially disruptive effects of the philosopher's vocation – particularly the effects on the family – come in the accounts of the Cynics.[112] Most

108 Vermes, *Scrolls*, 97.
109 Betz, 'Krieg'. For an interesting study of the eschatological significance of suffering and asceticism at Qumran, see Thiering, 'Suffering'.
110 So too, Coppens, 'Le Célibat', 302–3: 'La préoccupation d'une pureté rituelle qui domine à Qumrân est absente chez le Christ, chez Paul et dans les Actes.'
111 In general, see Nock, *Conversion*, 164–86; Hengel, *Leader*, 25–33. The phrase 'conversion to philosophy' comes from Nock.
112 Cynicism was founded by the ascetic philosopher Diogenes of Sinope (c. 400–325 BCE). It flourished in the third century BCE and experienced a revival in the first and second centuries CE. Evidence of the prevalence of wandering Cynic philosophers trying to make a living by begging in a city like Rome comes in the hostile account of Dio Chrysostom 32.8–10. For a general account of the tenets of Cynicism, see Armstrong, *Philosophy*, 117–19; Baldry, *Unity*, 101–12. For an exploration of the variety of ways of being a Cynic and the

explicit is the witness of the Stoic philosopher Epictetus (c. 55–135 CE), himself a pupil of the first-century Stoic Musonius Rufus.

In *Discourses* III.xxii, Epictetus gives a detailed and certainly Stoicizing account of the ideal Cynic,[113] in which he warns an interlocutor against the unpremeditated taking up of the Cynic philosopher's strenuous calling to be a 'scout' (κατάσκοπος) of what is good for man and what is evil.[114] Significantly, the cost of the Cynic vocation is presented repeatedly in relation to the philosopher's family ties. In order to be free for the task, what is required is radical detachment from family, property and all social customs and conventions; and to be a Cynic philosopher is to accept the call to live that out in practice. As Epictetus puts it:

> And how is it possible for a man who has nothing, who is naked, without home or hearth, in squalor, without a slave, without a city, to live serenely? Behold, God has sent you the man who will show in practice that it is possible. 'Look at me', he says, 'I am without a home, without a city, without property, without a slave; I sleep on the ground; I have neither wife nor children, no miserable governor's mansion, but only earth, and sky, and one rough cloak. Yet what do I lack? Am I not free from pain and fear, am I not free?'[115]

A little later in the *Discourse*, Epictetus' interlocutor asks specifically if the Cynic philosopher marries and has children. His reply is noteworthy, among other things, for its length. Clearly, the idiom of marital and family ties allows Epictetus considerable scope to address the issue of the philosopher's true goal and allegiance. To quote once more:

---

range of opinions in Cynic self-understanding, see Malherbe, 'Self-Definition', 48–59. For (what is in my view) a rather too enthusiastic attempt to interpret the gospel traditions in Cynic terms, see Downing, 'Cynics'; Downing, *Jesus*, esp. chs. III and IV. A view similar to Downing's is taken by Droge, in 'Call Stories'.

113 See Malherbe, 'Self-Definition', 50: 'Epictetus's description has often been taken to represent the true Cynic without due allowance being made for his Stoicizing or for the fact that he is presenting an ideal.' This point is important to register; but it is unnecessary for the present purpose to try to distinguish the Stoic elements from the Cynic, or the ideal Cynic from the real. The awareness of the implications for family ties of conversion to philosophy, as expressed by Epictetus, is what interests us here.

114 *Discourses* III.xxii.24ff., 38, etc.

115 *Ibid.*, III.xxii.45–8 (Loeb Classical Library translation).

But in such an order of things as the present, which is like
that of a battle-field, it is a question, perhaps, if the Cynic
ought not to be free from distraction (ἀπερίσπαστον),
wholly devoted to the service of God, free to go about
among men, not tied down by the private duties of men, nor
involved in relationships which he cannot violate and still
maintain his role as a good and excellent man, whereas, on
the other hand, if he observes them, he will destroy the
messenger, the scout, the herald of the gods, that he is. For
see, he must show certain services to his father-in-law, to
the rest of his wife's relatives, to his wife herself; finally, he
is driven from his profession, to act as a nurse in his own
family and to provide for them. To make a long story short,
he must get a kettle to heat water for the baby, for washing
it in a bath-tub; wool for his wife when she has had a child,
oil, a cot, a cup (the vessels get more and more numerous);
not to speak of the rest of his business, and his distraction
(περισπασμόν). Where, I beseech you, is left now our king,
the man who has leisure for the public interest?[116]

From these passages we may draw the following inferences about
Epictetus' view of the vocation of the Cynic philosopher. First, it is
a demanding vocation which requires total commitment as 'the
messenger, the scout, the herald of the gods'. Second, this vocation
justifies – indeed, necessitates – freedom from distracting ties[117] and
obligations, especially ties of family, property and a settled existence. Whereas for the majority, marriage is the norm, for the Cynic
it is the exception – that of Crates and Hipparchia being a case in
point.[118] Third, the Cynic calling involves the renunciation of a
particular family and an identifiable citizenship in order to benefit
the common good and to foster the ideal of the unity of mankind.[119]
Significantly, the renunciation of a particular family makes possible
participation in a universal family. As Epictetus says:

[116] *Discourses* III.xxii.69–72.
[117] Note Paul's use of the adverb ἀπερισπάστως in 1 Cor. 7.35. For the argument
that Paul is using Stoic ideas and terminology to counter the ascetics at
Corinth, see Balch, 'Debates'. He cites the Epictetus passage on pp. 430–1.
[118] See *Discourses* III.xxii.76.
[119] See Baldry, *Unity*, esp. 108–12, who argues that this ideal – more prevalent in
the Cynicism of the imperial period – was only ever a minor theme in Cynic
philosophy, the main focus being the healing of the individual soul and the
self-sufficiency of the true sage.

Man, the Cynic has made all mankind his children; the men among them he has as sons, the women as daughters; in that spirit he approaches them all and cares for them all. Or do you fancy that it is in the spirit of idle impertinence he reviles those he meets? It is as father he does it, as a brother, and as a servant of Zeus, who is Father of us all.[120]

Three other sources confirm the picture from Epictetus about the incompatibility of the Cynic way of life and normal ties of marriage, family and household. From the *Cynic Epistles*,[121] there is a letter to Zeno attributed to Diogenes (Epistle 47), but coming probably from the first century BCE,[122] which deals exclusively with the question of marriage and child-rearing. Its opposition to both is unequivocal:

One should not wed nor raise children, since our race is weak and marriage and children burden human weakness with troubles. Therefore, those who move toward wedlock and the rearing of children on account of the support these promise, later experience a change of heart when they come to know that they are characterized by even greater hardships. But it is possible to escape right from the start. Now the person insensitive to passion, who considers his own possessions to be sufficient for patient endurance, declines to marry and produce children.[123]

Lucian of Samosata (born c. 120 CE), writing of one of his own teachers, the Cynic philosopher Demonax, includes the following biographical apophthegm in which, once again, the question of marriage is at issue: 'When Epictetus rebuked him [Demonax] and advised him to get married and have children, saying that a philosopher ought to leave nature a substitute when he is gone, his answer was very much to the point: "Then give me one of your daughters, Epictetus!"'[124]

Finally, but by no means exhaustively, Diogenes Laertius, writing in the first half of the third century CE, gives extended treatments of, *inter alios*, the founders of Cynicism, in his compendium the *Lives of Eminent Philosophers*. Once again, the anti-social, unconventional, individualistic and afamilial character of Cynic lifestyle

---

[120] *Discourses* III.xxii.81–2.   [121] See Malherbe, ed., *Epistles*.
[122] *Ibid.*, 15.
[123] Text and translation *ibid.*, 178–9.
[124] Lucian, *Demonax* 55 (Loeb Classical Library translation).

and practice comes to the fore. In his account of Diogenes of Sinope, for example, considerable emphasis is placed on the fact that Diogenes' quest for the simple life and the return to nature leads him to abandon a settled, household-based existence and to live and sleep in open, public places.[125] Furthermore, in his teaching, this same Diogenes is distinctly hostile to the acquisition of wealth, as well as to marriage and child-raising. Concerning the latter, the following anecdote is typical: 'Being asked what was the right time to marry, Diogenes replied, "For a young man not yet: for an old man never at all."'[126]

What conclusions may we draw from this evidence of the Cynic hostility to marriage and family ties? First, it is important to register the fact that we have here a philosophical tradition, going back well into the Hellenistic period and lasting through to the first centuries of the Common Era, in which the quest for freedom and a life of simplicity, in harmony with nature and indifferent to the throes of fortune, has an explicitly anti-social and anti-familial corollary. So if the subordination of family and household ties in the gospels is not unprecedented in the biblical and Jewish traditions, it is not unprecedented in Hellenistic and Greco-Roman traditions either. Followers of Jesus both before and after Easter will not necessarily have been surprised, therefore, at the obligation laid upon them to be willing to subordinate kinship ties and household duties.

Second, while the similarities appear to be strong – especially between, say, Epictetus' portrait of the homeless, vagabond existence of the ideal Cynic, on the one hand, and the gospel traditions about the Son of Man who has nowhere to lay his head and who calls disciples to abandon their kin and follow him, on the other – it is important equally to acknowledge the differences.[127] For example, and to speak in necessarily general terms, where Cynicism is explicitly anti-social and opposed – or at best, indifferent – to marriage and family ties *per se*, the gospels are communal and take household institutions and family ties for granted – witness Jesus' prohibition on divorce or the teaching on respect for parents; where

[125] Diog. Laert. VI.22–3.
[126] *Ibid.*, VI.54 (Loeb Classical Library translation). See also, *ibid.*, VI.29: 'He would praise those who were about to marry and refrained ... [and] those also who purposing to raise a family do not do so.'
[127] See Hengel, *Leader*, 30: 'Jesus too demands complete freedom of the person who follows him; though of course on the basis of an entirely different kind of reasoning and of a different objective.' So too, Downing, 'Cynics', esp. pp. 588–9.

Cynicism involves renunciation of kinship ties as the price of individual freedom (ἐλευθερία)[128] and self-sufficiency (αὐτάρκεια), the gospels call for their (temporary) subordination as the price of the eschatological mission inaugurated by Jesus; where the Cynics adopt a deliberate asceticism as an integral part of the wise man's revolt against culture and return to nature, the gospels speak more of involuntary deprivation and hardship in consequence of faithful missionary discipleship; and where the Cynics seek to reform the individual by a highly provocative onslaught on civilized conventions and popular opinion, there is in the gospels a positive summons to Israel and the nations to personal and social reform in preparation for the advent of God.

6   The Stoics

If the Cynics may be characterized as a kind of 'left-wing Stoicism', it is useful also to illustrate attitudes to family and household ties in the writings of Stoics from the relevant period. What we find, in general terms, is a greater social conservatism on the part of the Stoics – a commitment to do one's duty as a citizen,[129] a corollary of which is a willingness to marry and raise sons. In fact, as Balch has shown, advice 'concerning marriage' is a recurring topos of Stoic literature.[130] I shall refer briefly to two Stoic writers, Musonius Rufus, the 'Roman Socrates' (born c. 30 CE)[131] and (once more) his pupil Epictetus.

In the teachings of Musonius Rufus, the question of marriage is addressed no fewer than three times.[132] What is striking, in comparison with the Cynics, is how positive is Musonius towards marital ties and the raising of children, and this, not only for the mutual benefit marriage brings to the partners involved, but also for the contribution it brings to the life and good order of the πόλις.[133]

---

[128] For an important study of Hellenistic ideas of freedom (as a background to Pauline thought), see Betz, 'Freedom'.

[129] Cf. Armstrong, *Philosophy*, 125–9, for an account of Stoic ethics.

[130] See Balch, 'Debates', who cites and discusses Epictetus, Hierocles, Antipater of Tarsus, and Musonius, as well as Paul.

[131] For a recent essay on Musonius' attitude to women and marriage, see Klassen, 'Musonius', 185–98; although I agree with Balch, 'Debates', 439, n. 35, that Klassen is anachronistic in describing Musonius as an 'egalitarian' – not to mention a 'feminist'!

[132] See Musonius Rufus XIIIA, XIIIB, XIV (= Lutz, 88–97).

[133] E.g. Musonius Rufus XIV (= Lutz, 93): 'Thus whoever destroys human marriage destroys the home, the city, and the whole human race.'

In particular, in relation to the question, 'Is marriage a handicap for the pursuit of philosophy?', Musonius' denial that it is so is clearly a polemic against the Cynic position. Musonius even uses the example of the Cynic philosopher Crates to support his argument: 'Crates, although homeless and completely without property or possessions, was nevertheless married; furthermore, not having a shelter of his own, he spent his days and nights in the public porticoes of Athens together with his wife.'[134] What for the Cynic position is an exception, for the Stoic becomes exemplary of the norm.

Nevertheless, it is also the case that, for Musonius, the philosophical quest for the good takes precedence over other ties of allegiance, including ties of filial piety. He addresses this in relation to the question, 'Must one obey one's parents under all circumstances?'[135] Here, while careful to defend the moral norm of obedience to parents, Musonius argues that there is a higher norm which justifies a son studying philosophy against the wishes of his father:

> If, then, my young friend, with a view to becoming such a man, as you surely will if you master the lessons of philosophy, you should not be able to induce your father to do as you wish, nor succeed in persuading him, reason thus: your father forbids you to study philosophy, but the common father of all men and gods, Zeus, bids you and exhorts you to do so. His command and law is that man be just and honest, beneficent, temperate, high-minded, superior to pain, superior to pleasure, free of all envy and all malice; to put it briefly, the law of Zeus bids man be good. But being good is the same as being a philosopher. If you obey your father, you will follow the will of a man; if you choose the philosopher's life, the will of God.[136]

Not surprisingly, the position adopted by Epictetus is similar to that of his teacher Musonius. While more approving of the Cynic option (as we have seen already) than Musonius, Epictetus also holds that marriage is a duty, and for the same reason: the welfare of the οἶκος and the πόλις.[137] Nevertheless, the philosopher's commitment to the good transcends even ties of filial respect:

134 Musonius Rufus XIV (= Lutz, 93).
135 Musonius Rufus XVI (= Lutz, 100–7).
136 Musonius Rufus XVI (= Lutz, 107).
137 See Epictetus, *Discourses* III.vii.19–28. A clear statement of Stoic social conservatism comes in II.xiv.8 (cited in Balch, 'Codes', 47): 'The result of this for

That is why the good is preferred above every form of
kinship. My father is nothing to me but only the good. 'Are
you so hard-hearted?' Yes, that is my nature. This is the
coinage which God has given me. For that reason if the
good is something different from the noble and the just,
then father and brother and country and all relationships
simply disappear.[138]

Here, then, are clear examples of a justification for the relativization of family – and specifically filial – ties in the thought of a
leading Roman Stoic philosopher of the first century and his pupil.
The call to subordinate family ties as a disciple of Jesus is a justification of a quite different kind, and reflects a different (i.e. eschatological) mood and ethos altogether. Nevertheless, that conversion
to philosophy, like conversion to Christianity, involved an allegiance higher than ties of kinship and household can fairly be
acknowledged.

7 Conclusion

The preceding survey of material from both Jewish and Greco-
Roman traditions is by no means exhaustive. On the Jewish side,
mention could be made also of biblical traditions which presuppose
the legitimacy of subordinating kinship ties out of obedience to the
divine will. From the torah, there is the call of Abram to 'Go from
your country and your kindred and your father's house to the land
that I will show you' (Gen. 12.1); the story of the sons of Levi who
execute God's judgment on the idolaters at Sinai, including their
own kin (Exod. 32.25–9; Deut. 13.6–11; 33.9); the Levitical regulation prohibiting the high priest from contact with a corpse, even that
of his own father or mother (Lev. 21.10–11), in spite of the customary obligation upon the son to bury his parents; and a similar
prohibition applies to the one who has taken the vow of the Nazirite
(Num. 6.6–8). From the prophets, Elisha's call to follow Elijah
requires him to abandon his ploughing with the oxen and to bid his
family farewell (1 Kgs 19.19–21); Jeremiah is instructed by divine

those who have so ordered the work of philosophy is ... that each person
passes his life to himself, free from pain, fear, and perturbation, at the same
time maintaining with his associates both the natural and the acquired relationships, those namely of son, father, brother, citizen, wife, neighbour, fellow-
traveller, ruler, and subject.'
[138] *Discourses* III.iii.5–6.

oracle not to marry a wife or to have children, as a sign of the judgment coming upon Judah (Jer. 16.1–2); and Ezekiel has his wife taken suddenly from him in death and is commanded by the Lord not to mourn for her, again as a sign to the people of the coming loss of Jerusalem and the temple (Ezek. 24.15–27). In addition, from the writings, there is the archetypal proselyte, Ruth, whom Boaz addresses with the accolade: 'you left your father and mother and your native land and came to a people that you did not know before' (Ruth 2.11).

From the Jewish apocryphal and pseudepigraphical traditions, there is Tobit, who breaks with his kinsfolk in captivity in Nineveh by refusing to eat the food of the Gentiles out of obedience to God (Tobit 1.10–12); the account of Abram, in Jubilees 11.14ff., who at the precocious age of fourteen shows his true piety by separating from his father 'so that he might not worship the idols with him', and tries (unsuccessfully) to convert his father from idol worship;[139] Asenath, whose conversion to the God of Joseph involves a complete break with her idolatrous religious heritage and brings upon her the enmity of her parents, kinsfolk, suitors and compatriots (Joseph and Asenath 11.4–6);[140] Judas Maccabaeus and his followers, of whom it is said that, in their war with Nicanor in defence of Jerusalem, 'their concern for wives and children, and also for brethren and relatives, lay upon them less heavily; their greatest and first fear was for the consecrated sanctuary' (2 Macc. 15.18); and the impressive rhetorical discourse known as 4 Maccabees, whose author mounts a sustained argument for devout reason's mastery over the emotions and exemplifies this by showing that adherence to the law transcends even familial affection (see 4 Macc. 2.9b-13), a principle graphically illustrated in the lengthy account of the martyrdom of the seven brothers and their mother resulting from their defiance of Antiochus' policy of enforced hellenization (4 Macc. 8–17).

In sum, there is no lack of material from the biblical and Jewish sources which provides further evidence for what we found in the analysis of Philo, Josephus and the Qumran documents: that, fundamentally speaking, allegiance to God and devotion to the will

---

[139] See also *Apocalypse of Abraham* 1–8, where the episode is developed at even greater length.
[140] See, most recently, Douglas, 'Liminality', esp. p. 37, where the author acknowledges the importance of 'the topos of disobeying or leaving one's parents or family for the sake of a higher good'; also, Kee, 'Joseph', 400.

of God transcend family ties and legitimate their subordination. Here is strong precedent, therefore, for the apparent 'hostility' to family in the context of discipleship of Jesus found in the gospels. When the anti-familial and subordinationist materials from the Cynic and Stoic sources are added, there is good reason for claiming that the gospel traditions to which we are about to turn resonate against a wider background.[141] Subordinating family and household ties to follow the eschatological prophet Jesus is a mode of action rooted deeply in the traditions of Jewish monotheistic faith and piety. Nor is it without analogies in Greco-Roman philosophical traditions to do with conversion to philosophy. Without such roots and analogies, it is doubtful that the gospel stories about the priority of discipleship of Jesus over kinship ties could have been at all meaningful to their hearers and readers, let alone prompt them to adopt such a demanding *modus vivendi* themselves.

[141] Note also the occurrence of the renunciation motif in Philostratus' *Life of Apollonius of Tyana*. In I.xiii, Apollonius gives away most of his property, and decides 'never to wed nor have any connexion whatever with women'; in IV.i, the mechanics at Ephesus leave their crafts and 'follow (ἠκολούθουν)' him; and in IV.xxxvii, there is the story of the testing of Apollonius' followers, in which 'some of them declared that they were ill, others that they had no provisions for the journey, [and] others that they were homesick (οἱ δὲ τῶν οἴκοι ἐρᾶν)'.

3

DISCIPLESHIP AND FAMILY TIES IN MARK

1 Introduction

One of the best ways of describing the ethos and self-understanding
of a religious community or movement is to analyse its attitudes to
natural ties. Such ties may be economic, geographical, racial or
familial; and they are the means by which a group identifies itself
and sustains itself. For a religious movement, discourse about
natural ties – and especially family ties – frequently constitutes a
major idiom of commitment and community. For example, attitudes to the family may function as a test of allegiance to the
charismatic leader. The subordination of the family may be part of
the cost of adherence. The religious community may come to represent itself in familial terms, as a kind of alternative family or
brotherhood, whose role norms and authority patterns are modelled
to some extent on those of the natural family. These, in general
terms, are the kinds of observations made by sociological observers
of sects and new religious movements.[1]

The aim of this chapter is to discuss the ethos and self-
understanding of the Marcan community by means of an analysis of
family- and household-related material in the Gospel of Mark. In
undertaking this analysis, I am working on the assumption which
undergirds all history-of-traditions and redaction-critical work on
the gospels, that the history of the tradition bears witness to the
history of the community which preserves it and passes it on. On this
view, the gospels are not only windows onto the historical Jesus:
they are also mirrors – to some extent, at least – of the communities
of believers in Jesus, communities which passed on and shaped the
tradition, in part, according to their own particular circumstances,

---

[1] See, for example, Harder, 'Life Style', 155–72; Wallis, *Salvation*, 74–90; Beckford, 'Typology', 41–55 ; Kilbourne and Richardson, 'Cults', 81–100.

needs and interests. I am assuming also that it is legitimate, in the interpretation of the gospel texts, to inquire after the intention of the evangelist, where 'evangelist' is understood as referring to the primary editor or author of the gospel in its final form. The two most common ways of distinguishing the intention of the evangelist are: first, separating the traditional and redactional stages of the formation of the gospel, on the assumption that editorial modifications will reflect the interests of the evangelist; and second, analysing the gospel as a literary whole in order to draw conclusions about the meaning of the story for the evangelist from the way it has been constructed.[2]

Classically, redaction criticism has adopted both of these approaches.[3] More recently, literary or narrative criticism has sharpened the gospel interpreter's focus on the second in particular, by attending to standard literary concerns such as plot, character development, setting, and use of rhetorical devices.[4] Although it is possible and legitimate to pursue literary concerns quite independently of historical questions about the gospel's original *Sitz im Leben*, it is in my view equally possible and legitimate to adopt an eclectic approach which combines classic redaction criticism and the more recent narrative criticism. After all, in the history of gospels scholarship, the latter can be seen as an organic development of the former.[5] Only in more dogmatic forms of structuralist analysis of biblical texts are historical (diachronic) concerns and authorial intent ruled out of court. The often surprisingly wooden results of such analysis argue in favour of interpretations which try to take seriously questions of historical context.[6]

So, if it is important, hermeneutically, to pay attention to the Gospel of Mark as a text, it is important also to locate that text historically and sociologically in relation to the audience or community for which it was composed. Obviously, this is an exercise in hypothetical reconstruction, and some circularity of argument is

[2] See further the rightly cautious essay on redaction criticism by Stein, 'Methodology'.
[3] See further Perrin, *Criticism, passim*.
[4] The literature is burgeoning. For a recent critical account, see Morgan, *Interpretation*, 203–68; and on Mark's Gospel, Rhoads and Michie, *Mark*; Best, *Mark*; and Iersel, *Mark*.
[5] So too, Perrin, 'Interpretation'.
[6] A useful account is Patte, *Exegesis*. For evaluation, see, *inter alios*, Thiselton, 'Structuralism', 329–35; Barr, 'Language', 48–52; and Morgan, *Interpretation*, 251–6.

unavoidable. Any conclusions about the Marcan community and the wider *Sitz im Leben* of the gospel can only be tentative, therefore.[7] But scholarly investigation builds upon a tradition; and there can be no doubt that the years since the advent of form criticism have brought considerable success in the elucidation of the communal dimension of earliest Christianity.[8] Form criticism of the gospels, with its concern to relate the various forms of the tradition to settings in the life of Jesus and the early church, has always been implicitly sociological.[9] Similarly, redactional investigations of the theologies of the evangelists have shown repeatedly the extent to which the gospels represent responses of a pastoral kind to crises and controversies in communities of second-generation believers.[10] More recently, attempts to sharpen the focus on the communal dimension of the New Testament documents generally, and of the gospels in particular, have made explicit use of methods and models drawn from the social sciences.[11] These have made possible the exploration of early Christianity as a 'social world in the making', where what is important is not texts in isolation, or theological ideas as somehow intelligible and significant on their own terms, or even the actions and teachings of persons of individual genius, but rather the way texts, beliefs and persons interact in a socially meaningful way.[12]

What follows, therefore, is an attempt at a more holistic study of the Gospel of Mark in which both literary and social scientific analysis will be used to interpret the stories and sayings to do with

[7] Note the warning of Kingsbury, 'Research', 105: 'Still, one thing is certain: the attempt to achieve a viable description of the Marcan community by assuming that the text of the Gospel reflects directly and throughout the circumstances of Mark's own day will not do; clearly, a more differentiated approach is needed.'

[8] See Barton, 'Community', 134–8; Barton, 'Communal Dimension'.

[9] See Bultmann, *Tradition*, 4: 'The proper understanding of form-criticism rests upon the judgement that the literature in which the life of a given community, even the primitive Christian community, has taken shape, springs out of quite definite conditions and wants of life from which grows up a quite definite style and quite specific forms and categories. Thus every literary category has its "life situation" (*Sitz im Leben*: Gunkel), whether it be worship in its different forms, or work or hunting or war.'

[10] See, for example, the essays on the gospels in Mays, *Gospels*; also, Achtemeier, 'Resources', 145–85.

[11] This is another massive growth area: witness the bibliographic article of Harrington, 'Exegesis', 77–85. To date, most progress has been made in Pauline scholarship, to which I myself have contributed. See Barton, 'Cross', 13–19; 'Resurrection', 67–75; 'Place', 225–46; 'Paul', 167–77.

[12] See the helpful methodological statement of Elliott, *Home*, 1–20.

family ties. I have chosen to focus upon the theme of family ties for
several reasons.

1. Mark devotes a significant amount of his narrative to family-
and household-related concerns, as will become evident below. So it
does not seem artificial to ask why and to what end. As Ieuan Ellis
puts it in a recent essay on the subject as a whole:

> The gospels are a distillation of material that has undergone
> transmission in the early Christian community's reflection
> on Jesus. It is fascinating to conjecture why his followers
> should have preserved these, and only these, stories about
> the relation of Jesus to the family, and what determined
> their choice in the matter.[13]

2. Redaction-critical study of Mark (and of the gospels generally)
has given most attention to questions of a doctrinal kind and, in
particular, to christology.[14] There is legitimate scope, therefore, for
a study which gives attention to questions of a social kind in Mark,
and which attempts by literary and social scientific methods to show
how the doctrinal and the social relate: to ask, in other words, what
christology and community have to do with each other according to
Mark. Important advances have been made already in this area,
especially by Howard C. Kee in *Community of the New Age: Studies
in Mark's Gospel* (1977).[15] Kee's study was one of the first successfully to combine redactional and sociological methods in gospels,
and especially Marcan, criticism.[16] But it gives relatively little attention to the material on family ties,[17] and methodologically it antedates the development of narratological approaches to the text.

3. As I pointed out in the Introduction, there is a growing
scholarly awareness of the impact of the household upon early
Christian faith and practice and, conversely, of the effects of conversion upon family ties. So far, discussion has focussed primarily upon
Pauline Christianity and the period after Paul, with important
studies on the letters of Paul, the Pastoral Epistles and 1 Peter. So

---

[13] Ellis, 'Jesus', 187.
[14] Note how christology dominates the survey by Martin, *Mark*, as well as the
essays collected in Tuckett, *Secret*, and in Telford, *Interpretation*.
[15] See also Kee's essay, 'Setting', 245–55.
[16] Mention should be made, however, of the very important earlier contribution,
although in the area of Johannine studies, by Meeks, 'Sectarianism', 44–72.
Here, too, the relation between christology and community is explored in a most
creative way, using literary and social science methodology.
[17] See Kee, *Community*, 109f., 153f.

far, the narrative material of the New Testament, namely the gospels, has not received sufficient attention in relation to the question of the relation of faith and family ties.[18]

2 The call to mission and the legitimation of detachment (Mark 1.16–20)

The story of the call of the disciples, in 1.16–20 (cf. 2.13–14), is of great importance for understanding the ethos of Marcan Christianity and its implications for family ties. The literary and sociological observations which follow are intended to show that this story may be interpreted properly, not only as an historical account of the beginnings of Jesus' public ministry in association with a group of supporters, but also as a story of paradigmatic significance for Mark, which functions – precisely because of its rootedness in the Jesus tradition – to provide a model of and a model for missionary discipleship in the evangelist's own day.

Form-critically, there can be little doubt that the tradition has been shaped according to the pattern of the biblical call story.[19] The tri-partite structure of the three episodes (1.16–18, 19–20; 2.13–14), each of which contains (i) a setting, (ii) a summons to follow and (iii) a response involving the renunciation of household and/or occupational ties, corresponds to that of the story of the call of Elisha by Elijah, in 1 Kgs. 19.19–21, a story which we know to have been influential in the formation of other parts of the gospels tradition (cf. Matt. 8.21–2 par. Luke 9.59–62).[20] This implies, at the literary level, that the call stories have a strong conventional quality. The appearance of the divinely appointed messenger, the authoritative summons to share his mission and the consequent subordination of otherwise legitimate commitments are elements which the Marcan stories share in common with the scriptural prophetic tradition. At the level of early Christian (including Marcan) theology, this has important implications. The mission of Jesus and his call to follow (even at the cost of family ties) are based upon clear

---

[18] A recent exception is Crosby, *House*. Also germane are Esler, *Community*; Koenig, *Hospitality*; Fiorenza, *Memory*.

[19] See, *inter alios*, Hengel, *Leader*, 4–5; Pesch, *Markusevangelium I*, 109ff.; Guelich, *Mark 1*, 49, and the works cited there. Best, *Jesus*, 168–9, is more cautious.

[20] See esp. Hengel, *Leader*, 16–18.

scriptural precedent; even more so, they are the fulfilment of scripture (Mark 1.2–3, 15). Consequently, they are the will of God (3.35).
But the implications are not only theological: they are sociological as well. For it can hardly be doubted that the preservation of
these stories and their shaping along conventional, biblical lines
made it possible for them to function in the traditioning communities, not only as models of discipleship in the period of Jesus' earthly
ministry, but also as models for missionary discipleship in the
period after Easter.[21] In short, there is reason to believe that one
important intention of the call stories is the legitimation of detachment from family and occupational ties for the sake of missionary
work.[22]

Redaction-critical analysis of this passage has been inconclusive.[23]
Mark's main contribution seems to have been his insertion of the
call stories at this point in the narrative.[24] In addition, E. Best[25] has
given good reasons for favouring the following material as redactional: (i) the entire initial clause in 1.16, Καὶ παράγων παρὰ τὴν
θάλασσαν τῆς Γαλιλαίας; (ii) the principal verb, εἶδεν, which
occurs in all three call stories (1.16, 19; 2.14); (iii) the parenthetical
ἦσαν γὰρ ἁλιεῖς, in 1.16; (iv) the link-words καὶ εὐθύς, in 1.18, 20;
and (v) the other participle expressing motion (cf. παράγων, v.16),
προβάς, in 1.19. These results are not unimportant, however.
With respect to the question of discipleship and family ties, certain
inferences seem reasonable.

First, the evangelist has seen fit to draw upon a tradition of the
call by Jesus of the first four disciples in which the leaving of
household and occupational ties is a prominent element. Second, he
has located the story at the very beginning of Jesus' public ministry.

---

[21] I am indebted for the distinction between 'models of' and 'models for' to
Geertz, *Interpretation*, 93–4.

[22] See the methodological statement of Theissen, *Followers*, 3–4: 'If we presuppose
that a tradition is genuine, we may assume that those who handed it down
shaped their lives in accordance with the tradition. If we assume that it
originated within the Jesus movement in the period after Easter, we can
presuppose that those who handed it down shaped the tradition in accordance
with their life. In either case the result is the same: there is a correspondence
between the social groups which handed down the tradition and the tradition
itself.' For further elaboration, see Theissen's essay on 'The Sociological Interpretation of Religious Traditions' in his *Setting*, 175–200.

[23] Typical is Gnilka, *Markus I*, 72: 'Markus hat die Perikope nahezu unverändert
gelassen und seine Intentionen vorab durch ihre Einordnung angedeutet.'

[24] So, Guelich, *Mark 1*, 49.   [25] Best, *Jesus*, 167–8.

This gives it an aetiological aspect, allowing the story both to explain how and why these disciples were chosen, and also to legitimate a particular mode of discipleship involving radical renunciation.[26] Third, the redactional setting in Galilee links this first story about the call of the disciples with two earlier episodes, Jesus' coming from Galilee to be baptized (1.9–11) and his coming back into Galilee preaching 'the gospel of God' (1.14–15). This link is not merely geographical. It conveys the profound connection in this gospel between theology, christology, eschatology and discipleship.[27] Leaving family and following Jesus is legitimate because he is the Son of God (1.11) who proclaims the coming of the kingdom of God (1.15). Nor is this leaving and following a mode of discipleship limited to the past and restricted to those first disciples. For the Galilean setting also points forward to the period after the resurrection (14.28; 16.7).[28]

The preceding form- and redaction-critical observations may be augmented by the following comments from a literary perspective. First we note the careful structure of the narrative as a whole. After the prologue (1.1–15), the gospel falls naturally into two parts: 1.16 – 8.26 and 8.27 – 16.8. The first part, which tells of Jesus' public ministry in Galilee, consists of three subsections: 1.16 – 3.12, 3.13 – 6.6 and 6.7 – 8.26. It is striking that each subsection begins with an episode involving Jesus and the disciples: the call story (1.16–20), the choosing of the twelve (3.13–19a) and the sending of the twelve on mission (6.7–13).[29] So disciples are with Jesus from the beginning, and developments in their role result from initiatives of Jesus. This structure gives the call stories in 1:16–20 (and 2:13–14) a programmatic quality.[30] It is noteworthy, therefore, that the disciples' renunciation of their household ties, in 1.16–20, corresponds

---

[26] See Pesch, *Markusevangelium I*, 108: 'Der Evangelist übernimmt ... eine ätiologische Jüngerlegende, welche zur Begründung und zur Anregung der Nachahmung der missionarischen Tätigkeit der Junger in Jesu Nachfolge erzählt wurde.'

[27] See Guelich, *Mark 1*, 49, who speaks slightly more narrowly of the 'interplay of Christology and discipleship'.

[28] The redactional status of Mark 14.28 and 16.7, and the interpretation of 'Galilee' in a predominantly symbolic sense, are views now widely held in Marcan scholarship. See, *inter alios*, Best, *Jesus*, 199–203; Best, *Mark*, 74, 76–8; Malbon, 'Jesus', 363–77; Freyne, *Galilee*, esp. 51–68.

[29] See Guelich, *Mark I*, xxxvi–xxxvii.

[30] So, too, Lane, *Mark*, 69–70, who draws upon Meye, *Jesus*, 83f., 99–110.

with the mission instruction to renounce possessions and depend upon the hospitality of others in 6.7–13.

Second, the sequence of the opening events is important and generates certain expectations. The prologue, which begins and ends with 'gospel' (εὐαγγέλιον) being announced and proclaimed (1.1, 15), and which presents in embryonic form the essential content of the gospel as a whole,[31] is followed by the authoritative summons of the disciples by the divine Son (1.11) to mission. This sequence – gospel proclamation with an ensuing summons to missionary discipleship – recurs repeatedly within the course of the narrative.[32] It also underlies the shape of the narrative as a whole: for, at the end, the heavenly messenger proclaims the gospel ('Ιησοῦν ... τὸν Ναζαρηνὸν τὸν ἐσταυρωμένον· ἠγέρθη) and commands the women to tell the disciples that Jesus 'goes before' them into Galilee, which the reader knows is the place of mission (6.6b–13).[33] Clearly, the sequence is a clue to the author's point of view. His whole narrative, which he himself designates τὸ εὐαγγέλιον (1.1), is a summons to give up everything, even one's own family, for the sake of 'following' Jesus in missionary preaching (13.10).

A third significant feature of the narrative is the sense of time. It is as if the evangelist is saying that extraordinary times demand extraordinary action.[34] John has been 'handed over' (παραδίδωμι): the time of his passion has arrived (1.14a). Jesus, having received the Spirit (1.9–11) and having defeated Satan in the wilderness (1.12–13), comes into Galilee proclaiming the fullness of time and the imminence of the kingdom of God (Πεπλήρωται ὁ καιρὸς καὶ ἤγγικεν ἡ βασιλεία τοῦ θεοῦ, 1.15a). We are witnessing here the introduction of an all-pervasive authorial conviction that history has reached a climax with the coming of Jesus 'the mightier one' (ὁ ἰσχυρότερός, 1.7) and that time is short (9.1).[35] Therefore, change is necessary (1.15b) and radical action required. The leaving of

---

[31] This is demonstrated well by Drury, using a form of structuralist analysis, in his 'Mark 1', 25–36; see also Hooker, *Message*, 1–16, who, however, restricts the prologue to vv. 1–13.

[32] Mark 2.13–14 is a good example. The summons to 'follow' (v. 14) is preceded by the crucial statement that 'he taught them' (ἐδίδασκεν αὐτούς), a redactional element of major christological import, which clearly provides the warrant for Levi's extraordinary compliance. See further, Achtemeier, 'Reflections', 465–81. Other examples of the sequence are 8.31–8; 9.30–50; 10.32–52.

[33] See Freyne, *Galilee*, 54–68.

[34] For a recent exploration of Mark's sense of time and its implications for Marcan ethics, see Via, *Ethics*.

[35] See further Robinson, *Problem*; and especially Kelber, *Kingdom*.

occupation, possessions and family in response to the call of Jesus is depicted in 1.16–20 as one such action. Normal work and everyday relations are for normal time. Their abandonment both reflects and is reinforced by a conviction that times have changed and a special time has come.

The repetition[36] of the basic call story (1.16–18) in 1.19–20 and 2.13–14 gives it an emphatic quality designed, perhaps, to overcome resistance to the idea of radical detachment for the sake of the kingdom of God, as well as to highlight the authority of Jesus and his word. The fact that Simon and Andrew respond 'immediately' (εὐθύς, 1.18) and that, once Jesus sees James and John, he calls them 'immediately' (εὐθύς, 1.20a) is emphatic also, conveying a sense of the sudden irruption of God's rule and, therefore, of God's new time.[37] This is reinforced further by the use of strong verbs of motion in relation to both Jesus (for example παράγων in 1.16a; 2.14a; and προβάς in 1.19) and the disciples (for example ἀφέντες ... ἠκολούθησαν αὐτῷ in 1.18; cf. 1.20; 2.14). Jesus, in Mark, is pre-eminently the one who is on the move, who leads his disciples 'on the way', and who 'goes before' them. The paradigmatic response of disciples is both negative and positive: to leave everything and to follow.[38]

From sense of time and repetition we turn to characterization. The central character, of course, is Jesus himself. He is God's Son (1.1, 11), has God's Spirit (1.10), and preaches the gospel of the kingdom of God (1.15).[39] As such, his word has great authority (ἐξουσία), as the first miracle story makes clear (1.21–8).[40] It is not surprising, therefore, that at his command, the fishermen (and the tax-gatherer) follow him. Their response reflects Jesus' authority. His authority legitimates their response. The ones called, in 1.16–20,

[36] On the possible significance of repetition in (mythological) narrative, see Meeks, 'Sectarianism', esp. at p. 144, drawing upon the insights of the social anthropologist Edmund Leach.

[37] On Mark's striking use of εὐθύς (42 times), primarily in the first half of the gospel, see Best, *Jesus*, 168.

[38] On the redactional intention of 'the way' (ἡ ὁδός) in Mark (esp. 8.27–10.52), see Swartley, 'Function', 73–86.

[39] There is a real sense, no doubt, that God is the main character, but Mark's understanding of the divine transcendence means that God remains off-stage, even though he intervenes at crucial points (e.g. 1.11; 9.7; 15.38) and is the subject of controversy (e.g. 12.13–17, 18–27, 28–34). See further, Donahue, 'Neglected Factor', 563–94.

[40] On the relation in Mark between Jesus' miracles and his authority as a teacher, see P. J. Achtemeier, 'Reflections', *passim*.

are the four (or three) whom the subsequent plot shows to be the most prominent among the twelve (1.29–31; 3.14ff.; 5.37; 8.29; 9.2; 10.35–45; 13.3; etc.), and it is noteworthy that they are identified by name. This prominence gives their behaviour in leaving natural ties to follow Jesus an exemplary status. There can be little doubt that Mark presents them as model disciples. Here the model is positive: elsewhere, it is negative (for example 10.32–3; 14.33ff.; etc.). Here they model positively Jesus' subsequent teaching on discipleship, addressed in a generalizing way to a much wider audience (8.34–8).[41] The fact that the first men called are two pairs (of brothers) may symbolize the subsequent practice of going on mission two-by-two (6.7).[42] If so, this would be further confirmation that the evangelist conceives of discipleship primarily in terms of itinerant mission.

A concluding comment from a sociological perspective is in order now. The story describes a new social world in the making: the advent of the authorized and tested agent of God who announces a new and climactic stage in time and with authority calls into being the nucleus of a renewed people summoned to mission. This story, part of the tradition about Jesus, has been incorporated into Mark's Gospel in the ways described already. Presumably, therefore, it was important both for the evangelist and for the life of his community. First, it roots their beliefs and practices in history, in the time of a revelatory 'beginning' (ἀρχή, 1.1). Second, it provides a basis of authority – Jesus himself and those called by him – for the persistence and development of their life together and their missionary activity (13.10; 14.9). Third, it provides a model for missionary activity which legitimates radical social detachment.

There is no sign, however, of antipathy toward familial and occupational ties *per se*. The motivation for leaving is presented, not in negative, anti-social terms, but in terms of the prophetic call to a mission to people of all kinds (2.15–17). Further, there is no indication that the leaving is to be a permanent state of affairs. On the contrary, shortly after the call of the disciples, Jesus enters the house of Simon and Andrew and heals Simon's mother-in-law, who herself reciprocates by showing hospitality (1.29–31). Again, in leaving to

[41] See Best, *Mark*, 49: 'What is said about the need to follow Jesus on the way of the cross is what needs to be said to all church members and not just to some sub-group of ministers within it.'
[42] So, *inter alios*, Pesch, *Markus I*, 114.

follow Jesus, the disciples do not destroy their means of livelihood
(as Elisha had done), nor do they leave their families bereft: Zebedee
still has the boat and the hired servants (1.20); and Simon and
Andrew still have their house (1.29), which now becomes a place for
serving and healing (1.31b, 32–4). So the social (and economic)
detachment which the story models and legitimates is not detachment at any cost and for any reason. Sociologically speaking, the
story represents the interests and self-understanding, not of an
anti-social movement, but of an innovatory, prophetic one. The
leaving of familial and occupational ties for the sake of Jesus and
the gospel (8.35b) dramatizes powerfully the movement's sense of
new priorities, while intimating, at the same time, what those new
priorities might cost in personal and social terms.

3   Jesus and his own family (Mark 3.20–1, 31–5; 6.1–6a)

The depiction of Jesus' relations with his own family is of undoubted importance for this study, given the centrality of Jesus to Mark's
understanding of the gospel, and given also his basic understanding
of discipleship as the *imitatio Christi* (for example 8.34ff.). There are
two important passages for assessing Mark's interpretation of Jesus
and his family: 3.20–1, 31–5 and 6.1–6a. We shall see that, in each
case, Mark's interpretation is somewhat hostile to the family of
Jesus. Advance warning of this derives from several preliminary
observations.

First, Mark provides no genealogies or birth narratives, unlike
Matthew and Luke; or any stories of Jesus' youth at home (cf. Luke
2.41–51). So neither Jesus' mother nor father is given any role in
salvation history. Nor are they depicted as disciples. The contrast
with the role accorded Joseph in Matthew and that accorded Mary
in Luke–Acts (and in the Fourth Gospel) is striking indeed.[43]

Second, the story of Jesus' rejection at Nazareth, in 6.1–6a, is the
final mention of Jesus' family in Mark. There is no rehabilitation
after the passion of the kind implied for Peter in 16.7 (cf. 14.28). Nor
is there a scene of caring reconciliation of the kind accorded Mary at
the foot of the cross, in the Fourth Gospel (John 19.25–7). Instead,
Jesus' family disappear from the scene when the story is still at a
relatively early stage. They disappear as finally as, at a later stage,

---

[43] See further, Brown, *Mary*, *ad loc.*; Fenton, 'Mother'; Fitzmyer, *Theologian*,
57–85; and Barton, 'Family'.

does another intimate of Jesus: Judas, one of the twelve (14.43). Fenton spells out the implications well: 'Neither flesh and blood nor physical proximity nor membership of the original group of disciples guarantees faith; nothing guarantees faith. It is God's gift and its reception cannot be presumed.'[44]

A third general consideration concerns the geography of Jesus' ministry. It is remarkable how early in the narrative Jesus leaves Nazareth (1.9a). Significantly, Nazareth is named prior to his baptismal commissioning in 1.9b–11, following which he does not return there but is driven by the Spirit into the wilderness (εἰς τὴν ἔρημον) instead (1.13). Nazareth, the town of his family, does not serve as the base for his ministry at any point. On the one occasion Jesus returns there (εἰς τὴν πατρίδα, 6.1), he is not made welcome but is met with unbelief. Capernaum, rather than Nazareth, becomes his base (1.21; 2.1; 9.33). It is there, rather than with his own kin, that he has his house (2.1; 3.20).[45] So from 1.9 to 10.1, when Jesus finally leaves Galilee for Judaea, his home base is Capernaum. That town, together with the community of the twelve called 'to be with him', replaces Nazareth and the community of Jesus' own family.[46]

Jesus' true family: Mark 3.20–1, 31–5 and parallels

The material in 3.20–35 is recognized widely to consist of both traditional and redactional elements, the respective identification of

---

[44] Fenton, 'Mother', 435. I am not persuaded, however, by Fenton's intriguing suggestion that Μαρία ἡ Ἰακώβου τοῦ μικροῦ καὶ Ἰωσῆτος μήτηρ, in 15.40 (15.47; 16.1), is a further (and damning) reference to the mother of Jesus. 1. If it is a reference to Jesus' mother, it is surprisingly ambiguous. 2. The women in 15.40–1 are disciples (ἠκολούθουν αὐτῷ καὶ διηκόνουν αὐτῷ). Jesus' mother is not described in these terms in Mark. Indeed, things are quite the contrary, on the evidence of 3.31–5 and 6.1–6a, discussed below. 3. The supposed link with 6.3 is tenuous. There, James and Joses are listed with Judas and Simon. In 15.40, we find James 'the younger' and Joses only. 4. Mary Magdalene and Salome and the 'many other women' are introduced here for the first time. It would be surprising if this were not the case for the second Mary also. 5. The three named women function in the narrative as replacements for the three men (Peter, James and John) who are noteworthy by their absence from the crucifixion. They are witnesses, however imperfect (ἀπὸ μακρόθεν, in 15.40): unlike the twelve.

[45] Mark 2.15, with the phrase, ἐν τῇ οἰκίᾳ αὐτοῦ, should almost certainly be added to the references, in the light of Malbon's excellent study, 'Mark 2.15', 282–92; and Malbon, *Space*, 117ff.

[46] See also Iersel, *Mark*, 93: 'Among all the spatial and geographical representations called up by the book, the two towns Nazareth and Capernaum are clearly one another's counterparts. In both places Jesus visits and teaches in the

which is notoriously difficult.[47] R. A. Guelich points out that
various literary forms are discernible in the text as it stands: two
pronouncement stories, one of which is a controversy narrative
(3.22–6), the other a biographical apophthegm (3.31–5); a parabolic
saying (3.27); a sentence of holy law (3.28–9); and 3.20–1 as,
perhaps, the remains of a biographical apophthegm.[48] At some
point in the history of the tradition, two larger units of material
appear to have developed, one relating Jesus' controversy with the
scribes from Jerusalem (3.22–30), the other the story of Jesus'
encounter with his family (3.21, 31–5). The principal concern here,
however, is the identification of Marcan editorial activity. We shall
see that the effect of Mark's redaction and composition has been to
sharpen the sense of the alienation between Jesus and his natural
kin.

Turning, then, to redactional analysis, which will demand most of
our attention in relation to this passage, we begin with 3.20–1. First,
3.20 is probably redactional. There is evidence of awkwardness in
the transition from the previous episode, since ἔρχεται is singular
and αὐτούς plural. The textual tradition shows an awareness of the
discrepancy by changing ἔρχεται to ἔρχονται.[49] The more difficult
reading is to be preferred, however. It prepares the way for the
accusations made against Jesus alone in the verses following
(vv. 21b–22).[50] The content of the verse is typically Marcan and
shows no evidence of an underlying source. The entry into a house
(εἰς οἶκον) compares favourably with 2.11, 26; 5.19, 38; 7.17, 30;
8.3, 26; 9.28.[51] For Mark, significantly, the house is a place of
withdrawal and private teaching in the ministry of Jesus (see also
10.10).[52] But it is also a place, as in 3.20, where a crowd gathers with

synagogue on the sabbath. In Capernaum Jesus meets with approval and
success ... In Nazareth Jesus is rejected ... All in all, Nazareth could be
described as Jesus' Galilean Jerusalem, a place fraught with opposition based
upon supposed knowledge.' From a linguistic approach, and focussing
especially on the phrase εἰς οἶκον in Mark, Kilpatrick reaches the same
conclusion, in 'Jesus', esp. p. 7.

[47] See, e.g., Gnilka, *Markus I*, 143ff. I have drawn especially upon Crossan,
'Mark'; the reply of Lambrecht, 'Relatives'; and Best, 'Mark III'.
[48] Guelich, *Mark 1*, 168. [49] ἔρχονται occurs in ℵ A X K Λ Δ Θ Π, etc.
[50] Note that καὶ ἔρχεται occurs redactionally also at 1.40; 5.22; 6.1; 14.17: cf.
10.46; 11.15,27, cited in Best, 'Mark III', 309–10, n. 1.
[51] So, Kilpatrick, 'Jesus', 3.
[52] See further, Best, *Jesus*, 226–7; and Malbon, 'Mark 2.15', 285ff.

inhibitory consequences (2.2).[53] The motif of not being able to eat because of the throng recurs at 6.31b (8.1).[54] Finally, πάλιν is a redactional link-word which refers back to the previous encounter with the crowds, in 3.7–12.[55]

Second, 3.21 shows signs of Marcan redaction of earlier tradition. In v. 21a, ἀκούσαντες is redactional by analogy with 2.1; 3.8; 5.27; 7.25; 10.47.[56] It links the action in v. 21a to the preceding verse. Of the remaining material, ἔλεγον γὰρ ὅτι ἐξέστη is accepted confidently by Pryke as one of many Marcan explanatory γάρ-clauses.[57] It is strikingly similar in form, content and location to the concluding explanatory clause in v. 30: ὅτι ἔλεγον, Πνεῦμα ἀκάθαρτον ἔχει.[58]

Mark 3.20–1 appears, therefore, to be a redactional seam linking separate traditional pericopae. Its meaning is not at all clear, however. Who is meant by οἱ παρ' αὐτοῦ (v. 21a)? Whence did they 'go out'? Who was the intended object of their action (since the αὐτόν in v. 21a is ambiguous)? Who is the subject of ἔλεγον (v. 21b)? And what is the appropriate translation of ἐξέστη (v. 21b)? All the exegetes agree on the ambiguity of the Greek. What is decisive, however, is the context in Mark. For only in Mark's version is the narrative constructed in his characteristic 'sandwich' pattern,[59] with the pericope of the Beelzebul accusation (vv. 22–30) inserted between the redactional seam and the story of Jesus and his family.[60] Following Brown *et al.*,[61] the structure of 3.20–35 may be presented as follows:

Introduction (20)
(A)   Jesus' 'own' set out to seize him (21)
        21a: 'His own' hear of his activity and set out to seize him
        21b: Their charge: 'He is beside himself.'
(B)   The dialogue between Jesus and the Jerusalem scribes (22–30)

[53] See also 4.1, and the comments on the redactional character of the ὥστε construction, in Pryke, *Style*, 117.
[54] Noted also by Fowler, *Loaves*, 77.   [55] So, Pryke, *Style*, 97.
[56] So, Crossan, 'Mark', 84; and Malbon, 'Disciples', 115.
[57] Pryke, *Style*, 126ff.
[58] *Ibid.*, 42, in agreement with Trocmé, *Mark*, 135–6.
[59] So, *inter alios*, Kilpatrick, 'Jesus', 7 (agreeing with Vincent Taylor); Guelich, *Mark I*, 169; Schweizer, *Mark*, 83; Brown, *Mary*, 54–9.
[60] Surprisingly, Wenham, 'Meaning', pays no attention to this stylistic pattern.
[61] Brown, *Mary*, 54.

22a: The first charge of the scribes: 'He is possessed by Beelzebul.'

22b: The second charge of the scribes: 'By the prince of demons he casts out demons.'

23–27: Jesus replies to the second charge of the scribes

28–30: Jesus replies to the first charge of the scribes

(A') Jesus' mother and brothers come and ask for him, resulting in the definition of who are his family (31–5).

The logic of Mark's ordering of the material is that the relatives of Jesus (= οἱ παρ᾽ αὐτοῦ interpreted in the light of vv. 31–5), having heard that Jesus (and the twelve) were being hindered by the crowd, set out (from Nazareth)[62] to take him into their custody, in the belief that he was mad. While they were coming and prior to their arrival, scribes from Jerusalem arrived and accused Jesus of demonic possession and of being the agent of Satan. Jesus replied by vigorously controverting both accusations and pronouncing a severe sentence on anyone who blasphemed against the Holy Spirit. Jesus' mother and brothers now arrive and send for him. But rather than heed *their* summons, Jesus identifies his true family as whoever does the will of God. The significance of the 'sandwich' pattern is crucial for understanding the sense of Mark's narrative, and we shall return to it shortly.

What of evidence of Marcan redaction in 3.31–5? It is possible that a traditional saying in v. 35 (somewhat analogous to the tradition in Luke 11.27–8) has been provided with a narrative setting by the evangelist.[63] Conversely, it is possible that the saying in v. 35 is a redactional composition and that the remaining material is mainly traditional.[64] More likely, however, Mark has taken over traditions which have been combined at the pre-Marcan stage and has made several editorial modifications of some significance.

Καὶ ἔρχεται (v. 31a) is a Marcan catchphrase recalling the first half of the unit preceding the interpolation (Καὶ ἔρχεται in v. 20a, and a form of ἐξέρχεσθαι in v. 21a).[65] This bridge between vv. 20–1 and 31–5 is an editorial means of identifying οἱ παρ᾽ αὐτοῦ with Jesus' 'mother and brothers'.

---

[62] So, too, *ibid.*, 55–6.

[63] So, e.g., Lambrecht, 'Relatives', 249–51; Bultmann, *Tradition*, 29–30.

[64] So, Crossan, 'Mark', 96–8.   [65] Kee, *Community*, 54.

The stylized depiction of the posture and distance from Jesus of his family relative to the crowd, in vv. 31a, 32a, 32b and 34a, is likely to be redactional. The family stand outside (ἔξω στήκοντες): the crowd is seated around him (ἐκάθητο περὶ αὐτόν). The relative postures and distance from Jesus symbolize degrees of faith and unbelief (cf. 2.4–5!). It is not at all coincidental that, in the first major block of teaching in this gospel (4.1–34), which follows immediately upon the passage under discussion, the crucial interpretation of the paradigmatic parable of the sower is addressed to οἱ περὶ αὐτὸν σὺν τοῖς δώδεκα (4.10b; Mark only). The evangelist clearly wishes his readers to assume that Jesus is addressing the same group as the one whom he had identified just previously as his true family.[66] It is to this privileged group alone that the 'secret' of the kingdom is revealed (4.11b). By contrast, 'for those outside (ἐκείνοις δὲ τοῖς ἔξω) everything is in parables' (4.11c). Given the predominantly redactional character of 4.10–12,[67] it is legitimate to assume that, in the mind of Mark, ἐκείνοις δὲ τοῖς ἔξω includes Jesus' natural kin, who are ἔξω (3:31b, 32b) also.[68]

The aorist participle περιβλεψάμενος, in v. 34a (Mark only), is redactional also. It is a characteristic action of the Marcan Jesus (3.5; 5.32; 10.23; 11.11). Here, it dramatizes further the distance between those in the 'circle' at his feet and his natural family.[69]

Another redactional element may be the use of ἰδού (v. 32b; cf. ἴδε, in v. 34b). Pryke has shown that ἰδού to Mark is 'more than a "mere interjection", and his sparing use of the word gives it an artistic forcefulness and finesse'.[70] It is used to express important new developments and points of challenge in the story to which the reader should give heed. Significantly, the second and fourth out of only seven occurrences (i.e. 3.32 and 10.28) serve to draw special attention to the negative implications of following Jesus for family ties.

---

[66] So, too, Kee, *Community*, 166; Best, *Temptation*, 117–18; Pryke, *Style*, 101; Marcus, *Mystery*, 89–95.

[67] See Bultmann, *Tradition*, 325 n. 1; Taylor, *Mark*, 254ff.; Pryke, *Style*, 156; Kee, *Community*, 41, 51. The indebtedness of Mark to an apocalyptic epistemology, both at 4.10–12 and *passim*, is demonstrated by Marcus, in 'Epistemology'.

[68] See further, Kelber, *Kingdom*, 25–6: 'This solidification of both the opposition and the *familia dei* causes an unforeseen division, because the dividing line does not naturally fall between friend and enemy, but consigns those who would above all others be expected to be on the inside, the family of Jesus, to the outside. It was Mark himself who with the aid of his interpolation technique conjoined relatives and scribes into this unlikely fraternity of shared hostility.'

[69] See Best, 'Mark III', 314–15.   [70] Pryke, 'ΙΔΕ', 419.

If we include v. 35, there is a fivefold reference to Jesus' mother
and brothers. Of these occurrences, the first and third (in vv. 31a,
33b) may well be redactional, the first providing part of the narrative framework and the third as part of a rhetorical question created
for the answer to which it points (in v. 34b). In general, and
especially from a literary point of view, ἡ μήτηρ αὐτοῦ καὶ οἱ
ἀδελφοὶ αὐτοῦ ... ἡ μήτηρ σου καὶ οἱ ἀδελφοί σου ... ἡ μήτηρ μου
καὶ οἱ ἀδελφοί μου ... ἡ μήτηρ μου καὶ οἱ ἀδελφοί μου ... ἀδελφός
μου καὶ ἀδελφὴ καὶ μήτηρ are catchphrases holding the narrative
together and drawing attention, by repetition and redundancy, to
the critical issue at stake – namely who constitutes Jesus' true
family? Robert Tannehill rightly points out how rhetorically powerful is this repetition.[71]

Verse 35, as Best has shown,[72] differs from vv. 31–4 in the following respects: a. 'Sister' is added to the list of kin terms, and the order
of terms is reversed: from mother–brother to brother–sister–mother.
b. The use of the personal possessive pronoun is limited in v. 35, by
contrast with its consistent use in vv. 32, 34. c. Whereas v. 34 is
absolute in identifying those around Jesus as his new family, v. 35 is
conditional: ὃς ἂν ποιήσῃ τὸ θέλημα τοῦ θεοῦ ...[73] d. The ὃς ἂν
introduction to the saying in v. 35 occurs frequently in Mark. Best
has shown in another essay that sayings of this form, sharing a
common theme of discipleship, 'existed as a collection prior to
Mark'.[74] e. An independent variant of v. 35 occurs in Luke 11.28 (cf.
2 Clem. 9.11). This provides grounds for suggesting that v. 35 represents an alternative version of a traditional saying. f. The narrative
would end quite satisfactorily at v. 34, with the identification of
Jesus' spiritual kin.[75] So v. 35 appears as an addition, rendering
Jesus' specific identification of his true kin applicable to a wider
audience including, of course, the readership of Mark's Gospel.[76] It
is difficult to decide, in the final analysis, whether v. 35 is an
originally independent logion added to vv. 31–4 (at either the pre-

[71] Tannehill, *Sword*, 166–71.   [72] Best, 'Mark III', 315.
[73] See Schweizer, *Mark*, 88: 'The last statement nearly cancels the startling com-
prehensiveness of the previous saying.'
[74] Best, 'Sayings Collection', 4. Of the eighteen examples he lists, one which occurs
in very close proximity to 3.35 is the saying in 3.29: ὃς δ' ἂν βλασφημήσῃ ...
[75] Crossan, 'Mark', 97.
[76] See Malbon, 'Disciples', 124–5: 'The pattern of movement from the disciples to
the crowd to the hearers/readers is suggested especially by ... Jesus' statements
of the "whoever" type, addressed within the story to the disciples and/or the
crowd, but reaching beyond.'

Marcan or editorial stage) or whether vv. 31–4 have been created as a narrative setting for v. 35.

Nevertheless, it is remarkable that the expansion of the kinship list to include 'sister' coincides with the reference to Jesus' natural mother and brothers *and sisters* in 6.3. This makes the two episodes mutually reinforcing, the one preparing the way for the other. The replacement of Jesus' natural family by his spiritual family in 3.20–1, 31–5 anticipates Jesus' rejection by his natural kin in his home town (6.1–6a). Remarkable also is the fact that the order of the kin terms in 3.35 (brother–sister–mother) coincides with the order of kin terms in the repeated, seven-member lists in 10.29 ('brothers or sisters or mother . . .') and 10.30 ('brothers and sisters and mother . . .'). This may be evidence of redactional harmonization, the effect of which is to make 3.35 an anticipation, not only of 6.1–6a, but also of the teaching about the cost of discipleship in 10.29–30. In other words, the climactic saying in 3.35 which identifies the true, spiritual family of Jesus prepares the way for both Jesus' rejection by his natural kin and Jesus' teaching that discipleship would be likely to cost his followers their ties of natural kin as well.

It was suggested earlier that 3.20–1, 31–5 have been intercalated to some purpose with the episode of Jesus' confrontation with the scribes in 3.22–30. This claim will be strengthened if evidence of redactional activity linking vv. 22–30 to the surrounding material can be demonstrated.

Mark 3.22 and 30 are cases in point. a. The Synoptic parallels agree against Mark in prefacing the Beelzebul accusation with an exorcism (Matt. 12.22–3 par. Luke 11.14). Mark alone prefaces the Beelzebul accusation with the accusation of the relatives (3.21b). b. Mark alone identifies Jesus' accusers as οἱ γραμματεῖς οἱ ἀπὸ Ἱεροσολύμων καταβάντες (3.22a). This represents two redactional interests: the enmity of the scribes (1.22b; 2.6, 16; 7.1); and Jerusalem as the place of mortal opposition to Jesus (10.32, 33; 11.1, 11, 15, 27).[77] c. The wording of the accusation is partly redactional. In Mark alone it is in two parts: ἔλεγον ὅτι βεελζεβοὺλ ἔχει and ὅτι ἐν τῷ ἄρχοντι τῶν δαιμονίων ἐκβάλλει τὰ δαιμόνια (3.22b). Of these two, only the second is paralleled in Matthew (12.24b) and Luke (11.15b). The first is unique to Mark and is parallel in form to the preceding accusation made by the relatives: ἔλεγον ὅτι ἐξέστη

⁷⁷ Crossan, 'Mark', 88–9.

(3.21b). Therefore, it is hardly coincidental to find that 3.30, at the conclusion of the pericope, conforms also to the redactional ὅτι ... form: this last explanatory clause is without Synoptic parallel and is formally similar to other editorial parenthetical clauses in Mark.[78]

These redaction-critical observations justify the following conclusions. First, since the accusations by both the relatives of Jesus and by the scribes are formally parallel, it appears that Mark is placing Jesus' relatives in the same category as the hostile scribes. Second, Trocmé seems to be right in suggesting that the parallels are not formal only. The accusations that Jesus is mad, that he is possessed by Beelzebul and that he has an unclean spirit are of a piece.[79]

Is it the case, then, that 'the severe condemnation by Jesus in vv. 28–9 of blasphemers against the spirit that is in him is directed, in the mind of the Evangelist, *at the family of Jesus as well as at the scribes of v. 22*'?[80] It is impossible to be certain. Crossan[81] agrees with Trocmé; but Lambrecht[82] thinks that Jesus' relatives are treated more leniently than the scribes, while Gnilka[83] argues that only against the scribes does Jesus direct his reply.

Several considerations lend weight to the Trocmé–Crossan view. The first concerns 3.23. V. 23a is almost certainly editorial: Καὶ ... ἔλεγεν αὐτοῖς is typically Marcan;[84] προσκαλεῖσθαι is a favourite Marcan term;[85] and ἐν παραβολαῖς is the essential feature of the Marcan Jesus' teaching (12.1).[86] So Mark has Jesus reply to his scribal opponents in parables. Now, according to 4.11, 'everything is in parables for those outside'. We saw earlier that, for Mark, 'those outside' include Jesus' own family. Consequently, both the scribes and the kinsfolk of Jesus seem to be in the same position vis-à-vis Jesus. They are outside the circle of his followers and they stand over against him.

A second consideration concerns the previously mentioned 'sandwich' pattern, the recognition of which goes back at least to C. H.

---

[78] Pryke, *Style*, 33, 42, 61.
[79] Trocmé, *Formation*, 135: 'It is the same libellous charge that Jesus' most implacable enemies simply formulate a little more brutally than his family, since any mental disorder was ascribed in those days to possession by an evil spirit.'
[80] *Ibid.*, 136 (Trocmé's italics). See also Best, 'Mark III', 316; Anderson, *Mark*, 123; Crossan, 'Mark', 89, 96, 98, 110; Pryke, *Style*, 42–3.
[81] Crossan, 'Mark', 98.   [82] Lambrecht, 'Relatives', 245–6.
[83] Gnilka, *Markus I*, 148–9.
[84] See 2.27; 4.2, 11, 21, 24; 6.10; 7.9; 8.21; 9.1.
[85] See 3.13; 6.7; 7.14; 8.1,34; 10.42; 12.43; and Pryke, *Style*, 51.
[86] See Räisänen, *Parabeltheorie*, 27 and *passim*.

Turner's discussion of Marcan parentheses in 1925.[87] For Turner, the significance of the pattern was primarily stylistic: the intercalation is related to the bracketing material topically rather than theologically. However, intercalations like 3.20–35 have been taken also as a literary device used to express an editorial interest. Von Dobschütz, for example, suggested that Mark's intention here was to contrast the loving concern of Jesus' family with the enmity of the scribes.[88] More recently, John Donahue, commenting upon this Marcan technique generally, has argued that: 'There is a dialectical relationship between the inserted material and its framework whereby the stories serve to interpret each other.'[89] He then tries to suggest that, apart from 5.21–43, all the intercalations express two major Marcan concerns: material about discipleship encloses material on Jesus' suffering and death. This is something of a *tour de force*, however, since it does not apply in every case, it is more likely (as Joanna Dewey points out) that intercalations may function variously,[90] and it is an explanation too general to do justice to the content of particular examples, including 3.20–35.

What, then, is the significance of 3.22–30 for Mark's portrayal of Jesus and his relatives in vv. 20–1, 31–5? Decisive, I think, is Mark's reordering of the Beelzebul tradition so that it comes to a climax with the 'sentence of holy law' in vv. 28–9: Ἀμὴν λέγω ὑμῖν...[91] Here, whereas Q distinguishes between speaking against the Son of Man as forgivable and speaking against the Holy Spirit as unforgivable (Matt. 12.32 par. Luke 12.10), Mark distinguishes between sins (including blasphemy) committed by 'the sons of men' as forgivable and blasphemy against the Holy Spirit as unforgivable. The effect of Mark's revision of the Son of Man tradition is to remove the idea that speaking against the Son of Man is a forgivable sin. On the contrary, Mark implies just the opposite. For Mark, Jesus is the Son

---

[87] Turner, 'Usage', 148. The other passages normally accepted as redactional intercalations are 5.21–43; 6.7–32; 11.12–26; see also 14.12–25 and 14.54–72. See further, Stein, 'Methodology', 193–4.

[88] Dobschütz, 'Erzählerkunst', 196.

[89] Donahue, *Are You the Christ?*, 42. For an excellent study of the redactional effect of intercalating the stories of the cleansing of the temple and the cursing of the fig tree in Mark 11.12–26, see Telford, *Barren Temple*.

[90] Dewey, *Debate*, 22.

[91] In the tradition, the saying about the unforgivable sin stood quite separate from Matt. 12.22–30, 43–5 par. Luke 11.14–28, at Matt. 12.32 par. Luke 12.10. Mark has placed it as the climax of the Beelzebul controversy; Matthew has followed the Marcan order while retaining some of the Q wording: so, Crossan, 'Mark', 94–5.

of Man on earth with all authority (2.10, 28), the 'strong man' (3.27) full of the Holy Spirit (1.8, 10, 12). In the Marcan perspective, therefore, to 'blaspheme' the Holy Spirit is to blaspheme the Son of Man, Jesus, through whom the Spirit is working powerfully. This is the sin which the scribes have committed, ὅτι ἔλεγον πνεῦμα ἀκάθαρτον ἔχει (3.30). As such, they are 'guilty of an eternal sin' and will never have forgiveness (3.29).[92]

These are harsh words. Nor may their severity be mitigated. T. A. Burkill has described Mark's Gospel aptly as 'damnation history';[93] and for the scribes and other Jewish leaders this is certainly so.[94] The 'holy law' form of the saying (in 3.28–9) is especially emphatic and one of eight redactional occurrences in Mark.[95] Mark places special emphasis on the sin of blasphemy.[96] And the words of judgment, ἀλλὰ **ἔνοχός** ἐστιν αἰωνίου ἁμαρτήματος in v. 29b, unique to Mark, are loaded heavily, since they anticipate the guilty blasphemy of the Jewish leaders at the trial of Jesus in judging Jesus to have blasphemed and thus to be 'worthy' (**ἔνοχον**) of death (14.64).[97]

If, then, 3.22–30 is 'damnation history' so far as the scribes are concerned, is it so for Jesus' family as well, given the setting of vv. 22–30 in vv. 20–35? The most appropriate answer is probably a qualified affirmative. The odium of blasphemy which the evangelist attaches to the scribes does extend, to some degree at least, to the story of Jesus and his family in the bracketing verses. As Guelich puts it: 'The severity of the scribes' charge finds its counterpoint in the warning against the unforgivable sin (3.28–30); the severity of the family's charge finds its counterpoint in a new definition of "family" (3.34–5).'[98]

---

[92] Crossan, 'Mark', 93–5; followed by Anderson, *Mark*, 124.
[93] Burkill, 'Blasphemy'.
[94] See 12.1–12, esp. v. 12: 'they perceived that he had told the parable against them'.
[95] See Pryke, *Style*, 74, 77; and Berger, *Amen-Worte*, 35–41.
[96] The noun βλασφημία (7.22; 14.64) and the verb βλασφημέω (2.7; 15.29) are Marcan favourites (see Crossan, 'Mark', 94). It is likely that the dual reference to blasphemies and blaspheming in 3.28b are editorial sharpening: καὶ αἱ βλασφημίαι, ὅσα ἐὰν βλασφημήσωσιν is redundant and syntactically awkward (see Berger, *Amen-Worte*, 36). The earlier form of the saying probably used the milder expression 'speak a word against' (as in Matt. 12.32a,b; Luke 12.10a): see Lambrecht, 'Relatives', 248, who speaks of 'Mark's radical interpretative rewriting' of an earlier Q form. On the biblical understanding of blasphemy, see Beyer, 'βλασφημέω', 621–5.
[97] ἔνοχος occurs in Mark only at 3.29 and 14.64.
[98] Guelich, *Mark I*, 171.

However, it needs to be remembered that: a. Jesus' relatives do not say specifically that he has an unclean spirit (v. 30); b. Jesus' words in vv. 23–9 are not directed specifically at them, since they are still *en route*; c. whereas the ὅς ἄν saying to the scribes is strongly negative in tone, the ὅς ἄν saying in the hearing (?) of Jesus' kin is positive. These observations are confirmed by Burkill's helpful distinction between relative and absolute kinds of unbelief in Mark's Gospel.[99] The guilt of the scribes is multiplied and confirmed by their part in the passion narrative, an episode in which the family of Jesus play no part, since they fade out of the story after 6.1–6a. At the end, their position is quite ambiguous. They are not there in support of Jesus: but neither are the twelve. They do not deny Jesus, like Peter: so there is no mention of their restoration (16.7). Nor do they betray Jesus, like Judas: so no awful woe is pronounced against them (14.21). In relation to the scribes and also to Judas, then, the unbelief of Jesus' family is relative only. Nevertheless, the dangerous proximity of their situation to that of the scribes is plain.[100]

A brief comparison with the Synoptic parallels confirms our findings about Mark by indicating that, in various ways, Matthew and Luke found Mark's hostility to the family of Jesus difficult to sustain.[101] a. Most striking is their omission of Mark 3.20–1. Neither Matthew nor Luke follows Mark in reporting that people close to Jesus set out to take him because they thought him mad. The effect of this is to reduce considerably the element of conflict in Jesus' relations with his natural kin. b. Luke relocates the episode of

---

99 Burkill, 'Blasphemy', 64–7. Kelber, *Mark's Story*, 26–7, misses this important distinction.

100 A linguistic point confirms this further. In 3.21, Jesus' family set out to 'seize' (κρατῆσαι) him. Κρατεῖν, in the sense of to 'seize' or 'capture', is used elsewhere in Mark only of major enemies of either John the Baptist (at 6.17) or of Jesus (12.12; 14.1, 44, 46, 49). (The one exception is the strange case of the seizing of the 'young man', in 14.51. But even here, the context is the narrative of the passion of Jesus. See Fleddermann, 'Flight', 415.) In all of these instances, κρατεῖν is part of the language of the passion, indicative of what John and Jesus suffer. Its use with respect to the intended action of Jesus' family implies that they, too, contributed to the passion, through their relative unbelief. Wansbrough, 'Mark III.21', overlooks this point completely in trying to argue that κρατῆσαι αὐτόν means 'to calm down the crowd'. Wenham, 'Meaning', 295–6, while noting Wansbrough's omission, fails himself to recognize that the object of κρατεῖν is nearly always Jesus, and that κρατεῖν + accusative in Mark is passion terminology: so the αὐτόν is unlikely to be the crowd.

101 For more detail, see Brown, *Mary*, 98–9 (on Matt. 12.46–50) and 167–70 (on Luke 8.19–21).

Mark 3.31–5 entirely (to Luke 8.19–21), so that the close analogies with the controversy between Jesus and the scribes, which Luke records at 11.14–23, are lost. c. In both Matthew and Luke, the inclusion of Q material after the warning about the unforgivable sin (Matt. 12.33ff. par. Luke 6.43–5; 11.29–32, 24–6) makes it impossible to imply, with Mark, that Jesus' own family are in danger of its commission. d. Whereas Mark has Jesus' kin issue a summons at a distance, Matthew has them reverently seeking to speak to him (12.46), and Luke has them wanting to see him but being prevented from so doing by the crowd (8.19–20). e. Neither Matthew nor Luke draws the pointed contrast between Jesus' family standing outside and the crowd of attentive followers sitting about him. Luke, indeed, makes the crowd sympathetic to the problem of access they are causing Jesus' mother and brothers (8.20)! f. Finally, unlike Mark, who is followed by Matthew in having Jesus begin his reply with an emphatic rhetorical question, 'Who are my mother and my brothers?', Luke has no rhetorical question at all. Nor does Luke have Jesus provocatively identify his spiritual family over against his natural one, in marked contrast to Mark and Matthew.[102] The reply of the Lucan Jesus can be interpreted more easily as including Jesus' natural kin (8.21). The same cannot be said for Mark and Matthew, although neither explicitly excludes them.[103]

Once again, the preceding form- and redaction-critical analyses may be augmented by observations from a literary-critical perspective. First, the characterization. a. Jesus' mother and brothers are not identified by name, as they are at 6.3. This makes possible a striking contrast with the naming of those whom Jesus wanted to be with him, in the immediately preceding episode (3.13–19). It also makes possible the metaphorical play on kinship whereby Jesus' true mother, brothers and sisters are identified in spiritual terms. b. The crowd (ὄχλος) is a composite character in its own right in Mark, as Elizabeth Malbon has shown.[104] Here, the crowd is cast in a very

[102] The emphatic use of forms of ἰδού, so important for Mark and Matthew, is noticeably absent from Luke's version.

[103] See also Brown, *Mary*, 59, n. 102: 'However, we cannot say that Mark means to exclude the natural family permanently from the following of Jesus. Presumably family members could become disciples on the same basis as anyone else.'

[104] Malbon, 'Disciples', e.g. p. 104: 'the crowd is also portrayed in the Gospel of Mark in both positive and negative ways in relation to Jesus and serves to

positive light. It is in the house with Jesus, in contrast to his relatives; it serves as a kind of mediating body between Jesus and his relatives; and it receives Jesus' teaching about the criterion for belonging to his true family. Worth noting also is the fact that this potential alternative family has an identity which is strongly inclusive; for, according to 3.7ff., the ὄχλος is constituted by people from a very wide geographical spread indeed.[105] Malbon's comment about the role of the crowd, from the point of view of the hearer/reader, is very apposite: 'both separately and together, the disciples and the crowd serve to open the story of Jesus and the narrative of Mark outward to a larger group – whoever hears or reads the Gospel of Mark'.[106] c. Jesus is undoubtedly the most important character. He is located, in spatial terms, both in the house and at the centre of the crowd of followers who are seated around him. He dominates the verbal action as well, making the climactic pronouncement which brings the episode to an end. Jesus' family, in contrast, is given no direct speech at all.

Second, the structure and sequence of the narrative. The two passages about Jesus and his family are bracketed between two passages about the twelve: 3.13–19 and 6.7–13. The former relates Jesus' summons and naming of the special group 'whom he wanted ... to be with him' (3.13–14). The latter tells of the sending out of the twelve on mission. This bracketing is very significant. It suggests that what takes place between the brackets is intended to prepare the twelve for their mission, to be some kind of an education. Not surprising in this respect, therefore, is the occurrence of Jesus' first extended teaching discourse containing parables of growth so obviously relevant to prospective missionaries (4.1–34). More surprising, however, are the two episodes about Jesus and his family which fall just inside each of the brackets. In general terms, this literary arrangement is used to convey two ideas. In relation to Jesus, the evangelist is implying that Jesus' relations with his own family are being superseded by his relations with his disciples; that those chosen by him have precedence now over those to whom he belonged 'naturally'; that his mission has priority over family ties.[107]

complement the disciples in a composite portrait of followers of Jesus'. See also Iersel, *Mark*, 58–9.
[105] See Iersel, *Mark*, 58.   [106] Malbon, 'Disciples', 104.
[107] So, too, Trocmé, *Formation*, 81–2, 134–5; and Anderson, *Mark*, 115, who entitles the whole section 3.13–6.6 'The Disciple Family of Jesus and "Outsiders"'.

In relation to the disciples, the evangelist is implying that the misunderstanding and rejection which mark the relations between Jesus and his family may well become the experience of the disciples in relation to their respective families also.

Third, the setting of the episode deserves attention too. The episode takes place after Jesus comes εἰς οἶκον (3.20). This setting is significant. Most obviously, Jesus' house is a place where his own kinsfolk might legitimately expect acceptance and recognition. Instead, they gain no access and their place is taken, as Jesus' true family, by the disciples (presumably) and the ὄχλος. 'The expected criterion for being an insider, being family, is cast out, and a new criterion is brought in.'[108]

Malbon has shown recently that the house as an architectural space in Mark is one of a number of such spaces which function symbolically in the narrative to convey the transformation and overturning of one order by another which the coming of Jesus represents. At the risk of oversimplifying her analysis, she detects a shift from the earlier part of the narrative (i.e. 1.21–6.4), where house and synagogue function in similar ways (as places of teaching, healing and controversy), to a stage where the house replaces the synagogue as the centre of teaching, to a final stage where the temple becomes dominant but only to be set in critical relation to a leper's house (14.3–9), the cross and an empty tomb.[109] Of particular importance to the present discussion is Malbon's observation that at 3.20–1, 31–5 and 6.1–6a, 'home and synagogue merge. When Jesus is "at home" ... his family thinks he is possessed and is joined there in this belief by the scribes. When Jesus is in the synagogue (6.2), those who know his family take offense at him ... This is a narrative turning point, and it is marked as such at the architectural level.'[110] After 3.35, Jesus ministers no longer in his own home, but in the homes of others instead (for example 5.38). After his rejection in 6.1–6a, Jesus no longer teaches in synagogues, but (again) in private homes (7.17; 9.28, 33; 10.10). 'By the close of the Gospel of Mark, no architectural space functions in its normal, expected way any longer. A house is no longer a family dwelling but has become a gathering place for the new community, replacing the rejected and rejecting synagogue.'[111] I agree with this conclusion. It does full justice to what is at least anticipated in the episode narrated at 3.20–1, 31–5.

[108] Malbon, *Space*, 130.   [109] *Ibid.*, 113ff.   [110] *Ibid.*, 115.
[111] *Ibid.*, 140.

What does this story about Jesus and his natural kin, as it is presented by Mark, suggest from a sociological perspective? A number of possibilities deserve consideration on the basis of the preceding reading of the text.

First, the new social world in the making which began with the story of the 'beginning' of the gospel and the call of the disciples by the authoritative agent of God is taken an important stage further. For now there develops a strong sense of social displacement and of the relativization of existing social norms as the process of community formation takes place. The newly chosen twelve (3.13–19) along with the many other followers of Jesus are placed at the centre, while the scribes are condemned and Jesus' own family are left 'outside'. As a paradigmatic story about Jesus, its undoubted function for the evangelist is to legitimate a change in self-understanding from a group whose identity is forged around natural ties of synagogue and family to a voluntary association[112] ('Whoever does the will of God . . .') whose most significant kinship ties are fictive only ('is my brother and sister and mother'). Such legitimation will have been of special importance for hearers and readers whose allegiance to Christ had brought them already into conflict with synagogue authorities and had earned them the enmity of their own kin, as 13.9–13 suggests.[113]

Howard Kee claims that, 'All genetic, familial and sex distinctions are eradicated in this new concept of the true family.'[114] But this is anachronistic and pushes the relatively slender evidence too far. All that the evidence of Mark's Gospel will allow is the claim that, according to the evangelist, obedience to the will of God revealed in Jesus relativizes family (and other) ties and creates the potential for a new, family-like community of God's people. Kee's view loses sight of the metaphorical dimension of 3.35; and makes nonsense of the support of the fifth commandment in 7.10–13 and 10.19, and the teaching on divorce in 10.1–12.

But have we done justice to the evidence that Mark's portrait heightens the tension between Jesus and his relatives? In particular,

---

112 So, too, Kee, *Community*, 107.
113 See Watson, 'Secrecy', 61: '"Suffering" in this context may be defined as the experience of society's hostility encountered by a group which has isolated itself from the norms, beliefs and values of that society. The separation of Mark's community from the surrounding society and its norms may be inferred from such passages as Mark 1.16ff., 3.31ff., 8.34ff., 10.29f., which stress the incompatibility of the call of Jesus with ordinary life in the world.'
114 Kee, *Community*, 109.

are those scholars right who suggest that Mark's hostile portrait of the family of Jesus (together with his negative portrayal of the disciples) is a reflection of the tradition of hostility in Mark's own day towards the leadership of the Jerusalem church, prominent amongst whom were Jesus' mother and especially James the Lord's brother?[115] If so, then a sociological interpretation of the narrative under consideration would consider it as a contribution to the intra-mural politics of the early Christian churches.

For a number of reasons, I am dubious about this hypothesis. First, at the level of methodology, greater caution is required in attempting to use the gospels as mirror-reflections of the ecclesiastical politics of the period of their respective final redactions. When Mark sets out to write 'the gospel of Jesus Christ' (1.1), it is *a priori* far more likely that he is concerned to preserve and pass on the tradition in a way which will summon his readers to faith and instruct them in the way of true discipleship after the pattern and according to the teaching of Christ. This, rather than contemporary ecclesiastical politics (about which we know notoriously little), seems to do more justice to the seriousness and profundity of Mark's narrative. In Mark 3.20–35, we have material which holds out the privilege of belonging to Jesus' true family to anyone who does God's will; material which shows that, historically,[116] Jesus was misunderstood even by those closest to him in kinship terms, with the ominous implications of what this might mean for followers

---

[115] See, e.g., Tyson, 'Blindness', esp. pp. 39, 41f.; Trocmé, *Formation*, 130–7, who speaks of the evangelist as 'an author passionately antagonistic to our Lord's family and hence to James' (p. 132); Crossan, 'Mark', *passim*, esp. p. 112: 'The polemic against the disciples and the polemic against the relatives intersect as a polemic against the doctrinal and jurisdictional hegemony of the Jerusalem mother-church although, of course, this was most likely all provoked by heretics within the Markan community'; Kelber, *Kingdom*, noting his appeal also to the comment of S. G. F. Brandon, on p. 27, n. 3: '"So categorical a repudiation of the blood-relationship and its replacing by discipleship-relationship is truly amazing, when it is recalled what the prestige of the blood-relationship to Jesus meant in the Jerusalem Church."'

[116] While I do not want to beg any questions about *historicity*, it is important not to neglect the importance of the dimension of *the past* in Mark's presentation of the gospel, not least because his readers may well have included contemporaries of Jesus. See Gnilka's similar concern for the historical dimension, in *Markus I*, 232: 'Diese Kritik kann nicht aus den Verhältnissen der markinischen Gemeinde abgeleitet werden, die sich angeblich gegenüber der Kirche von Jerusalem, die hegemoniale Ansprüche gestellt habe und in der die Familie Jesu dominierte, durchsetzen wollte. Die Kritik reflektiert einfach die auch anderswo bezeugte ablehnende Haltung der Familie, insbesondere der Herrenbrüder (Joh 7,1ff), die erst nachösterlich zum Glauben kamen.'

of Jesus; and intercalated material (vv. 22–30) which shows what a short step it is for misunderstanding (of Jesus' hidden messiahship)[117] to lead to outright and blasphemous hostility to Jesus and to the Spirit of God. On this reading, it is difficult to imagine that the leadership of James the Lord's brother in the Jerusalem church is uppermost in the mind of Mark![118]

Second, the hypothesis is dependent on a thematic linking of Jesus' relatives viewed negatively and his disciples viewed negatively. On the one hand, however, both 3.20–1, 31–5 and 6.1–6a are set in narrative contexts which portray Jesus' disciples in a positive light over against his kinsfolk (see, respectively, 3.13–19 and 6.7–13). On the other hand, as the latter instances show, the portrayal of the disciples is not consistently negative, which is what the hypothesis requires. Indeed, 14.28 and 16.7, both redactional texts, clearly imply the enlightenment and rehabilitation of the disciples after the resurrection.[119] Fallible the disciples may be: consistent failures they are not.[120] So, *contra* the view of T. J. Weeden and others,[121] the disciples are poor material for a hostile polemic against the apparently hated leaders of the Jerusalem church.

Third, if stories about the family of Jesus are meant to evoke the leadership of James the Lord's brother at Jerusalem, we might expect him to be singled out, in the way Peter is, for example. But this does not occur. Mark 3.31–5 refers only to Jesus' 'brothers'; and

---

[117] Grässer, 'Nazareth', 19, is on the right lines, I think, in seeing the episode in relation to Mark's christology and the *Messiasgeheimnis*: 'In the same way as people are always astonished when they see the powerful actions of Jesus, but do not understand anything ... so also with the Pharisees and scribes (iii. 6, 22, 30), the disciples (iv. 41), even the family of Jesus (iii. 20f., 31–5), and his countrymen (vi. 1–6) ... But in their very unbelief they reveal to the reader "the incognito of the son of God" (E. Käsemann).'

[118] There is surely a chronological problem here as well. Why should Mark, writing in the late sixties or early seventies CE, be polemicizing against leaders who were now dead? On the weakness of the evidence of Hegesippus (quoted by Eusebius) for an hereditary succession of bishops in Palestine, beginning with James the Lord's brother and followed by Symeon a cousin of the Lord and of James, see Campenhausen and Chadwick, *Jerusalem*, 3–19. Mark would have concurred with von Campenhausen's opening remark (p. 3): 'In Christianity physical descent and spiritual kinship seem to have little to do with each other.'

[119] See Catchpole, 'Silence'.

[120] Excellent on this is Malbon, 'Fallible Followers'; likewise, Tannehill, 'Disciples', esp. pp. 139ff.

[121] Weeden, *Mark*, and those cited in n. 115 above.

in 6.3, James is merely listed alongside Joses, Judas and Simon, none of whom actually figure as actors in their own right in the story.[122]

I conclude, therefore, that Mark's account of Jesus, his disciples and his relatives ought not to be interpreted as a kind of subtle allegory[123] of ecclesiastical politics in the post-Easter period. Such interpretations positively distract our attention from the plain sense of the narrative: Jesus brought into being a new community based, not on ties of blood and heredity, but a voluntary association, open in a quite novel way to anyone who repents, believes in the gospel (1.15), and does the will of God (3.35).[124] Jesus' own family were blind to what God was doing in him and attempted to restrain him. Even worse, scribes from Jerusalem sought to undermine his divine authority by accusing him of demonic possession. For Mark's reader, the message is that the familial and official opposition experienced by Jesus is to be the expectation of members of Jesus' new family, as well.

I have suggested that we have in this episode evidence of a new social world in the making and the conflict this generates. Can we be more precise, however, about the cultural values which underpin the social dynamics of the story? A recent study by David May is helpful in this regard.[125] On the basis of an anthropologically well-grounded assumption that shame and honour are two pivotal values of first-century Mediterranean culture, and that honour may be either ascribed (through birth or inheritance) or acquired, May argues that Mark 3.20–35 is a study in acquired honour. This is especially significant for understanding the motivation of the various actors in the social drama. Thus, in going out to take Jesus, his mother and brothers are seeking to protect their honour, since what Jesus does reflects upon them.[126] Jesus' response to their 'call'

[122] See Burkill, *New Light*, 239: 'In the story of the rejection in the patris (6.1ff.) it is not the close relatives of Jesus but *hoi polloi* who take the initiative against him – and so it can hardly be maintained that the members of his family are put in the worst possible light.'
[123] See also Malbon, 'Disciples', 123: 'Yet the Gospel of Mark is not an allegory in which a group of characters in the story may be equated with a group of persons beyond the narrative.'
[124] On the hermeneutical importance of 3.35 for understanding Mark's theology of discipleship, see Donahue, 'Neglected Factor', 584–7.
[125] May, 'Shame/Honor'. May draws heavily upon the ground-breaking work of Bruce Malina, esp. *World* and *Origins*.
[126] See May, 'Shame/Honor', 85: 'it was the possible social repercussions of Jesus' aberrative behavior that motivated his family. Just as one might today hurry an eccentric relative out of public scrutiny because of public perception and guilt by association, Jesus' family was concerned about their honor rating.'

(v. 31) is crucial. Significantly, he does not specifically uphold their honour (by compliance), but neither does he shame them. Instead, he appeals to a higher, legitimating norm (v. 35) as the basis for acknowledging other people as now his true family. In effect, ascribed honour as the basis of social relations is subordinated to the honour acquired by doing the will of God. At the end, the primary emphasis is, not upon the discrediting of Jesus' relatives, but upon 'Jesus as honorable and the new family as a center for loyalty, relationship and reciprocity'.[127] The story of Jesus and his family expresses the evangelist's firm conviction that the basis of relations in the people of God has been reconstituted once and for all.

Jesus in Nazareth: Mark 6.1–6a and parallels

The story of Jesus' return to his hometown, in Mark 6.1–6a, is the second important passage for assessing Mark's interpretation of Jesus' relations with his own family. As we shall see, it is noteworthy again both for the strong evidence of editorial activity and for the negative light which is thrown upon Jesus' family ties. In a number of ways, this episode confirms and develops the evangelist's critical stance towards ties of natural kinship.

From a form-critical perspective, Bultmann considered this passage to be a biographical apophthegm: 'a typical example of how an imaginary situation is built up out of an independent saying', the dominical saying in this case coming, not at the end (where it would be 'normally'), but in the middle, at 6.4 (cf. Luke 4.24; John 4.44; *Gospel of Thomas* 31; and P. Oxy. 1.5, for other occurrences of the sayings tradition).[128] This is useful in so far as it draws attention to 6.4 as a focal point of the story, at least in the pre-Marcan tradition. But to clarify the meaning of the saying and of the episode as a whole from the evangelist's point of view, we must turn to redactional and literary analysis.

In his excellent study of 1970, Erich Grässer draws attention to a number of 'unmistakable rents and gaps' in Mark's narrative, the explanation for which is best found at the redaction-critical level.[129]

---

[127] *Ibid.*, 86.   [128] Bultmann, *Tradition*, 31; cf. Guelich, *Mark 1*, 306.
[129] Grässer, 'Nazareth', with the quotation from p. 5. Grässer's results compare favourably with Crossan, 'Mark', 98–104 (apparently written independently of

i. In spite of the specific mention of the disciples in 6.1b, they play no part in the rest of the story. ii. The reference to the 'mighty works' (v. 2c) conflicts with the sole emphasis on Jesus' teaching, in v. 2a, b. iii. There is also a dislocation between the reactions to Jesus: ἐξεπλήσσοντο (v. 2b) implies a positive response, whereas ἐσκανδα-λίζοντο (v. 3b) signifies a strong negative response. iv. The prover-bial reference to the fate of the *prophet* (v. 4) contradicts the view of Jesus as a teacher of wisdom and a miracle-worker in v. 2. v. The elaboration of the proverb with καὶ ἐν τοῖς συγγενεῦσιν αὐτοῦ καὶ ἐν τῇ οἰκίᾳ αὐτοῦ is difficult to reconcile with the fact that Jesus' family are the subject of dialogue at v. 3a, not participants in it. vi. The outright failure spoken of in v. 5a contradicts both the attes-tation of 'mighty works' in v. 2, and the weak exceptive clause (εἰ μὴ ὀλίγοις ἀρρώστοις ... ἐθεράπευσεν) in v. 5b.[130]

The solution to these literary problems lies in the analysis of Mark's redaction of an oral[131] or written[132] source. The scope and character of this redaction may be summarized as follows. (i) The close similarities between 6.1–2a and 1.21, 22, 27 show that the synagogue setting, the description of Jesus teaching there and the response of astonishment are all redactional.[133] The phrase εἰς τὴν πατρίδα (v. 1a) is probably a redactional assimilation to the prover-bial ἐν τῇ πατρίδι (v. 4b).[134] The statement καὶ ἀκολουθοῦσιν αὐτῷ οἱ μαθηταὶ αὐτοῦ in v. 1b has no Synoptic parallel and is typically Marcan.[135] It expresses the evangelist's view that Jesus chose the

Grässer), and Lambrecht, 'Relatives', 252–3. Otto Betz has attempted a wholesale rebuttal of Grässer's *redaktionsgeschichtlich* approach in 'Jesus in Nazareth'. Resisting what he calls the 'highflown literary and theological speculations' of the redaction critic, Betz offers a *traditionsgeschichtlich* approach which seeks to evaluate the narrative as a unity, and establish its meaning against the backdrop of the biblical Jubilee tradition (Lev. 25.10). In my view, his own analysis is unsatisfactory, however. 1. He ignores evidence of Marcan redaction. 2. He harmonizes the gospel accounts, especially when he reads the Jubilee Year theology of Luke's Sermon at Nazareth into Mark 6.2a. 3. His appeal to a scriptural backdrop appears forced, at points. 4. No attention is given to the narrative and rhetorical aspects of Mark's story. Such themes as discipleship, unbelief, falling away, and Jesus' hidden messiahship are left undeveloped.

130 Grässer, 'Nazareth', 5–7; cf. the anticipation of these observations in Light-foot, *History*, 188, n. 2.
131 So Schweizer, *Mark*, 123; cf. Grässer, 'Nazareth', 7.
132 So Crossan, 'Mark', 98ff.
133 Grässer, 'Nazareth', 9ff.; Pryke, *Style*, 78, and 62 (on the genitive absolute in 6.2a), 79 (on the ἄρχομαι + infinitive construction in 6.2a), and 80 (on ἤρξατο + διδάσκειν, also in 6.2a); also Gnilka, *Markus I*, 228.
134 Grässer, 'Nazareth', 10.   135 *Ibid.*, 10, n. 6.

disciples – in particular, the twelve – to be 'with him' (3.14) in order that, having learnt from him,[136] they might engage in a mission of preaching and healing (3.14–15; 6.7–13). In this instance, they learn, through the experience of the rejection of Jesus in his hometown and amongst his familiars, that mission is undertaken in the shadow of the cross: something made explicit in 8.34–8.[137]

Evidence of Marcan redaction in vv. 2b–3 is difficult to establish. Commentators such as Pesch[138] accept, on the basis of the roughly parallel versions in Luke 4.22b and John 6.42 (where πόθεν occurs twice), that we have here early tradition which reflects the barriers to accepting Jesus' authority posed by his occupational and familial background and his place of upbringing.[139] It is unlikely that problematic material of this kind, with its potentially damaging christological implications, would be a post-Easter creation of the Christian community. Nevertheless, the failure to mention Jesus' father may be significant redactionally. The irregularity of calling Jesus ὁ υἱὸς τῆς Μαρίας (6.3a) has been recognized widely,[140] particularly since both Luke and John have Jesus identified as 'son of Joseph' (Luke 4.22; John 6.42), and Matthew removes the double offence (of Jesus as τέκτων, whose father is unknown) by calling Jesus ὁ τοῦ τέκτονος υἱός (Matt. 13.55a)! Rather than posit a dogmatic interest in the virgin birth on Mark's part,[141] or fall back on the likelihood of Joseph's death by this time,[142] it seems more satisfactory to accept that the omission is consistent with Mark's positive lack of interest in Joseph generally (3.31–5), since for Mark,

---

136 See Meye, 'Secret', 68: 'The specific office of the Twelve is to receive the words and witness of the historical Jesus who functioned as their teacher. They receive both his words and acts and their interpretation.' Best, 'Mark's Use', would not agree with Meye in so confining this 'office' to the twelve alone.

137 Note ἀκολουθεῖν in 8.34 (twice), as in 6.1.

138 Pesch, Markusevangelium I, 318–19.

139 For a discussion of one part of the evidence, see Stendahl, 'Quis et Unde?', 56–66. The issue of Jesus' origins is a recurring theme in the Fourth Gospel, in particular: e.g. 6.42; 7.25–31; 8.13–20; 9.24–34; cf. 1.45–6; 7.15, 40–4. These are discussed in Jonge, 'Jewish Expectations', 246–70.

140 The expression is used only here in the entire NT. Note Vincent Taylor's comment that 'it is contrary to Jewish custom to describe a man as the son of his mother, even when the father is no longer living, except in insulting terms': Mark, 299–300. A comprehensive treatment is McArthur, '"Son of Mary"', with a full treatment of the textual variants on pp. 47–52; see also, Brown, Mary, 61–4.

141 So, Brown, Mary, 62–3.

142 Contra Brown, Mary, 64; and Schweizer, 'υἱός', 363. Note that Joseph's (alleged) death did not hinder reference to him in the other three gospels.

Jesus is the Son of God.[143] Alternatively, it may be, as Crossan suggests, that the omission of Joseph serves to sharpen the hostility between Jesus and the other members of his family: his mother, Mary; his brothers, named in 6.3; and his sisters, unnamed.[144]

[K]αὶ ἐσκανδαλίζοντο ἐν αὐτῷ in 6.3c is probably redactional. Certainly, it occurs as a comment of the narrator. Certainly also, σκάνδαλον terminology very quickly became an important component of Christian vocabulary for describing the rejection of the Messiah because of unbelief.[145] So the occurrence of ἀπιστία in v. 6a comes as no surprise. Mark himself uses the terminology elsewhere, at 4.17 and 14.27, 29 (see also 9.42, 43, 45, 47), where again it has christological connotations. Its meaning in early Christian usage generally is quite harsh, and Mark is no exception. As Grässer says: 'Σκανδαλίζειν by no means signifies only "to feel offended", but it signifies a denial of faith ... of eschatological importance.'[146] Significantly, there is no Lucan parallel since Luke wishes to portray Jesus' 'inaugural address' in his hometown as a triumph: σκανδαλίζειν and ἀπιστία, not to mention Jesus' consequent inability to perform a miracle, find no mention in Luke 4.16ff. Finally, Jesus' reply in 6.4 appears not to match adequately the christological and eschatological force of ἐσκανδαλίζοντο. It would serve better as a response to the doubt-inspired questioning of vv. 2c–3b. On these grounds, it seems reasonable to attribute καὶ ἐσκανδαλίζοντο ἐν αὐτῷ to Marcan redaction.[147]

So Mark appears to 'raise the stakes' in this story of Jesus' rejection in Nazareth. The people from his own hometown refuse to acknowledge God's Son powerfully at work in their midst. In so doing, they are representative of the response to Jesus of the nation as a whole. It is striking in this connection that, in terms of the narrative structure of the gospel, the rejection at Nazareth at the end of a cycle of teaching and miracle stories (3.13–5.43) parallels the ending of the first cycle of teaching and miracle stories, where 'the Pharisees went out, and immediately held counsel with the Herodians against him, how to destroy him' (3.6).[148]

Although we are told of Jesus' teaching in the synagogue (6.2), the

---

[143] So, Robinson, *Problem*, 81, n. 1.   [144] Crossan, 'Mark', 105.
[145] See Stählin, 'σκάνδαλον', esp. 344ff.
[146] Grässer, 'Nazareth', 16.   [147] So also, *ibid.*, 16.
[148] Anderson, *Mark*, 157. See also Lightfoot, *History*, 186–8, who points out that 6.1–6a represents the final appearance of Jesus in a Galilean synagogue and that, quite unlike the first appearance (1.21–8), the reaction is negative: a premonition of things to come.

only saying attributed to him is the proverbial word of v. 4.[149] The introduction, καὶ ἔλεγεν ... ὅτι, is an editorial bridge.[150] The saying itself clearly functions as the climax of the story. Jesus is speaking in response to the rejection, and expresses a truth dire in its connotations. What is striking about the Marcan version, further-more, is the long, tripartite form of the saying: εἰ μὴ ἐν τῇ πατρίδι αὐτοῦ καὶ ἐν τοῖς συγγενεῦσιν αὐτοῦ καὶ ἐν τῇ οἰκίᾳ αὐτοῦ (v. 4b). This is especially rhetorical and emphatic. Luke (4.24) and John (4.44) have only the first part; Matthew the first and second (13.57b). What is more, the reference to the prophet's lack of honour among his kin and in his own house is not justified by what has gone before.[151] In v. 3a, Jesus' family is cited merely as part of the argument of a third party; whereas in v. 4, his family is included in the culpability of the third party! It seems legitimate to conclude, *contra* Pesch,[152] that καὶ ἐν τοῖς συγγενεῦσιν αὐτοῦ καὶ ἐν τῇ οἰκίᾳ αὐτοῦ is an editorial expansion of traditional material widely attes-ted.[153]

The reason for the expansion is not difficult to discover. The previously noted links between this story and 3.20–35 point the way. Mark's editorial expansion in 6.4 is a deliberate reminder of the earlier story. There, Jesus' mother and brothers are left standing outside: here, his mother and brothers (now identified by name)[154] and sisters are included among those of his hometown who respond to him with unbelief. Their unbelief in 6.1–6a makes prophetic

149 For history-of-religions parallels from Dio Chrysostom, Apollonius of Tyana and Epictetus, see Pesch, *Markusevangelium I*, 320.
150 Pryke, *Style*, 78.
151 So too, Grässer, 'Nazareth', 16; Lambrecht, 'Relatives', 253.
152 Pesch, *Markusevangelium I*, 320–1. Pesch cites Gen. 12.1 (LXX), which does indeed have a triadic form strikingly similar to Mark 6.4 : Ἔξελθε ἐκ τῆς γῆς σου καὶ ἐκ τῆς συγγενείας σου καὶ ἐκ τοῦ οἴκου τοῦ πατρός σου ... But even if Mark 6.4 does have a traditional form, it could still have been introduced by the redactor as especially emphatic, and consistent with 3.20–35. The differences between Mark and the other gospels also count against Pesch's view.
153 In addition to the canonical versions already cited, there is the *Doppelspruch* in *Gospel of Thomas* 31: 'Jesus has said: There is no prophet who is received in his own village; a physician is not wont to cure those who know him' (Hennecke/Schneemelcher, *NT Apocrypha*, I, 109). No doubt the *Doppelspruch* has been formed from Luke 4.23, 24. See further, Grässer, 'Nazareth', 8; and Gnilka, *Markus I*, 229, n. 11.
154 See Crossan, 'Mark', 103, who draws special attention to the conjunction of the traditional list of names in 6.3 and the redactional 'relatives' in 6.4: 'This means that the list of personages in vi.3 has been turned from respectful indication in the tradition to specific indictment in the redaction.'

Jesus' identification of a new family of brothers and sisters and mothers, in 3.35.

Vv. 5–6a are a mixture of tradition and redaction. V. 5a, because it contradicts the later conception of Jesus' unlimited power, is early tradition. Both the other Synoptists have modified the stark confession of Jesus' powerlessness (οὐκ ἐδύνατο . . .): Matthew implying that Jesus did not want to work many miracles (13.58); Luke implying that this was not part of the divine plan (4.25ff.).[155] V. 5b is probably editorial. It stands in tension with the absolute statement in v. 5a, a tension which Matthew resolves by omitting v. 5b entirely. Form-critically, v. 5b is a negative version of the summaries of healing which are characteristic of Mark (1.32–4; 3.7–12; 6.53–6).[156] Perhaps Mark intended the mention of a few healings to be a rebuke to those who had rejected him: he acts in spite of them.

Finally, v. 6a is probably redactional as well.[157] It cannot easily be reconciled with Jesus' acceptance of the situation as proverbial (v. 4). Instead, it returns our attention to the σοφία and δυνάμεις of the redactional v. 2. In spite of what they have heard and seen, Jesus' own people do not believe. They are culpably blind. Jesus' visit to his hometown ends on the damning note of ἀπιστία.[158] The contrast with the salvation and healing which come to the father and his demoniacal son, in 9.23–4, is striking: for there the father's faith makes healing possible. The οὐκ ἐδύνατο of 6.5a gives way to πάντα δυνατὰ τῷ πιστεύοντι . . . πιστεύω· βοήθει μου τῇ ἀπιστίᾳ of 9.23b, 24b. An anonymous man shows the kind of faith in Jesus which Jesus' own family so obviously lack. Mark 6.6a is the only place in the gospel where Jesus is said to be 'amazed' (ἐθαύμασεν). That the object of his amazement should be the unbelief of his own kinsmen is telling indeed. Equally telling is the fact that, under the cloud of ἀπιστία, Jesus' family now pass entirely from Mark's narrative.[159]

---

155 Grässer, 'Nazareth', 17.
156 Gnilka points out, in *Markus I*, 229, n. 13, that the terminology of v. 5b (θεραπεύειν and οἱ ἄρρωστοι) points forward to the disciples' mission, in 6.13.
157 *Contra* Gnilka, *Markus I*, 229. See Burkill, 'Damnation History', 55, who presents a strong case for Marcan redaction at v. 6a.
158 From a narrative-critical perspective, this is the obvious ending. Crossan's attempt, in 'Mark', 105, to make v. 6b the conclusion is unconvincing, as the effect would be to soften the shock generated in v. 6a. Rather, v. 6b is an editorial transition which prepares the way for the calling and sending of the twelve, in 6.7ff.
159 In an important discussion of ἀπιστία in Mark, Burkill, 'Blasphemy', 54f., observes that the sequence of the narrative, with the apostolic mission follow-

We may conclude, with some assurance, that Mark 6.1–6a provides evidence of the same redactional tendency evident in 3.20–35. Taken together, the two episodes reflect a development by the evangelist in a negative direction of the portrayal of Jesus' relations with his own family. The depiction of Jesus' mother and brothers as οἱ ἔξω and in dangerous proximity to the position of the Jerusalem scribes, in 3.20–35, grows now to a depiction of their attitude as one of open ἀπιστία. We are close, perhaps, to the 'ethical dualism' of the Johannine prologue: εἰς τὰ ἴδια ἦλθεν, καὶ οἱ ἴδιοι αὐτὸν οὐ παρέλαβον (John 1.11).

Several observations from a literary-critical perspective reinforce these findings. We turn first to narrative sequence. The story comes at the end of a section of narrative devoted to Jesus' miraculous acts (4.35–5.43). The outstanding success of Jesus' miracle-working both in the Gentile territory of the Decapolis (5.20; cf. 5.1) and back in Galilee contrasts markedly with the almost total failure of his ministry in his hometown.[160] This contrast is brought to our attention, not only by the ordering of the material (which is unique to Mark), but also by the narrative itself: for, in context, the 'mighty works' (δυνάμεις) of 6.2 must refer back to the miracles recounted in 4.34–5.43. The people's confession of Jesus' power makes their hard-heartedness and Jesus' failure among them all the more striking, especially since it follows hard upon Jesus' most miraculous cure in this gospel, the raising of Jairus' daughter from the dead (5.21–4, 35–43). It is as if Mark is saying the greater the signs, the greater the misunderstanding.[161]

As mentioned earlier, this episode comes immediately prior to the sending out of the twelve on mission (6.7–13), just as 3.20–35 comes immediately after the call of the twelve to be with Jesus (3.13–19).[162] Again, the sequence is unique to Mark. From it we may infer that the rejection of Jesus in his hometown is paradigmatic for Mark's understanding of mission. Jesus' experience shapes expectations about the kinds of experience which his followers will share. Hence the teaching of Jesus in 6.11: 'And if any place will not receive you

ing the people's rejection of Jesus through *apistia*, corresponds with Paul's view that the hard-heartedness of the Jews in rejecting the Messiah led to world-wide mission (see Rom. 11.20).
160 Anderson, *Mark*, 157.   161 Iersel, *Mark*, 85ff.
162 Note that 3.13–15 and 6.7 are linked at the linguistic level, with προσκαλεῖσθαι, δώδεκα, ἐξουσία and ἀποστέλλειν occurring in both. See Best, 'Mark's Use', 15.

and they refuse to hear you, when you leave, shake off the dust that is on your feet for a testimony against them.'[163] It may be the case also that the evangelist wishes to imply a causal link between Jesus' rejection at Nazareth and his sending out of the twelve. Perhaps it is that, having learnt this lesson about being rejected most strongly by one's own kin, they are ready now for mission themselves.[164]

Second, there is the setting. The temporal setting is the sabbath (6.2a). We know from 2.28 that Jesus the Son of Man is 'lord of the sabbath'. But 6.1–6a shows that Jesus' own familiars do not acknowledge this. For them, he is not the Son of Man, but 'the son of Mary' (6.3). The spatial setting is the synagogue. This is ominous. The previous reference to Jesus' presence in a synagogue (3.1–6) is an episode charged with conflict: Jesus looks around 'with anger'[165] at those who would accuse him; and they go out from the healing in the synagogue intent on destroying him. The hardness of heart Jesus finds in the synagogue on that occasion (3.5) parallels the unbelief that Jesus meets in the synagogue of his *patris* on this occasion.

Third, we turn to the rhetoric of the narrative: in particular, the use of irony. There is irony, for example, in the contrast between the recognition and acclamation Jesus receives both in Gentile territory and in other parts of Galilee and the unbelief he encounters in his hometown. Even sharper, however, is the irony of the words of the people in the synagogue, in response to Jesus' teaching (6.2b–3a). Like the chief priests and the scribes at the crucifixion, who mock Jesus as 'the Christ, the King of Israel' (15.32) without knowing the truth of what they say, the audience in the synagogue mock Jesus' wisdom and power, thinking that they understand who he really is. Bas van Iersel puts it well: 'All in all, Nazareth could be described as Jesus' Galilean Jerusalem, a place fraught with opposition based upon supposed knowledge.'[166]

The characterization merits consideration as well. a. The disciples are mentioned in the introduction (6.1b), only to play no active role in the episode. They are there in the background, in the role of followers of Jesus being prepared for the mission he will give them later. They are silent, passive witnesses of what happens to Jesus in his hometown. b. The action proper focusses on Jesus, and he is effectively alone in his encounter with his compatriots. They are identified only as the 'many' (πολλοί), and they ridicule Jesus on the

---

[163] Anderson, *Mark*, 165.   [164] See Gnilka, *Markus I*, 228.
[165] The only occurrence of ὀργή in Mark comes at 3.5, in this synagogue setting.
[166] Iersel, *Mark*, 93.

basis of what they think is all there is to know about him. But it is to Jesus that the final, emphatic word is given, in which he identifies his role with that of a prophet (6.4); and his is the last reaction to be narrated (6.6a). c. The grace of Jesus is not thwarted completely by the blindness of the 'many', however. There remain, in contrast to the many, 'a few sick people' (εἰ μὴ ὀλίγοις ἀρρώστοις) whom Jesus heals (6:5b). The note of sorry irony remains to the end.

The episode in Jesus' *patris* can be illuminated from a sociological perspective, as well. For a central concern of the story is that of Jesus' identity and, by implication, the identity of his followers also.

According to social scientific theory, personal identity in traditional societies particularly is an answer, not to the question, 'Who am I?', but to the question, 'Whom do I belong to?' Personal identity is a matter, that is, not so much of individual, existential discovery, but of what is given in membership of a group.[167] The most significant group for defining personal identity is the family or household.[168] That conception is what lies behind the knowing question of Jesus' synagogue audience: 'Is not this the carpenter, the son of Mary and brother of James and Joses and Judas and Simon, and are not his sisters here with us?' (6.3a).The assumption revealed here is that the identity of Jesus is a matter simply of locating him in relation to his familial group. Having done this to their satisfaction, Jesus' interlocutors know that Jesus is 'one of them'; in which case, his wisdom and miracle-working powers must be fraudulent, and so they take offence at him (6.3b).

But the identity of Jesus, according to Mark, is not defined satisfactorily by locating him in relation to his kinship group. According to Mark, there is an important sense in which Jesus is not 'one of them'. From the very beginning of Mark's narrative, the identity of Jesus is defined otherwise, as the Son of God (1.1, 11; etc.), the Spirit-empowered agent of the kingdom of God (1.8, 10,

---

167 See further, Pitt-Rivers' analysis of the anthropology of honour in Mediterranean societies, in *Shechem*; Malina's discussion of honour and shame and of 'the first century personality', in *World*, 25–70; also, Leach, *Anthropology*, ch. 5 (on 'debt, relationship, power') and ch. 6 (on 'marriage, legitimacy, alliance').

168 See Garnsey and Saller, *Empire*, 148, speaking of imperial Roman society: 'The place of a Roman in society was a function of his position in the social hierarchy, membership of a family, and involvement in a web of personal relationships extending out from the household. Romans were obligated to and could expect support from their families, kinsmen and dependants both inside and outside the household.' On the biblical material, see Countryman, *Dirt*, 148ff., 168ff.

12; etc.), the Holy One of God (1.25), the Son of Man (2.10, 28; etc.), and so on. Furthermore, as we have seen, Jesus gathers around himself an alternative group, in relation to whom his different identity is more appropriately defined, and these μαθηταί, who include a smaller group called 'the twelve' (οἱ δώδεκα), are presented as Jesus' *true* family, in the episode we discussed earlier (3.31–5).

Hence, the crisis which is precipitated by Jesus' return to his hometown. It is a crisis over competing conceptions of the identity of Jesus: that is, over competing views of who Jesus belongs to (and, conversely, of who belongs to Jesus). Having been away, having developed a work of teaching and charismatic healing, even across 'the sea' in the Gentile region of the Decapolis, Jesus comes εἰς τὴν πατρίδα αὐτοῦ, with disciples in train, and takes the initiative immediately by teaching in the synagogue on the sabbath. The response of Jesus' compatriots is predictable and understandable. They attempt to maintain their own sense of the identifiable, familiar world by effectively denying the reality of his divine wisdom and mighty works and by reclaiming Jesus as 'one of them', locating him back in one of their kinship groups. Their taking offence is an attempt to put Jesus in his place, which is the place ascribed to him by virtue of his ties of natural kinship. Jesus, however, will not be put in his place, for his sense of identity and of belonging is different. Jesus' sense of identity and role as a προφήτης (6.4) expresses his sense of belonging above all to God, as his 'Son', and derivatively, his belonging to those who acknowledge his prophetic vocation, especially those who 'follow' him. The corollary of this is that refusal to acknowledge Jesus as prophet and to 'honour' him as such results in a mutual distancing in social relations. The people take offence and disqualify themselves from becoming recipients of the power at work in Jesus; Jesus, on the other hand, responds with a proverb of intense disaffection, is unable to heal more than a very few sick people (and perhaps only then by way of rebuke to the many), and expresses amazement at the people's 'unbelief'.

The possible sociological significance of this episode, as narrated by Mark for the audience of Mark, is considerable, and takes further what was said before about early Christianity as a social world in the making. For what we have here is the story of yet another episode in the life of Jesus the authoritative Son of God, in which his divine vocation sets him at odds with those to whom he is tied by kinship and cohabitation. The message of Mark for his readers, those who 'believe' and 'follow' in a later generation, is twofold. First, the coming of Jesus and the kingdom of God disturbs previously taken-for-granted conceptions of personal identity and patterns of society, and therefore causes conflict. Second, the coming of Jesus and the conflict thus created generate a new social world based, not on the ascribed solidarity of kinship and household ties, but on the solidarity acquired by becoming a follower of Jesus and a doer of the will of God.

4   Discipleship and family ties (Mark 10.28–31)

This twofold message is confirmed in a striking way in the next piece of Marcan material to which we should turn: Mark 10.28–31. Peter's forthright statement to Jesus, 'Lo, we have left everything and followed you', exemplifies the disruption and reordering of social patterns caused by Jesus' summons to discipleship; and Jesus' promise, in reply, of houses and households 'one hundredfold' exemplifies the coming into being of a new solidarity bound together by ties of discipleship rather than of kinship and marriage. So what, in the previous major section of the discussion, we inferred from the two episodes to do with Jesus, we find confirmed and reinforced in material dealing directly with the implications of becoming a follower, material which, as we shall see, also picks up and takes further the story of the call of the disciples, in 1.16–20 (2.13–14), with which we began.

Mark 10.28–31 comes at the conclusion of a larger block of tradition, the episode of Jesus and the rich man (10.17–31), which itself belongs to a sequence of didactic material, beginning at 10.1 and addressing discipleship issues of a broadly household-related nature: marriage and divorce (vv. 2–12), the place of children (vv. 13–16), and possessions (vv. 17–31). It is agreed widely that this collocation of tradition is probably pre-Marcan.[169] Focussing on the third pericope in the sequence (vv. 17–31),[170] we note how mixed is the material from a form-critical perspective. The story of the rich man (vv. 17–22) is a 'genuine apophthegm'[171] and stands satisfactorily on its own. This has been expanded by the addition of diverse logia to do, variously, with the difficulty (especially for the rich) of

---

[169] See Best, *Jesus*, 99, and the literature cited there.
[170] See, for more detail, *ibid.*, 110–19.
[171] Bultmann, *Tradition*, 21.

entry into the kingdom of God (vv. 23–5); the necessity of divine aid for human salvation (vv. 26–7); the manifold reward which will come to those who renounce all for Jesus' sake, a promise conveyed in the form of a sentence of holy law (vv. 28–30); and a final, 'floating' logion (Matt. 20.16 and Luke 13.30) about eschatological reversal (v. 31). The broad thematic concern binding this material together is that of how to act in relation to wealth and possessions (including household possessions) in order to inherit 'eternal life'.

But Mark has not taken over the tradition without modification, as redaction criticism demonstrates. We need not linger over 10.1–16, except to observe that the opening verse is almost certainly a redactional seam: v. 1a, by analogy with 7.24a; v. 1b, because of the characteristically Marcan portrayal of Jesus in a teaching role (1.21, 22; 2.13; 4.1, 2; 6.2, 6, 34; 8.31; 9.31; 11.17; 12.35).[172] This opening is important for what follows, by augmenting the already-present sense of seriousness. The teaching which Jesus gives in chapter 10 is given one step further along the way to Jerusalem and the passion: 'the region of Judaea and beyond the Jordan' (v. 1a). Further, what he gives to the crowds and to the disciples is messianic *didache*: instruction in how to live prior to the coming of the Son of Man (13.26). The willingness to practise radical renunciation, to which Peter bears witness and which Jesus commends, comes at the climax of this *didache*.

Turning to 10.17ff., we note that, though the biographical apophthegm of vv. 17–22 is largely traditional, there are indications that Mark has so edited the material as to bring to prominence the theme of discipleship. Thus, the introductory adverbial clause, Καὶ ἐκπορευομένου αὐτοῦ εἰς ὁδόν, depicts Jesus setting out 'on the way', which is a discipleship motif;[173] and the depiction of Jesus in motion reminds us of the call stories (1.16, 19; 2.14). The summons which Jesus makes, in v. 21 (καὶ δεῦρο ἀκολούθει μοι), could well be redactional. Its omission would do no harm to the sense and continuity of the story, but it would have the striking effect of removing almost completely the discipleship element in the story. Its terminology, furthermore, is reminiscent of the call stories (1.17–18 – δεῦτε ὀπίσω μου ... ἠκολούθησαν αὐτῷ). Finally, the concluding γάρ-clause (v. 22b) is characteristically Marcan.[174] In this context,

172 See further, Achtemeier, 'Reflections', esp. 472–6; also, France, 'Teaching'.
173 So, Swartley, 'Function'.   174 Pryke, *Style*, 126–7.

its effect is to draw specific attention to the heavy obstacle to discipleship created by attachment to possessions.[175]

Mark 10.23–7 is a combination of tradition and redaction, which elaborates on the theme of possessions. The traditional element is the teaching in vv. 23b, 25 about how hard it is for the rich to enter the kingdom of God. The redactional elements are most likely: a. the sudden introduction of the disciples (v. 23a; cf. v. 27a) so that the teaching is addressed to them, reminiscent of the earlier vv. 10–11 (4.10–12); b. the recurring expressions of astonishment by the disciples at the teaching of Jesus (vv. 24a, 26a); c. the generalizing expansion of Jesus' teaching in the direction of disciples in general (not just rich ones), in v. 24b, reminiscent of the earlier teaching on how to enter the kingdom, in vv. 13–16; d. the generalizing teaching at the end, in v. 27b.[176] What is noticeable again is Mark's redaction of the tradition in a way which sharpens the focus on the disciples and on discipleship.

This brings us to 10.28–31. Again, this is material loosely connected to what goes before: this time, by way of contrast with the episode of the rich man unable to renounce his possessions. V. 28 has strong claim to be entirely redactional. In v. 28a, we note the typically prominent role accorded Peter,[177] as well as linguistic and syntactical clues like the use of ἄρχομαι as an auxiliary plus a verb of speaking in the infinitive (here, λέγειν).[178] As for v. 28b, ἰδοὺ ἡμεῖς **ἀφήκαμεν** πάντα καὶ **ἠκολουθήκαμέν** σοι, the occurrence of both ἀφίημι and ἀκολουθεῖν indicates Mark's redactional intention to evoke the story of Peter's call by Jesus (1.16–18), which has, ἀφέντες τὰ δίκτυα **ἠκολούθησαν** αὐτῷ.[179]

The saying of Jesus in vv. 29f., with its ἀμὴν λέγω ὑμῖν form is traditional, at least as far as ἑκατονταπλασίονα.[180] (The versions in Matthew and Luke omit the repetition of the household list.) Even within this material, however, the motive, expressed in the form, ἕνεκεν ἐμοῦ καὶ ἕνεκεν τοῦ εὐαγγελίου, is likely to be redactional

---

175 Best's comment, *Jesus*, 110, is fair: 'For Mark the rich man is a potential disciple; the kind of ties which may have held back such enquirers from full commitment are given in vv. 29f.'
176 See further, *ibid.*, 110–12.
177 See Brown, *Peter*, 58–64.
178 See, Pryke, *Style*, 79, 81.
179 Best, *Jesus*, 36–7, points to the redactional use of ἀκολουθεῖν in 2.14, 15; 6.1; 10.32, 52; and 15.41, as well as here, in 10.28.
180 Bultmann, *Tradition*, 110.

by analogy with 8.35.[181] Luke's ἕνεκεν τῆς βασιλείας τοῦ θεοῦ, in
Luke 18.29, may be closer to the original. But what of the emphatic
repetition of the household list, in v. 30? If it is Marcan redaction,
then we have important evidence of Mark's interest in the household theme. It is impossible to be certain, but, with Best,[182] I am
inclined to accept it as redactional. Note that the list is not repeated
slavishly. Fathers are omitted from the hundredfold reward, a
Christianizing modification reflecting belief in God as the only
Father (11.25; 14.36; also, Matt. 23.9).[183] Significantly, neither is
mention made of fathers among Jesus' list of spiritual kin in 3.35.
Note also that there is an addition: μετὰ **διωγμῶν**. This phrase
comes as no surprise. It is reminiscent of the interpretation of the
Parable of the Sower (at 4.17 – θλίψεως ἢ **διωγμοῦ** διὰ τὸν λόγον).
It is consistent also with the suggestion of hospitality denied, in 6.11,
and with the prophecy of kinship-related persecution, in 13.12. By
repeating the household list (with modifications), Mark is able to
specify the reward that comes, emphatically, νῦν ἐν τῷ καιρῷ τούτῳ,
and to distinguish the eschatological reward to come in the future:
'eternal life' (v. 30b). The ζωὴ αἰώνιος motif skilfully links the end
of this episode to the beginning (v. 17b) and produces an effective
reversal so characteristic of this gospel. The rich man will not inherit
eternal life because his possessions are a stumbling block: the
disciple who renounces 'everything' (πάντα) will inherit eternal life.
To reinforce the idea of eschatological reversal, Mark then adds the
traditional logion of v. 31.

What, in sum, do these redactional modifications signify? First,
there is a consistent orientation of the tradition in the direction of
messianic *didache* for disciples. Second, there is a particular concern
about the hindrance to discipleship created by attachment to possessions. Third, this concern is generalized: from possessions, which
may be a matter primarily relevant to the wealthy, to 'everything',
which broadens the demand to everyone.[184] The disciple's whole life
as constituted by his/her kinship and household ties is what discipleship of Jesus demands. Fourth, attention is drawn to the fact that
renunciation of this kind will bring persecution. It will bring also

---

[181] See further, Trocmé, *Formation*, 159, n. 1, for a discussion of the phrase,
including the textual variants of 8.35.

[182] Best, *Jesus*, 114.   [183] So too, Robinson, *Problem*, 81, n. 1.

[184] See also, Schmeller, *Brechungen*, 108: 'Das ursprüngliche, radikale Anliegen
der verarbeiteten Traditionen wird zwar entschärft und ausgeweitet, aber im
Kern noch festgehalten.'

membership of many families on the basis of spiritual ties and, in the end, eschatological reward.

Observations from the perspective of literary criticism reinforce this interpretation considerably. Once again, we begin with sequence and setting. The episode of the rich man and the teaching which follows, in 10.17–31, come towards the end of Mark's important central section, 8.27–10.45. This section is presented as a journey from Caesarea Philippi to Jerusalem, is structured systematically around three predictions of the passion (at 8.31; 9.31; and 10.33–4), and provides the context for instruction of the disciples (understood as ones who 'follow' Jesus) in the 'way' of discipleship.[185] It is no coincidence, therefore, that one of the effects of the Marcan redaction, analysed above, is to orient the traditional story about the rich man in precisely this direction. Mark wants to say that leaving family and household for Jesus' sake is not confined to time past, in the days of Jesus. On the contrary, it is of the essence of discipleship in the post-Easter period, as well.

The episode immediately precedes the third and most detailed passion prediction, in 10.32–4. These verses are heavy with the motifs of revelation, passion christology and passion discipleship, not least in (the entirely redactional) v. 32: Ἦσαν δὲ ἐν τῇ ὁδῷ ἀναβαίνοντες εἰς Ἱεροσόλυμα, καὶ ἦν **προάγων** αὐτοὺς ὁ Ἰησοῦς, καὶ ἐθαμβοῦντο, οἱ δὲ **ἀκολοθοῦντες** ἐφοβοῦντο.[186] The juxtaposition of the story of the rich man and its didactic sequel (vv. 17–31) with the third passion prediction (vv. 32–4), redolent as it is with implications for those who 'follow', has the powerful effect of casting Jesus' teaching about renunciation of family in the shadow of Mark's passion christology. No wonder, then, that belonging to a new, eschatological solidarity of spiritual kin is qualified by the μετὰ διωγμῶν. This is entirely consistent, furthermore, with the messianic *didache* Jesus imparts after the first passion prediction, where following Jesus is interpreted in terms of the dominant, passion symbol of cross-bearing (8:34).

Next, we consider the sense of time. It is significant that there are virtually no chronological markers. The previous one comes back at 9.2, the reference to the theologically significant 'after six days'

---

185 See, in general, Schweizer, 'Portrayal'. I have discussed this material in more detail in my chapter on Mark, in Barton, *Spirituality*.
186 See Best, *Jesus*, 120–2; Catchpole, 'Silence'; Malbon, *Space*, *ad loc.*

(cf. Exod. 24.15–16).[187] This lack gives the material in this whole central section a certain trans-historical quality. What is narrated is a matter not just of times past (the perspective implied at 10.6a!). The pace of this central section is different, too. Whereas εὐθύς occurs some thirty-two times prior to 8.27–10.45, it occurs only three times within that material, and all three occurrences come in the story of the exorcism of the demonized boy (9.15, 20, 24). The effect of this is to slow the pace and thereby reinforce the trans-historical quality of the narrative and of the teaching within it. Nevertheless, in the specific episode under discussion, Jesus draws a distinction between the present and the future: νῦν ἐν τῷ καιρῷ τούτῳ . . . καὶ ἐν τῷ αἰῶνι τῷ ἐρχομένῳ (10.30). This distinction is important. It signifies that what Jesus promises begins to be experienced in the present epoch of history. The call to a life of radical renunciation is not understood as a call out of historical existence. Likewise, the promise of belonging to a new solidarity is a promise to be realized within history; and μετὰ διωγμῶν is a sharp reminder of the 'adulterous and sinful' nature of the present generation (8.38; 9.19).[188]

Characterization plays an important part in our story, as well. Taking a cue from 10.1, we begin with the crowds (ὄχλοι) who gather around Jesus 'again' (πάλιν).[189] In fact, they are never far away. Significantly, at the beginning of Mark's central section, Jesus' momentous words about the nature of discipleship are addressed to the crowd, as well as to his disciples (8.34ff.). The crowd are found with the disciples again in the episode of the demonized boy (9.14ff.). They gather yet again beyond the Jordan with Jesus and his disciples (10.1, 10). And on the road out of Jericho, they are there still, once more alongside the disciples (10.46). Their recurring presence with Jesus' disciples makes them of more than marginal interest.[190] In relation to 10.1–31, they function in several ways. First, they give the action and Jesus' teaching about discipleship an open, public dimension. This implies that discipleship is open to all: it is not restricted to an elite, not even the twelve. Second, they function as potential disciples, the 'sheep without a shepherd' (6.34), the 'many' last who will be first (10.31) and whom

---

[187] Iersel, *Mark*, 128.   [188] See Robinson, *Problem*, 80–1.

[189] See Rhoads and Michie, *Mark*, 134–5. But particularly useful is Malbon, 'Disciples', which effectively controverts Best, 'Role'.

[190] *Contra* Best, *Jesus*, 100: 'The crowd plays no part in the subsequent story and acts only as a foil to prepare the way for the secret teaching of the disciples in vv. 10–12.'

the Son of Man came to serve (10.45). That is why Jesus teaches them as well as his disciples (10.1b). Third, they function as a kind of bridge between the narrative and the reader.[191] What Jesus addresses to them is addressed through them (and the disciples) to the audience of Mark. That is why the ὃς ἄν form, or an equivalent generalizing form, is so common in Jesus' teaching. In 10.1–31, it comes in the teaching on marital ethics (v. 11), on receiving the kingdom like a child (v. 15), and on renunciation of family and household (vv. 29f.). In the latter instance, it is especially noteworthy that what appears to be a claim made by Peter for an apostolic elite (v. 28) is generalized in a radical way to apply to 'anyone'. For Mark, it is the reader who is in mind. Malbon's comment is apt: 'What the Markan narrative says about discipleship it says to all. Both separately and together, the disciples and the crowd serve to open the story of Jesus and the narrative of Mark outward to the larger group – whoever has ears to hear or eyes to read the Gospel of Mark.'[192]

The characterization of the man who comes to Jesus, in vv. 17–22, need not detain us long, since his story is told mainly to preface the teaching to the disciples which follows. It is a cameo portrait of someone who by all appearances is 'first' in deserving eternal life – he runs to Jesus, kneels before him, addresses him with due respect, testifies to being observant in keeping the commandments, and even evokes Jesus' love (the only character in Mark to do so!) – but who in the end makes himself 'last' because renunciation of his 'great possessions' is a cost too high for him to pay in order to become a follower of Jesus. As such, he is an object lesson of someone who, in the terms of the preceding pericope, is unable to become 'like a child' (10.13–16). He also functions as a contrast with other figures whose cameos Mark presents: the blind beggar who becomes a follower 'on the way' (10.46–52), the poor widow who puts 'her whole living' into the temple treasury (12.41–4), and the anonymous woman who anoints Jesus in the leper's house (14.3–9).[193] More immediately, though, he contrasts with Peter and those like him – including some among Mark's readers? – who have 'left all' and followed Jesus.

The disciples and Peter especially are prominent characters in 10.1–31, whose main function is to be foils to Jesus and recipients

---

[191] See Malbon, 'Disciples', 110, 124–6.   [192] *Ibid.*, 126.
[193] On the latter episode, see Barton, 'Mark'.

thereby of his teaching.[194] Typically for Mark they are cast in an ambivalent light. In vv. 10–12, they require amplification, in private, on Jesus' outright prohibition of divorce; in vv. 13–16, they earn Jesus' indignation for attempting to deny the children access to him; in vv. 23ff., they are repeatedly amazed at Jesus' teaching on the danger of wealth; and Peter's somewhat inappropriate (though not necessarily untrue) interjection, in v. 28, meets only with an indirect, generalizing response on the part of Jesus (vv. 29–31). In the symbolic terms of the healing of the blind man at Bethsaida (8.22–6), they are characters whose vision of Christ and of discipleship is only very gradually and haltingly coming into focus.

Finally, there is Jesus himself. In line with 10.1b ('and again, as his custom was, he taught them'), Jesus is portrayed as a teacher of supreme authority. He controverts the Pharisees and relativizes the torah in his teaching against divorce (vv. 2–12); overrules his disciples in order to bless the children and pronounce on how to enter the kingdom (vv. 13–16); sees through the appearances of the rich man and summons him to true obedience (vv. 17–22); and pronounces again on how to enter the kingdom and on the renunciation required (vv. 23–31). The actions of Jesus are equally authoritative. He journeys relentlessly towards Jerusalem (vv. 1a, 17, 32); blesses the children by 'taking them in his arms' (ἐναγκαλισάμενος αὐτά: v. 16; cf. 9.36) and 'laying his hands upon them'; and looks with divine prescience at his interlocutors (vv. 21a, 27; cf. v.23a). The dominance of Jesus as the central character, together with the great weight given to his teaching (augmented by the twofold occurrence of the ἀμὴν λέγω ὑμῖν in vv. 15, 29), generates a very strong sense of the authority of Jesus and his words (9.7b!) and, in consequence, the imperative of obedience and trust. For the reader, there is, in other words, a basis in the characterization for accepting the legitimacy of the demand for the renunciation of family and household ties, as well as the legitimacy of the alternative familial solidarity which takes their place.[195]

It is important, finally, to bring sociological insights to bear on this material in 10.1–31. Once again, the most helpful model is that of early Christianity as a social world in the making.

---

[194] See further, Rhoads and Michie, *Mark*, 89–95; Tannehill, 'Disciples', esp. 148ff.; Malbon, 'Disciples'.
[195] See Tannehill, 'Disciples', 149: 'Not only the authority of the teacher but also the emphasis and openness ... allow this material to function as direct teaching

Jesus, cast in the role of founder of a 'new covenant' community (10.45; 14.22–5) and authoritative teacher of the will of God, gives instruction in three areas crucial for constructing and maintaining an alternative social world: marriage rules,[196] the place of children and the control of property. Notably, this messianic *didache* is bare of casuistry.[197] There is little accommodation to the legacies of history and tradition and the complexities of individual cases. What is in view, instead, is the establishment of an eschatological community whose ordering expresses both God's intention for creation ἀπὸ δὲ ἀρχῆς κτίσεως (10.6a) and what is appropriate in view of the coming of the kingdom of God (cf. 10.14, 15, 23, 24, 25). The lack of casuistry, and the appeal instead to 'first principles' as a basis for reflection and social organization, are indicative of the fact that this is teaching for what is envisaged as an alternative society, itself the precursor to life in 'the age to come' (10.30).

The novelty of this alternative is conveyed forcefully in the reactions to the teaching. Thus, the teaching on marriage and divorce is presented in the form of a controversy story, where Jesus' hostile interlocutors are (not for the first time) those guardians of the society's legal and traditional boundaries, the Pharisees (10.2a; cf. 2.16, 24; 3.6; 7.1, 3, 5; 12.13).[198] The prohibition of divorce, on the grounds that the marriage partners 'are no longer two but one flesh' (10.8b), is so absolute that the disciples then feel the need to inquire further, 'in the house' (εἰς τὴν οἰκίαν). In this significant setting, itself symbolic of an alternative society focussed no longer around temple and synagogue,[199] Jesus confirms his prohibition of divorce by putting it another way: divorce and subsequent remarriage,

---

to the reader, not just teaching to the first disciples. This is also promoted by the generality of much of the teaching.'

[196] For an important study of the teaching of Paul in this respect, see Yarbrough, *Gentiles*.

[197] See, in general, Verhey, *Reversal*, 78ff., noting esp. p. 79: 'The norm is no longer the precepts of Moses but the Lord and his words (8.38). "The commandment of God" still holds, of course (7.8; cf. 10.19), but it is simply not identical with any manipulable code or casuistry, even one based on the law. The law is summarized in the great principles of loving God and the neighbour (Mark 12.28–34).' Similarly, Houlden, *Ethics*, 45: 'For this writer, then, as for John, it appears that facing and settling moral problems, in the everyday sense, was not a primary concern. He had no eye for casuistry.'

[198] See Saldarini, *Pharisees*, esp. 150–1, speaking of the Pharisees in Mark: 'Jesus and the Pharisees did not argue over theological issues which were of interest to a limited number of Jews, but rather for control over the community.'

[199] See Malbon, 'Mark 2:15', noting her conclusion on p. 287: 'But the dominant architectural marker of the Gospel of Mark is house.'

instigated by either partner, constitutes adultery (10.10–12). In relation to marriage and divorce rules prevailing in both Jewish and Greco-Roman society at the time,[200] this teaching represents a degree of moral strictness and a level of moral demand which will have marked out clearly the social group which adhered to it. The Pharisees' hostility and the disciples' (implied) incomprehension testify to this distinctiveness.

Similarly, in the two episodes following. The reaction of the disciples to those (presumably 'the crowds' of 10.1) who were bringing children (παιδία) to Jesus shows that they have yet to understand the implied inversion of ways of defining status and honour in the kingdom of God and in the society which lives in anticipation of that kingdom (10.13f., noting κωλύειν in v. 14 and at 9.38, 39). The classic exploration of this inversion comes immediately after the third passion prediction, in teaching once again addressed to woefully blind members of Jesus' inner circle (10.35–45). There is a counter-cultural aspect to Jesus' messianic *didache*: and the welcome Jesus accords to the παιδία, in contrast to the resistance of the disciples, gives this graphic expression.[201]

Resistance occurs in the third episode, also. The rich man expresses resistance to Jesus' summons to radical renunciation of wealth by refusing the invitation to 'follow' and by going away sorrowful (10.22). The repeated astonishment of the disciples at Jesus' teaching that it is difficult for the rich to enter the kingdom is a form of resistance, as well. It expresses the culturally induced expectation that prosperity and the honour it brings are blessings from God.[202] So, if not the rich, 'Then who can be saved?' (10.26b). The sequel, based on the major theological presupposition of the sovereignty of God, with whom 'all things are possible' (10.27), implies that salvation comes to 'anyone' who renounces all for the sake of Jesus and the gospel (10.28–31).

If, then, the teaching about marriage and divorce, children and possessions represents an attempt by Mark to provide the basis for an alternative society – supplementing what comes elsewhere in the

---

[200] On which, see, e.g., Derrett, 'Teaching'; Catchpole, 'Divorce'; Banks, *Jesus*, 146–59.

[201] On the status and treatment of children in Jewish and Greco-Roman society, see Weber, *Jesus*; and Wiedemann, *Adults*.

[202] See Schmidt, *Hostility*, 60: 'The OT declares that wealth is a confirmation of God's covenant with his people, a reward for keeping the terms of his covenant.' Also, Hauck/Kasch, 'πλοῦτος, κτλ', 323ff.

gospel about sabbath observance, purity rules,[203] power relations
and the like – it is important to be more specific about what he has in
mind particularly in relation to family and household ties. This
brings us back to the saying of Jesus in 10.29–30, which contains a
number of clues. First, as noted earlier, the saying is unrestricted in
its application: οὐδείς ἐστιν ὅς ἀφῆκεν ... What Peter says of the
apostolic band is generalized in the rejoinder of Jesus. This implies
that leaving family and household has to do, not just with itinerant
missionary activity of the kind referred to in 6.7–13 (1.16–20), but
that it has to do, more fundamentally, with conversion and discipleship – in Mark's terms, with becoming a follower of Jesus the one
who 'goes ahead' (10.32; 14.28; 16.7).[204] Second, the motive for
leaving is ἕνεκεν ἐμοῦ καί ἕνεκεν τοῦ εὐαγγελίου. The only other
occurrence of this phrase comes in 8.35, in a context (at the beginning of Mark's central section) of fundamental teaching about the
nature of Christian discipleship, addressed widely to τὸν ὄχλον σὺν
τοῖς μαθηταῖς (8.34a). This strengthens the likelihood that discipleship generally is what Mark has in mind in 10.29 also. Part of the
cross the follower of Jesus (in any generation) may have to bear is
the cost to family and household ties arising out of his/her transfer
of allegiance to Christ and to the solidarity of Christ's new covenant
people. Third, missionary activity is not ruled out, whether of an
itinerant form or not. This dimension of discipleship is evoked by
the introduction of Peter and his saying, reminiscent of 1.16–20; by
the reference to τὸ εὐαγγέλιον, which, for Mark, is something to be
preached (1.14; 13.10; 14.9); and by the allusion to persecution,
which implies public testimony, by analogy with 13.9–13. Fourth,
there is the significant reference to 'fields' (ἀγροί). This is reminiscent, from outside Mark, of the cameo story of Barnabas, in Acts
4.36–7,[205] who 'sold a field (ἀγροῦ πωλήσας) which belonged to
him, and brought the money and laid it at the apostles' feet'. This is
depicted as a prime example of the κοινωνία of the Jerusalem
church. A similar *Sitz im Leben* fits the Marcan material well. The
person in Mark's audience who becomes a follower of Christ at the
cost of his natural kin and household possessions, including lands,
will be compensated from within the fellowship of the new, eschatological family (3.34–5), by the sharing of property and income.

---

[203] On which, see the excellent interdisciplinary study of Neyrey, 'Purity'.
[204] See Best, *Jesus*, 113; and *contra* Pesch, *Markusevangelium II*, 144–5, who takes
the text to refer to early Christian *Wanderradikalismus*.
[205] See Gnilka, *Markus II*, 93.

Nevertheless, it should be pointed out that this material reflects no animosity to family and household ties *per se*, something we had cause to observe in relation to earlier pericopae, as well. Instead, their significance is made relative to cross-bearing discipleship for the sake of Jesus and the gospel. The fact that fictive families and households constitute the disciple's reward, at least with respect to life before the End, shows that such ties are a fundamental and taken-for-granted aspect of Mark's 'social philosophy'. What is proposed is not an alternative social pattern to replace the household (of the kind which became established at Qumran, for instance), but alternative households to compensate (and more so) for those left behind. This conclusion is reinforced by the observation that the saying of Jesus in 10.29f. does not envisage the leaving of wives (diff. Luke 18.29b). Separation of this kind would certainly imply a rejection of the historical mode of existence expressed in marital relations and family ties, in anticipation, perhaps, of that state in 'the age to come' when 'they neither marry nor are given in marriage, but are like angels in heaven' (12.25). But this option is not chosen. Indeed, as we have seen, marriage relations are reaffirmed strongly, and divorce initiated by either partner is prohibited (10.2–12). Nor is this an ideal only. Paul provides evidence that an itinerant apostle like Peter travelled in the company of his wife (1 Cor. 9.5). In sum, if the Marcan narrative holds out the prospect of social marginalization for followers of Jesus and preachers of the gospel in the time before the End, it also holds out the prospect of social integration into Jesus' eschatological family, and provides specific messianic *didache* to give that integration a foundation in authoritative Jesus tradition.

5 'A passion prediction for Mark's community' (Mark 13.9–13)

In the discussion earlier of Jesus' relations with his family and *patris*, we observed that the tension, misunderstanding and hostility evident there were heavy with implications for the disciples' relations with their own kin. This becomes explicit in the remarkable discourse of Mark 13.5–37, at vv. 9–13, a paraenetic section described recently by Helen Graham as, 'a passion prediction for Mark's community'.[206] It is to this material that we turn now as the

---

[206] Graham, 'Prediction', 18–22.

final piece of evidence in the gospel bearing directly on the theme of discipleship and family ties, material which serves as an elucidation of the dark phrase, μετὰ διωγμῶν (10.30), in the teaching about discipleship examined immediately above.

It is not possible here to go into the complicated tradition-history of Mark 13, about which an enormous amount has been written already.[207] Suffice it to say that, from a form-critical perspective, traditional sayings from Jewish and early Christian apocalyptic sources, with frequent allusions to biblical texts, have been brought together to constitute an extended, eschatological discourse. Hugh Anderson's summary is useful:

> It is probably best therefore to think of Mark 13 as an amalgam of authentic sayings of Jesus, like the prophecy of the Temple's ruin (verse 2) or the denial of knowledge of the day or hour of the end (verse 32), and the pronouncements of a Jewish or Christian prophet or prophets, worked together and developed gradually by the Church and given its final shape by the Evangelist himself.[208]

The main elements are: a. an introduction in two parts, in the first of which Jesus prophesies the destruction of the temple (13.1–2), and in the second of which the disciples ask when this will happen and what will be the sign (13.3–4); b. a warning about false messiahs (13.5–6); c. prophecy about the beginning of the End-time woes (13.7–8); d. a second warning, this time about persecution of members of the believing community (13.9–13); e. prophecy about 'the desolating sacrilege' (Dan. 12.11) and how to survive in the tribulation to follow (13.14–20); f. the warning about false messiahs and false prophets repeated (13.21–3); g. prophecy about the signs of the End and the coming of the Son of Man (13.24–32; cf. Dan. 7.13); and h. concluding paraenesis (13.28–37), which consists of two parables – the fig tree (vv. 28–9) and the door keeper (vv. 33–7) – separated by three logia concerning the imminence of the End

---

[207] See the survey of the literature in Pesch, *Markusevangelium II*, 264–8, noting the warning comment on p. 264: 'Seit den drei großen Untersuchungen zu Mk 13 von L. Hartman (1966), J. Lambrecht (1967) und R. Pesch (1968) ist die Diskussion in kritischer Auseinandersetzung mit ihnen und durch zahlreiche eigenständige Beiträge weiter gefördert worden; sie hat sich jedoch keineswegs auf eine communis opinio zur Interpretation des schwierigen Kapitels des Mk-Ev hin bewegt.'

[208] Anderson, *Mark*, 290.

(v. 30), the perduring authority of Jesus' words (v. 31), and the unknown time of the End (v. 32). Just to list the main elements demonstrates the strange collocation of forms which have amalgamated in the history of the tradition. Fundamentally, as Hartman and others have shown,[209] we have here an apocalypse which itself is 'a revision of apocalyptic traditions'.[210] Its basic thrust is 'historicizing' and 'actualizing': the reappropriation of biblical (especially Danielic) apocalyptic and the tradition of the eschatological sayings of Jesus for the instruction and encouragement of believers in the post-Easter period of the *Endzeit*.

From a redactional point of view, there are a number of factors which indicate the importance of this material for the evangelist. I list these first, before going on to discuss likely redactional modifications of the tradition.

a. It is the longest continuous speech of Jesus (or anyone else) in this gospel.[211] This of itself makes the material in 13.5–37 especially noteworthy. b. It appears as an intrusion into the narrative sequence, which otherwise would flow smoothly from Jesus' prophecy of the temple's destruction (13.1–2) to the plotting of the chief priests and scribes to kill him (14.1–2). c. Its juxtaposition with the passion narrative immediately following allows the discourse to function as a prophetic disclosure of the true significance of the passion, as Lightfoot showed.[212] It also allows the passion narrative to serve as an exemplification of the teaching in chapter 13.[213] In relation to 13.9–13, the passion of Jesus is a theodicy in terms of which Mark and his community are able to interpret experiences of persecution of their own.

Turning, second, to Mark's redaction of the tradition, we note that there are strong indications that Mark is trying to temper an apocalyptic fervour emphasizing imminent End-expectation.[214]

---

[209] Hartman, *Prophecy*, esp. 145–77, 235ff. Hartman considers Mark 13, in both its apocalyptic and paraenetic elements, to be a kind of 'midrash' on Daniel (esp. Dan. 7, 11, 12), with other scriptural prophetic material incorporated at points, as well. See also, Kee, *Community*, 44–5; and, for an attempt to draw sociological implications from Mark's indebtedness to Daniel, see Kee, 'Setting', 245–55.

[210] Kelber, *Kingdom*, 109.   [211] Grayston, 'Mark XIII', 375.

[212] Lightfoot, *Message*, 48–59.

[213] See Grayston, 'Mark XIII', 386–7.

[214] See Cousar, 'Eschatology', who goes too far, however, in distinguishing Mark's views from those of contemporary apocalypticists. More nuanced is Hooker's assessment of ἀρχὴ ὠδίνων (13.8c): 'Some have described this

Hence the strong redactional qualifiers, ἀλλ' οὔπω τὸ τέλος (v. 7b) and ἀρχὴ ὠδίνων ταῦτα (v. 8c), early in the discourse,[215] together with the emphasis on the suddenness but fundamentally unknown timing of 'that day', in the all-important ending of the speech (vv. 32–7). This is relevant to understanding vv. 9–13, which may be seen as an attempt to dampen apocalyptic enthusiasm by sober warnings about persecution and the likelihood of martyrdom in the *Endzeit*. Such an interpretation is borne out by the following points.

The opening imperative, βλέπετε δὲ ὑμεῖς ἑαυτούς (v. 9a), is agreed generally to be Marcan redaction.[216] Its effect is to draw the reader's attention away from fixation upon signs of a cosmic nature to what the approach of the End will mean for him/her.[217]

The addition of the παραδιδόναι sayings (vv. 9b, 11a, 12a) sets traditional apocalyptic motifs (at vv. 8, 12b) firmly within the *theologia crucis* framework of the passion narrative.[218] This word became an integral part of early Christian passion terminology at an early stage, subsequently developing apologetic and soteriological connotations.[219] As Lightfoot pointed out, '[it] is almost always a word of sinister meaning in Mark, implying the delivery of someone or something good to an evil power'.[220] In Mark's passion narrative, it occurs ten times (at 14.10, 11, 18, 21, 41, 42, 44; 15.1, 10, 15). It is used also in the Marcan prologue with reference to the passion of

section as anti-apocalyptic ... It would be more accurate to describe it as anti-apocalyptic-fervour; as intended to dampen down wild enthusiasm which saw any disaster as the prelude to the Last Days' ('Trial', 84). See also, Kelber, *Kingdom*, 113ff., who identifies Mark's opponents as Christian false prophets who taught a realized eschatology focussed (mistakenly) upon Jerusalem, based on the assumption that the destruction of the temple had initiated the parousia: 'Mark is opposed to the prophets both because they miscalculated the time and because they chose the wrong place' (p. 116).

215 In support of Marcan redaction is Lambrecht, *Redaktion*, 113–14, 258.
216 See Pryke's list, in *Style*, 21; also, Pesch, *Markusevangelium II*, 283.
217 Grayston, 'Mark XIII', 383ff., makes the distinction between second person plural (as in v. 9a) and third person (as in v. 12) pivotal for his reconstruction of the history of the tradition. He considers the apocalyptic material to be subsequent addition to a nucleus of 'fairly simple instructions for an expected development of an actual situation of the Church [which] advised non-involvement because the End was near' (p. 385). Later, the evangelist incorporated this 'pamphlet with its apocalyptic supplement' into his gospel as a way of making the crucifixion an hermeneutical control upon potentially dangerous End-time expectation.
218 On the possibility that vv. 8, 12 belonged originally together and were expanded subsequently in the pre-Marcan tradition to include the key-word παραδιδόναι sayings of vv. 9, 11, see Hartman, *Prophecy*, 168, n. 78, followed by Graham, 'Prediction', 20.
219 See further, Perrin, 'Use'.   220 Lightfoot, *Message*, 52.

John the Baptist (at 1.14). So its use three times in 13.9–13 is obviously intended to align the experience of the disciples with the mortal enmity suffered first by John and then by Jesus.

The editorial insertion of the logion of v. 10 implies that the End will not come until the gospel is preached 'first' (πρῶτον) to all nations.[221] Further, its insertion here implies that Mark conceived of the judicial court as an inevitably significant location for gospel proclamation (cf. εἰς μαρτύριον αὐτοῖς, in v. 9b). This is why inspiration by the Spirit is so important: for it is the Spirit who empowers the defendant to deny him/herself and confess Christ (v. 11; cf. 14.62).[222]

The conclusion to the section, v. 13b (ὁ δὲ ὑπομείνας εἰς τέλος οὗτος σωθήσεται), which forms a redactional frame with v. 9a,[223] ends the paraenesis on the theme of endurance. This is sober warning enough. But in the Marcan context, endurance εἰς τέλος probably refers both to the Last Day (its sense in the tradition) and to the point of death in martyrdom.[224] Hence, εἰς θάνατον ... καὶ θανατώσουσιν αὐτούς in v. 12. Such also is the endurance shown by Jesus in the passion; and it is noteworthy there that Jesus refuses to save himself (15.30ff.; cf. 8.34ff.). Instead, he denies himself, endures to the end, and is vindicated by God: precisely the pattern of expectation in 13.13b (... οὗτος σωθήσεται).

Vv. 12–13a bring these sober warnings to a head. Previously, the agents of 'handing over' have been anonymous. Now, they are identified as members of the disciple's own family. Pesch's comment is apt: 'Die Nennung der engsten Blutsverwandten als der Verfolger, welche die Auslieferung und sogar den Tod der Verfolgten betreiben, bedeutet eine starke Steigerung.'[225] Finding no direct

---

[221] On 13.10 as Marcan redaction, on grounds of terminology (esp. ἔθνη, πρῶτον, δεῖ, κηρύσσω, εὐαγγέλιον) and parenthetical form, see Pryke, *Style*, 53–4; also, Taylor, *Mark*, 507–8; Lambrecht, *Redaktion*, 127–30; Pesch, *Markusevangelium II*, 285. Hooker's comment on the role of this saying in its context is apt ('Trial', 88): 'the reference to preaching in 10 serves the same function as the comment in 7 that the End is not yet: the emphasis is on endurance instead of urgency'. So too, Cousar, 'Eschatology', 329.

[222] In association with this, Iersel, '*Community*', 27–8, makes a convincing case for interpreting 3.28–9 (blaspheming against the Holy Spirit) as referring to apostasy from Christ in a judicial forum; i.e. abjuring Christ in court in disobedience to the prompting of the Spirit. As apostasy, the 'unforgivable sin' is precisely that referred to in Heb. 6.4–6.

[223] So, Pesch, *Markusevangelium II*, 283.

[224] So, Gnilka, *Markus II*, 192; Hooker, 'Trial', 87; Pesch, *Markusevangelium II*, 287; Schweizer, *Mark*, 272.

[225] Pesch, *Markusevangelium II*, 286.

support in the Book of Daniel, it appears that the originators of the tradition have drawn upon the prophets for a motif relatively common also in apocalyptic literature.[226] Hartman draws particular attention to Targum Jonathan on Mic. 7.2 – 'A man delivers up his brother to destruction' – in addition to Mic. 7.5f.: 'Put no trust in a neighbour, have no confidence in a friend ... for the son treats the father with contempt, the daughter rises up against her mother, the daughter-in-law against her mother-in-law; a man's enemies are the men of his own house.'[227] This incorporation of scriptural tradition makes vv. 12–13a especially weighty. For Mark, it is the disciple able to endure persecution, prosecution and death, even at the hands of his/her own kinsfolk, who will be saved. It is striking that being handed over εἰς θάνατον is mentioned only in this saying about kinship enmity, a severity reinforced by the saying following, where μισεῖν is used for the one and only time in this gospel (v. 13a). In its Marcan context, being hated ὑπὸ πάντων refers especially to rejection by one's own familiars.[228]

The foregoing observations point to the following broad conclusions. First, 13.9–13 represents part of an attempt by the evangelist, writing in an apocalyptically charged atmosphere, to warn his audience that the End has not come yet, and that the time before the End will be one of tribulation for the followers of Jesus. Helen Graham is justified, therefore, in designating this material as 'a passion prediction for Mark's community'. In danger of being carried away by End-time fervour and apocalyptic speculation, the Marcan Jesus urges that in the time of the 'not yet' (13.7), the

---

[226] There is a version in Q of the same tradition (Luke 12.52–3 par. Matt. 10.35–6). However, it is unnecessary, with Lambrecht (*Redaktion*, 137–8, 257), to posit Q as Mark's source. This hypothesis raises more problems than it solves. See the comments of Reicke, 'Test', 214ff. For the motif of kinship enmity in Jewish apocalyptic, see 1 Enoch 99.5; 100.1f.; Jubilees 23.16, 19; 2 Esdras 16.24; Syriac Baruch 70.6 – cited in Schweizer, *Mark*, 265. For the prophets, Hartman (*Prophecy*, 168) cites Ezek. 38.21; Amos 1.11; Hag. 2.23; Zech. 7.10; 14.13; Mic. 7.2, 5–6.

[227] Hartman, *Prophecy*, 168–9, 213–14. According to Hartman, vv. 8, 12 may have consisted of a 'midrash' combining Isa. 19.2 and Mic. 7.2ff. V. 13a, likewise, draws upon Mic. 7.6, which LXX renders, 'a man's enemies are all the men in his house'; and Targum Jonathan renders, 'those who hate a man are the men ...'.

[228] Contrast Matt. 24.9b, where πάντων is qualified by τῶν ἐθνῶν. Schweizer, *Mark*, 271, is right: 'In the apocalyptic scheme (e.g. vs. 8) the word "everyone" referred to the nations of the whole world, as in Matthew 24.9. In Mark, however, "everyone" refers to the members of the persecuted person's family and his fellow citizens.'

serious and all-important task of preaching to all nations must be carried forward. The task is a serious one, in part at least, because it will lead to persecution both in the synagogues and sanhedrins of the Jews and in the courts of the Gentiles. Vv. 9 and 11 constitute paraenesis for the persecuted follower on trial for his/her life and called upon to abjure 'the name' (v. 13a).

Second, the evangelist emphasizes the severity of the persecution by warning that members of the disciple's own family will be his/her mortal enemies. In vv. 12–13a, traditional prophetic and apocalyptic material about intra-familial enmity has been woven into an overall paraenesis on martyrdom based upon the key-word, παρα-δίδόναι. It is clear that Mark conceives of discipleship and mission to Gentiles in the Last Days as divisive of ties of natural kinship.

Third, as a prominent part of a 'farewell speech' addressed in private to representative disciples and intended as a prophetic reve-lation of eschatological events which will be precipitated by his death, 13.9–13 (together with the speech as a whole) is directed at the situation in Mark's own day.[229] It is this which explains an important difference between the otherwise closely linked suffering of Jesus and of disciples. Whereas Jesus is 'handed over' by the leaders of the Jews and by Pilate, in a particular situation in time past, disciples will be 'handed over' by their own kinsfolk. This generalizes the threat of persecution. It also makes the warning as applicable to Gentile as to Jewish believers – an observation rele-vant, of course, to the possibility of a non-Palestinian provenance of Mark's Gospel.

It is important to supplement these primarily history-of-traditions findings from a literary-critical perspective. Here, once again, we turn from the traditio-historical model of the text as an edited collection of pericopae to the model of the text as a literary com-position, the meaning of which arises out of the response of the reader to the text in its final form.

We begin with the setting. The spatial setting of the revelatory discourse is elaborated in two ways. First, Jesus comes out of the temple (13.1a). The temple (τὸ ἱερόν) is the dominant architectural space in the whole of the Jerusalem section of the gospel narrative. Jesus' first act upon entering Jerusalem is to enter the temple and look around at everything (11.11), before withdrawing to Bethany

---

[229] So too, Marxsen, *Mark*, 166ff.

for the night. On the following day, Jesus returns to Jerusalem, re-enters the temple and brings the temple commerce to a halt (11.15–19). On the third day, *en route* once more to Jerusalem and finding the fig tree withered, Jesus calls for faith in God of the kind expressed in the mountain-moving prayer, where '*this* mountain' (τῷ ὄρει τούτῳ) clearly refers to the mountain of the Jerusalem temple soon to be destroyed (11.20–5).[230] Once in Jerusalem, Jesus engages in extended (and controversial) teaching in the temple (11.27–12.44; esp. 11.27b; 12.35a, 41). At 13.1, Jesus leaves the temple: but the private teaching of 13.5–37 is imparted in a location specifically described as κατέναντι τοῦ ἱεροῦ (13.3a; cf. κατέναντι τοῦ γαζο-φυλακίου, in 12.41), and concerns the elaboration of Jesus' prophecy in 13.2 that the 'great buildings' of the temple complex will shortly be thrown down. So the temple setting effectively unites the whole narrative from 11.1 to 13.37: and Jesus' relation to the temple is cast in a consistently negative light (see also 14.58; 15.29). That the apocalyptic warning of kinship enmity and universal hatred of disciples comes against the backdrop of the doomed temple, a temple with which Jesus has broken decisively,[231] allows us to interpret that enmity as arising, at least in part, out of a sense of outrage among Jews at a perceived abandonment of Judaism by Jesus' followers.

The second aspect of spatial setting reinforces the first. Jesus delivers the private revelation seated on the Mount of Olives opposite the temple (13.3a). That Jesus is seated evokes his role in Mark as authoritative teacher of the will of God (cf. 4.1, the introduction to Jesus' other main discourse in Mark). The Mount of Olives setting is evocative also.[232] As a mountain, it is a place traditionally associated with divine revelation. This mountain, more specifically, was the scene of Ezekiel's vision of the glory of the Lord (Ezek. 11.23); and, according to Zech. 14.4, it was to be the place where the Lord would appear to initiate the eschatological judgment. Josephus, furthermore, gives it specific messianic significance, associating it

230 See further, Telford, *Barren Temple*, 95–119. On p. 119, Telford quotes with approval the statement of R. E. Dowda: 'The temple is the mountainous obstacle which is to vanish before the faith of the gospel movement. The temple system, with its corrupt clericalism and vested interests, is to be removed in the eschatological era, which is now being experienced.'
231 So too, Kelber, *Kingdom*, 111 – 'Jesus' second speech forms the culmination of this anti-Jerusalem, anti-temple thrust (Chaps. 11–12)'; also, Telford, *Barren Temple*, 39; Iersel, *Mark*, 153.
232 See Malbon, *Space*, 32–3; Iersel, *Mark*, 160.

with the activities of the Egyptian false prophet (in *Antiquities* XX.169). Finally, in Mark's own narrative, the Mount of Olives is the place to which Jesus returns with the disciples after the Last Supper (14.26), there to prophesy in messianic terms of the striking of the shepherd and the scattering of the sheep (14.27; cf. Zech. 13.7). So the eschatological woes which Jesus prophesies in chapter 13 begin to be fulfilled, on the same mountain, with the arrest of Messiah Jesus and the scattering of his disciples, in chapter 14. The strong eschatological and messianic associations of the setting are undeniable. For the reader, this reinforces the sense that the persecution and kinship enmity spoken of in 13.3–13 are of eschatological significance and presage the End itself.

The temporal setting is complex and overlapping. At one level, the sayings are a kind of farewell discourse set in (authoritative) time past, in the period of Jesus' ministry immediately after the teaching in the temple (13.1a) and two days before the Passover and the passion (14.1ff.). At the level of the content of the discourse, the temporal setting is time future, in response to the question of the disciples, in 13.4, 'Tell us, when will this be?' At the level of Mark's readers, the setting is time fulfilled, the time of their own past, present and future. Hence, the important aside to the reader – ὁ ἀναγινώσκων νοείτω – in 13.14; the collocation of historical references, in vv. 5b–22, unparalleled elsewhere in Mark; the multiplicity of imperatives, whose relevance extends well beyond Jesus' four immediate addressees; and the concluding, generalizing imperative, ὃ δὲ ὑμῖν λέγω **πᾶσιν λέγω** γρηγορεῖτε (13.37). The overwhelming sense that we have in this discourse, more clearly than in any of Jesus' previous teaching (but cf. 9.1), prophecy and paraenesis directly addressed to the time of the readers of Mark,[233] gives his warnings about persecution and kinship enmity particular seriousness. This is reinforced by the recognition that, in terms of the flow of the narrative, this discourse takes place in what we might call 'time out'. It functions as a kind of extended aside of such importance that it brings the narrative virtually to a halt, and for no short space of time, at a point of considerable tension.

From setting we turn to considerations of rhetoric. First, Jesus' eschatological teaching is a private discourse (κατ᾽ ἰδίαν, in v. 3) addressed to a select inner circle. The stress on privacy is the

---

[233] So too, Kelber, *Kingdom*, 109ff.; Iersel, *Mark*, 160ff.; Achtemeier, 'Reflections', 469.

evangelist's way of signalling a significant revelation to privileged persons (cf. the occurrences of κατ' ἰδίαν in 4.34; 6.31, 32; 7.33; 9.2, 28).[234] Rhetorically, the privacy motif functions as an invitation to the reader to share the privileged intimacy of the select addressees. It also heightens the tension surrounding Jesus' words. The weight of the words as esoteric disclosure is augmented by the setting of withdrawal and the narrowing of Jesus' audience.[235]

The speech is striking also for the absence of hostile questions from outsiders.[236] Elsewhere, Jesus' teaching comes generally in conflict situations marked by hostile questions: the cycle of controversy stories, in 11.27–33; 12.13–17, 18–27, 28–34, for instance. In chapter 13, at the outset, the marvelling exclamation of a disciple at the magnificence of the temple buildings provokes the customary rhetorical retort of Jesus, the preface to an authoritative saying about the temple's destruction (13.1–2). Then, after the change of scene and addressees, come the disciples' two questions at 13.4, which give the necessary impetus to the discourse,[237] but more importantly, involve the readers by giving voice to their own (eschatological) concerns. Otherwise, there are no intrusive interrogatives in what becomes Jesus' longest address. This suggests that the teaching in 13.5–37 'was composed not for apologetic purposes but for the instruction of Christians ... to help [them] come to terms with certain experiences and to understand them in the light of the gospel they proclaimed'.[238]

From a rhetorical and compositional perspective, endings are points of high tension, as Frank Kermode has shown.[239] Mark 13 is no exception. It serves as a kind of farewell address, preparing the

---

[234] So too, Schweizer, 'Anmerkungen', 41. These disclosures take the form either of teaching (so, 4.34 and 13.3) or miracles (6.30–44; 7.3; 9.2, 28). See also, Kee, *Community*, 53; and, in support of interpreting these disclosures within the framework of ideas of Jewish apocalyptic (esp. Daniel), see Freyne, 'Disciples', 7–23.

[235] Private settings which function similarly to mountains in Mark are desert places, houses, the boat, the sea, a garden, and 'the way'.

[236] On the important rhetorical function of questions in Mark, see Rhoads and Michie, *Mark*, 49–51.

[237] See Marcus' interesting observation (in *Mystery*, 91) on the questioning of Jesus about the Parable of the Sower by the disciples, in 4.10: 'For Mark, then, part of faithful listening is asking questions appropriate to Jesus' teaching ... the hiddenness of the kingdom makes inquiry necessary. Because Satan opposes God's action and blinds human beings (4.15–19), only those who penetrate beyond surface appearances can see the kingdom's advent.'

[238] Grayston, 'Mark XIII', 376.   [239] Kermode, *Ending*.

disciples for the time when their master has been taken.[240] This is the significance of the redactional introduction, Ὁ δὲ Ἰησοῦς ἤρξατο λέγειν αὐτοῖς, in 13.5a.[241] The recurring imperative, βλέπετε (vv. 5, 9, 23, 33), twice accompanied by the emphatic, second-person plural pronoun, ὑμεῖς (vv. 9, 23; also, ὑμᾶς, in v. 5), reinforces the tension. Further, not only does the teaching come towards the end of the narrative, but it is also teaching about the End and its coming. Hence, the fourfold occurrence of the syntactical pattern of temporal clause + imperative (using ὅταν in vv. 7, 11, 14, and τότε ἐάν in v. 21).[242] The paraenesis to the disciples is directed specifically to the events and circumstances of the End-time. It constitutes nothing less than a reinterpretation of history for the benefit of an audience prone, perhaps, to being 'led astray' by false messiahs claiming that the End has come already (vv. 5–6, 21–2). No previous teaching of Jesus in Mark has focussed so exclusively on this subject.[243]

A final observation about the rhetoric of Mark 13 concerns significant links with Mark 4.[244] Each of these major pieces of messianic *didache* is placed strategically at similar distances from the beginning and ending of the narrative. Each contains teaching given in private to disciples (4.10, 34). In each, the teaching has a 'riddling' quality, the decipherment of the riddles (or parables) serving to separate insider from outsider. There are intriguing similarities of content, also. To give but one instance, chapter 4 speaks of the sower who sows the word (τὸν λόγον, 4.14) and of the irrepressible growth of the grain until the harvest, which is the advent of the kingdom of God (4.26–9). Chapter 13 speaks similarly of the preaching of the gospel (τὸ εὐαγγέλιον) to all nations (13.10) and of the advent of the Son of Man, whose approach is likened to the ripening of the fig tree (13.26–7, 28–9). Such similarities become significant for our purpose when it is noticed that the hostilities spoken of in 13.9–13 are anticipated in the reference to 'tribulation or persecution ... on account of the word' in 4.17. This shows that

---

[240] Hooker, 'Trial', 80–1, points to literary precedents for such farewell speeches: Gen. 49 (Jacob), Deut. 32 (Moses), 1 Chr. 28 (David), The Testaments of the Twelve Patriarchs, The Assumption of Moses, and (as a New Testament analogy) Acts 20 (Paul). Strikingly also, the Farewell Discourse in the Fourth Gospel occurs at the same point in the narrative as in Mark: between Jesus' final teaching in the temple and the beginning of the passion narrative (John 13–17).

[241] As redactional, see Pryke, *Style*, 79, 81; Kee, *Community*, 44.

[242] Grayston, 'Mark XIII', 376.

[243] See France, 'Teaching', 121.   [244] See Iersel, 'Community', 17–19.

the warning in 13.9–13 is not an isolated or inconsequential one. On the contrary, it is an important element of the two major speeches of Jesus in Mark.

Finally, some brief comments on the characterization are in order. Jesus dominates, once more. He is cast, again, in the role of authoritative teacher, and is addressed as such in the scene-setting (13.1b).[245] He is cast also as eschatological prophet able to reveal the course of the events and woes of the *Endzeit*: hence, προείρηκα ὑμῖν πάντα, in v. 23b. This prophetic knowledge allows him to warn about impostors, counter eschatological anxiety (μὴ θροεῖσθε in v. 7; cf. 2 Thess. 2.2), and give instruction on the witness, endurance and vigilance required of the believer in the time of testing before the parousia of the Son of Man and the in-gathering of the elect.

The only other characters identified by name are the four disciples – Peter, James, John and Andrew (v. 3) – precisely the four whom Jesus called to follow him, in 1.16–20. The same inner circle (minus Andrew) is the recipient of other major eschatological disclosures in Mark: the resurrection of Jairus' daughter (5.35–43), the transfiguration (9.2–9; again, a mountain setting, as at 13.3), and the Gethsemane episode (14.32–42). Far from being cast in a negative light, as the representatives – in almost allegorical fashion – of a false ('divine man') christology or a false ('realized') eschatology,[246] these disciples are depicted as Jesus' privileged audience, the select recipients of words of revelation of such authority that they 'will not pass away' (v. 31b).[247] The fact that they may not fully understand what Jesus says (here, as elsewhere), or that they subsequently demonstrate that they have not learnt the lesson of vigilance which Jesus has tried to impress upon them (14.27–31, 50, 66–72), shows

---

245 See 4.38; 5.35; 9.17, 38; 10.17, 20, 35; 12.14, 19, 32; 14.14. Note Achtemeier, 'Reflections', 473, on *didaskalos*: 'In Mark, this word is restricted in its application to Jesus. Jesus so identifies himself and is so identified by disciples, religious officials and others.'

246 The views, respectively, of Weeden, *Mark*, and Kelber, *Kingdom*. Marcus, *Mystery*, 91, n. 55, rightly points out that Mark 14.28 and 16.7 present insuperable difficulties for the view that Peter and the twelve represent Mark's opponents.

247 See Freyne's important essay, 'Disciples', esp. pp. 8–12, in which attention is drawn to the apocalyptic Book of Daniel where revelation to a select, but representative, group – another foursome, in fact (i.e. Daniel and his three companions) – is shown to be quite characteristic, in a manner that bears close comparison with the private revelations to (members of) the twelve, in Mark: 'the singling out of individuals for "depth" experiences that apply to the whole group is very much a feature of the apocalyptic mode' (p. 12).

only that they – even they – are fallible,[248] and that they do not yet
have the 'key' to the mystery of Jesus and the will of God: namely
the cross and resurrection, still to come in the narrative. In narrative
terms, the narrowing of the audience to this select group, who have
been with Jesus from the outset, serves above all to heighten the
significance of Jesus' teaching and therefore to invite a greater
attentiveness on the part of the reader. That the select group are a
group of fallible people increases the reader's sympathetic identification with them and invites the reader to learn from their mis-
takes.[249] This invitation to attentiveness and identification becomes
explicit in the discourse itself: 'And what I say to you I say to all:
Watch' (v. 37; cf. v. 14b).

Our final step must be to see what light can be thrown upon this
'passion prediction for the community' from a sociological perspective. If we take further our suggestion that Mark's Gospel is
intended to foster the development of the (alternative) social world
of his Christian audience, the material in chapter 13 is particularly
pertinent because it appears to relate in a more transparently direct
way to the situation of that audience. We need to consider the
implications of the material both for relations with outsiders and for
relations with insiders.

On the well-grounded assumption that Mark is written for a
persecuted community (cf. 4.17; 8.34–9.1; 10.30, 38–9; 13.9–13;
14.66–72),[250] with the destruction of Jerusalem and the temple either
a realistic possibility for the very near future or a cataclysmic event
of the recent past, the authoritative prophecy and paraenesis of
Jesus in 13.9–13 (and in the discourse as a whole) function sociologically to legitimate counter-cultural behaviour and to provide a

---

[248] So, Malbon, 'Fallible Followers'; Malbon, 'Disciples'; Tannehill, 'Disciples';
Best, 'Role'.

[249] See Best, *Jesus*, 12: 'Many of Mark's readers may have already failed through
public or private persecution or through other causes; the failure of the
historical disciples followed by their eventual forgiveness and known success as
missionaries (e.g. Peter) would then be a source of great encouragement.'

[250] See further, Iersel, 'Community'; Weeden, *Mark*, 81–2. For the view that
Mark's story of Peter's denial was intended as a contribution to widespread
pastoral and disciplinary problems in the nascent Christian communities,
caused by persecution, see Lampe, 'Denial', 346–68, and Lampe, 'Discipline',
357f. For a compelling picture of synagogue discipline as the *Sitz* in which
believers in Jesus were required to anathematize him, see Derrett, 'Cursing
Jesus'.

theodicy for the suffering which that will bring. The legitimation takes the form of a private revelation to a privileged, specially representative, inner circle of the divinely foreordained events of the *Endzeit*, central to which is the revelation that, under the divine sovereignty, 'the gospel must first (πρῶτον δεῖ) be preached to all nations' (v. 10). It is this preaching of the gospel to Gentiles as well as Jews, along with the conversion and cross-bearing discipleship consequent upon that preaching, which is counter-cultural. It is counter-cultural because it is a divinely authorized summons to repentance and to membership in a 'new covenant' community in view of the in-breaking of 'the kingdom of God' (1.14–15; 6.12), a kingdom which relativizes the claims of all other powers and authorities (11.27–12.44)[251] and, in place of the law and the temple, constitutes what Kelber perceptively calls 'a new place and a new time'.[252] The new place is anywhere which can be understood as being 'on the way' with Jesus, or 'following' Jesus. The new time is the eschatological time of 'the age to come', already begun with the coming of Jesus, the Son of God.

Counter-cultural beliefs and behaviour inevitably generate resistance from the preservers of the status quo, especially in times of national upheaval, and it is that resistance of which Jesus warns, in 13.9–13: formal judicial action within both Jewish (εἰς συνέδρια καὶ εἰς συναγωγάς) and Gentile (ἐπὶ ἡγεμόνων καὶ βασιλέων) spheres of authority,[253] compounded at the domestic level by the mortal enmity of the disciple's own kin and, in general, by the experience of universal hatred. But with the warning comes also the theodicy: God is in sovereign control and will save those who endure to the point of martyrdom (vv. 13b, 20; cf. 10.26–7); the divine presence, in the form of the Holy Spirit, is promised to enable self-denying confession of Christ (v. 11); and the example of the endurance and vindication of Jesus, set forth in the narrative which follows (14.1–16.8), shows that the passion of members of the believing community is by no means in vain.

In terms of the ethos and dynamics of the community itself, such prophecy and paraenesis are intended, in all likelihood, both to

---

[251] See Verhey, *Reversal*, 77: 'Jesus' authority calls Mark's community into the uncompromising and uncomfortable status of a counterculture, a new covenant community standing in contrast to both the established religious authorities and the established civil authorities.'

[252] Kelber, *Kingdom*; see also, Malbon, *Space*.

[253] So too, Pesch, *Markusevangelium II*, 284.

sustain the community in the time of eschatological testing[254] and to act as a control on the eschatological enthusiasm generated by the (anticipated or actual) destruction of the temple, as suggested earlier. Yes, the End is near: but it is 'not yet'. So, beware of false messiahs and false prophets making claims to the contrary and attempting to usurp power in the community on the basis of those claims. Jesus is the true Messiah and prophet whose revelatory words (unlike those of other claimants) 'will not pass away'. The priority in the time before the End is, not 'signs and wonders' (v. 22; cf. v. 4), but preaching the gospel and being willing to accept the onerous consequences, as does Jesus himself. In opposition to the tendency to reduce the eschatological tension by claims that the Messiah has returned and the End has come, the Jesus of Mark maintains the tension by repeated warnings (βλέπετε ... γρη-γορεῖτε) and by asserting emphatically that claims to know the time of the Day of the Lord are groundless, since it is known by the Father only (v. 32). Thus, claims to knowledge of apocalyptic secrets are controlled by making Jesus alone the authoritative seer (whose knowledge is itself limited!), and by limiting Jesus' audience to a privileged and authentic circle of followers – the four leading disciples and, by identification with them, the readers of Mark. Likewise, claims that the End has arrived are tempered by the sombre disclosure that the End-time birthpangs have only begun, and that persecution and enmity, even from the believer's own close kin, lie in store on account of the gospel and 'the name'.

6 Conclusion

By way of concluding our analysis of the theme of discipleship and family ties according to Mark, it is necessary to attempt to summarize the main points of the preceding discussion. This will serve as the basis for the next stage of the study: a comparison with the handling of the theme in the Gospel of Matthew.

1. At the level of methodology, it is, I think, fair to say that the attempt at a more holistic approach to the interpretation of the Marcan text has been vindicated. The combination of insights from traditio-historical, literary-critical and sociological approaches has not resulted in artificial and disjointed analysis. On the contrary, the

---

[254] See Marcus, *Mystery*, 122: 'knowledge of mysteries [both in the Qumran literature and in Mark's gospel] *upholds* the elect community in the eschatological testing and *saves* it from destruction' (Marcus' italics).

approaches have been found to be complementary. Thus, as well as drawing inferences from Mark's handling of the tradition, the analysis has been enriched by responding as a reader to the Marcan text as a literary composition, and by developing an hypothesis at the sociological level about the kind of meaning and function the text might have had in the putative first-century audience or community for which it was written.

2. Mark's Gospel reveals a persistent interest in the implications for household and family ties of discipleship of Jesus. It appears at the outset, in the paradigmatic story of the call to discipleship of Simon and Andrew, James and John, where following Jesus requires leaving behind occupation, possessions and family. It appears in the equally significant stories of Jesus' fraught relations with his own family and *patris*, heavy as these stories are with implications for any who follow him. It comes again in the context of messianic *didache* on cross-bearing discipleship, where Peter's testimony to have left all is interpreted specifically in terms of household ties and applied to followers generally. Finally, in Jesus' prophetic 'farewell discourse' devoted to paraenesis for the elect in the testing time before the End, a particular warning is given of persecution of believers so virulent that even their own close kin will hand them over to a martyr's death.

3. There is no evidence that Mark is anti-family or is hostile to ties of natural kinship *per se*. On the contrary (to take but one example), Jesus' prohibition of divorce presupposes the continuing validity – indeed, the radical renewal – of household relations, at least in the present age. Furthermore, to those who leave household and family for his sake, Jesus promises, not no households, but households one-hundredfold. Rather than describe Mark as anti-family,[255] therefore, it is appropriate to put his emphasis in positive, eschatological terms: the new priorities and new forms of solidarity established by the coming of the kingdom and the imminence of the End.

4. To put it another way, household ties and kinship-related identity are strongly relativized. They are relativized, first, by belief in the breaking in of the kingdom of God with the coming of Jesus the Son of God, who establishes the nucleus of a new covenant community open to the Gentiles. This new covenant community is understood as the eschatological family of Jesus constituted, not on the basis of inheritance and blood ties, but on the basis of active

---

[255] See the view of Kee, *Community*, 109, cited earlier.

obedience to the will of God. They are relativized also by the call to follow Jesus in a life of faith and radical detachment enabling participation in the all-important preaching of the gospel to all nations. Third, they are relativized by the story of Jesus himself, rejected not only by the leaders of his own people, but also by the people of his own hometown, and by the members of his own family.

5. Furthermore, Mark is pessimistic about blood ties. The memory of Jesus' relations with his family provides no grounds for optimism, a point confirmed emphatically by the testimony of Jesus concerning the prophet's lack of honour 'in his own country, and among his own kin, and in his own house' (6.4). On both occasions when Jesus addresses the matter in his teaching, it is to warn of household-related persecution (10.30; 13.12). Jesus' last word on the matter makes this very apparent. The time before the End – which is the time of Mark and his audience – is to be a time when households are divided and in bitter conflict on account of 'the name'. The 'passion of the Marcan community' is the passion arising out of public and domestic persecution provoked by testimony to the gospel. The likely historical setting of this persecution is the crisis of identity and belief for Jews and Christians in the period of the destruction of Jerusalem and the temple.

6. From a sociological viewpoint, Mark's presentation of discipleship and family ties is helpfully understood in terms of the model of early Christianity as a social world in the making. In these terms, Mark's Gospel is suggestive of a strongly counter-cultural group ethos, heavily indebted to the world-view and traditions of Jewish apocalyptic. At the personal level, the believer's identity is defined, no longer primarily in relation to his/her ties of natural kinship and household belonging (since here, the expectation is more one of resistance and conflict), but in terms of ties of fictive or spiritual kinship to Jesus. At the social level, honour is a commodity, no longer ascribed by heredity and blood ties, but acquired by voluntary solidarity with fellow 'mothers', 'brothers' and 'sisters' in the new, eschatological family of followers of Jesus. The effect of Mark's presentation is: first, to legitimate the subordination of household ties for the sake of Jesus and the gospel mission; second, to authorize the practice of a new kind of voluntary solidarity and integration whose norms and boundaries transcend those established by heredity and consanguinity; and third, to provide a theodicy (based upon revelation) for experiences of kinship-sponsored marginalization and persecution.

7. In seeking Mark's motive for giving prominence to Jesus' relations with his family, no convincing evidence has arisen to encourage support for the view of Trocmé, Crossan, Weeden, Kelber and others, that Jesus' family and the twelve represent opponents of Mark in the Jerusalem church. On the one hand, the portrayal of the twelve is by no means consistently hostile or negative: rather, they are more aptly described as fallible followers, learning – however reluctantly and incompetently – the true meaning of discipleship of the suffering Son of Man in ways which speak vividly and directly to followers of Jesus of a subsequent, turbulent generation. On the other hand, the portrayal of the family of Jesus in no way justifies a kind of allegorizing interpretation according to which Mark's hidden motive is to snipe at Mary the mother of Jesus and James the brother of the Lord and leader of the Jerusalem church. Far more in keeping with the manifestly kerygmatic concerns of the gospel itself – christology and discipleship at the turn of the ages – is the view that his family's misunderstanding of Jesus exemplifies the mystery of the kingdom and the hiddenness of Jesus' messiahship, and that his rejection at Nazareth is an anticipation both of his own final rejection in Jerusalem and of the kinship-related hostility that awaits any who follow Jesus 'on the way' in the *Endzeit*.

4

DISCIPLESHIP AND FAMILY TIES IN MATTHEW

1 Introduction

In the previous chapter, we saw that the evangelist Mark gives considerable prominence to Jesus' relations with his own family and to the implications of discipleship of Jesus for family ties. In general terms, we saw that Mark's Gospel evinces a counter-cultural ethos. Jesus as the divine agent of the kingdom of God engages in a prophetic mission which brings him into conflict with his own family and fellow-countrymen. Disciples of Jesus have to subordinate family ties in order to be with him and (especially in the post-Easter period) to engage in mission for the sake of Jesus and the gospel. Following Jesus, even at the cost of household-based security and identity, brings the disciple into a new kind of family not determined by blood-ties, the eschatological family of Jesus open to 'whoever does the will of God'. This radical reordering of values and social identity generates fierce resistance, especially from the disciple's kinship group. Mark's story of Jesus serves to legitimate the Christian community's counter-cultural stance and to provide a theodicy for the persecution it suffers in consequence.

Now we turn to Matthew's story of Jesus in order to see how Matthew understands the implications of discipleship for family ties. We do so for the following reasons. First, even a superficial glance reveals that this gospel shows no diminution of interest in the theme of discipleship and family ties. On the contrary, not only does Matthew take over the relevant Marcan tradition, but he also includes other tradition not available to him from the earlier gospel – most notably, the Q tradition at Matt. 8.18–22 = Luke 9.57–60, and Matt. 10.34–6, 37–9 = Luke 12.51–3; 14.26–7, as well as tradition unique to Matthew (19.10–12).

Second, analysis of the relevant Matthean material makes possible a comparison with our findings about Mark and the putative

Marcan community. Such comparison may serve to confirm or correct inferences which were drawn about the ethos of Marcan Christianity. It will serve also to show the kind of developments which took place in early Christian reflection upon the tensions generated within household groups by becoming a follower of Messiah Jesus.

Third, study of discipleship and family ties in Matthew will contribute to our understanding of Matthew's Gospel itself and, in particular, the ethos of Matthean Christianity. This is an area of continuing and current growth in Matthean studies, but the relative number of studies from a sociological perspective is surprisingly small,[1] and there is still scope for more intensive work on the particular theme of family ties. The latter claim is supported by the witness of two recent surveys of Matthean scholarship,[2] as well as of Ulrich Luz's authoritative essay on 'The Disciples in the Gospel according to Matthew'.[3]

Fourth, and finally, turning to Matthew gives us another opportunity to test out the interdisciplinary approach to the reading and interpretation of the text which we attempted in the chapter on Mark. The vast majority of scholarship on Matthew since 1945 has taken either a history-of-traditions approach within which redaction criticism has been dominant,[4] or a history-of-religions approach setting Matthew in relation to contemporary Judaism of various kinds.[5] The recently published first volume of the new International Critical Commentary, on Matthew 1–7 (1988), is a monument to the enduring significance of this work.[6] Only in the last decade has the hegemony of these approaches from within the historical paradigm begun to give way to a greater pluralism of approaches; so that now work on Matthew from a literary-critical[7] or a social scientific perspective[8] is being undertaken. The discussion which follows will attempt to take this kind of pluralism further.

Methodologically, there is no doubt that a redaction-critical

[1] See Stanton, 'Damascus Document', 85–6.
[2] Stanton, 'Origin and Purpose'; and Senior, *Matthew*.
[3] Luz, 'Disciples'.   [4] The classic study is Bornkamm *et al.*, *Tradition*.
[5] A recent exponent is Przybylski, *Righteousness*.
[6] Davies and Allison, *Matthew I*.
[7] E.g. Kingsbury, *Story*; and Edwards, *Story*. Freyne, *Galilee*, interestingly juxtaposes literary and historical approaches. He too (pp. 6–13) discusses the greater pluralism of current approaches to gospels interpretation generated by the advent of literary-critical and social scientific readings.
[8] E.g. White, 'Grid and Group'; and, most recently, Overman, *Gospel*.

approach is on safer ground with Matthew than with Mark. This is recognized widely. On the well-grounded assumption of Marcan priority,[9] observation of the ways in which Matthew modifies his Marcan source allows inferences to be drawn about Matthew's particular concerns.[10] The same procedure may be applied, although more tentatively, to Matthew's redaction of Q.[11] The material unique to Matthew is important as an indicator of the evangelist's interests also, whether or not such material comes from the redactor's own hand. But it would be a mistake to assume that only in the alterations – even could these be established with assurance – are the evangelist's interests to be found. As G. N. Stanton points out: 'If we concentrate on the distinctive elements introduced by the evangelist, we fail to appreciate that he frequently uses his traditions with little or no modification simply because he accepts them and wishes to preserve them and make them part of his portrait of Jesus and of his message to his own Christian community.'[12]

But as well as the separate parts of Matthew, we need to pay attention to the whole, to Matthew's Gospel as a composition to be read and interpreted in its final form, as text.[13] We need, that is, to move from the gospel as window onto the past (or present) world(s) outside the text or onto the earlier stages of the tradition behind the text to the gospel as a self-contained narrative which invites the reader, by appropriate rhetorical means, to enter its story world and engage with its implied author, plot, setting and characters.[14] That

---

[9] See the now classic defence by G. M. Styler, in Moule, *Birth*, 285–316; and, most recently, Davies and Allison, *Matthew I*, 98–114.

[10] See Kingsbury, *Matthew* 19: 'Matthew receives traditional materials and interprets them by redacting them, through expansion, rearrangement, abridgment, clarification, omission, and substitution. The grand result is that he creates a new literary document which narrates the gospel afresh to meet the needs of the church to which he belongs.'

[11] For an important defence of the Q hypothesis, see Fitzmyer, 'Priority', 131–70; and see critical surveys of the alternatives in Stanton, 'Origin and Purpose', 1899–1903; and Davies and Allison, *Matthew I*, 115–21.

[12] Stanton, 'Origin and Purpose', 1896. See Luz, *Matthew 1–7*, 74: 'Thus the evangelist even theologically continues to a large extent thoughts of his two main sources. Matthew is the disciple or, better, the heir of his theological fathers, Mark and Q.'

[13] An early attempt at 'composition criticism', though not from within the literary-critical paradigm, is Thompson's excellent monograph, *Advice*, on Matt. 17.22–18.35.

[14] See Kingsbury, *Story*, 2. See also Ben Meyer's perceptive essay, 'Challenges', noting the three challenges of reader-response theory to historical-critical method, mentioned on p. 11: 'First, there is the challenge to historical-critical

is why the techniques of literary criticism are valuable.[15] Not only so. From a sociology of knowledge point of view, it is fair to ask, why has the story been told *this* way? Whom is the author seeking to influence or persuade, and to what end(s)? These are sociological questions, plausible answers to which may deepen our understanding of the text by making us aware of various levels of possible meaning and significance. So there is a legitimate place for sociological criticism, as well. We have seen the value of applying these various perspectives to the text of Mark. Now we take the experiment a stage further by turning our attention to Matthew.

2   The call of the two pairs of brothers to discipleship (Matt. 4.18–22 par. Mark 1.16–20)

The first episode directly relevant to our theme is the story of the call of the disciples, which Matthew has taken over from Mark. Whereas Matthew is known at other points for his willingness to abbreviate Mark,[16] the same cannot be said here. Rather Matthew preserves the Marcan tradition basically intact. If it was important for Mark's understanding of discipleship, it is so for Matthew as well. Form criticism adds nothing to the points made in relation to Mark 1.16–20, so we move directly to redaction-critical observations, in particular to Matthew's modifications of his source.

Matthew brings the two call stories into much closer formal similarity with each other by making the ending of the second episode symmetrical with the ending of the first, thus: οἱ δὲ εὐθέως ἀφέντες . . . ἠκολούθησαν αὐτῷ (vv. 20, 22). The effect of this change is significant. The close symmetry of the two episodes strengthens their paradigmatic quality for the reader of Matthew. It is as if Matthew is signalling that repentance in response to the coming of the kingdom (4.17) is to be like this: leaving everything immediately and following Jesus in radical obedience to his call.[17]

> exegetes to cut the last of their underground ties with positivism. Second, there is the challenge to attend intensely and consistently to the implied author or the voice of the text . . . Third, there is the challenge to discover, not a plurality of senses, but the fulness, the multidimensionality, of the sense of the text.'
>
> [15] A recent essay which applies this form of narrative criticism to discipleship in Matthew is Edwards, 'Uncertain Faith'. The theme of family ties plays no part, however, in Edwards' reading.
>
> [16] This has been demonstrated, especially for the miracle stories, by Held, in 'Matthew', 165–229.
>
> [17] See Luz, *Matthew 1–7*, 199: 'The reader is made to feel that this is exactly the way it is when one is called by Jesus.'

In a most emphatic – because redundant – way, the redactor inserts on both occasions a description of the pairs of men as 'two brothers' (δύο ἀδελφούς, vv. 18, 21). This, in addition to the fact that he follows Mark in identifying the second of each pair as the brother of the first (καὶ Ἀνδρέαν τὸν ἀδελφὸν αὐτοῦ ... καὶ Ἰωάννην τὸν ἀδελφὸν αὐτοῦ). Consistent with this is Matthew's version of the list of the names of the twelve, in 10.2–4 (par. Mark 3.16–19). Here, we note two things. First, Andrew is brought from fourth to second place and identified as Peter's brother (ὁ ἀδελφὸς αὐτοῦ) (10.2; diff. Mark 3.18). Second, the naming of James and John 'his brother' (ὁ ἀδελφὸς αὐτοῦ) is brought into strict parallel with the naming of Simon and Andrew, by the omission of the 'Boanerges' parenthesis (10.2; diff. Mark 3.17b).[18] The overall effect is that the first part of the discipleship list is brought into conformity with the call stories. It is apparent, therefore, that the kinship term ἀδελφός is important to Matthew.[19] Interestingly, it occurs most often in Matthew of the four gospels.[20] In my view, this is because the depiction of the first and most prominent disciples as 'brothers' has special significance at the level of the evangelist's ecclesiology. For Matthew, repentance and following Jesus bring the follower into a community that is best understood as a brotherhood.[21] As we shall see, this fits well with other material in this gospel. In 12.49, for example, Jesus points specifically to his disciples (diff. Mark 3.34a) and calls them his mother and his brothers; in 23.8 (Matthew only), Jesus says ('to the crowds and to his disciples', 23.1), 'you are all brothers'; and in his first resurrection appearance, Jesus instructs the two women to 'go and tell my brethren (τοῖς ἀδελφοῖς μου) to go to Galilee' (28.10; Matthew only), where the reference is quite clearly to the eleven disciples (28.16).

Matthew also differs from his source in his depiction of Zebedee. In 4.21, he makes it clear from the outset of the episode that the father of James and John was with them in the boat. This is in

---

18 See Gundry, *Matthew*, 182–3.
19 See also Matt. 20.24 par. Mark 10.41, where Matthew substitutes 'the two brothers' for Mark's 'James and John'; and similarly at Matt. 26.37 par. Mark 14.33. See Davies and Allison, *Matthew I*, 395.
20 According to Morgenthaler, *Statistik*, 68, the word count is: Matthew 39 times, Mark 20 times, Luke 24 times, and John 14 times.
21 So too, Gnilka, *Matthäusevangelium I*, 102: 'In der Berufung der Brüderpaare, die gemeinsam in die Nachfolge eintreten, soll man die neue geistige Bruderschaft, die neue geistige Familie erkennen (12, 50), zu der sich Gemeinde konstituiert.' See also Kingsbury, 'Peter', 77–80.

contrast to Mark, who refers to Zebedee's presence only when the two brothers leave and follow (Mark 1.20b). The effect of this earlier mention of Zebedee 'their father' being with them makes the brothers' abandonment of the boat and 'their father' all the more radical. Consistent with this is the omission of the 'hired hands' (μισθωτοί) (Mark 1.20b). Zebedee, according to Matthew, is left behind alone. Nor is there time for leave-taking, a possibility which Mark's version (with εὐθύς modifying ἐκάλεσεν, not ἀφέντες) leaves slightly open.[22] James and John leave 'immediately', just as Simon Peter and Andrew have done. Zebedee is left decisively behind. In paradigmatic terms, their entry into the brotherhood of followers of Jesus displaces their commitment to their father.

We have here an anticipation of subsequent material in Matthew (discussed below) which speaks specifically of the subordination of filial piety to the greater obligation of discipleship. In 8.21–2, a disciple is refused permission to bury his father; 10.35 speaks of division between a man and his father; 12.50 omits earthly fathers from Jesus' new family; and in 19.27, Peter testifies to having left 'everything' to follow Jesus. It seems fair to say that we begin to see in 4.18–22 evidence of a redactional process reflecting commitment to an understanding of community as a brotherhood whose claims take priority over family (and occupational/household) ties and where patriarchal authority patterns are relativized (cf. 23.9). Historically, this would contrast strikingly with contemporary developments in Pharisaic piety where, as Neusner has shown,[23] it was precisely into the sphere of the household that the Pharisees transferred the duties of the holy life after the destruction of the Jerusalem temple.

Another modification worth noting is Matthew's use of ἀκολουθεῖν at the end of the second call story (diff. Mark 1.20b – ἀπῆλθον ὀπίσω αὐτοῦ) as well as of the first (where ἠκολούθησαν αὐτῷ comes from Mark 1.18). This reflects the evangelist's preference for this verb,[24] since, for him, ἀκολουθεῖν has a particular conno-

---

22 Note that, if the form critics are right in seeing the gospel call stories as modelled especially upon the call of Elisha by Elijah, in 1 Kgs. 19.19–21, then the fact that the disciples follow 'immediately' is in marked contrast with the elaborate leave-taking of his kin practised by Elisha prior to going after Elijah (see esp. LXX and Josephus, *Antiquities* VIII.354). See further, Hengel, *Leader*, 16; Davies and Allison, *Matthew I*, 393.

23 Neusner, *Politics*, 83, 146; Neusner, *Trends*, 31.

24 According to Morgenthaler, *Statistik*, 70, the word count is: Matthew 25 times, Mark 18 times, Luke 17 times, John 18 times.

tation. Kingsbury has shown that Matthew uses this verb in both its literal sense of going after someone and in its metaphorical sense of going after someone as a disciple.[25] The metaphorical connotation is unambiguous where two factors characterize its use: a demand for personal commitment, such as a summons by Jesus; and an indication that there is a 'cost' involved. It is these factors precisely which are evident in the uses of the verb in 4.20, 22, as also in 9.9 (= Mark 2.14), 19.29 (diff. Mark 10.29), and elsewhere. So the repetition of ἠκολούθησαν αὐτῷ in 4.22 brings the second episode into conformity with the first and heightens the paradigmatic quality of both. The call stories express for the evangelist what it means to be a disciple of Jesus: unqualified personal commitment, even at the cost of occupational and family – including filial – ties.

The fact that ἀκολουθεῖν occurs again immediately after in the description of the response of the crowds (ὄχλοι) to Jesus' threefold ministry of teaching, preaching and healing (4.23–5, at v. 25) is likely to be significant (8.1; 12.15; 19.2; 20.29), especially since both crowds and disciples are present to hear the Sermon on the Mount (5.1). For Matthew, discipleship is open to all, disciples are drawn from the crowds, and the radical demands of discipleship – expressed paradigmatically in the call stories and including the subordination of family ties – are laid upon all.[26]

I take the paradigmatic character of 4.18–22 to be indicated by yet another redactional modification: the name Simon is augmented by the qualifier τὸν λεγόμενον Πέτρον (v. 18).[27] This occurs also, and significantly, at the inauguration of the mission to Israel, when the names of the twelve 'apostles' are listed: the first is Σίμων ὁ λεγόμενος Πέτρος (10.2). The Marcan parallel to the latter has something quite different: Simon is named Peter by Jesus (Mark 3.16; Matt. 16.18!), and the juxtaposition of the two names occurs here for the first time. So in Matthew, Simon is known as Peter from the very

---

[25] Kingsbury, 'Verb', 56–73, as well as the studies cited in his n. 1. Classic is Bornkamm, 'Stilling', 54–5.

[26] See Luz, *Matthew 1–7*, 201: 'following on the part of the disciples does not distinguish them from the people who are sympathetic to Jesus, but the people, by following, belong together with the disciples. We have here a first indication of the structure of the Matthean community, in which there is neither a special group of followers nor a constitutive structure of office.' Contrast Kingsbury, 'Verb', 61, who argues, less persuasively in my view, that the following of the crowds is literal only and lacks connotations of discipleship.

[27] In Brown, *Peter*, 76 n. 172, the authors note: 'The usage of "Peter" is about five times as frequent as the usage of "Simon" in Matthew, and indeed antedates the giving or explaining of the name "Peter" in 16.18.'

beginning. The evangelist's concern here is primarily christological and ecclesiological: Peter (and the twelve) are the link with Jesus, and it is upon Peter that Jesus will build his church (16.18). Just as importantly, the model of discipleship represented by the story of the call of Peter (and the others) applies to the church founded upon him. Schweizer puts it well: 'Peter says and hears *in an exemplary way for all disciples* what every disciple could say and hear ... [Likewise,] everything that is said and given to the twelve applies in principle to all future disciples of Jesus.'[28]

In 4.18–22, therefore, Jesus is calling to follow him the ones – the plural is justified if Simon Peter is *primus inter pares*[29] – upon whom the new community of Christ's *ekklesia* will be established. It is important to notice the communal tenor of Matthew's ecclesially oriented interpretation here, for the effect is to qualify the possibility that Matthew's primary idea of discipleship in the post-Easter period is (to use Theissen's term) of *Wanderradikalismus* ('wandering radicalism').[30] In Matthew's day and in the changing circumstances of his community, what may have been important was, not so much to challenge people to take up an itinerant, homeless lifestyle in literal imitation of Jesus and the disciples, as to argue that, from the start, Jesus was engaged in building a new community with Peter and the twelve, and that membership in that community would be a demanding and costly affair.[31] It is as if Matthew is saying, 'If that is what following Jesus cost them – a life of homeless itinerancy – what will it cost us?' In Matthew's day, the idea of leaving occupation and family may have had more to do with the cost of joining the brotherhood of the Christian *ekklesia* than with becoming an itinerant, mendicant preacher.

We ought not to draw too sharp a distinction, however. This gospel evinces a major commitment to mission to the Gentiles (28.16–20).[32] Thus, joining the brotherhood may have required participation in itinerant mission or the support of those so engaged. The call stories will have been able to 'speak' both to all followers of Jesus in Matthew's day who had made the transfer into the brotherhood of Jesus' new family (cf. 12.46–50) and to those who were transferring

---

[28] Schweizer, 'Church', 136 (Schweizer's italics).

[29] So, Kingsbury, 'Peter', 71.

[30] See Theissen, 'Wanderradikalismus', available in translation, as Theissen, 'Radicalism'.

[31] See further, Keck, 'Ethos', 38–44.

[32] See Hare, *Persecution*; also, Hare and Harrington, 'Disciples', 359–69.

also from a settled, household existence to one of itinerant mission. In terms of the scholarly debate over the *Sitz im Leben* of Matthew, we ought in my opinion to resist the temptation to polarize. On the evidence so far – and, of course, much more needs to be examined – it is not sufficient to say, either that Matthew's community is an itinerant, charismatic group of social fringe-dwellers,[33] or that Matthew is engaged in the conservative task of 'community consolidation'.[34] Rather, some combination of the two may represent a more accurate *Sitz*. This would see the evangelist engaged both in consolidating the pattern of life and self-understanding of the brotherhood and in encouraging mission and missionaries.[35]

From the evidence of Matthew's editorial modifications of his Marcan source and its possible significance for understanding the Matthean *Sitz im Leben*, we turn to a literary-critical analysis of how the episode communicates as a piece of narrative. As in the chapter on Mark, attention will focus mainly on literary features like setting, plot, characterization and rhetoric. Methodologically, it is important from a literary-critical point of view to interpret the text of Matthew as a discrete text in its final form, independent of any traditio-historical links with Mark or other sources. Nevertheless, where appropriate, literary points of a comparative kind will be made.

The setting of the call stories in Matthew is important. Following immediately upon 4.17, the call of the disciples comes at a structural turning-point in the narrative as a whole. Kingsbury has shown that 4.17, with its formulaic beginning, Ἀπὸ τότε ἤρξατο ὁ Ἰησοῦς, marks one of two such turning-points, the other being 16.21, since it too begins, Ἀπὸ τότε ἤρξατο ὁ Ἰησοῦς. According to Kingsbury,

---

[33] This is the tendency of Schweizer's 'Observance', esp. pp. 226–9, although it is important to note that Schweizer limits the identification of the charismatic prophets: 'Some particularly gifted members of the Church are probably following Jesus in a more literal way . . . wandering from place to place to serve and to teach the Church' (p. 229). See also his essay, 'Church', 141.

[34] Keck, 'Ethos', 39ff.; also, Kingsbury, 'Verb', 62–70.

[35] Kingsbury himself admits ('Verb', 73) that the situation was probably more complicated when he concludes that Matthew's community was in a 'transitional' stage, where the ethic of itinerant radicalism remained relevant for missionaries as well as for those facing persecution, but the majority were no longer able to interpret it literally. In his more recent essay, 'Peter', 78–9, he distinguishes 'at least two groups' within Matthew's church (apart from the 'false prophets'): itinerant missionaries engaged in preaching to Jews and Gentiles, and a resident group of those who teach.

the topical outline of the gospel is as follows: (1) the Person of Jesus Messiah (1.1–4.16); (2) the Public Proclamation of Jesus Messiah (4.17–16.20); (3) the Suffering, Death, and Resurrection of Jesus Messiah (16.21–28.20).[36] On this reading, 4.17 marks the beginning of Jesus' proclamation to Israel, a period which comes to a climax with Peter's confession of Jesus as 'the Christ the Son of the living God' at Caesarea Philippi (16.13–20). Whether or not we accept in full Kingsbury's tripartite structure for the gospel,[37] a good case can be made for regarding 1.1–4.16 as Matthew's prologue, ending with the climactic fulfilment quotation of Isa. 9.1–2.[38]

If this is so, then the location of the call stories at the very start of the narrative of Jesus' public ministry to Israel is significant. The disciples are with him from the beginning. Conversely, he is with them from the beginning. He does not engage in mission on his own: nor (after Easter) will they (28.20b). This solidarity between Jesus and the disciples, which continues into the period of the church, is a fundamental motif of the work as a whole.[39] As we shall see, this solidarity is given expression in kinship terms: at the 'vertical' level, Jesus is *the* Son of the heavenly Father (3.17), and disciples are sons of God (cf. 5.9, 45; 13.38); and at the 'horizontal' level, disciples are members of the spiritual family of Jesus (12.49–50), and belong to the brotherhood of the Christian *ekklesia* (23.8).[40] Further, this immediate association of the Messiah and his disciples creates the expectation that they will do what he does: and this is borne out. If Jesus is the light (4.16), his disciples are to be likewise (5.14a). If Jesus preaches the kingdom and heals the sick (4.23), his disciples will also (10.7–8a).

With respect to spatial setting, it is worthy of note that the call stories and the material which surrounds them reveal a strong sense of place. Most importantly, the first disciples are called 'by the Sea of Galilee' (4.18a). Galilee, for Matthew as for Mark, is a place charged with meaning. Its full significance cannot be explored

[36] Kingsbury, *Structure*, 1–37.
[37] For a discussion of alternatives, see Stanton, 'Origin and Purpose', 1903–6; Senior, *Matthew*, 20–7; Gundry, *Matthew*, 10–11. A recent corroboration of the Kingsbury position, from a specifically literary-critical approach, is Bauer, *Structure*, esp. pp. 73–108.
[38] Amongst recent works adopting this view are Senior, *Invitation*, 20–52; and Gnilka, *Matthäusevangelium I*, 1–98.
[39] See further, Frankemölle, *Jahwe-Bund*, chs. 1–2.
[40] So too, Kingsbury, *Story*, 104.

here.[41] Suffice it to note the following. First, Galilee unites the story of Jesus from beginning to end (2.22; 28.16). Second, references to Galilee frame the story of Jesus' mission to Israel (4.12–17, 23; 15.29–31). It is where he heals (for example 4.23–5; 8.1–4, 5–13, 14–17; 9.1–8; etc.); it is where he gives four of the five great discourses (19.1); it is where he begins to reconstitute the people of God and graces them with God's presence, over against Jerusalem and the temple (cf. 9.9–13; 9.35–11.1; 12.1–8, 15–20; etc.); it is where he first pronounces judgment on Israel (for example 11.20–4; 12.38–42, 43–5; etc.) and encounters the opposition that will come to a head in Jerusalem (for example 9.3, 34; 12.14); and it is where he returns after his resurrection to commission the eleven for mission to all nations (28.16–20). But Galilee is important for the story of the disciples, as well. Thus, and in significant parallel to the story of Jesus – imitation, almost – Galilee unites the story of the disciples from beginning to end. It is where they are called to be fishers of men (4.18–22), and it is where, after the resurrection, that call is given its recapitulation and decisive interpretation (28.16–20). Further, again like Jesus, the mission of the disciples to Israel occurs in Galilee (10.1–42); and this strikingly open-ended mission (diff. Mark 6.30!) is an anticipation of the Galilee-inspired mission to all nations in the post-resurrection period.

In sum, Galilee functions in Matthew's story as the place of eschatological hope: of mission and ministry, first to Israel and then to all nations. The reduplication of the Galilee experience of Jesus in the Galilee experience of the disciples reinforces the sense that discipleship involves the imitation of Christ – since Christ himself is the exemplary disciple (11.25–30). It also provides the eschatological and messianic context of meaning for a discipleship which is radical enough to require the renunciation of occupation and family: '"The land of Zebulun and the land of Naphtali, toward the sea, across the Jordan, Galilee of the Gentiles – the people who sat in darkness have seen a great light, and for those who sat in the region and shadow of death light has dawned"' (4.15–16).

What we have discovered about the eschatological significance of the spatial setting is reinforced by the temporal setting of the call stories. In a word, that setting is one of fulfilment (cf. 1.22; 2.15, 17, 23; 3.15; 4.14; 5.17). The fulfilment of the divine will in the dawning of the kingdom of heaven with the coming of God's Son, revealed

---

[41] See further, Freyne, *Galilee*, 70–90; Kingsbury, *Story*, 27–9.

beforehand in scripture, is an idea writ large in Matthew's first part
(1.1–4.16).[42] It is an idea which Matthew holds in common with
Mark, but which Matthew elaborates, primarily for apologetic
reasons,[43] at much greater length and with the help of carefully
organized formula quotations. Its bearing on the call stories is
twofold. First, in so far as it identifies Jesus as the long-awaited
Messiah, the true Israel, the Son of God, it endows him with the
authority to make the summons. Second, and on the same basis, it
justifies the fishermen's extraordinary response: 'Immediately, they
left . . . and followed him.'

From setting, we turn, next, to considerations of plot. The call of
the fishermen is preceded by events in the narrative of major import,
not only for christology, but for discipleship as well. I cannot go
into this in detail here, but make the following general observations.
First, the birth of Jesus generates division and conflict: the wise men
from the East come and worship (2.1ff.); Herod 'and all Jerusalem
with him' are troubled (2.3), and a fierce pogrom takes place
(2.13–18) of such virulence that Joseph and his family flee to Egypt
and return subsequently, not to Judaea, but to Galilee (2.22–3).
Likewise, John the Baptist's appearance in the wilderness preaching
the breaking in of the kingdom of heaven (3.1–2) – a precise
anticipation of the proclamation of Jesus (4.17b) – provokes division: many repent and are baptized (3.5–6), but the 'Pharisees and
Sadducees' are condemned (3.7–10). Conflict marks the appearance
of Jesus also: the contest with Satan which follows Jesus' baptism
(4.1–11). Finally, before Jesus begins preaching and choosing disciples, John is arrested (Ἰωάννης παρεδόθη, 4.12). There is a narrative pattern here which conveys the message that the coming of the
kingdom is both salvation and judgment,[44] and that envoys of the
kingdom – both Jesus and the disciples – will suffer from the
hostility provoked by its proclamation. We shall see subsequently
that this hostility has a strong familial dimension in Matthew
(10.21–2, 34–9).

The call comes directly after Jesus' initial preaching in Galilee of
the breaking in of the kingdom of heaven (4.17). Quite clearly, this

[42] So too, Luz, *Matthew 1–7*, 156–64, esp. p. 162.
[43] See Stendahl, '*Quis et Unde?*'.
[44] See Brown, *Birth*, 183, speaking only of Matt. 1–2: 'Thus understood, ch. 2 is
the necessary completion of ch. 1 in the sequence of revelation, proclamation,
and twofold reaction, a sequence that gives to the infancy narrative its status as
a gospel in miniature. The gospel is the good news, but that gospel must have a
passion and rejection, as well as success.'

plot sequence is intended to make the point that leaving all to follow Jesus is the appropriate response to the overwhelming eschatological reality which Jesus proclaims.[45] The call stories are paradigmatic of what discipleship means at the turn of the ages.

After they go with Jesus, he engages in a Galilee-wide mission of teaching, eschatological preaching and healing, as a result of which 'great crowds followed him' (4.23–5). Then comes Jesus' first major discourse, addressed to the crowds in general, and to the disciples in particular (5.1–7.29). Once more, the plot sequence is contrived in order to make a point.[46] It is a theological point about grace and obligation. First comes the revelation of 'God with us' in Jesus the Son (1.23), the call to follow and the teaching/preaching/healing throughout Galilee: so all is of grace. Then comes the obligation. Following Jesus into the life of the kingdom of heaven requires radical obedience, the nature of which is spelt out in the Sermon on the Mount. In fact, the call stories anticipate this and prepare the way for it. For the willingness of the fishermen to leave 'immediately' (εὐθέως twice!) their occupations, possessions and family ties is exemplary of the kind of wholehearted obedience which the Sermon aims to inculcate in every disciple (for example 6.24–34).[47]

Our third area of literary-critical analysis is that of characterization. We must be careful not to find what is not there, however. For it is striking that, whereas considerations of setting and plot make an important contribution, the characterization is minimal. The overwhelming focus is on Jesus, as it has been from the very beginning (1.1). In 4.18–22, Jesus is the person of authority; and the initiative lies with him. He is the one who comes 'walking by the Sea of Galilee', who 'sees' the two pairs of brothers, and who issues the call to follow – which is also a call to mission. He alone speaks: there is no dialogue. The response of the fishermen is to him only.[48]

---

[45] So too, Luz, *Matthew 1–7*, 200.

[46] Note the divergence from Mark at this point. Where Mark (1.21ff.) proceeds from the call of the fishermen to the events in Capernaum (including the exorcism in the synagogue and the healing of Peter's mother-in-law), Matthew inserts the Sermon on the Mount at the beginning of Jesus' ministry, with the Capernaum healings coming after.

[47] See also Kingsbury, 'Verb', 72–3: 'The ethic Matthew held up to contemporary Christians is that of the "greater righteousness" (5.20) ... Within the framework of this ethic, those logia of Jesus which speak of the abandonment of home, family, and goods, give illustration on [*sic*] the person of the first disciples of Jesus of the character of discipleship, of being single-heartedly devoted to God.'

[48] Precisely the same is true of the story of the call of Matthew, in 9.9.

Concerning those called we are given the barest outline: their
names and kinship ties as brothers and/or sons, their occupational
activities as fishermen when Jesus appears, and their immediate and
positive response to his summons. No hint is given of character
development or of motivation or of conflict, in order to help explain
their response. All we have is Jesus' call to repentance in view of the
dawning of the kingdom (4.17b), and his word of command to
follow. But, for the narrator, that is enough. For Matthew, questions of individual psychology and personal motivation are not the
issue here, in the way that they may be elsewhere (for example 5.46;
6.2, 5, 7, 16; etc.). Rather, from what we as readers know so far, they
are four ordinary working men going about their everyday labour.
It is people such as these whom Jesus calls and who obey. The
representative, paradigmatic role of the four fishermen, seen in these
terms, is transparent.[49] In terms of the narrative sequence, they are
the kinds of people of whom and to whom it might be said, 'Blessed
are the poor in spirit, for theirs is the kingdom of heaven' (5.3ff.).[50]

A sociological perspective on the call story episode in Matthew is
in order now. As with Mark, the family ties material in Matthew is
approached most helpfully in terms of the model of early Christianity as a social world in the making. We need to ask, that is, what
each episode expresses about the self-understanding of early Christianity in its Matthean form, about relations between members of
Matthew's church, and about relations with outsiders. Is there a
discernible corollary between Matthew's interpretation of Christ
and the kingdom of heaven, on the one hand, and Matthew's
understanding of the communal life of the people of God, on the
other?

Presumably, Matthew has taken over, almost unaltered, the
Marcan tradition of the call of Peter, Andrew, James and John
because for him also it has the potential for contributing significantly to the process of community building and community
maintenance. First, it roots the origins of the community in the past,
in the epoch-making time of the ministry of Jesus and of the twelve.
In an author and a group which set enormous store on the authority
of Jesus' words (7.24; 9.7b; 28.20a), the saying of Jesus – 'Follow

---

49 So too, Overman, *Gospel*, 135: 'The disciples in Matthew lack sharp contours,
with little or no personal and biographical information provided about them.
The disciples are models (*Vorbild*) for the members of the community.'
50 See Kingsbury, *Story*, 107.

me, and I will make you fishers of men' (4.19) – is a constant reminder of the group's primary *raison d'être*: discipleship of Jesus in mission to all people in view of the new reality of the kingdom of heaven.

Second, it roots the community in the call of the apostles, that is, of the twelve. Not unlike Luke–Acts (Acts 1.15–26), assurance about the apostolic foundations of the church is important to Matthew.[51] In this episode, we have the call of the four named first in the list of apostles, in 10.2–4. Subsequently, in Matthew's redaction of the story of the call of the tax-collector (Mark 2.13–14 par. Matt. 9.9), the man's name is changed from Levi, a non-apostolic figure, to Matthew, the apostle (10.3, Μαθθαῖος ὁ τελώνης).[52] Pre-eminently, of course, there is Simon Peter, the one named first here, and subsequently in the list of the twelve apostles in 10.2, and whom the author regards as the apostolic foundation-stone of the Christian *ekklesia* (16.18). So stories such as the one in 4.18–22 link the second generation of believers – the brotherhood of the Matthean community – with the first generation, pre-eminent among whom are Peter and the twelve. It is they whom Jesus chooses to be with him from the beginning of his Galilean ministry; it is they whom Jesus teaches about the kingdom of heaven; and it is they who pass on and interpret the significance of Jesus' teaching to the next generation.

Third, the call stories legitimate an understanding of Christian discipleship as involving a commitment to Jesus radical in its social consequences. This is true for Mark, as we saw. It is the case for Matthew, as well. The in-breaking of the kingdom of heaven and the call to follow Jesus establish priorities which transcend the mundane obligations of occupation and family life. That is certainly the message of Matthew to his readers; and it corresponds closely with what the Jesus of Matthew teaches elsewhere about the demand of God for wholehearted devotion to the kingdom (for example 6.19–24, 25–33; 19.16–30). The contours of these radical social consequences will be spelt out later. Here, we may suggest that the evangelist's repeated use of the kinship term ἀδελφός provides some grounds for inferring that, in his day, transference

---

[51] See, however, Luz, 'Disciples', 108–9: 'In contrast [to Luke] Matthew consistently avoids the title apostle, even where he is speaking of the mission of the twelve. Why? the reason may be as follows: the members of his community could identify with the *mathetai* but not with the *apostoloi* who had already become by that time figures of the past.' I do not myself see that this follows. Why is it not possible to identify with figures of the past?

[52] So Luz, *Matthäus II*, 42; *contra* Gundry, *Matthew*, 166.

into the brotherhood of the Christian *ekklesia* may have taken place at the cost of ties of the believer's natural family – something which we saw in the Introduction to have been the case from elsewhere in early Christian literature.

3 The cost of following Jesus the Son of Man (Matt. 8.18–22 par. Luke 9.57–60, 61–2)

If we take the material in its sequence in Matthew, the next episodes directly relevant to the theme of discipleship and family ties come immediately before the story of the stilling of the storm (8.23–7), in 8.18–22. Here we are dealing, not with tradition taken over from Mark, but with Q material, on the grounds that there is an almost verbatim parallel in Luke 9.57–60 (61–2). We shall see that Matthew has incorporated this non-Marcan tradition because it makes possible further exposition of the nature and cost of discipleship, an exposition begun in the call stories.

In form-critical perspective, and including the additional episode in Luke 9.61–2, we have here three biographical apophthegmata[53] linked together by the common theme and terminology of 'following' and a common two-part structure: an anonymous person asks permission – in two cases with a proviso – to follow Jesus; and each time, Jesus answers with a warning which challenges the expectations of the questioner. Redaction criticism will show that the respective evangelists embroider the details and provide their own distinctive settings; but the common, paradigmatic form of each pericope is evident, and in each case, a memorable Jesus logion provides the abrupt, even shocking, climax.

It is worth noting that these three pericopae in Q[54] correspond substantially to the call stories in Mark. Common aspects are: the 'ideal scene' character of the episodes; the theme of 'following' and its implications, not least for family ties; the centrality accorded Jesus' powerful – and usually metaphoric or hyperbolic – word; and

---

[53] Bultmann, *Tradition*, 28–9; see also Hengel, *Leader*, 3–5.

[54] For our purpose, it is not necessary to come to a firm decision on whether or not Luke 9.61–2 should be designated Q. Certainly, it is formally and thematically identical with the two preceding pericopae, so there is good reason for attributing it to Q – as, for example, do Hengel, *Leader*, 3–4, nn. 4–5; and Marshall, *Luke*, 408–9, who also gives a useful account of three alternative ways of accounting for Luke 9.61–2! Manson, *Teaching*, 122, attributes the pericope to Special Luke (L), as does Fitzmyer, *Luke I–IX*, 833.

the parallels in form and content to the story of the prophetic call of Elisha by Elijah, in 1 Kgs. 19.19–21. So we can see that traditions to do with following Jesus and its implications circulated widely in the early church. It is not difficult to understand why: the reason is the fundamentally hortatory concern of Christian preachers and pastors to show believers of the second generation what discipleship of Jesus always involves. 'Here a concrete situation brings to symbolic expression the truth that "to follow" Jesus "sets the disciple free from every duty, permits him no further obligation, but requires of him a surrender securing him wholly to Jesus alone."'[55]

Turning to evidence of Matthean redaction, in so far as this may be discerned both from a comparison of the versions in Matthew and Luke and from observations of distinctive Matthean composition, we note the following.

Contrary to Manson's claim that there is no reason why Matthew should omit the third discipleship pericope (Luke 9.61–2),[56] it may be said that its absence from Matthew is coherent from a redactional viewpoint. First, Matthew's tendency to abbreviate his sources is well known.[57] Second, an additional pericope which merely reiterates the one preceding it would only disrupt the narrative flow between vv. 18 and 23.[58] Third, the sequence of two pericopae serves an important rhetorical function, by allowing complementary stories to interpret each other as, for instance, the closely parallel call stories do, in 4.18–22.[59] This latter point will be taken further below.

The respective settings are different and likely to be redactional. For Luke, the triad of encounters about discipleship constitutes an ideal introduction to his Travel Narrative (9.51–19.46). Luke 9.57a is a redactional beginning which links 9.57b-62 to the whole section from 9.51 on (τοῦ **πορεύεσθαι** εἰς Ἰερουσαλήμ ... Καὶ **πορευομένων** αὐτῶν ἐν τῇ ὁδῷ...).[60] In Matthew, however, the pericopae

---

[55] Bultmann, *Tradition*, 29 (quoting A. Schlatter).   [56] Manson, *Teaching*, 122.
[57] See Kingsbury, *Matthew*, 18. Such abbreviation is illustrated well in Matthew's handling of the storm-stilling, in 8.23–7 par. Mark 4.35–41: on which, see Iersel and Linmans, 'Storm', 24.
[58] Hengel, *Leader*, 4, n. 4.
[59] See Kingsbury, 'On Following', 51–2; also, Gundry, *Matthew*, 154: 'The tradition includes a third dialogue ... But Matthew has his wheat and his tare, his true disciple and false. The third dialogue therefore vanishes.' Note, however, that Kingsbury and Gundry take opposite positions on which character is the 'wheat' and which is the 'tare'! I shall argue below that neither is right.
[60] Marshall, *Luke*, 409.

are inserted, remarkably, into a long section of narrative (8.1–9.35) devoted almost entirely to recounting the miraculous 'works' (11.2) of the Messiah. Further, whereas the pericopae in Luke prepare for the sending out on mission of the seventy-two (Luke 10.1–16), in Matthew they precede the miracle of the stilling of the storm (8.23–7), the effect of which is to reinterpret the miracle story in terms of Matthew's understanding of discipleship and the church, as Bornkamm's classic study showed.[61]

Another important difference, related also to the setting of the pericopae in Matthew, concerns the preface, in v. 18. By contrast with Mark 4.35, the Matthean Jesus issues a command to go over to the other side of the sea: ἐκέλευσεν ἀπελθεῖν . . .[62] This enables the theme of Jesus' authority – which is the warrant for following him wherever he leads – to come to the fore. Thus, whereas Mark has the disciples taking him 'as he was, in the boat' (Mark 4.36), Matthew depicts Jesus himself making the embarkation, with the disciples 'following' after him into the boat (8.23). The redactional point is clear. Discipleship means following Jesus wherever he leads and at any cost – even the cost of household and kinship ties – because he is the one who has all authority (8.27; 28.18).

Matthew also transfers to v. 18 the reference in Mark 4.36a to 'the crowd'.[63] The effect is striking. In Mark, the disciples and Jesus are in the boat already and, since the day is at an end, they leave the crowd behind on the shore (4.36a), even though 'other boats' are with him, as well (4.36b). According to Matthew, however, Jesus gives a command to go over to the other side, not because evening has come, but as a result of 'seeing the crowd' (8.18a). Since ἐκέλευσεν lacks a direct object, and since the only group specifically mentioned is the crowd, it appears that the evangelist envisages Jesus seeing the crowd and ordering *it* to cross with him to the other side![64]

---

61 Bornkamm, 'Stilling'; Held, 'Matthew', 202; Iersel and Linmans, 'Storm', 24–8; and Luz, *Matthäus II*, 20–30, who treats 8.18–27 as one section, under the heading, 'Nachfolge in den Sturm'.

62 On Matthew's preference for κελεύειν, see 14.9, 19, 28; 18.25; 27.58, 64; and Gundry, *Matthew*, 151. According to Morgenthaler, *Statistik*, 112, it occurs thus: Matthew 7 times; Mark never; and Luke once. The point, for Matthew, is to put the initiative firmly with Jesus.

63 Matthew also may have changed Mark's ὄχλον to πολλοὺς ὄχλους, as several strong textual variants attest. Metzger's *Commentary*, 21, gives ὄχλον only a D rating.

64 According to Bauer–Arndt–Gingrich, *ad loc.*, when κελεύω occurs with the infinitive alone and no object in the accusative, 'everything else must be supplied from the context'. Matt. 8.18b (ἐκέλευσεν ἀπελθεῖν) is a case in point.

This interpretation is reinforced by two further observations. First, the 'disciples' have not been referred to specifically since 5.1; and there they are introduced as a kind of inner circle, after Jesus has gone up the mountain to teach, having seen 'the crowds' (Ἰδὼν δὲ τοὺς ὄχλους; cf. 8.18a, Ἰδὼν δὲ ὁ Ἰησοῦς ὄχλον). In Mark, it is the relations between Jesus and the disciples which is given greatest prominence in the material leading up to the storm-stilling. They are with him in the boat on the sea as he teaches in parables (Mark 4.1–2, 10, 35–6), and it is to them 'alone' that the secret of the kingdom is revealed. Matthew, by contrast, emphasizes Jesus' ministry of word and deed to the 'great crowds'. Noteworthy here are the redactional references to them, in 7.28 and 8.1.[65] The former speaks of the astonishment of οἱ ὄχλοι at Jesus' teaching. The latter speaks of the ὄχλοι πολλοί who 'followed him' and who become beneficiaries of his ministry of healing and further teaching. Second, the crowd in 8.18a is described as being περὶ αὐτόν. In Mark, this phrase is used of the crowd which constitutes Jesus' true family (Mark 3.32; diff. Matt.). In other words, the περὶ αὐτὸν ὄχλος is a positive designation of disciples of Jesus (cf. Mark 4.10). Matthew removes it from his source at Mark 3.32 and places it here, in 8.18a, so as to imply that the crowd 'around him' are potential disciples, at least.[66]

On these grounds, then, it is not at all surprising that Jesus commands the crowds to cross the sea with him. They have 'followed' him previously (4.25; 8.1). Will they 'follow' him now, even across deep waters? The interrogative is justified fully by the pericopae on discipleship which Matthew now inserts in vv. 19–22. For, in the context of vv. 18 and 23–27, these two pericopae constitute the basis for a challenge and a sorting out: who from among the crowd is willing to accept the cost of becoming a true disciple?[67] That a

[65] See Gundry, *Matthew*, 151.
[66] This conclusion concurs with Minear's important study, 'Disciples', 31f., from which I quote: 'Far from being an amorphous and neutral category, the *ochloi* played a highly positive role as followers of Jesus, accepting his prophetic authority and accompanying him from the beginning to the end of his career ... From the standpoint of Matthew, these *ochloi* represented a major objective of Jesus' ministry in all its aspects: healing, exorcism, preaching, teaching, suffering. They represented therefore a major purpose of God in sending his son to claim the fruits of his vineyard.'
[67] See Thompson, 'Reflections', 372, who also argues that Jesus is portrayed as summoning the crowd: 'he seems to invite his hearers to make a deeper commitment by crossing the lake with him' (n. 21). Opposed to this interpretation is Kingsbury, 'On Following', 46–7.

sorting out takes place is implied by the fact that it is specifically οἱ μαθηταὶ αὐτοῦ who follow Jesus into the boat (which, incidentally, appears suddenly on the scene for the first time, in 8.23; diff. Mark 4.1), as well as by the fact that there is only one boat to get into (diff. Mark 4.36b)!

This brings us to the next important difference in Matthew's version. Prompted, as it were, by Jesus' command to go over to the other side, two people come from out of the crowd and address Jesus in sequence. In contrast to Luke's account, each is identified: the first is a 'scribe' (γραμματεύς), the second, ἕτερος τῶν μαθητῶν. The dialogues between each of these men and Jesus allow Matthew to indicate the criteria of true discipleship: a willingness to count the cost of identification with the rejected Son of Man (v. 20), and a willingness to accept the heavy and total demand of disciple-ship even to the point of the radical subordination of family ties (v. 21).

But how are we to determine whether the two interlocutors of Jesus are understood by the evangelist in a particular way? Matthew is not explicit on this, so it is impossible to be certain – and perhaps, from a rhetorical point of view, that is the point: to leave the challenge open. Literary-critical analysis will help on this score. Redaction critics, however, have come to at least three different conclusions, in a debate which is still current. In the first place, some, like Kingsbury, argue that the interlocutors are in a relation-ship of contrast: the 'scribe' is portrayed negatively and the 'dis-ciple' positively.[68] Others, like Gundry, agree that 'scribe' and 'disciple' are contrasted, but reverse the evaluation: the willing Christian scribe is the 'wheat' in Matthew's church, and the disciple who wishes to delay following represents the 'tares' in Matthew's church, the ones who lack absolute commitment.[69] A third option, argued most recently by Orton, is that Matthew understands both 'scribe' and 'disciple' in a positive light: 'the link between both scribes and disciples for Matthew is both close and positive.'[70]

It is not possible here to analyse all the arguments and evidence in detail. Nor is it necessary if, as Orton says, 'the double logion is

---

[68] See Kingsbury, 'Verb', 59–60; and, most recently, his 'On Following', *passim*.

[69] See Gundry, *Matthew*, 151–2.

[70] Orton, *Scribe*, 35–7, quoting from p. 37. Of course, these three positions do not exhaust scholarly ingenuity! Thompson, 'Reflections', 372, n. 22, tries to find a mediating position: '[although] not yet a disciple, he is inclined to cross over to the other side of the lake with Jesus'.

preserved for what Jesus says, not for the example (positive or
negative) presented by the enquirers'.[71] Nevertheless, since the
identifying labels 'scribe' and 'disciple' belong to the Matthean
redaction, some editorial interpretation is implied. In my view,
Orton's position has most to commend it, for the following briefly
stated reasons.

a. On a plain reading of the narrative, there are no compelling
grounds for contrasting 'scribe' and 'disciple', or for evaluating the
two inquirers in either of the (contradictory) ways proposed by
Kingsbury or Gundry. It would be compelling, for instance, if Jesus
unambiguously commended one and rebuked the other: but he does
not. It would be compelling also if one or other of the two turned
away from following, as is the case explicitly with the rich young
man – another discipleship story – in 19.16–22 (at v. 22). But, on the
contrary, the sequel is: 'And when he got into the boat, his disciples
followed him' (8.23). b. Both inquirers are associated with the
crowd(s) which Matthew has introduced into the setting (v. 18a) and
which he understands positively, as we have seen. c. Matthew brings
the two episodes into closer stylistic conformity. Each has a clear,
two-part structure of: statement/request by an inquirer (identified),
and response by Jesus with a formulaic introduction (καὶ λέγει αὐτῷ
ὁ Ἰησοῦς . . . ὁ δὲ Ἰησοῦς λέγει αὐτῷ).[72] Also, the second introductory phrase, ἕτερος δὲ τῶν μαθητῶν (v. 21a), looks as if it is
intended to increase this conformity by linking together 'scribe' and
'disciple'.[73] As with the pair of call stories, in 4.18–22, it seems
legitimate to interpret this stylistic conformity as implying a correspondence in the meaning of the pair of discipleship stories, as well.
d. Both the terms used to address Jesus – διδάσκαλος and κύριος –
are terms of respect. Matthew has introduced the first along with the
identification of the man as a 'scribe' because it is natural for a
scribe to recognize Jesus as a teacher; and, in return, he is given
teaching about the Son of Man (v. 20). Certainly, διδάσκαλε may be
a form of address used by outsiders or enemies of Jesus (12.38;

---

[71] Orton, *Scribe*, 36.

[72] The greater symmetry has been achieved mainly by moving ἀκολούθει μοι from
the beginning of the second pericope to the end (Matt. 8.22b; diff. Luke 9.59a).
Note also Matthew's use of the present tense of λέγειν to introduce the sayings
of Jesus, rather than the aorist (so Luke). Gundry, *Matthew*, 152, comments:
'The historical present tense implies that Jesus is speaking also to the church.'

[73] Orton, *Scribe*, 36; Gundry, *Matthew*, 151–2; *contra* Kingsbury, 'On Following',
48, 53.

22.16, 24, 36);[74] but so may κύριε (7.21, 22)! Conversely, Jesus applies the term διδάσκαλος to himself (23.8; also 10.24–5; 26.18), and it is self-evident in this gospel that Jesus plays the role of teacher and commands his disciples to do so also (28.20).[75] e. Γραμματεύς in Matthew may be the designation of a disciple. Indeed, on the basis of the uniquely Matthean material in 13.51–2 and the redacted saying in 23.34 (diff. Luke 11.49), where the term is used of true followers of Jesus and members of the church, we should say more strongly that ideally, γραμματεύς expresses what is for Matthew something quintessential about the scholarly, exegetical, inspired and prophetic nature of Christian discipleship which his own gospel writing seeks to exemplify.[76] That there are scribes who do not conform to the ideal – and they are the ones Matthew associates especially with the Pharisees – does not contradict this. The scribe introduced in 8.19a is not obviously one of these. On the contrary, the context of discipleship points in a positive direction.[77]

We turn now to the two sayings of Jesus, which constitute the climax of the respective pericopae, to ask about the meaning of these Q logia in their present context in Matthew.[78] With respect to the saying about the homeless Son of Man (8.20 par. Luke 9.58),

---

[74] A point emphasized by Kingsbury, 'On Following', 51.

[75] See Orton, *Scribe*, 36; Gundry, *Matthew*, 152.

[76] This is the burden of Orton's entire study: *Scribe*, esp. chs. 1, 6, 7.

[77] Kingsbury argues that, by contrast with the call stories (4.18–22), the story of the scribe has pejorative overtones because it is the scribe, and not Jesus, who takes the initiative. 'In Matthean perspective, the words "I will follow you wherever you go" cease to be simply an appeal to become someone's disciple and constitute an arrogation to oneself of Jesus' peculiar authority. The problem with the scribe is that he would "enable himself" to become Jesus' disciple ... [For Matthew] it is impossible for anyone, apart from Jesus' enabling call, to enter upon and to sustain the life of discipleship (4.18–20, 21–22; 9.9)' ('On Following', 49, 51; see also Kingsbury, 'Verb', 60). Against this: 1. It is not at all clear that Matthew is concerned here with a theological debate over 'grace versus works'. 2. Even on Kingsbury's terms, do not the call stories themselves, together with the numerous miracle stories – all of which precedes the discipleship pericopae – provide a sufficient demonstration of grace and authority to which the scribe's offer may be interpreted as an appropriate response? And does not Jesus take the initiative in (the redactional) v. 18? 3. The Gospel as a whole depicts many people who are viewed positively in the initiative they take in appealing to Jesus (e.g. 8.2, 5; 9.2, 18, 27; etc.). 4. The point of both pericopae (8.18–22) is revealed above all in the storm-stilling which follows (vv. 23–7): belonging to the Christian community is tough and testing and demands faith in Jesus. On the latter, see Iersel and Linmans, 'Storm', 25–6.

[78] A good case for the authenticity of the logion as a saying of the historical Jesus is presented by Casey, 'Jackals'.

several observations are pertinent. First, the idea that 'the Son of man has nowhere to lay his head' has a controlling effect on the wider narrative. Matthew interprets the saying literally.[79] Thus, in his version of the storm-stilling, the reference in Mark 4.38 to Jesus sleeping ἐπὶ τὸ προσκεφάλαιον is omitted (8.24b).[80] Jesus is portrayed as the exemplary disciple who does what he himself teaches (in contrast, of course, with the 'hypocrites' of 6.2, 5, 16; 7.5; etc.). Followers, by extension, are those who are willing to imitate Jesus by adopting a homeless, itinerant lifestyle also. The costliness of discipleship of this kind is conveyed well in the vulnerability of the disciples in the boat, utterly exposed to the violent storm. The contours of this violence are given a specifically familial shape soon after, in the missionary discourse (10.21–2, 34–8).

Second, Lindars points out that this is the first mention of the Son of Man in Matthew.[81] He goes on to say that 'there is nothing in the context to suggest that it means to him anything more than a self-reference on Jesus' part'.[82] I find this surprising, because it does not go far enough. In view of the evangelist's widely recognized attraction to Son of Man as a christological title drawn from the Book of Daniel,[83] and in view also of the apocalyptic element in the story (immediately following) of the σεισμὸς μέγας in the sea (8.24),[84] it seems likely that the logion as interpreted by Matthew implies a strong element of eschatological crisis. The homelessness of the Son of Man expresses that crisis, especially because his situation contrasts so unfavourably with that of creatures – foxes and birds – whom it was common in the ancient world to despise.[85] The evangelist, on this reading, intends the saying to be a warning to

---

[79] So too, Luz, *Matthäus II*, 24: 'Matthäus Jesu Heimatlosigkeit buchstäblich versteht.'

[80] So too, Iersel and Linmans, 'Storm', 24.

[81] Lindars, *Son of Man*, 116–17.

[82] *Ibid.*, 117.

[83] Lindars himself says (*ibid.*, 130): 'The proliferation of sayings in which Jesus speaks of himself as the apocalyptic Son of Man is thus due to Matthew's interest in apocalyptic.' Instances of this proliferation are 10.23b; 13.37, 41; 19.28; 24.30; 25.31.

[84] Bornkamm, 'Stilling', 56, cites in support of an apocalyptic interpretation: Matt. 24.7; 27.54; 28.2; also, Rev. 6.12; 8.5; 11.13, 19; 16.18.

[85] See Hoehner, *Herod*, 343–7; and Casey, 'Jackals', 8–9. Texts indicating a negative evaluation of foxes include: Neh. 4.3; Ps. 63.10; S. of S. 2.15; Lam. 5.18; Ezek. 13.4; Enoch 89.42 – and of birds: Gen. 40.17; Deut. 28.26; 1 Sam. 17.44, 46; 2 Sam. 21.10; 1 Kgs. 14.11; 16.4; 21.24; Ps. 79.2; Isa. 18.6; Jer. 7.33; 16.4; 19.7; 34.20; Ezek. 29.5; 31.13; 32.4; 39.4, 17. I owe these references to a personal communication from Professor D. R. Catchpole.

the would-be follower that the homelessness (which, as with the response to Wisdom, in Enoch 42.1ff., signifies rejection)[86] of the Son of Man will be his lot as well in this End-time epoch.

Can any particularly Matthean nuances be detected similarly in the second logion, in 8.22b? The complete verbal agreement between Matt. 8.22b and Luke 9.60b shows that Matthew has been quite content to preserve the Q tradition of Jesus' reply intact: ἄφες τοὺς νεκροὺς θάψαι τοὺς ἑαυτῶν νεκρούς.[87] Nevertheless, Matthew's understanding of the logion is indicated in several ways. First, the saying is preceded immediately by the important summons of Jesus, ἀκολούθει μοι (diff. Luke, where it comes at the opening of the pericope, in 9.59a).[88] As Kingsbury has shown, the use of ἀκολουθεῖν qualifies the saying as a clear expression of Matthew's understanding of discipleship: it involves cost and commitment.[89] In contrast with the call of Elisha by Elijah (1 Kgs. 19.19–21), the true disciple of Jesus is not permitted to go 'first' and fulfil his familial obligations. The word of Jesus has an authority which gives him precedence even over family ties.[90]

Second, Jesus' refusal to allow the disciple to go and bury his father is quite consistent with the abandonment of their father by James and John when Jesus called them (4.22). In other words, for this evangelist, the Q logion contributes to an important theme in the self-definition of God's new people: that of the church as a new family (12.46–50) or brotherhood (23.8), for whom there is only one Father, the One in heaven (6.9; 23.9). The 'dead' who bury their dead are, therefore, those who do not obey the will of the Father in heaven as it is revealed authoritatively in the call of the Son on earth to follow him.[91]

---

86 On the close parallels with Wisdom's difficulty in finding a place to dwell, see Gnilka, *Matthäusevangelium I*, 311–12. He cites Enoch 42; 94.5; Job 28.21; Baruch 4.20ff.; *et al.* On Matthew's Wisdom christology generally, see Suggs, *Wisdom*, where particular attention is drawn to 11.19, 25–7, 28–30.

87 The conclusion in Luke 9.60c (σὺ δὲ ἀπελθὼν ... θεοῦ) is Lucan redaction, according to Marshall, *Luke*, 412.

88 Marshall, *Luke*, 411, thinks the Matthean version is original. It seems more likely – although certainty is impossible – that Matthew has relocated the summons as a way of bringing the two episodes into formal parallel with each other: so, Gundry, *Matthew*, 153; and Hengel, *Leader*, 4.

89 Kingsbury, 'Verb', 57–62.

90 On the authority of Jesus' word in Matthew, see 7.28–9; 8.3, 8, 13, 16b, 32; 9.2–8, 9, 22, 29–30; etc. It is a prominent theme in this whole section: see further, Thompson, 'Reflections', *passim*.

91 This is to give greater precision to the more general interpretations of the logion by such scholars as Hengel, *Leader*, 7–8, and Beare, *Matthew*, 214. Beare merely

But perhaps the most striking way of approaching the Matthean interpretation of this saying is by setting it in relation to Matthew's understanding of the torah. We need not dwell for long on this evangelist's strong commitment to an understanding of discipleship as doing the will of God (for example 5.17–20, 21–48; 12.46–50; etc.). Active obedience to God's will as revealed in, and fulfilled by, Jesus is the essential response to the divine grace, also revealed in Jesus.[92] Whether 'righteousness' (δικαιοσύνη) so conceived represents an apologetic response by the evangelist to criticism from Pharisaic rabbis in the synagogue communities outside, or whether it is more a pastoral response to fragmentation and dissipated commitment within his own community, is difficult to decide with certainty.[93] We need not exclude either possibility. What is certain is that, for Matthew, it is the teaching and example of Jesus which defines 'righteousness', and this teaching gives central place to works of love (5.43–8; 7.12; 19.19b; 22.34–40; 24.12; and the double appeal to Hos. 6.6 in 9.13 and 12.7).[94] On this basis, Jesus' refusal to allow the disciple to go 'first' and perform what was taken for granted in antiquity generally as a fundamental work of love and filial piety – the burial of a father by his son – is provocative and shocking.[95]

However, it would be a false step to interpret the logion as indicating Matthew's opposition to filial piety and ritual observance. Elsewhere in this gospel, both filial piety (15.4–6; 19.19a) and ritual observance (6.16–18; 23.2–3a, 23; also, 15.17; diff. Mark 7.19b) appear to be taken for granted as valid expressions of obedience to the will of God. Nevertheless, the controlling factor for Matthew is not the law, but Jesus the Son of God who 'fulfils' the law (5.17).[96] The controlling interest is not 'righteousness' *per se*, but being a disciple, which means above all to 'follow' Jesus.[97] As we have seen, the

takes the whole saying as an extravagant way of saying, 'let that matter take care of itself'.

92 See further, Przybylski, *Righteousness*, 105ff.

93 Amongst the vast literature, see further, Barth, 'Law'; Schweizer, 'Observance'; Hammerton-Kelly, 'Attitudes'; and the surveys of Stanton, 'Origin and Purpose', 1934–7; and Senior, *Matthew*, 47–55.

94 See esp. Barth, 'Law', 75–85. Barth concludes (p. 85): 'The love commandment is for him the centre and supporting basis for the whole of the law and the prophets, and therefore it is made the principle of interpretation.'

95 Hengel, *Leader*, 8–14, gives full details of the 'break with law and custom' which the saying of Jesus represents; also, Sanders, *Jesus*, 252–5.

96 See Banks, 'Understanding', esp. pp. 229–32, on the meaning of πληροῦν.

97 See the important statement of Przybylski, *Righteousness*, 115: 'The concept of righteousness does not pervade Matthean theology. For example, it plays no crucial role in the Matthean view of the nature of salvation. Matthew's religious

logion at hand is set firmly within an exploration by Matthew of the theme of discipleship.[98] What we have, then, is a saying which does not set filial piety aside *tout court*, but relativizes it strongly by setting it within a different frame of reference: that of being a follower of Jesus in the short and troubled (8.24–5!) time before the End when mission to all nations is the over-riding priority.

Literary criticism is concerned, not with how a redactor has modi-fied his sources, but with how an author has told a story. It approaches the text, not as a window onto the mind of the evangelist or the situation of the (hypothetical) community, but as an invita-tion to the reader to enter the enchantment of a narrative world. This is our concern now, in relation to these two discipleship episodes.

The setting is intriguing because it is surprisingly vague. From 4.12ff., we know that Jesus 'withdraws' to Galilee and lives in (someone's house in) Capernaum, that he calls four fishermen at the Sea of Galilee, that he teaches the crowds and disciples on 'the mountain' (unspecified) (5.1; 8.1) and from there returns to Caper-naum, where he heals the centurion's servant (8.5–13), enters Peter's house – where he has accepted domicile? – and heals Peter's mother-in-law (8.14–17); and then, with the sudden appearance of the crowd 'around him', he gives orders to depart to 'the other side' – pre-sumably of the Sea of Galilee (cf. 8.24, 28; 9.1). The form critic is likely to see the relative ambiguity of the setting as the result of the loose juxtaposition of previously independent pericopae. The redac-tion critic will draw attention to the overall geographical unity supplied by the references to Galilee, as we have seen already. From a reader-response perspective, however, where it is incumbent on the reader to find the meaning precisely in the 'gaps' in the text, this ambiguity has a dislocating, disorienting effect. But perhaps this is the point. Jesus is the Son of Man who (astonishingly) has nowhere to lay his head, but who leads the way into the boat and onto the stormy sea. The disciple is one who is able and willing to accept the dislocations and disorientations which come with following the homeless Son of Man: and, as the two encounters show, such dislocations are likely to be strenuous, involving a disturbance of domicile and family ties.

self-understanding is that of a disciple doing the will of God as distinct from that of a righteous person doing righteousness.'
[98] Emphasized also by Thompson, 'Reflections', 371–8.

The narrative sequence and structure are important and 'tell-tale' also. As is recognized widely,[99] 8.1–9.34 presents Jesus as 'Messiah of deed' just as 5.1–7.29 presents Jesus as 'Messiah of word': the words and deeds of Jesus are the powerful and unified expression of the coming of God's Son and the breaking in of the kingdom of heaven. The telling of Jesus' power in word and deed provides strong justification and incentive for discipleship (8.18–22). It also provides a model for engagement in mission (9.35–11.1).

Within 8.1–9.34,[100] it is not just a 'Messiah of deed' who is presented, however. The power of Jesus' word continues to be of critical importance. Thus, in the trio of miracle stories (in 8.1–17) which precede our material, Jesus' word is decisive in the first two (8.3b, 8b-9, 13), and the third concludes with a summary statement saying that Jesus 'cast out the spirits with a word (λόγῳ), and healed all who were sick' (8.16b). Because the authority of Jesus' word is so manifest, the focus of attention in vv. 18–22 has to be on what Jesus says there also: for it is the Son of God and Servant of Yahweh (v. 17) who speaks. Discipleship of Jesus is grounded in his word – his word of call (8.22; 9.9) and his word of instruction (8.20, 22b; 9.10–12, 14–17).

The way in which the two discipleship episodes containing Jesus' authoritative sayings preface the story of the storm-stilling (vv. 23–7) turns the latter into something of an appendage,[101] a vivid evocation of the life of discipleship in the company of Jesus the Κύριος. Once again, the focal point is the dialogue,[102] culminating in Jesus' strong rebuke, 'Why are you afraid, O men of little faith?' (vv. 25–6a). This, in turn, provides a clue to the preceding material: to follow the homeless Son of Man requires faith; and to follow Jesus without reservation or condition requires faith also.

Concerning characterization, little needs saying. Jesus dominates throughout: moving from place to place, healing the sick, giving orders, and summoning followers even to forego fundamental duties of filial piety. But this Jesus is a figure of paradox.[103] Not only is he a person of divine authority. He is also a person of divine humility: 'the Son of man has nowhere to lay his head' (8.20b). We could say, in fact, that his authority arises out of his humility. That is why he is,

---

[99] See Stanton, *Gospels*, 61–2.

[100] See further, Thompson, 'Reflections', *passim*.

[101] So too, Held, 'Matthew', 204.

[102] See also Iersel and Linmans, 'Storm', 26: 'Hereby all direct discourse becomes a dialogue between Jesus and his disciples.'

[103] See also Luz, *Matthäus II*, 23–4.

in the portrayal of Matthew, both 'Lord' and exemplary disciple. The two would-be disciples serve as foils to Jesus and as lessons in discipleship. The one makes an offer which Jesus' reply shows to be ill-considered. The other offers a conditional discipleship when the demand of Jesus and the kingdom is for commitment which is unconditional.[104]

The already-observed importance of the dialogue in each episode calls for a comment on the rhetoric of this material. The stark brevity and the close formal similarity of the two episodes give them an emphatic and paradigmatic force. They communicate in a very direct way to the reader, in a manner which is reinforced by the relative lack of historical particularity.

Each episode consists of a dramatic, one-to-one encounter between Jesus and an interlocutor,[105] and follows a pattern of the interlocutor's offer/request followed by Jesus' reply. The emphasis, rhetorically, falls upon Jesus' heavy and disturbing demand, in the face of which a decision by each individual follower has to be made. Interestingly, we are not told explicitly how the two individuals respond, so the narrative tension remains unresolved:[106] an effective way of leaving with the implied reader the question of how he/she would/should respond in the light of Jesus' demanding call.

In each dialogue, the interlocutor's offer/request is, at face value, laudable or eminently reasonable – to follow Jesus anywhere, to perform time-honoured duties of filial piety. Precisely as such, these offers and requests have the effect of rendering Jesus' responses intensely disturbing and uncongenial. Tannehill puts this well:

> The text makes agreeing with Jesus difficult by placing his words in contrast with the sensible point of view which, by and large, we also share. It is deliberately trying to make things hard for us in order to block the natural tendency to simply add discipleship to the configuration of duties and values by which we live. Discipleship is not merely another

---

[104] See Bornkamm, 'Stilling', 54: 'Both cases are concerned, however, with ἀκολουθεῖν, in the one case in the warning against an unconsidered decision and in the other in the summons to a radical decisiveness.'

[105] This is a narrative device used extensively, of course, in the Fourth Gospel, e.g. the encounters between Jesus and Nicodemus, Jesus and the Samaritan woman, Jesus and Martha, Jesus and Mary, Jesus and the Father (?), Jesus and Pilate, etc. The rhetorical effect there also is to make these characters representative figures. See further, Collins, 'Figures – I' and 'Figures – II', and Culpepper, *Anatomy*, ch. 5.

[106] See Tannehill, *Sword*, 158.

commitment which we may add to the long list of our commitments but is *the* commitment, demanding a reordering of our lives from the bottom up. We are forced to recognize this by the conflict of perspectives within these little dialogues.[107]

The rhetorical structure of Jesus' respective replies heightens this sense of the challenge to the values of the everyday world represented by Jesus' call. The first reply hinges upon an antithesis between the natural order of things – that foxes and birds have places to dwell – and the eschatological order of things – represented by the homelessness of no less than the Son of Man. The second reply hinges upon a devastating pun: ἄφες τοὺς νεκροὺς θάψαι τοὺς ἑαυτῶν νεκρούς. In context, 'the dead' referred to first are those who fail to respond to the breaking in of the kingdom of heaven by following Jesus. But Jesus' words do not constitute an argument: for puns do not work like that. Rather, they are a verbal thunderbolt, focussing upon an extreme and normally deserving case, intended to crack open people's perception of the way things are.[108]

The sociological dimension of these discipleship pericopae in Matthew remains to be examined. First, the overwhelming concentration on the authority of Jesus, seen already in the call stories, and developed in the portrayal by Matthew of Jesus as Messiah in word and deed, is maintained and reinforced.[109] The implication of this focus, at the sociological level, is to justify acceptance of this authority over against alternative claims and claimants. This constitutes the basis for the formation of an alternative society, in which the story of Jesus and the words or commandments of Jesus become accepted as the normative point of reference and, correspondingly, other norms are at best relativized and at worst displaced altogether. If we envisage Matthew and his group or audience developing their

---

[107] *Ibid.*, 159.
[108] See Tannehill, *Sword*, 165: 'The interplay between request and reply, and the forceful way in which Jesus' words are formulated, make us sharply aware of the tension between the customary and reasonable, on the one hand, and what Jesus demands, on the other. We might be able to accept the idea that the demands of the kingdom are total as a general statement, but these little stories allow us no refuge in general statements.'
[109] See Gundry, *Matthew*, 203–4, who points out that the theme of Jesus' authority prominent in the Sermon on the Mount (chs. 5–7) is 'carried out' in chs. 8–9, just as the theme of opposition and persecution in the discourse of ch. 10 is 'carried out' in chs. 11–12.

sense of corporate identity in a post-70 situation within which formative Judaism is taking shape under the authority and leadership of the Pharisaic party,[110] this concentration on the authority of Jesus and his words is quite understandable.[111]

Consistent with this are the implications of Jesus' reply to the disciple who would delay following in order to go first and bury his father, in accordance with the norms of the law and religious custom. For the call to follow Jesus is the new and absolute norm which takes priority even in extreme instances like the obligation to bury the dead. The extremity of the instance is a vivid representation of the absolute exclusiveness of the authority of Jesus. Whereas the Pharisees are engaged in relocating authority from the cult and temple, now destroyed, to the torah (as interpreted by the Pharisees themselves) and household (now sacerdotalized),[112] Matthew is engaged in relocating authority in Jesus, the Jesus tradition (as contained in the gospel) and the brotherhood of the church (where Jesus is present). Here, the demands of law and custom in respect of filial piety and of household relations generally are relativized strongly. The point, of course, is not that Jesus and those who follow him dishonour their parents or refrain from their obligations to the dead. Rather, it is a matter of competing claims to legitimate authority as the basis for reconstituting the people of God: the torah (interpreted by the Pharisees) and household piety (interpreted in sacerdotal terms), or Jesus, the commandments of Jesus, and the Christian brotherhood.

But if this discipleship material contributes to a sociological understanding of authority in Matthew and his audience, it also sharpens our perception of the ethos of Matthean Christianity. For these two episodes elicit the suggestion that Matthean Christianity has a certain afamilial character. Jesus' first reply calls for a more serious consideration of the demanding nature of true discipleship, and does so by appealing to his own state of homelessness. Jesus' second reply shows that following him is not compatible ultimately with a social and religious system which accords first priority to the

---

110 See further, Overman, *Gospel*, esp. ch. 2; and Stanton, 'Judaism'.

111 See Crosby, *House*, 76–98, where the question of authority is addressed explicitly also.

112 See the account of the Pharisees given in Neusner, 'Two Pictures', esp. p. 536: 'The setting for observance was the field and the kitchen, the bed, and the street'; Neusner, *Judaism*, 45–61. Important also is the anthropological approach to the study of the temple and the torah as 'redemptive media' in Second Temple Judaism, by Isenberg in 'Power' and 'Millenarism'.

demands of family ties. As we shall see subsequently, these sayings
are not isolated. A similar afamilial – or, perhaps better, suprafamilial – emphasis comes in the mission discourse, where Jesus says, 'He
who loves father or mother more than me is not worthy of me; and
he who loves son or daughter more than me is not worthy of me'
(10.37). Matt. 19.12, furthermore, has that uniquely Matthean
saying of Jesus about those 'who have made themselves eunuchs for
the sake of the kingdom of heaven'. If that is taken together with the
emphasis this gospel gives to the need for strenuous self-discipline
and singleminded commitment to Jesus for the sake of the Christian
brotherhood and the mission to all nations, it seems legitimate to
infer both a certain distancing from normal household patterns and
lifestyle, and a communal ethos which deprecates family ties. In
terms of our understanding of the self-definition of the Matthean
church, this – at the very least – tolerance of an afamilial ethos is
significant. In relation to insiders, it makes possible the development
of a religious group membership of which is determined no longer
by family ties and the activity of which is not constrained within the
order of the household. So Gentiles can belong now, as well as Jews;
and itinerant patterns of discipleship are free to develop (in imitation of Jesus), alongside more settled patterns.[113] In relation to
outsiders, and to formative (Pharisaic) Judaism in particular, such
an ethos marks off church from synagogue. For where the Pharisees
are seeking to restore Israel on the basis of an intensification of
torah piety in the context of the home and family life, Matthew and
his group are claiming to be the true Israel on the basis of discipleship of Jesus and obedience to that 'greater righteousness' the
demands of which transcend household religion and piety.

4   'Not peace but a sword': mission and family ties (Matt. 10.16–23 par. Mark 13.9–13; Matt. 10.34–6 par. Luke 12.51–3; Matt. 10.37–8 par. Luke 14.26–7)

The sayings relevant to the theme of discipleship and family ties
which come next in the sequence of Matthew's story of Jesus are the

---

[113] My interpretation here runs in the opposite direction to that of Riches,
'Sociology', who argues that Matthew has redacted radical Q tradition preserved in groups of wandering charismatics in such a way that 'patterns of
behaviour which were basically anomic are being bracketed off, allowing for an
increasing normalization of the community' (p. 270). The same position is
taken by Keck, in 'Ethos', 38–44. Rather than 'bracketing off' the radical Q
tradition of Matt. 8.18–22 par. Luke 9.57–60, Matthew has given it signal

ones about persecution which Matthew has drawn from his two main sources and incorporated into an important section which runs from 9.35 to 11.1, the major part of which is Jesus' second extended discourse (10.5b–42), the so-called 'missionary discourse'. Within this discourse, there are three pieces of sayings tradition particularly relevant: 10.21–2, 34–6 and 37–8. Since these occur together in Matthew, in the one discourse, it is most appropriate if we handle them together in the analysis below. As we shall see, the radical implications of discipleship for family ties conveyed already by the call stories (4.18–22) and the sayings on discipleship which preface the storm-stilling (8.18–22) are taken considerably further in the teaching of the Matthean Jesus about mission. The issue is a *leitmotif* which comes to the fore regularly throughout the gospel.

Source- and form-critical analysis may be limited to the following summary. Matthew's account of the naming and sending out of the disciples and of the mission charge is a composite of (mainly) sayings material from a variety of contexts in Mark (3.13–19; 6.6b–11, 34; 13.9–13; cf. 8.34–5; 9.37, 41) and Q (for example Matt. 9.37–8 par. Luke 10.2; Matt. 10.15 par. Luke 10.12; Matt. 10.26–33 par. Luke 12.2–9; Matt. 10.34–6 par. Luke 12.51–3; Matt. 10.37–8 par. Luke 14.26–27), as well as of sayings lacking independent testimony (for example Matt. 10.5–8, 23, 24–5, 41). Thus, while many of the independent logia may go back to Jesus or the early church,[114] the compilation must be attributed to the evangelist. Beare puts it well:

> The charge itself is in Matthew a compilation of sayings, many of which are not appropriate to the context and cannot have originated in such a context . . . Jesus may have supplied some or all of the words in one context or another . . . but it is the gospel writer who has arranged them as seemed good to him, fitting them into a pattern of his own designing, like an artist setting the tesserae into a mosaic.[115]

Redaction criticism attempts to interpret the material from

prominence, not least by using it to exemplify the nature of true discipleship as a preface to his little 'parable' of the church in the End-time, the story of the storm-stilling.

[114] Bultmann, *Tradition*, 145, rather arbitrarily designates the sayings in Matt. 10.5–16 and par. as 'Church Rules' which come from the post-Easter period.

[115] Beare, 'Mission', 2.

Matthew's point of view as that is revealed in both his handling of sources and in his composition and overall organization of the text. Naturally, we shall focus on the family ties sayings; but the broader context has to be kept in mind as well.

The first important observation is that 9.35–11.1 is a unified piece of material which 'interrupts' the flow of the text. The statement in 11.2 which tells of the imprisoned John hearing about τὰ ἔργα τοῦ Χριστοῦ refers back naturally to the miraculous works performed by Jesus in 8.1–9.34. On this view then, 9.35–11.1 is an editorial insertion. The principle behind the insertion is compositional. As is well known,[116] Matthew is a careful organizer of his tradition and follows a regular pattern of blocks of narrative followed by blocks of discourse in rotating sequence, there being five major discourses in all (chs. 5–7, 10, 13, 18, 23–5), each of which ends with a version of the formula, 'And when Jesus had finished these sayings ...' (7.28; 11.1; 13.53; 19.1; 26.1). This compositional technique allows Matthew to present his version of the gospel of Jesus topically, as well as chronologically, an important feature which makes his work look like a manual for disciples of a generation after Jesus and the twelve.[117] The first discourse teaches the values of the kingdom, the second – which is our present concern – teaches about eschatological mission and its consequences, the third and central discourse teaches in parables what the kingdom of heaven is like, the fourth addresses questions to do with the right ordering of life within the brotherhood of members of the kingdom, and the final discourse begins with the woes on the scribes and Pharisees and goes on to a revelation about the coming of the kingdom and of judgment at the end of time. Significant is the fact that these five main discourses appear to be related to each other thematically (and also in terms of length) in chiastic fashion.[118] In broad terms, if the first has to do

---

[116] See Davies and Allison, *Matthew I*, 58–72 for an excellent survey of theories about the structure of Matthew; also, Ellis, *Matthew*, 8–25; Stanton, *Gospels*, 60–2.

[117] See Dobschütz, 'Matthew', esp. pp. 25–6: '[Matthew] aims in this Gospel to provide the Christian community with a kind of church order and catechism of Christian behaviour.' Also, Minear, *Teacher's Gospel*, 12–23, noting the opening comment: 'The author of this Gospel was a *teacher* who designed his work to be of maximum help to *teachers* in Christian congregations' (p. 3, Minear's italics). From a literary-critical perspective, see recently, Lincoln, 'Matthew'.

[118] See Davies and Allison, *Matthew I*, 60 and n. 27; also, Ellis, *Matthew*, 12–13; Stanton, *Gospels*, 61.

with who will enter the kingdom, the fifth has to do with who will be
left out of the kingdom; if the second concerns how to engage in
mission, the fourth concerns how to practise community; and at the
centre are the crucial parables of the kingdom, which not only speak
of a division and a separation but also mark a turning-point in the
ministry of Jesus.[119]

The unity of 9.35–11.1 as a Matthean construction within this
overall framework is clear.[120] First, just as 4.23 (–25) is a redactional
summary statement in narrative form which paves the way for the
first discourse, so 9.35 – which is a verbatim repetition of 4.23 – is a
redactional summary statement which paves the way for the second
major discourse, in 10.5b-42. Second, 9.35 is closely analogous to
11.1b, since both refer to Jesus teaching and preaching in the cities;
so these two editorial statements frame the 'missionary discourse'.
Third, 11.1a is one of Matthew's formulaic endings, which is tailor-
made at the same time to what has come immediately before. The
use of διατάσσω (only here in Matthew) is appropriate to the content
of the discourse – mission instructions. Also, the reference to 'his
twelve disciples' harks back to 10.1a ('And he called to him his
twelve disciples ...'). Fourth, and most obviously, 9.35–11.1 has a
unity of theme: Jesus teaches his disciples about mission, as part of
his own mission.

The section 9.35–11.1 has an internal structure of its own, as
Weaver has shown.[121] This may be represented as follows: i. A
narrative introduction (9.35–10.5a) consisting of various materials
which Matthew uses to describe actions of Jesus which pave the way
for the discourse. ii. The discourse on mission (10.5b-42), itself
consisting of three parts,[122] each of which ends with a formulaic,
'Truly, I say to you' saying (10.15, 23, 42) to do with eschatological
warning or promise. The three parts are: instructions on mission
(10.5b-15); warnings about persecution and how to respond
(10.16–23); and encouragement not to fear, in view of the disciples'
relationship to Jesus (10.24–42). iii. A narrative conclusion (11.1)
which links the discourse directly back into the continuing mission
of Jesus.

---

[119] See Kingsbury, *Parables*, who distinguishes 13.1–35 from 13.36–52, and
demonstrates that 13.1–35 marks a turning-point for the Matthean Jesus: from
the unbelieving Jews to the disciples (who represent the church).

[120] See Luz, *Matthäus II*, 74–5.   [121] Weaver, *Discourse*, esp. ch. 3.

[122] Luz, *Matthäus II*, 76 distinguishes only two main parts in the discourse –
vv. 5b-23 and 24–42 – but also considers the first part to be subdivided between
vv. 5b-15 and 16–23.

It has long been recognized that 9.35–11.1, carefully arranged as it is, has a number of puzzling features which raise the question how to interpret the text. Thus, although Jesus sends out (ἀποστέλλω, 10.5, v. 16) the twelve ἀπόστολοι (10.2), they are not reported as actually going or returning![123] Instead it is Jesus himself who, at the end, goes on 'to teach and to preach in their cities' (11.1b). This contrasts strongly with Matthew's Marcan source, according to which the twelve are sent out two-by-two (6.7), go out preaching, exorcising and healing (6.12–13), and subsequently return to report to Jesus 'all that they had done and taught' (6.30). Mark is followed in this by Luke, who likewise has the apostles depart on mission and return (9.6, 10). Luke's additional story of the sending out of the seventy (-two) also has them return and report to Jesus (10.17). In Matthew's version, however, they do not go out. In fact, the μαθηταί are not mentioned explicitly again until the sabbath controversy story, in 12.1–8 (at v. 1b). Their departure and return are substituted for by the extended – it is much longer than the comparable material in Mark and in either of the Lucan versions – discourse of Jesus and the continuation of his mission. Clearly, it is Jesus' instructions and his mission which are of supreme importance for Matthew.[124] A mission of the disciples in Galilee during the ministry of Jesus has no interest. Their mission must wait.

It is unclear how much of the discourse has to do with mission proper. If some parts are relevant to mission – and this is particularly true of vv. 5b–15, with its roots in Mark and Q mission sayings – other parts are not especially so, and could be just as relevant to discipleship generally. Indeed, Beare claims that the opening verses of the discourse are but 'a prelude to a more general discourse on the responsibilities, the dangers, and the rending conflicts of Christian discipleship in a hostile world'.[125] Similarly, Luz states: 'Manche Worte der Aussendungsrede sprechen die sogenannten Wanderradikalen an, d.h. Jünger unterwegs (10, 5f. 9–14. 23. 40), andere dagegen richten sich ausdrücklich an seßhafte Christen (10, 41f). Die meisten Worte können unterschiedslos von Wanderradikalen und von seßhaften Gemeindegliedern auf sich bezogen werden.'[126] For this reason, and encouraged by the observation that the addressee of the discourse is fundamentally the

---

[123] See Beare, 'Mission', 1–3.
[124] See Gundry, *Matthew*, 190: 'For him, the actuality of the disciples' mission pales before Jesus' instructions.'
[125] Beare, 'Mission', 3.   [126] Luz, *Matthäus II*, 78–9.

μαθητής (9.37; 10.1, 24–5, 42; 11.1), Luz concludes emphatically: '*Wir nennen sie darum Jüngerrede, nicht Aussendungsrede.*'[127]

The discourse appears contradictory and anachronistic at points.[128] First, the twelve are instructed explicitly to go, neither to Gentiles nor to Samaritans, but 'to the lost sheep of the house of Israel' (10.5–6). Apparently, theirs is to be a mission to Israel only, just as Jesus' mission is to Israel only (15.24). In the second part of the discourse, however, as well as issuing the warning about being 'handed over' to (Jewish) councils and being flogged in 'their synagogues', Jesus also says that 'you will be dragged before governors and kings (ἡγεμόνας δὲ καὶ βασιλεῖς) for my sake, to bear testimony before them and the Gentiles (καὶ τοῖς ἔθνεσιν)' (10.18; diff. Mark 13.9). This seems to imply a mission whose scope is much broader than Israel alone: more appropriate, therefore to a post-Easter setting (28.19a, πάντα τὰ ἔθνη).[129] Second, whereas the sending out implies a mission within the context and duration of Jesus' own ministry, the subsequent warnings about persecution envisage an extended duration: 'he who endures to the end (εἰς τέλος)'; and, 'before the Son of man comes (ἕως ἂν ἔλθη ὁ υἱὸς τοῦ ἀνθρώπου)' (10.22b, 23b). Third, the phrase 'in their synagogues (ἐν ταῖς συναγωγαῖς **αὐτῶν**)' (10.17; diff. Mark 13.9; cf. Matt. 4.23; 9.35; 12.9; 13.54; and 23.34, with ὑμῶν) implies an alienation from the synagogue communities hard to reconcile with the time of Jesus but quite feasible a generation later.[130] Fourth, the virulence of the persecution predicted by Jesus comes as a surprise in the context of his own time. Jesus himself experienced such mortal hostility only at the end of his ministry, with the trial(s) and crucifixion. It is much more likely that the persecution of his followers began from that point on than that it took place beforehand (cf. John 16.2).[131] Fifth, the designations προφήτης and δίκαιος in 10.41, together with οἱ μικροί in 10.42, look more like technical terms for church members of different kinds than terms for disciples of the historical Jesus.[132] Finally, much of the teaching, especially from 10.16 on, loses any close connection with the

---

127 *Ibid.*, 79 (Luz's italics). Similarly, Bornkamm, 'End-Expectation', 18.
128 See further, Weaver, *Discourse*, 13–16. Her whole first chapter is relevant.
129 See Stanton, 'Judaism', 275.
130 See Kee, 'Transformation', 15, 20–3; and Overman, *Gospel*, 60–2.
131 See Stanton, 'Judaism', 276–7.
132 See Gundry, *Matthew*, 203: 'Consequently, we have a hierarchical list descending from the apostles (v. 40) through Christian prophets and teachers of righteousness (v. 41) to ordinary church members (v. 42).'

ostensive setting – the sending out of the twelve to Israel – and contains instead sayings in the third person of potentially quite general application: ὁ δὲ ὑπομείνας εἰς τέλος οὗτος σωθήσεται (10.22b); Οὐκ ἔστιν μαθητὴς ὑπὲρ τὸν διδάσκαλον (10.24); Πᾶς οὖν ὅστις ὁμολογήσει ἐν ἐμοὶ (10.32); Ὁ φιλῶν πατέρα ἢ μητέρα ὑπὲρ ἐμέ (10.37), and so on.[133]

The main implication of the preceding is that Matthew has taken an event in the life of Jesus and the twelve – the sending out on a mission to Israel as part of Jesus' own mission – and made it transparent of the life of the church in his own day.[134] As Stanton puts it: 'In Matthew 10 the evangelist sets out his account of the sending out of the disciples by the historical Jesus, but it is clear that at the same time he is portraying Christian disciples in his own day who have been sent out "to make disciples of all nations" (28.19). The evangelist has a "dual perspective".'[135] Just as the other major discourses bring the living and powerful words of the historical Jesus to bear, theme by theme, on the situation and self-understanding of Matthew's church, so also does the discourse on eschatological mission, addressed to the twelve disciples in their role as representatives of the true Israel (19.28). The fact that the disciples do not go out has a dual effect. It gives absolute primacy to Jesus, to what he commands, and to his own example; and it pushes the carrying out of his commands into the future. That future is the time between the resurrection of Jesus and his return in judgment as the Son of Man. It is the time when the disciples will have been taught fully (13.51–2; 26.1a) and will be able, therefore, to 'disciple' the nations by teaching them all the commandments of Jesus (28.19–20). It is the time of Matthew's church and of Christianity of the second generation, when the Lord is now sending out labourers into the End-time harvest (9.37–8).[136]

Understood thus, as teaching of Jesus re-presented for a mission-oriented church, the material on family ties is particularly impor-

---

[133] See Weaver, *Discourse*, 16.

[134] See the views cited in Weaver, *Discourse*, 22–3.

[135] Stanton, 'Judaism', 275. See also Brown, 'Mission', 80: 'In Mt 9.35–11.1 the Evangelist has Jesus address his community in the person of the twelve disciples, and in the point-for-point assimilation of their missionary functions with those of Jesus, who sends them out, the Matthean community must be able to see the delineation of its own missionary task.' Note, however, that Brown argues (rather tenuously) that, on the basis of this central section of Matthew, the responsibility of the Matthean community in mission was to Israel alone. This seems to me irreconcilable with 28.19.

[136] See also, Luz, 'Disciples', 100–1.

tant. The bringing together into this one discourse of scattered sayings from both Mark (13.12–13a) and Q (Luke 12.51–3; 14.26–7), which all speak in various ways of the painful – even disastrous – consequences for family ties of following Jesus, is especially noteworthy. This is the greatest concentration of such material in the whole of Matthew. It is legitimate to infer from this that Matthew envisages Jewish-Christian mission to Jews and Gentiles as being extremely costly in terms of domestic and kinship relations, and that the subject is of particular pertinence to the evangelist and his audience.[137]

Just the opposite view is taken by Meeks, Keck and Riches in several recent studies.[138] They suggest that Matthew has interpreted the tradition in a more socially conservative direction, taking sayings which (in Mark 13) refer to the future mission of the disciples and its effects until the coming of the Son of Man, and setting them within the more restricted confines of the mission of the twelve to Israel during Jesus' lifetime, an event of the past. This shift is explicable in terms of the evangelist's pastoral strategy, aimed at controlling (or even suppressing) rather anti-social itinerant charismatic activity on the part of some who are either church members or who have come in from outside. By analogy with the context in which the early Christian *Haustafeln* were developed,[139] such a reinterpretation of the tradition might have apologetic motives also: to defend Matthew's church against the charge (from the synagogue?) that following Jesus was an outrageous threat to family ties and filial piety. In either case, we may be seeing – so it is argued – the effect of an urban environment and ethos upon Matthew's handling of a tradition which originated in a quite different setting. Referring specifically to Matt. 10, Meeks says:

> Matthew has lifted 10.17–22 from Jesus' apocalyptic prediction of future disturbances in Mark 13.9–13. The changed context has the effect of removing the predicted difficulties from the reader's future, placing them in the community's past experience. Verses 40–42, moreover,

[137] See Gnilka, *Matthäusevangelium I*, 398: 'Dieses Motiv muß ihm wichtig gewesen sein. Ist es erlaubt, die Vermutung zu äusern, daß sich hier eine besondere Erfahrung der mt Christen ausdrückt?'
[138] See Meeks, *Moral World*, 136–43; Keck, 'Ethics'; and Riches, 'Sociology'. The influence of Theissen's understanding of early Christian *Wanderradikalismus* is important here, and is acknowledged explicitly by both Keck and Riches.
[139] See Balch, *Wives*, esp. part II; and Verner, *Household*.

emphasize the reward for those who receive the wanderers, not for the wanderers themselves. Discipleship in Matthew is not identical with imitation of the ascetic life of Jesus or his twelve special missionaries. Thus, for all the church's inevitable retrojection of its own experiences into the time of Jesus, this author does find ways to accord the past an integrity of its own.[140]

However, such an interpretation flies in the face of the evidence set out above, which suggests that, far from bracketing off the instructions of Jesus for mission to Israel and its inevitable consequences in persecution and rejection, Matthew gives them considerable prominence as one of the major discourses, precisely because of their direct relevance to the followers of Jesus in Matthew's own day, when a mission to both Israel and the Gentiles is taking place 'until the Son of man comes'.[141] Indeed, it is in my opinion more accurate to interpret the Matthean redaction and composition as taking the tradition in a more radical direction. Rather than restricting the mission with its radical social consequences to a limited circle and to an event in the time of Jesus, Matthew specifically leaves its fulfilment open – to the time after the resurrection and as the responsibility, not just of the twelve, but of disciples generally (cf. 9.37–8; 10.24–5, 32–3, 42). This is the value of Luz's claim that we are dealing here fundamentally with a discourse on discipleship, relevant to all in Matthew's audience, not just to 'wandering radicals': 'Wanderradikalismus ist eine besondere Möglichkeit christlicher Vollkommenheit (19, 16–30) ... Den Auftrag zur Mission verstand Matthäus als Aufgabe der gesamten Kirche und die Existenz als Wandermissionar als Möglichkeit des Gehorsams für jeden Christen. So gilt die *These: Die Jüngerrede ist der grundlegende ekklesiologische Text des Matthäusevangeliums.*'[142]

---

[140] Meeks, *Moral World*, 141. See Riches, 'Sociology', 270: 'the tension between the norms of the predominantly itinerant stage of the movement and the daily demands of urban life on the more stable communities of Matthew's generation were softened (i) partly by portraying Jesus' more radical commands as being directed specifically to the founder group within the community; (ii) partly by modifying the sense of Matt. 6.25ff so that it now reads as an injunction to subordinate daily cares to the needs of the community ... That is to say, patterns of behaviour which were basically anomic are being bracketed off, allowing for an increasing normalization of the community.'

[141] See Brown, 'Representation'; Stanton, 'Judaism', 274ff.; Gundry, *Matthew*, 194. For Matthew's interest in the return of the Son of Man, cf. 16.27–8; 24.30, 34; 25.31; and 26.64.

[142] Luz, *Matthäus II*, 79, 154 (Luz's italics).

The first of the three sayings on the implications of discipleship for family ties comes at 10.21–2a, in the second main part of the discourse (10.16–23), the main concern of which is to warn about persecution and to give instruction on how to respond.[143] The change in direction is indicated by the striking contrast in the use of the metaphor of the sheep. According to the commissioning in the first part, the disciples are sent 'to the lost sheep of the house of Israel' (10.6). The second part, however, begins by identifying the disciples as the sheep, with those amongst whom they go as the wolves (10.16)! This sets the sombre tone for what follows. It is here that Matthew introduces sayings of Jesus which he has drawn, almost verbatim, from the eschatological discourse of Mark 13 (at vv. 9–13).

Several redactional modifications signal Matthew's own under-standing. i. Matthew has 'Beware of men (Προσέχετε δὲ ἀπὸ τῶν ἀνθρώπων)' (v. 17a; diff. Mark 13.9a). The threats to the disciple on mission, it is implied, may come from any quarter, just as the disciple is to bear witness in any quarter (vv. 32–3). ii. 'You will be beaten in synagogues (εἰς συναγωγὰς δαρήσεσθε)' becomes 'they will flog you in their synagogues (ἐν ταῖς συναγωγαῖς **αὐτῶν μασ-τιγώσουσιν** ὑμᾶς)', the effect of which is to imply official synagogue disciplinary action against Jewish-Christian missionaries (23.34),[144] as well as to align the fate of the disciple with that of his Lord (20.19).[145] iii. Matthew takes the reference to τὰ ἔθνη in Mark 13.10 (which he otherwise omits) and adds it to the saying about being dragged before governors and kings (v. 18), implying that good will come out of evil. Persecution in the synagogues and appearing before foreign rulers is not in vain: rather, it is εἰς μαρτύριον αὐτοῖς **καὶ τοῖς ἔθνεσιν**. Clearly, the seeds of Gentile mission are being sown already in these instructions on mission to Israel. iv. In the teaching on not being anxious about what to say when brought to trial, Matthew identifies the source of the disciple's inspiration as τὸ πνεῦμα **τοῦ πατρὸς ὑμῶν** τὸ λαλοῦν ἐν ὑμῖν (v. 20b; diff. Mark 13.11 – τὸ πνεῦμα τὸ ἅγιον). This reinforces the teaching in the Sermon on the Mount about not being anxious in view of the care of the heavenly Father (cf. 6.31–4). It also prepares for the warning to come about kinship enmity, by reminding the disciple that his true family is that over which God is Father.[146] v. The warning of mortal

---

[143] See Weaver, *Discourse*, 90–1.

[144] See Harvey, 'Forty Strokes', 90–4.

[145] See Gundry, *Matthew*, 192.

[146] *Ibid.*, 193.

enmity from members of the disciple's own family (v. 21) is taken over from Mark unaltered, except for Matthew's use of the adversative δέ in place of Mark's καί. The same is true of the warning of universal hatred (v. 22a), and the promise of eschatological salvation to the one who endures (v. 22b). vi. The saying which ends this section of the discourse (i.e. v. 23) does not come from Mark, however. Rather, it is a Matthean composition which, with its reference to the coming of the Son of Man, summarizes the following part of Mark's eschatological discourse (Mark 13.26), while at the same time adapting it to the theme of persecution and mission.[147] Hence, his use of διώκω, common in the Sermon on the Mount (5.10, 11, 12, 44; also 23.34); the motif of flight from persecution (2.13; 23.33); the predominance of references to πόλεις (10.11, 14, 15; 23.34);[148] and the focus on Israel as the object of mission (23.34). The point of the saying is to conclude the section (vv. 16–23) on a relatively positive note: persecution serves to foster mission as the disciple 'flees' from one city to the next; and in spite of the persecution and kinship enmity, the mission to Israel is to continue 'until the Son of man comes'.

The second and third sayings about discipleship and family ties in the discourse come in its third section (vv. 24–42), at vv. 34–6, and 37–8. Weaver has demonstrated perceptively that, where the focus of the first section is on mission and of the second is on persecution, the focus of this third section is on relationships: 'The theme is announced in 10.24–25, a proverbial saying which defines the relationship of the disciples to Jesus. The section concludes in 10.40–42 with a sequence of verses which (1) establishes a bond linking the disciples to Jesus and to "the one who sent [him]" (10.40) and (2) spells out the implications of that bond for all those who receive the disciples (10.41–42).'[149] The main point of the section is to show that persecution arises out of the disciple's relationship to Jesus and through him to the Father, that this relationship provides grounds for fearless endurance and witness, and will, in the end, bring sure reward.

In between the introductory statement (in vv. 24–5) setting out the relationship between the disciple and Jesus (as διδάσκαλος, κύριος and οἰκοδεσπότης) and the concluding sayings on the reward which will come to those who 'receive' with hospitality missionary dis-

---

[147] Ibid., 194–5.   [148] See Kingsbury, Matthew, 97.
[149] Weaver, Discourse, 104.

ciples of Jesus (vv. 40–2), there are two groups of sayings, each of which begins in a formally similar way, with a negative command (vv. 26, 34).[150] The first group is vv. 26–33, and begins, Μὴ οὖν φοβηθῆτε αὐτούς (v. 26a). The threefold repetition of the command not to fear (vv. 26, 28, 31) makes emphatically clear that this group of sayings is intended to deal with fear arising out of persecution. It does so on the basis of an appeal to the sovereignty of God (v. 28) and to his providential care as 'your Father' (vv. 29–31), reinforced by a solemn promise/warning that acknowledgment (or denial) of Jesus before men will be reciprocated by Jesus before his Father (vv. 32–3). The second group is vv. 34–9, which begins, Μὴ νομίσητε (v. 34a). The thrust of this sequence of sayings is to focus on the personal and domestic consequences of fearless missionary discipleship. It is here that the two Q sayings about family ties are placed, side-by-side.

When we turn specifically to 10.34–6, a comparison with Luke's version of the tradition makes possible several suggestions about Matthean redaction, although the precise identification of Q is difficult.[151] i. The verbal parallel between 10.34a and Luke 12.49a (ἦλθον βαλεῖν ... ἐπὶ τὴν γῆν) suggests that Matthew has retained a shorter form of the tradition, omitting both the 'fire' and 'baptism' sayings (Luke 12.49, 50) and drawing upon the material which was more pertinent to his theme of discipleship and its implications for family ties, and so combining Luke 12.51–3 and Luke 14.26–7.[152] ii. Matthew's opening imperative, Μὴ νομίσητε (v. 34a), is redactional, both on the basis of the formal parallel with v. 26a, mentioned above, and by analogy with 5.17a.[153] It highlights Jesus' role as authoritative teacher. iii. The triple occurrence of ἦλθον + infinitive, in vv. 34a, b, 35a, represents the editorial refining of the tradition into a more formal pattern. The first two occurrences (v. 34a, b) bring the two halves of the saying into antithetical parallelism, precisely in the form which occurs in 5.17. The repeated use of ἦλθον throws the focus upon the theme of Jesus as the

---

150 *Ibid.*, 104–5.
151 Note Marshall's comment on the Lucan parallel (12.49ff.), in *Luke*, 545: 'The matter is complicated by the fact that Luke's use of sources here is also a puzzle, and hence we cannot tell what order there may have been in any source that he was following. Nor is the line of thought within the section obvious.'
152 So too, Manson, *Sayings*, 120; Marshall, *Luke*, 545; Beare, *Records*, 85; Black, 'Violent Word', 115. For an alternative, which posits Luke 12.49–50 as L, see Fitzmyer, *Luke X–XXIV*, 994.
153 See Bultmann, *Tradition*, 155; Gnilka, *Matthäusevangelium I*, 393.

Coming One (cf. 3.11) and the consequences of his coming.[154] In Luke, by contrast, the concern is with the signs of the times (cf. Luke 12.49–56). iv. βαλεῖν comes from the tradition (Luke 12.49a), but it is also a favourite word of Matthew.[155] It is used twice in 10.34 – Luke has the weaker δοῦναι once, in 12.51a – and is rabbinic in style.[156] v. Similarly, ἐπὶ τὴν γῆν is traditional (cf. Luke 12:49a), but also a Matthean favourite (diff. ἐν τῇ γῇ, in Luke 12:51a). The phrase links the saying in v. 34 with v. 29b (Matt. only) and also constitutes an antithesis with the material immediately preceding (vv. 32, 33), where confessing/denying Jesus before men is rewarded by acknowledgment/denial by 'my Father who is in heaven'. vi. Matthew uses (the traditional?) μάχαιρα (diff. διαμερισμός, in Luke 12.51b)[157] to bring the saying into conformity with Ezek. 38.21b: 'every man's sword will be against his brother'. Its effect is to heighten the contrast with εἰρήνη and to emphasize the likelihood of violence provoked by the Coming One. It is likely also that μάχαιρα has overtones of an apocalyptic kind for Matthew. It is a symbol of End-time turmoil and judgment.[158] vii. The nature of the turmoil is elaborated in vv. 35–6 in scriptural terms, with the allusion to the prophetic lament of Mic. 7.1–7, especially v. 6: 'for the son treats the father with contempt, the daughter rises up against her mother, the daughter-in-law against her mother-in-law; and a man's enemies are the men of his own house'. Luke's version is a free paraphrase which

---

[154] See Gundry, *Matthew*, 199.

[155] According to Morgenthaler, *Statistik*, 82, βάλλειν occurs as follows: Matthew 34 times; Mark 18 times; Luke 18 times.

[156] See Gundry, *Matthew*, 199.

[157] See the threefold occurrence of μάχαιρα in 26.52 (Matthew only).

[158] Black, 'Violent Word', 117–18, follows Betz, 'Krieg', esp. 129–30, in interpreting the language of the sword against the background of the Jewish holy war tradition, a tradition kept alive at Qumran, and justified scripturally on the basis of such texts as Exod. 32.27–9 and Deut. 33.6–11. In this context, and on the lips of Jesus, the saying in 10.34 represents a claim by him to be the agent of God's End-time wrath, bringing the sword of judgment against Belial and all his followers in heaven and on earth. Rather than being a political Zealot, the analogies with Qumran show Jesus as an 'apocalyptic Zealot'. It is not surprising, furthermore, to find the Johannine Apocalypse describing the triumphant Christ as having a sharp, two-edged sword (ῥομφαία δίστομος) proceeding out of his mouth (Rev. 1.16; 2.12, 16; 19.15, 21). Against this background in apocalyptic circles of the first century, both Jewish and Christian, it is not unlikely that Matthew, who himself shows an attraction to apocalyptic ideas and images, interprets μάχαιρα in similar terms. However, it is not clear that he understands missionary discipleship in conventional holy-war terms, given the priority of the love commandment in his gospel, and the fact that the mission is to Gentiles as well as to Jews. See further, Betz, 'Sinai-Tradition'.

considerably expands the OT text and introduces deliberate numerical calculation (Luke 12.52–3). Matthew's version conforms more closely to Mic. 7.6 but, as Stendahl points out, it is not possible to ascertain whether the deviations from the LXX imply greater proximity to the MT.[159] viii. To Matthean redaction we can attribute the ἦλθον opening (of v. 35a); the infinitive διχάσαι (cf. διαμερισθήσονται in Luke 12.53a), which is appropriate to Matthew's use of 'sword';[160] and the strange substitution of ἄνθρωπος for υἱός, to form an *inclusio* with the ἄνθρωπος of v. 36.[161] In addition, it is worth noting that Matthew's κατά + genitive (contrast ἐπί in Luke) follows from his use of διχάσαι, and has the effect of sharpening the note of conflict. Matthew alone concludes (v. 36) with the final statement from Mic. 7.6 καὶ ἐχθροὶ τοῦ ἀνθρώπου **οἱ οἰκιακοὶ αὐτοῦ** (LXX: ἐχθροὶ ἀνδρὸς πάντες οἱ ἄνδρες οἱ ἐν τῷ οἴκῳ αὐτοῦ). The use of the relational term οἱ οἰκιακοί is significant,[162] for it recalls the saying in the thoroughly redactional v. 25b (diff. Luke 6.40), 'If they have called the master of the house (τὸν οἰκοδεσπότην) Beelzebul, how much more will they malign those of his household (**τοὺς οἰκιακοὺς αὐτοῦ**).' The redactional aim implicit here is to reinforce the idea that discipleship involves membership of the household of Jesus and is likely to bring division between the disciple and the members of his natural kin-group household.

As already noted, Matthew follows 10.34–6 with additional Q material on the same theme (10.37–8 par. Luke 14.26–7). There is a logic to the juxtaposition. Where vv. 34–6 speak of what Jesus has come to do and its implications for a person's household ties, vv. 37–8 draw out the corollary for household allegiance and ethics from the disciple's point of view. The disciple is not to love his kinsfolk – which is the same as not loving his own life (v. 39) – 'above' (ὑπέρ) Jesus.[163] These two aspects are related by compositional means, as well: for the three κατά-clauses in v. 35 parallel the three

---

159 Stendahl, *School*, 90.
160 According to Stendahl, *ibid.*, 90, n. 3, διχάζειν is a *hapax legomenon*, both in Matthew and in the NT as a whole.
161 So, Gundry, *Matthew*, 199. On the use of ἄνθρωπος, note the interesting comment of Gnilka, *Matthäusevangelium I*, 395: 'Am Anfang steht es für "Sohn". Sollte damit eine bestimmte Perspektive angedeutet sein? Daß sich die Bekenner zum Christentum vornehmlich in der jüngeren Generation finden und sie ihre Hausgenossen als Feinde erfahren?'
162 The term οἰκιακός occurs only at Matt. 10.25, 36 in the NT as a whole.
163 For interesting history-of-religions parallels in the Stoicism of Epictetus, see *Dissertations* III.3.5; and in Judaism, see Josephus, *Ant.* XI.145–7; *Bell.* 2.134 – cited in Luz, *Matthäus II*, 140, n. 46.

statements in vv. 37–8 which end, οὐκ ἔστιν μου ἄξιος (diff. Luke).[164]

The differences between the Matthean and Lucan versions are extensive. The following observations relate specifically to evidence of Matthean redaction of the underlying Q tradition. i. As with 10.34–6 par., Matthew's version is shorter and more carefully arranged. We have just noted the threefold pattern of vv. 37–8, with the repeated concern about what disqualifies a person from being 'worthy' of Jesus. The identification of who is ἄξιος is an important concern of Jesus' instruction in this very discourse (vv. 10, 11, 13 bis). The disciple on mission is 'worthy' of material sustenance, and must try to find 'worthy' (i.e. Christian) households[165] in the towns or villages he visits who will provide that sustenance. In return, he gives – significantly, in view of v. 34! – εἰρήνη (v. 13). The point being made in vv. 37–8 is that what qualifies the disciple as 'worthy' is loving Jesus more than his own natural family. ii. Whereas Luke's version speaks of 'hating' one's kinsfolk (Luke 14.26), Matthew has the apparently weaker form of not 'loving [kinsfolk] more than [me]' (v. 37). This change from μισεῖν-terminology to φιλεῖν-terminology is probably Matthean redaction. It conforms well with the evangelist's overall concern to distinguish inadequate from adequate forms of love, where φιλεῖν is used of the former (cf. 6.5; 23.6; 26.48) and ἀγαπᾶν of the latter (cf. 5.43, 44, 46; 19.19; 22.37, 39).[166] The avoidance of μισεῖν – which is probably a literal translation of the underlying Aramaic[167] – conforms also with the evangelist's pejorative use of the term elsewhere (cf. 5.43f.; 6.24; 10.22; 24.9, 10). But the sense of the Matthean form ought not to be distinguished sharply from that of the tradition. Citing Gen. 29.31ff. and Deut.

---

[164] So, Gundry, *Matthew*, 200. See also Goulder, *Midrash*, 351: 'The climax – he who loves parents more than me, he who loves children more than me, he who does not take his cross after me – bridges beautifully from the Mic. text to Mark 8.34f.'

[165] See Gundry, *Matthew*, 188, who points out that the evangelist makes explicit what is not so in Mark and Luke: that the disciple is to seek out the house of a fellow-believer (v. 11; diff. Mark 6.10) and stay there. He says, interestingly: 'Nevertheless, the explicitness of Matthew agrees with his emphasis on Christian brotherhood. Thus, instead of staying wherever they can find hospitality, the disciples are to stay where the proclamation of the kingdom has already found a favorable reception. In Matthew we are reading about itinerant ministry in evangelized communities rather than about itinerant ministry in unevangelized communities.'

[166] Note that the noun ἀγάπη occurs only once, in 24.12 (Matthew only), and there the concern is about 'love' growing cold in the Last Days.

[167] So, Manson, *Sayings*, 131.

21.15ff., T. W. Manson says: 'In the Old Testament ... "love" and "hate" stand side by side in contexts where it is obvious that "hate" is not to be taken in the literal sense, but in the sense "love less".'[168] It is precisely this connotation which Matthew captures in his version. It is not that the disciple's kinsfolk are to be set outside the bounds of his love, but rather that devotion to Jesus is given absolute priority. Such an expression of religious devotion is rooted deeply in the biblical tradition – at Deut. 33.8–9, for example.[169] iii. Matthew's version refers to the close kin in two pairs, representing the older and younger generations, respectively: πατέρα ἢ μητέρα ... υἱὸν ἢ θυγατέρα (v. 37a, b). Luke's longer catalogue of seven nouns in the accusative linked by καί may be a combination of Q and Mark 10.29 at this point (Luke 14.26). This would explain the occurrence of 'children', 'brothers' and 'sisters': the reference to the 'wife' would then be Lucan redaction by analogy with 18.29b (diff. Mark).[170] Matthew's ὑπὲρ ἐμέ is reminiscent of 10.24 (Matthew only) and is likely to be redactional: a natural consequence of the comparative ἤ-form, but which highlights the radical implications of devotion to *Jesus*[171] for kinship ties. iv. 10.38 par. Luke 14.27 is an originally independent logion (Mark 8.34) which has been joined to the preceding material already in Q. As noted earlier, Matthew has brought it into conformity with the two parts of the family ties saying, via οὐκ ἔστιν μου ἄξιος (10.38b). He has made it also into a discipleship saying specifically, by using ἀκολουθεῖν (diff. Luke). This is of a piece with the recurrent linking of the theme of discipleship and its implications for family ties which we have found also in 4.18–22 and 8.18–22 (cf. 19.27–9). For Matthew, loving Jesus more than father, mother, son or daughter is of a piece with a willingness to endure persecution to the point of martyrdom for Jesus' sake (vv. 38–9).

The focus on the overwhelming pre-eminence of Jesus and the disciple's relationship with Jesus, even to the point of subordinating family ties and losing one's life for Jesus' sake, comes to a climax on

---

[168] *Ibid.*, 131.

[169] The use of this biblical tradition as part of the ideology of holy war at Qumran is noteworthy. See n. 158 above; also Gnilka, *Matthäusevangelium I*, 395–6, who observes an important difference from Qumran: 'Sie bedeutet also nicht eine Trennung von der Familie in einem grundsätzlichen Sinn, wie das für die Essener-Mönche von Qumran verlangt war (vgl. 1QS 6,2ff. 19ff; Josephus, bell. 2,120ff), denen aber auch der Konfliktfall bekannt ist (1QH 4, 9; 4QTest 16ff).'

[170] See Jeremias, *Theology I*, 224, n. 2.

[171] Note the recurrence of the personal pronoun (first person) in 10.37–8.

a positive note, in vv. 40–2. Where the first section ended on a
negative note, with teaching about the judgment which will fall on
those who do not 'receive' (δέχομαι) with hospitality the Christian
preacher (vv. 14–15), the third section ends by focussing on the
eschatological 'reward' (μισθός) which will come to those who do
'receive' (δέχομαι) such a person.[172] The principle of relationship is
stated first (cf. vv. 24–5), since this establishes the moral and conceptual basis upon which hospitality is to be extended: 'He who receives
you receives me, and he who receives me receives him who sent me'
(v. 40 par. Mark 9.37b). Then follows another saying carefully
structured in two parallel parts, unique to Matthew (although not
necessarily redactional[173]), in which reciprocal reward is promised
to those who 'receive' a προφήτης and to those who 'receive' a
δίκαιος (v. 41a, b).[174] Surprisingly, however, the final – and
authoritative[175] – word of Jesus, both in the sequence and in the
whole discourse, is on behalf of 'one of these little ones (τῶν μικρῶν
τούτων) ... because he is a disciple (εἰς ὄνομα μαθητοῦ)' (v. 42;
diff. Mark 9.41 – ἐν ὀνόματι ὅτι Χριστοῦ ἐστε). Even a cup of
cold(!) water given to one such[176] will bring reward to the giver.

This conclusion to the discourse is important. To the missionary
disciple faced with mortal hostility from his own kin (vv. 21–2a) and
called to subordinate family ties in order to follow the One who
severs one family member from another (vv. 34–6, 37–8), these are

---

[172] Gundry, *Matthew*, 201–2, suggests that the 'receiving' referred to in v. 40 has to
do with 'harboring those who are fleeing persecution (v. 23)'. I think that this is
too narrow an interpretation. The connotations of hospitality generally are
much stronger: cf. vv. 8b–14, and the reference to the cup of water, in v. 42a;
also, 25.35ff., 42ff.

[173] See Luz, *Matthäus II*, 149: 'Mt hat hier ein judenchristliches Logion aufge-
nommen.'

[174] Matthew can use these terms as a pair to refer to OT figures, as at 13.17 and
23.29. In 10.41, however, their application is to Christians (who, no doubt, are
understood as fulfilling the roles of the OT figures). This is confirmed by the
saying of Jesus in 23.34, where προφῆται are sent by Jesus himself and are,
therefore, itinerant proclaimers of the kingdom of heaven. The identity of the
δίκαιοι is more difficult to clarify, especially since 'righteousness' is demanded
of all disciples in Matthew (5.20), and 'the righteous' can refer likewise to all
disciples (e.g. 13.43, 49; 25.37, 46). Gundry, *Matthew*, 202, makes the plausible
suggestion that, in the context of instruction about mission, the δίκαιοι of
10.41 are (Christian) teachers of 'righteousness' (28.19). See further, Schweizer,
'Church', 130–3, 137–8; Weaver, *Discourse*, 120–1.

[175] Note the ἀμὴν λέγω ὑμῖν form of the saying; cf. 10.15, 23.

[176] For the identity of the 'little ones' as ordinary members of the Christian
brotherhood, see 18.6, 10, 14; and the discussion in Gundry, *Matthew*, 202–3;
Schweizer, 'Church', 138–9; Luz, *Matthäus II*, 152–3.

words intended to give encouragement by fostering solidarity: the solidarity of hospitality within the Christian brotherhood exercised, not only towards people of status like προφῆται and δίκαιοι, but also and especially towards ordinary members with no special status – the μαθηταί. The characteristic Matthean ethic of humility comes to the fore here (5.5; 19.30; 21.5), since it is this ethic, given practical expression in works of love towards ordinary members of the fellowship, which makes a more profound solidarity possible (cf. 18.1–5; 23.8–12).[177]

From a redaction-critical point of view, we have seen how carefully Matthew the evangelist has edited and organized his sources in order to re-present the story of Jesus' mission to Israel and his sending out of the twelve on mission in a way that is transparent for his own mission-oriented church a generation or so later. Above all, we have noted the prominence given to the theme of discipleship and family ties in Jesus' teaching, in a way which suggests that the consequences for members' households of the Jewish-Christian mission of Matthew's church are a pressing concern. Now, we proceed from an analysis of the evangelist as editor to an analysis of the evangelist as author, and from the text as an accretion of sources to the text as literature.

The narrative sequence and setting are especially important from a literary-critical perspective.[178] As already noted, the discourse in 10.5b–42 is framed firmly within a narrative context of the Galilean mission of Jesus to Israel (9.35a; 11.1b). Leading up to the discourse, Jesus 'sees' the crowds with prophetic insight, has feelings of compassion towards them, bereft as they are of a messiah to lead them (9.36), speaks to the disciples of the scarcity of labourers to help in the eschatological harvest of God's people (9.37), instructs them to beseech 'the lord of the harvest' to send out labourers (9.38), calls to himself the twelve and authorizes them to perform exorcisms and healings (10.1), and sends them out (10.5a). The fact that they do not go out, either immediately or at any point subsequently in narrative time, creates a disjunction in the narrative, the effect of which is to pose sharp questions to the implied reader: Why do the disciples not go out immediately? When will they go out? Why is the reader confronted instead with a lengthy discourse,

---

[177] See Gerhardsson, *Ethos*, 33–62.
[178] A point made especially by Weaver, *Discourse*, 22–3 and *passim*.

parts of which appear either anachronistic or only indirectly relevant? And why is it that Jesus alone goes on from there 'to teach and
preach in their cities' (11.1b)?

The answers to these questions lie at the heart of Matthew's
achievement as a communicator. First, the disciples do not go out
because they are not ready to go out. Their preparation is as yet
partial only. They have not been instructed fully, either by Jesus'
ministry of word (cf. 26.1 – **πάντας** τοὺς λόγους τούτους; 28.20a
– **πάντα** ὅσα ἐνετειλάμην ὑμῖν), or by the example of his life, and
especially his passion and resurrection – events still to come in the
narrative sequence.[179] Second, as to when the disciples will go out,
the non-occurrence of the mission of the twelve during the lifetime
of Jesus together with the commissioning of the eleven after the
resurrection at the end of the narrative (28.16–20) implies that the
mission will take place – if at all – outside narrative time: that is to
say, in the time between the resurrection of Jesus and his coming as
the Son of Man at the end of the age (cf. 10.22b, 23b; 28.20b).
Significantly, this is the time of the implied reader. It is also the time
when Jesus is himself indubitably 'the Lord of the harvest' who
sends out the labourers. As such, the sending out of the eleven on
mission after the resurrection, anticipated as it is in the sending out
of the twelve in Jesus' pre-resurrection ministry, is an invitation to
the implied reader to complete what the narrative leaves incomplete,
by engaging in mission as Jesus has commanded.[180] Third, the
functions of the lengthy discourse, when seen in this light, are
several. It focusses attention where attention is needed: not on the
actions of the disciples, but on the authoritative instruction of Jesus.
It also points beyond itself: to a time when mission will involve
testimony before Gentiles as well as Jews; to a time of acute persecution for which only the passion of Jesus at the hands of fellow-Jews
and Gentiles will prepare his followers; and to a time of itinerant
mission independent of Jesus' physical presence, when the provision
of hospitality by fellow-believers will be an imperative. Finally, only
Jesus himself engages in mission immediately following the discourse because he is himself the model disciple, the one who does

---

[179] So too, *ibid.*, ch. 4.
[180] So too, *ibid.*, 152: 'Since the mission of "the eleven disciples" extends from the
resurrection of Jesus to the end of human history, and since the temporal
location of the implied reader likewise lies between these two points, it is now
clear that the boundaries between the story world of the text and the real world
of the implied reader have disappeared ... [T]he implied reader him/herself is
drawn by this route into the ongoing mission of "the eleven disciples".'

what he himself teaches, and who therefore becomes the model for his followers to imitate.[181] Thus, having authorized the disciples to 'heal the sick, raise the dead, cleanse lepers, cast out demons' (10.8; cf. 10.1), it is Jesus himself who can testify to John's disciples that it is through him (Jesus) that 'the blind receive their sight and the lame walk, lepers are cleansed and the deaf hear, and the dead are raised up' (11.5). Above all, having warned the disciples that they will be 'handed over' to sanhedrins, flogged, brought before governors and kings to bear testimony, and put to death (10.17ff.), it is Jesus himself to whom this happens, in the narrative of the passion (26.47ff.). The principle conveyed in the narrative is the principle enunciated by Jesus in the discourse: 'A disciple is not above his teacher, nor a servant above his master; it is enough for the disciple to be like his teacher, and the servant like his master' (10.24–5a).

To turn next to characterization, much is implicit in what has been said already. As in the passages discussed previously, Jesus is the central character and the focus is on his authority. He is the one who teaches in synagogues, preaches and heals, who calls the twelve, gives them authority and sends them out on mission, and who himself continues the mission. Above all, he is the one who gives instruction in missionary discipleship, at the climax of which claim is made to a quality of allegiance from his followers which surpasses even their allegiance to their own close kin and calls even for a willingness to accept death for his sake (10.34–9).

The disciples, by contrast, are cast in a role of privileged dependence. The initiative lies, not with them, but with Jesus. They do not even go out on mission; so they cannot report back on what they have done. Instead, they remain with Jesus, pray as he instructs them to do, respond to his call, receive authority from him, and listen without interruption or question to the teaching he gives. In a word, they are learners (μαθηταί) in the presence of their teacher (διδάσκαλος) who is none other than the divine Son of the heavenly Father (10.32–3). When they themselves have been instructed fully, they in turn will be able to 'disciple' (μαθητεύειν) others, teaching what Jesus has taught them (28.19–20). That particular attention is paid to the twelve (10.1, 2, 5; 11.1) arises out of the fact that they represent Israel (19.28), and it is appropriate, therefore, that they be sent on mission to Israel. The fundamental category, however, is

---

[181] As Weaver, *ibid.*, 126, puts it: 'The example of Jesus' own life provides the necessary basis for interpreting the commission given to the disciples.' See further, pp. 146–7.

'disciple' (μαθητής) (9.37; 10.1, 24, 25, 42; 11.1), for this expresses most clearly the identity and character of the follower of Jesus as one who is instructed in the way of Jesus (13.52; 27.57; 28.19f.).[182]

The crowds, treated *en masse*, are a significant character also: for it is when Jesus sees the crowds that his compassion is aroused and the sending of the disciples on mission is initiated (9.36). Their position is a needy one, characterized by the doubly emphatic 'harassed and helpless' (Ezek. 34.5) and 'like sheep without a shepherd' (cf. Num. 27.17; 1 Kgs. 22.17; 2 Chr. 18.6). For the narrator, it is likely that they symbolize the people who are to be discipled from all nations.[183]

Our previous text (8.18–22) contained sayings of Jesus clearly designed to shock: 'Let the dead bury their own dead.' The family-ties sayings of Jesus' instructions in Matt. 10 likewise merit examination from the point of view of rhetoric.[184] The use of repetition is widespread and emphatic. In vv. 34–6, there is the threefold series of ἦλθον-sayings which pose, in a quite provocative and hyperbolic fashion, the claim that the purpose – not just the consequence – of Jesus' coming is to split families asunder.[185] There is also the threefold series of opposed (cf. κατά) kinship pairs which serve as focal instances of the schism within families which allegiance to Jesus brings: 'a man against his father, and a daughter against her mother, and a daughter-in-law against her mother-in-law' (v. 35). This is followed, in vv. 37–8, by another series of three statements which end, οὐκ ἔστιν μου ἄξιος, the first two of which teach a love for Jesus which takes precedence over love for members of the natural family.

Together with repetition, there is antithesis reinforced by striking metaphor: 'Do not think that I have come to bring peace on earth; I have not come to bring peace, but a sword' (v. 34). The denial (twice!) that Jesus has come to bring peace is startling enough (cf. 5.9; 10.13; also, Luke 1.79; 2.14; 19.38; Acts 10.36): even more startling

---

[182] See Luz, 'Disciples', esp. 99–105, 108–9, noting the comment at pp. 104–5: 'In the first Gospel, the disciples are basically designated as hearers of Jesus' message ... [D]iscipleship is always related to the teaching of the historical Jesus.' See also Orton, *Scribe*, 151 (on μαθητευθείς in 13.52).

[183] So, Gundry, *Matthew*, 180.   [184] See further, Tannehill, *Sword*, 140–4.

[185] Tannehill's comment (*ibid.*, 143) is apt: 'Obviously this is not a general summary of Jesus' mission; it is not meant to be. But the choice of this manner of speech is significant. The text contradicts our desire to think of such family divisions as temporary or accidental ... It claims that such divisions are inherent in Jesus' mission.'

is the use of the concrete metaphor 'sword', in place of 'war', a metaphor itself drawn from the biblical tradition (cf. Isa. 3.25; 22.2; 51.19; 65.12; Jer. 5.12; 14.12–13, 15–16, 18) and extended by the use of the infinitive διχάσαι, in v. 35a. As it occurs here in Matthew, the metaphor has eschatological rather than political/military connotations.[186] The End-time divisions and familial strife traditionally associated with the time before the coming of the Messiah[187] are linked here with the coming of Jesus. There can be little doubt that they have direct associations also with the experience of Matthew's implied readers.

We conclude our discussion of the family-ties material in the 'missionary discourse' by drawing out some inferences for the sociological interpretation of Matthew's Gospel. First, in so far as 9.35–11.1 points forward to, and is transparent of, the situation of Matthew's audience, it is reasonable to infer that the church of Matthew is engaged in a mission to all nations, Jews as well as Gentiles, in what are regarded as the days before the End and the coming of the Son of Man. The stories of the call of the disciples to become 'fishers of men' and of the sending out of the twelve on mission to Israel and thence to the Gentiles are now finding their explicit fulfilment and implementation in the post-Easter period in the life of Matthew's mission-oriented group of followers of Jesus. The social corollaries of mission in relation to members' family ties are twofold. On the one hand, as we saw in 4.18–22 and 8.18–22, mission requires the radical subordination of family ties and obligations for the sake of the kingdom of heaven. This gives Matthew's group a certain afamilial or suprafamilial ethos, as we have seen. In view of the coming of the kingdom and of the Messiah, family ties do not matter in the way they once did. What matters more is following Jesus as a disciple and belonging to the brotherhood of the church. On the other hand, participation in mission involving the subordination of family ties generates persecution – precisely from those who have been displaced. This is the focus of concern in the discourse in chapter 10, especially from v. 16 on. It is summed up in v. 36 (Matt. only), taken from Mic. 7.6: καὶ ἐχθροὶ τοῦ ἀνθρώπου οἱ οἰκιακοὶ αὐτοῦ. Belonging to the household of Jesus

---

[186] So, Luz, *Matthäus II*, 136–9.
[187] Luz, *ibid.*, 138, n. 41, cites Jubilees 23.16, 19f.; 1 Enoch 100.2; 4 Ezra 6.24; Sota 9.15; bSanh 97a.

(v. 25b) brings separation and fierce hostility from the household of one's natural kin.

Second, the focus on the authority of Jesus and his words, with Jesus himself as the model for missionary discipleship, and mission in the post-Easter period firmly rooted in the pre-Easter mission of Jesus, provides the basis for the reinforcement of an alternative identity and an alternative focus of loyalty. The mission is not only authorized by Jesus, but also in a very specific sense the continuation of the same mission. This legitimates the subordination of family ties, for Jesus is the Son of the heavenly Father come to inaugurate the kingdom of heaven. It provides also a powerful theodicy in a context of kinship-sponsored persecution: for does not the tradition of the sayings of Jesus about mission contain the words, 'I have not come to bring peace, but a sword'? It is here that Matthew's Gospel comes closest, perhaps, to adopting an anti-familial stance. Certainly, the line between a suprafamilial and an anti-familial stance may be a fine one and, in practical circumstances, easily open to confusion. The words of Jesus in vv. 34–6, indebted as they are to the Jewish holy-war tradition and to the prophetic lament of Mic. 7.6, are provocative, intended to confront the reader in the most forceful way with the potentially catastrophic impact of the coming of Jesus upon family ties. But in context, any suggestion that the Jesus of Matthew is opposed to the household and to family ties *per se* is undermined by two observations: first, that the deep ambivalence towards kinsfolk springs from dire experiences of kinship-sponsored persecution (vv. 21–3); second, that the issue is one of ultimate allegiance, not of social policy – hence, 'He who loves father or mother *more than me* is not worthy of me' (v. 37).

An important parallel to this apparent hostility to the family is Matthew's well-known hostility towards the Jews and especially towards the Pharisees (cf. 3.7; 5.20; 6.1–18; 8.11–12; 21.43ff.; 22.1–10; 23.13–39; 27.25). Such hostility is understandable if we envisage an historical context for Matthew in which the brotherhood of followers of Jesus for which the gospel is written has its roots in Judaism and the communities of the synagogue, and is undergoing the traumatic process of a parting of the ways, while at the same time continuing to engage in a mission to Israel.[188] Given

---

[188] See further, Stanton, 'Judaism', and the studies cited there; most recently also, Kee 'Transformation', esp. 20–4; and Overman, *Gospel*, esp. ch.3.

the familial basis of religious belonging and identity in Judaism, the specifically household-based piety of the Pharisees,[189] and the common practice of locating synagogue meetings in private homes,[190] it is inevitable that the parting of the ways between the Jewish συναγωγή and the (predominantly) Jewish-Christian ἐκκλησία places tremendous strains upon family ties in cases where transfer from the one to the other does not take place along family lines but instead divides one family member from another. The attempt to maintain synagogue discipline in the face of such a transfer[191] and the virulence of the intrafamilial strife it generates are reflected explicitly in 10.17–23, 34–9. Thus, it is no coincidence that in G. N. Stanton's account of this process of separation, a kinship metaphor seems so appropriate: 'The evangelist is, as it were, coming to terms with the trauma of separation from Judaism and with the continuing threat of hostility and persecution. Matthew's anti-Jewish polemic should be seen as part of the self-definition of the Christian minority *which is acutely aware of the rejection and hostility of its "mother", Judaism.*'[192] The evidence of the Gospel in general, and of the 'mission discourse' of chapter 10 in particular, suggests that the parting of the ways at the broader socio-religious level of the synagogue is being played out time and again in the microcosm of the household. Only such an explanation as this helps to explain Matthew's recurring interest in discipleship and family ties and his considerable ambivalence – even pessimism – about them.

5   Jesus, his family and his hometown (Matt. 12.46–50 par. Mark 3.31–5; Matt. 13.53–8 par. Mark 6.1–6a)

The next pericopae directly relevant to our theme are two more episodes taken over from Mark, the one to do with Jesus' true

---

[189] See Neusner, *Politics*, 82–90; Neusner, *Formative Judaism*, 77–83.

[190] See further, Kee, 'Transformation', *passim*, noting the comment at p. 9: 'Thus there is simply no evidence to speak of synagogues in Palestine as architecturally distinguishable edifices prior to 200 CE. Evidence of meeting places: "Yes", both *in private homes* and in public buildings. Evidence of distinctive architectural features of a place of worship or for study of Torah: "No"' (my italics).

[191] On which, see Harvey, 'Forty Strokes'.

[192] Stanton, 'Judaism', 274 (my italics). See also Overman, *Gospel*, 142, speaking about Matthew 23: 'It is perhaps here, more than anywhere else in his Gospel, that Matthew exposes the sectarian nature and stance of his community over against the dominant *parent group* in his setting, the Jewish leadership referred to as the scribes and the Pharisees' (Overman's italics).

family, the other to do with Jesus' rejection in his *patris*. The importance which Matthew (like Mark) attaches to Jesus both as teacher of his disciples and example for his disciples explains why Matthew has retained these two apophthegmata. But his re-presentation of Jesus' relations with his own family is significantly different from Mark's, as we shall see. The pertinent form-critical observations have been made already, in the analysis of Mark, so in each case, we begin with redactional analysis, paying particular attention to Matthew's modifications of his Marcan source.

Jesus' true family (Matt. 12.46–50 par. Mark 3.31–5)

From a redaction-critical perspective, the following editorial modifications are important. Most striking is Matthew's omission of the ambiguous and disturbing material in Mark 3.20–1, where Jesus' relatives (most likely) set out to seize Jesus, believing him to be mad. Correspondingly, Matthew begins, not with Jesus' mother and brothers 'coming' (as in Mark 3.31), but with the more static picture of them 'standing outside' (12.46, 47). The effects of these changes are twofold. First, they remove the damaging information that Jesus' own people thought him mad, and so remove the element of conflict in Jesus' relations with his kinsfolk. Second, they destroy the 'sandwich' structure of Mark's narrative which brought into damning juxtaposition the belief of the family that Jesus was mad and the claim of the scribes from Jerusalem that he was possessed (Mark 3.20–1, 22–30, 31–5).[193]

The distance between Jesus and his own kin is reduced further by modifications of Mark 3.31–2. First, the crowd is not seated stereotypically περὶ αὐτόν (as in Mark 3.32, 34; cf. 4.10), and Jesus' kin are not distinguished from the crowd as sharply as in Mark. The stylized contrast between the inner circle of the crowd (seated) and the family of Jesus outside (standing) all but disappears.[194] In Matthew, the crowds (plural) are more a part of the setting: Ἔτι αὐτοῦ λαλοῦντος τοῖς ὄχλοις (12.46a). Second, Jesus' kin do not summon him, as in Mark 3.31b. Much more deferentially, they 'seek to speak to him' (12.46b, 47b).[195]

---

[193] So too, Brown, *Mary*, 98–9.
[194] Note also that, in 12.48a, Jesus does not address the crowd over against his kinsfolk. Instead, he speaks to an anonymous individual.
[195] The status of 12.47 is uncertain textually. It is missing from codices ℵ and B and from the older Syriac versions. So v. 47 could be a later gloss assimilating

Whereas Mark has Jesus identify as members of his new family the crowd sitting around him (Mark 3.34a), Matthew has Jesus 'stretching out his hand *toward his disciples*' (... ἐπὶ τοὺς μαθητὰς αὐτοῦ – 12.49a). This is most significant.[196] Jesus' true family are the disciples, those who follow him wherever he goes (4.18–22; 8.18–22). The point of this alternative identification is clear: it reinforces the ecclesiological imagery of brotherhood introduced in the call stories (4.18–22; 10.2). The μαθηταί, who in Matthew's depiction are paradigmatic of the members of his own group, are to see themselves as a brotherhood, members of the true Israel, and belonging to the family of Jesus the divine Son.[197]

Characteristically, Matthew replaces θέλημα τοῦ θεοῦ (Mark 3.35) with θέλημα τοῦ πατρός μου τοῦ ἐν οὐρανοῖς (12.50). The strong emphasis on the fatherhood of God in the First Gospel, with its christological corollary of Jesus as the divine Son of God, provides a profound theological basis for an ecclesiology centred on the idea of brotherhood and of the church as the true, spiritual kindred of Jesus.[198] For Matthew, as for Mark, membership of this family is not by natural ties, but by doing the will of the heavenly Father, with Jesus the Son as the authoritative revealer and teacher of the Father's will. Thus, the disciple has been taught by Jesus to pray, Πάτερ ἡμῶν ὁ ἐν τοῖς οὐρανοῖς ... γενηθήτω τὸ θέλημά σου, ὡς ἐν οὐρανῷ καὶ ἐπὶ γῆς (6.9–10). Jesus also teaches them, in a later discourse, to 'call no man your father on earth (ἐπὶ τῆς γῆς), for you have one Father, who is in heaven (εἷς ... ὁ πατὴρ ὁ

---

to the parallels in Mark and Luke, and smoothing the way for the reference, in v. 48, to 'the man who told him'. See Beare, *Matthew*, 284; Hill, *Matthew*, 222; Gnilka, *Matthäusevangelium I*, 470, n. 1. However, Metzger, *Commentary*, 32, regards its omission from some MSS as accidental, the result of *homoeoteleuton* (λαλῆσαι ... λαλῆσαι). Metzger's view is followed by Gundry, *Matthew*, 249, and Luz, *Matthäus II*, 286.

[196] Note also that the gesture of Jesus reinforces the focus of the saying on the disciples. For another instance, also unique to Matthew, where Jesus stretches out his hand to a disciple (Peter!), see 14.31. I do not find convincing Gundry's view (*Matthew*, 249) that Matthew equates the crowds with the disciples. For Matthew overall, the disciples come from the crowds (8.18–22), but they are hardly identical with the crowds. For the distinct presence of the disciples, see earlier 11.1 and 12.1, 2.

[197] See Gnilka, *Matthäusevangelium I*, 471: 'Weil die Rede sich auf die Jünger bezieht, ist ihre Gemeinschaft, ist letzliche Gemeinde als Familie konzipiert.'

[198] See further, Kingsbury, *Matthew*, 41, 79, 101; also, Sparks, 'Fatherhood', 251–5. Bauer, *Structure*, 62, draws attention both to 12.50 and to 17.24–7 as the two places where Matthew interprets the language of sonship in terms of the relation between Jesus and his disciples, based on the prior relationship of Jesus as Son of the heavenly Father.

οὐράνιος)' (23.9). So the modification of Mark we find in Matt. 12.50 expresses a theological/ecclesiological tendency widespread in this gospel (cf. 7.21; 18.14; 21.31; 26.42). The μαθηταί, who 'represent' Matthew's church, are drawn from many families into one family: the family called into being by Jesus who is ever with them (28.20)[199] and who teaches them the will of their one Father who is in heaven (11.25–7).

This brings us to the last major modification: to do with the order of the pericopae. Like Mark, Matthew places the story prior to Jesus' parable discourse (Matt. 13 par. Mark 4). Unlike Mark, however, Matthew precedes the story with material from Q (Matt. 12.38–42 par. Luke 11.29–32; Matt. 12.43–5 par. Luke 11.24–6), in which Jesus speaks words of judgment on 'this evil generation', as part of a sustained attack on the Pharisees in response to their accusation that Jesus owes his authority to Beelzebul (Matt. 12.24ff. par. Mark 3.22ff.). The effect of this reordering, from a redactional viewpoint, is twofold. First, it further separates the story of Jesus and his family from the Beelzebul controversy – stories which are closely linked in Mark, as we have seen. Second, it allows the story of Jesus' identification of his true family to serve as a positive contrast to the condemnation of the '(scribes and) Pharisees' (12.2, 14, 24, 38) and 'this evil generation'. In this way, 12.46–50 functions in a similar way to 11.25–30, where, once again, the positive and gracious words of Jesus (the divine Wisdom) both to the Father and to 'the weary and heavy laden' contrast with his words of judgment upon unrepentant Israel (cf. 11.16–19, 20–4).[200]

In sum, the effect of Matthew's editorial activity is to give this biographical apophthegm from Mark a primarily ecclesiological slant. In Mark's version, what dominates is that evangelist's passion christology, expressed through the negative portrayal of Jesus' family and the distance which Mark creates between Jesus' natural kinsfolk and his true, eschatological kinsfolk. Matthew softens this polemical edge substantially.[201] What is important for him is not a

---

[199] See Trilling, *Israel*, 30: 'Auch für seinen Jüngerbegriff ist das persönliche Verhältnis zu Jesus, die Bindung an seine Person grundlegen.'

[200] See Kingsbury, *Parables*, 16; also, Bauer, *Structure*, 92–3; Howell, *Story*, 140–1.

[201] So Beare, *Matthew*, 284, is mistaken, in my view, in heading this section, 'Jesus Repudiates His Family'. That is much more the Marcan picture. Likewise, Kingsbury is unjustified (*Story*, 75) in stating: 'And last, like the others in Israel, even the family of Jesus deserts him, which leaves the disciples as the only ones who adhere to him (12:46–50).'

hostile depiction of the family of Jesus in the interest of christology, but the identification of the disciples – over against unrepentant Israel and its leaders, the Pharisees – as Jesus' true family in the interest of ecclesiology.[202]

In any case, it would be unusual for Matthew to maintain the harsh portrayal of Jesus' family found in Mark, given Matthew's account of the birth of Jesus where Mary and Joseph are cast in such a positive light. As Brown *et al.* put it:

> In the logic of Matthew's Gospel, Jesus' mother had virginally conceived her son; she knew of an angelic message that he would save his people from their sins; she had seen how God had protected him from the wicked king and had planned geographically his destiny, bringing him to Nazareth. She could scarcely show such misunderstanding of his mission to think that he was beside himself.[203]

From redaction-critical analysis, we turn again to literary criticism. The setting deserves comment. The temporal setting, according to 12.1, is the sabbath. Significantly, what takes place this sabbath, however, is not rest and the celebration of the divine *shalom*, but controversy and strife. This happens because Israel, and in particular the Pharisees, refuses to acknowledge that a new time has dawned and that the Son of Man, who is 'lord of the sabbath' (12.8), has come. This sets the tone for 12.46–50. Jesus' words of judgment upon the Israel that has rejected him are the prelude to his identification here of the true people of God who will take Israel's place.

The spatial setting is unclear. What we do know is that it is not 'their synagogue' (12.9), since the result of Jesus' healing of the man with the withered hand is the Pharisees' determination to destroy him (12.14): and so Jesus makes a prudent withdrawal, followed by the 'many' (12.15). The consequence of this is that when Jesus identifies his true, eschatological family, an abandonment of the synagogue has taken place and an opposition to the synagogue is implied. Interestingly, immediately after our episode, Matthew as narrator clarifies the spatial setting when he says: 'That same day

---

[202] That μαθηταί refers to a body of people larger than the twelve is clear from the inclusive identification of the μαθηταί here as Jesus' brothers and sisters and mothers.

[203] Brown, *Mary*, 99.

Jesus went out of the house' (13.1). It is almost as if, having identified his true family over against Israel, Matthew now identifies the spatial corollary: not the synagogue, but the house (οἰκία) (cf. 13.36a).

Observing the narrative structure is enlightening also. A good case can be made for setting 12.46–50 within the wider context of 11.1–16.20, where the narrator presents the response – both positive and negative – to the mission of Jesus to Israel, a mission itself set out in 4.17–11.1.[204] Within this framework, the demanding teaching about family ties which Jesus lays upon his disciples in 10.37–8 finds its exemplification with respect to Jesus himself, in 12.46–50, with Jesus' identification of his true family as 'whoever does the will of my Father in heaven' (v. 50). Matthew 12.46–50 comes at the point of transition from narrative (broadly speaking) to the parables discourse. These parables (and their interpretation) refer time and again to a process of eschatological sorting out (cf. 13.3–9, 18–23, 24–30, 36–43, 47–50). They are, therefore, an apt rejoinder to Jesus' rejection by Israel in chapters 11 and 12. They are also an apt reinforcement of Jesus' signalling of the identity of those who belong to him by virtue of their obedience to the Father's will, in 12.46–50.[205]

The effectiveness of the episode at the level of communication is a function of rhetorical factors.[206] The amount of repetition is significant in pointing to the central theme. Thus, Jesus' mother and brothers are referred to no fewer than five times (accepting v. 47 as authentic). The first two occurrences are prefaced by ἰδού, the one spoken by the narrator (v. 46), the other by the anonymous interlocutor (v. 47). The third occurrence comes in the form of a startling rhetorical question from Jesus in the rather deliberate, two-part form, τίς ἐστιν ἡ μήτηρ μου καὶ τίνες εἰσὶν οἱ ἀδελφοί μου; (v. 48b). The fourth also begins with an ἰδού in a way which gives Jesus' words an adversative sense, as if to say, 'Not those people are my mother and brothers, but these!' The fifth is an expanded form in reverse order: 'brother and sister and mother' (v. 50). 'Brother' (ἀδελφός) is listed first here, probably because that is the kinship term of greatest ecclesiological significance for the narrator. The addition of ἀδελφή together with μήτηρ is gender-inclusive, and,

---

204 See Bauer, *Structure*, 84–95; also, Howell, *Story*, ch. 3, esp. 128–45.
205 See Kingsbury, *Parables*, 15–16.
206 See Tannehill, *Sword*, 165–71 (commenting on the rhetoric of the Marcan parallel).

together with the gesture towards the disciples, indicates that Jesus' reply is to be interpreted at the metaphorical level.

The words and actions of Jesus completely dominate the episode. Jesus' mother and brothers (unnamed; cf. 13.55) remain off-stage. Communication takes place through an anonymous intermediary, so that Jesus replies, not to them, but to him. The only non-verbal action is that authoritative gesture of Jesus in 'stretching out his hand toward his disciples' (v. 49a). And Jesus speaks the final, conclusive word which announces that others belong to his family: namely those who do the will of 'my Father' (v. 50). This is a word of all-inclusive scope and generalizing intent. As such, it is a direct appeal to Matthew's reader, as well.

The episode narrated at 12.46–50 has important sociological implications which may be expressed quite succinctly and which reinforce the sociological inferences drawn earlier. On the assumption that Matthew's Gospel can be understood as a contribution to the social world-building of the Christian audience for which it is written, 12.46–50 is interpreted plausibly as providing a foundation in the tradition of the sayings of Jesus for the development of a common identity constituted along the lines of a spiritual family. Membership of this family is not a matter of heredity and blood ties. They are thrown, disturbingly, into question: 'Who is my mother, and who are my brothers?' The normally taken-for-granted familial identity and allegiances are taken for granted no longer. Now, belonging becomes a matter of action rather than ascription: 'Whoever does the will of my Father in heaven is my brother, and sister, and mother.' Spiritual kinship comes from radical and wholehearted obedience, not to any earthly patriarch (cf. 23.9), but to the Father in heaven.

That is the ideal basis for community, according to the Jesus of Matthew; and it is one which relativizes strongly – though by no means replaces – community based upon marital and household ties. Such an ideal basis for community makes possible a diversity of roles and social patterns. It also makes innovation possible. Now Jewish believer can enter into association with Gentile believer (cf. 28.19–20). Now an itinerant, homeless missionary existence has a legitimate place alongside, and in co-operation with, a settled, household-based existence (cf. 10.5–15). Now it is honourable to be so devoted to the kingdom of heaven that the single life becomes a legitimate option (19.10–12). This latter point will engage our attention further in subsequent discussion.

Jesus in his hometown (Matt. 13.53–8 par. Mark 6.1–6a)

Attention to Matthean modification of Mark and to Matthew's own compositional activity reveals the following. Matthew follows Mark in setting Jesus' teaching in parables immediately after the story about Jesus' true family (Matt. 13.1–52 par. Mark 4.1–34). Then, having used already the miracle stories from Mark 4.35–5.43 (at Matt. 8.23–34; 9.18–26), he once again draws upon his Marcan source at Mark 6.1–6a, the story of Jesus' rejection in his hometown, Nazareth (2.23; 4.13). The result is a typically Matthean sequence of discourse followed by narrative, the discourse coming to a formulaic closure, at 13.53a (cf. 7.28; 11.1; 19.2; 26.1). This is the first significant difference from Mark: the direct juxtaposition of the parables of the kingdom and the story of Jesus' rejection in the town of his upbringing.

The effect of the new sequence of the material in Matthew is striking. To understand it more clearly, however, it is necessary to back-track: for 13.53–8 stands at the end of a longer section running from the end of the second major discourse (i.e. 11.2–13.52). This section has two major parts, as Kingsbury has shown.[207] The first runs to the end of chapter 12 and has as its central theme the rejection of Jesus. As we have just seen, the story which brings this part to an end is that of Jesus' identification of his true family, the μαθηταί. So the μαθηταί are identified and accepted, over against the people of 'this generation' (cf. 11.16–19), the unrepentant cities of Galilee (11.20–4) and the unbelieving (scribes and) Pharisees (12.1–45). There is a sorting out taking place, as Jesus' dramatic gesture in stretching out his hand towards the μαθηταί shows (12.49). They are the ones he has called into the brotherhood of his family, and they have come to him (11.28–30).

This sorting out is reflected further in the second part, 13.1–52. For the parables themselves are constructed carefully in a sequence which distinguishes between the ὄχλοι (13.2, 34) who do not understand (especially 13.10–17) and the μαθηταί who do (13.51; cf. vv. 10, 36). There are eight parables in all, arranged chiastically.[208] After the 'parable about parables'[209] and its interpretation, there follow six kingdom parables in two groups of three and, finally, the Parable of the Householder. The first four parables are addressed

---

[207] Kingsbury, *Parables*, 15–16.
[208] See Wenham, 'Structure'; Orton, *Scribe*, 138–9.
[209] So, Gundry, *Matthew*, 250.

ostensibly to the ὄχλοι (13.3–23, 24–30, 31–2, 33), the second four to the μαθηταί (13.44, 45–6, 47–50, 51–2). Most noticeable is the separation indicated at v. 36 (Matthew only): Τότε ἀφεὶς τοὺς ὄχλους ἦλθεν εἰς τὴν οἰκίαν. καὶ προσῆλθον αὐτῷ οἱ μαθηταὶ ἀυτοῦ. Noticeable also is the fact that, in the six kingdom parables, the first to the ὄχλοι is the Parable of the Tares (13.24–30) which speaks of a future sorting out, and the first word to the μαθηταί privately in the house gives the key to this sorting out (13.36–43). Furthermore, the last parable of the six (the Dragnet) corresponds with the first: just like the latter, it concerns a future sorting out of the good from the bad (13.47–50). Following the Parable of the Dragnet, the disciples are marked out unequivocally as the ones who understand (13.51), and this is confirmed in a solemn way by Jesus in his likening of the 'scribe trained for the kingdom of heaven' to a wise householder (13.52). Coming as it does immediately before the story of Jesus' rejection in his hometown (in 13.53–8), the contrast is powerful. The theme of the failure of the ὄχλοι to understand, see and hear (13.13–15) is developed further now, with reference to those even closer to Jesus, his familiars in the *patris*.

The fact that the disciples claim, in 13.51, to understand Jesus' teaching may explain their omission from the narrative following. Mark's statement, καὶ ἀκολουθοῦσιν αὐτῷ οἱ μαθηταὶ αὐτοῦ (Mark 6.1b), is missing from Matthew. Apparently, Matthew removes them from possible association with 'their synagogue' (13.54), and from possible complicity in 'their unbelief' (13.58). The disciples are set apart from the Jews of Jesus' *patris* and from Jesus' family by blood, a separation for which Matt. 12.46–50 and Matthew 13 have prepared us. Alternatively, their omission may be the result of editorial abbreviation of his source. Whatever the case, the lack of mention of the disciples has the effect of focussing attention more clearly on the reaction of the people to Jesus himself – in contrast, for instance, to the reaction of the Pharisees to Jesus' disciples, in 12.1ff.

As we have seen already, the phrase 'in *their* synagogue' (13.54; diff. Mark 6.2) is Matthean redaction (4.23; 9.35 – both major redactional summaries; also, 12.9).[210] It expresses the distance, in his own day, between church and synagogue (10.17). Clearly, its occurrence here is ominous for the kind of reception Jesus will

---

[210] Gnilka, *Matthäusevangelium I*, 513.

receive, even though it is the synagogue of his hometown. In the context of the gospel as a whole, this is the last time Jesus appears in a synagogue.[211]

Jesus' audience responds with a sequence of questions, which Matthew has reordered subtly so that their focus shifts away from a concern about the nature of Jesus' σοφία and δυνάμεις to a concern with their origin.[212] Hence, the first and last of the five questions are parallel: **πόθεν τούτῳ** ἡ σοφία αὕτη καὶ αἱ δυνάμεις ... **πόθεν** οὖν **τούτῳ** ταῦτα πάντα; (13.54c, 56b). The reader is being reminded of the controversy provoked earlier by Jesus' enemies, the Pharisees, who were imputing to Beelzebul Jesus' power to exorcise (12.22–32). Like the Pharisees, the compatriots of Jesus do not understand that his power comes from the Spirit of God (12.28).[213]

The three middle questions all relate to Jesus' kin by blood. They reflect the people's unbelief. Rather than confess him as Son of God, they know him only as 'son of the carpenter' (13.55a; diff. Mark 6.3a). Rather than understand that Jesus' mother and brothers and sisters are, not his kin by blood, but whoever does the will of the heavenly Father (12.50), they know him only as member of a much more clearly definable family circle whom they can name (13.55) and whose location is 'with us' (πρὸς ἡμᾶς – 13.56). Jesus' brothers are no longer the four named by his compatriots: they are instead the four Jesus himself has called to follow him (4.18–22).[214] And Jesus' sisters are not 'all' (πᾶσαι 13.56a; Matthew only) there in the *patris*: rather, they are women like (subsequently) the Canaanite woman who responds to Jesus in faith (15.21–8).[215]

Matthew's version of Jesus' reply to his compatriots (in 13.57b par. Mark 6.4) has one important modification: the omission of καὶ ἐν τοῖς συγγενεῦσιν αὐτοῦ. The evangelist may have considered it redundant in view of the subsequent phrase, καὶ ἐν τῇ οἰκίᾳ αὐτοῦ; and, by omitting the second of the three phrases, he achieves a pair of phrases in parallel: εἰ μὴ ἐν τῇ πατρίδι καὶ ἐν τῇ οἰκίᾳ αὐτοῦ. But there may be more to it than that. First, the omission of Jesus' 'own

---

[211] Luz, *Matthäus II*, 386.
[212] Matthew abbreviates the series of questions in Mark 6.2, and omits the 'What ...?' questions altogether.
[213] See Gundry, *Matthew*, 283.
[214] Gnilka, *Matthäusevangelium I*, 514, suggests that the naming of James first may reflect his later role as leader of the church in Jerusalem. In my view, however, the distinction between Jesus' family by blood and his true, spiritual family is the evangelist's primary point.
[215] See Howell, *Story*, 143–4.

kin' serves to soften any implied criticism of them. This would be quite consistent with what we found in the Matthean redaction of Mark 3.20–1, 31–5 (particularly in the omission of 3.20–1). It would be consistent also with the very positive light in which this evangelist casts both Joseph and Mary in the birth narrative. Second, the omission may reflect yet again the influence of 12.46–50, where Jesus' true kin are identified once and for all.[216]

The conclusion of the story has undergone major modification. In Matthew's version, there is no suggestion that Jesus' healing power is limited by the unbelief of his compatriots. Rather, because of their unbelief and therefore in judgment upon them, Jesus refuses to do 'many mighty works'. By not receiving Jesus, in faith, as the Son of God, the people of his *patris* have forfeited the salvation conveyed by his δυνάμεις. So his *patris* has become like the cities of Galilee: having refused to repent in the light of Jesus' mighty works, it stands under judgment (11.20–4). Matthew has begun this whole section (11.2–13.52) with Jesus responding to John's inquiry by citing his mighty works and gospel proclamation and concluding, 'And blessed is he who takes no offense at me (μὴ σκανδαλισθῇ ἐν ἐμοί)' (11.6). At the end of the section, Jesus' own compatriots in Nazareth witness for themselves his wisdom and mighty works; but they take offence at him – καὶ ἐσκανδαλίζοντο ἐν αὐτῷ.[217] So no blessing comes upon them. They do not belong to Jesus' true family.

We ought not to be surprised, therefore, at one other difference. Whereas Mark moves on to the sending out of the twelve on mission (Mark 6.6–13), Matthew, who has used this material earlier (in 9.35; 10.1, 9–11, 14), moves on to the death of John at the hands of Herod (14.1–12 par. Mark 6.17–29). The juxtaposition thus achieved is unlikely to be coincidental. Rather, John's 'rejection' by Herod parallels Jesus' rejection in his *patris*. Not only so. It also points forward to the ultimate rejection of Jesus by the whole nation (27.25), of which the experience in his hometown is a premonition.[218]

In sum, we have seen how Matthew uses the Marcan story of Jesus in Nazareth to conclude an important and central section of

---

[216] See Gundry, *Matthew*, 284.

[217] According to Morgenthaler, *Statistik*, 140, σκανδαλίζειν is used most frequently by Matthew (Matthew 14 times; Mark 8 times; Luke twice), as also is σκάνδαλον (Matthew 5 times; Mark never; Luke once). Interestingly, Matthew 13 contains three uses of this terminology – in 13.21 (par. Mark 4.17); 13.41 (Matthew only); and 13.57 (par. Mark 6.4).

[218] So too, Luz, *Matthäus II*, 386.

his gospel. It serves as a reiteration of Jesus' experiences of opposition and rejection in chapters 11 and 12, at the end of which Jesus
identifies the μαθηταί as his true family. Yet further, it expresses in
narrative form the separation, underlying the parables in 13.1–52,
between those who understand and those who do not. Jesus' compatriots are clearly among the latter – as also, in the subsequent
episode, is Herod and ultimately, the *laos* as a whole. But Matthew
softens any criticism of Jesus' natural family which Mark may have
implied. This is partly because of the high esteem in which he holds
Joseph[219] and Mary; partly also because of the much more neutral
depiction of Jesus' mother and brothers, in 12.46–50.

From Matthew's handling of Mark, we turn to literary-critical
concerns. Little need be added about narrative structure to what has
been said above about the way Matthew has positioned the episode
of Jesus' rejection in his hometown at the end of the parables
discourse and prior to the story of the death of John the Baptist. The
theme of the rejection of Jesus by Israel which the narrator develops
from 11.2 on, linked closely as it is with Jesus' turning instead to the
(understanding) disciples, marked so clearly at 13.36 (16.21ff.), is
taken further in this episode. The resounding 'Yes' of the disciples
to Jesus in 13.51 contrasts with the equally resounding 'No' of his
compatriots to him in 13.53–8 (at v. 57a). Further, that their rejection of Jesus anticipates his subsequent death at the hands of Israel
at the end of the narrative is signified by the story of the death of
John the Baptist at the hands of Herod in the next episode.[220]
   The rhetoric of the episode is significant for its irony. It is a case of
Jesus' compatriots showing their lack of understanding by their
claim to know. In so doing, they bear witness to the truth of Jesus'
words in the parable discourse: 'For to him who has will more be
given . . . but from him who has not, even what he has will be taken
away' (13.12). Through their claim to be able to understand Jesus by
identifying his earthly ties, they show that they have no understanding of Jesus' heavenly ties. That this lies at the heart of the matter is
reinforced by the concentric pattern of their rhetorical questions (in
13.54b-6b): a series of three kinship questions – relating Jesus
emphatically to his father (v. 55a), his mother and four brothers
(v. 55b) and his sisters (v. 56a) – is bracketed on either side by two

---

[219] Note that, in contrast to Mark, Matthew includes a reference to Joseph, in
13.55a (diff. Mark 6.3): οὐχ οὗτός ἐστιν ὁ τοῦ τέκτονος υἱός;
[220] See Howell, *Story*, 141–2.

πόθεν τούτῳ questions to do with the source of Jesus' wisdom and mighty works (vv. 54b, 56b). This in turn is bracketed by two references to Jesus. The first is a general summary statement: 'and coming to his own country he taught them in their synagogue' (v. 54a). The second, parallel reference has Jesus' direct speech – and it consists of words of condemnation: 'A prophet is not without honour except in his own country and in his own house' (v. 57b). The overall chiastic pattern[221] brings the references to Jesus and the references to his kinsfolk into stark opposition. Jesus' compatriots assert his kinship identity as strongly as possible: but he denies his kinship identity just as strongly by proverbial appeal to a prophet's fate.

The point of view of the narrator is made clear in the commentary which the narrator provides on the attitudes of Jesus' compatriots. This commentary shows a significant shift in a negative direction as the episode is played out. First, 'they were astonished (ἐκπλήσσεσθαι αὐτούς)' (v. 54b), an expression which is used of the crowds elsewhere (cf. 7.28; 22.33) and has neither explicitly positive nor negative connotations. Then, at the conclusion of the barrage of questions about Jesus' identity, the narrator comments, καὶ ἐσκανδαλίζοντο ἐν αὐτῷ (v. 57a). Finally, as the conclusion to the episode as a whole, the narrator states that Jesus 'did not do many mighty works there, because of their unbelief (διὰ τὴν ἀπιστίαν αὐτῶν)' (v. 58). Astonishment – 'stumbling' – unbelief: that is the progression in the position of the compatriots from the narrator's point of view. The same progression characterizes Israel as a whole as the wider story unfolds. Counterposed to that progression, however, is the process of the instruction and enlightenment of Jesus' true family, the disciples, a process which reaches an important point of definition at 13.51–2, and comes to a climax at 16.13–20.

The sociological implications of the rejection at Nazareth remain to be discussed. The fundamental point, from a sociological perspective, is the same as that made already in our discussion of Mark 6.1–6a, in the previous chapter. What is at stake in this story is competing conceptions of the identity of Jesus,[222] where personal

---

221 Luz, *Matthäus II*, 383.

222 See Kingsbury, *Story*, 75–7, who shows that, 'entwined with the motif of repudiation in 11:2–16:20 is the motif of wonderment and speculation in Israel about the identity of Jesus. This motif of Jesus' identity serves the sub-plot of

identity is a social given, determined by where the person comes from and what kinship web the person belongs to. Thus, when Jesus returns to his hometown, the issue of his identity and status naturally comes to a head. The result is a sharp conflict of perception about Jesus. His σοφία and δυνάμεις place in question the assumptions which Jesus' townspeople make about who he is on the basis of what they know already about him – who he belongs to, his father's occupation, and so on. This generates a crisis which can be resolved either by acknowledging Jesus' new identity and changed status or by reasserting the conventional categories. To do the former would involve a change in the perception, not only of Jesus, but of themselves as well, since social identity is defined reciprocally. In Matthean terms, this would involve 'repentance' and 'faith'. But Jesus' townspeople do the latter. They attempt to deny Jesus' divine authority by reasserting conventional categories of residence, occupation and kinship. In Weberian terms, whereas Jesus demonstrates the attributes of one who claims charismatic authority, his compatriots refuse to acknowledge that authority, appealing instead to the legitimating norms of traditional authority.[223] Jesus' response, in turn, is equally uncompromising: as it must be if he is to maintain his claim to divine authority and to the honour due to a prophet. Their refusal to recognize him is met by Jesus' reciprocal refusal to be their benefactor: 'And he did not do many mighty works there, because of their unbelief' (13.58).

For Matthew's audience, such an episode from the life of Jesus is likely to have reinforced considerably the suprafamilial ethos of the faith and lifestyle to which they are being encouraged to commit themselves. If Jesus is represented as being rejected by his familiars, this is no more than what he himself has predicted already for his followers (cf. 10.34–6). Likewise, if his identity is defined satisfactorily no longer in terms of place of origin, occupation and kinship ties, neither can it be for them (cf. 4.18–22; 8.18–22; 12.46–50).

6 Eunuchs for the sake of the kingdom (Matt. 19.10–12)

From the episode which serves as a sequel to the third major discourse (13.53–8), we turn to the episode which immediately

conflict in Matthew's story because Israel shows itself to be ignorant of who Jesus is.' Kingsbury's literary point is important from a sociological perspective, as well.

[223] See Weber, *Theory*, esp. 324–63.

follows the fourth major discourse: Jesus' teaching about divorce (19.1–12). This is the next block of material in Matthew containing sayings directly relevant to our theme of discipleship and family ties.

Form-critical analysis is relatively straightforward. 19.1–12 is a reworking of Mark 10.1–12[224] and has the form of a controversy dialogue[225] in public which has been expanded by the addition of explanatory sayings in private. There is a loose narrative setting (vv. 1–2); opponents of Jesus appear and ask a question with male-volent intent (πειράζοντες, v. 3); Jesus controverts his opponents and the encounter ends with a climactic λέγω δὲ ὑμῖν saying (vv. 4–9); and in an addendum, Jesus takes his teaching further for the disciples in response to an intervention by them (vv. 10–12). There is good reason to locate the origins of the controversy dialogue proper (i.e. vv. 3–9 par. Mark 10.2–12) within a *Sitz im Leben Jesu*;[226] just as there is good reason also for locating the origins of the startling 'eunuch saying' within a *Sitz im Leben Jesu*, as Moloney has shown.[227] No doubt, the controversy over the divorce law was preserved subsequently because of its pertinence to the ordering of the social life of the nascent communities, sometimes in dialogue and controversy with neighbouring synagogue communi-ties, sometimes arising out of problems generated by the conversion of Gentiles (cf. 1 Cor. 7.10ff.).[228] The 'eunuch saying' may have been preserved because it could hardly have been forgotten, or because it legitimated the ascetic lifestyle of early Christian 'wandering charismatics',[229] or because it helped the church address the question of what to do about eunuchs seeking membership (cf. Acts 8.26–40).[230] Be that as it may, our primary concern is to interpret the material as it stands, in its present context in Matthew.

Whereas form criticism operates by breaking the text down into its

---

224 For a comprehensive traditio-historical analysis, see Catchpole, 'Divorce'.
225 Bultmann, *Tradition*, 26–7.
226 See Catchpole, 'Divorce', esp. 110–27; Banks, *Jesus*, 146–59.
227 Moloney, 'Matthew 19, 3–12', 50–3, in agreement with J. Blinzler. Thus: 'J. Blinzler has convincingly argued that in this same type of situation Jesus was called "eunuch!"'. Given the importance of marriage and the production of children it appears more than probable that there was something about the life-style of Jesus of Nazareth which caused his opponents to call him a eunuch in a derogatory and abusive sense' (p. 51).
228 See, on the latter, Dungan, *Sayings*, Part II; also, Yarbrough, *Gentiles*.
229 So, Theissen, 'Radicalism', citing Matt. 19.12 on p. 85.
230 See Schneider, 'εὐνοῦχος', 768; Brooks, *Community*, 108.

various constituent units, the boundaries of which are determined
along formal lines of literary analysis, redaction criticism focusses
on the creative editorial and compositional process by which an
evangelist has shaped his materials into a gospel. Matt. 19.1–12 is an
interesting case in point, for here we observe substantial Matthean
modification of Mark, the addition of the 'eunuch saying' at the
end, probably taken from an independent source of Jesus-logia, and
an overall setting significantly affected by the evangelist's compositional method.

Mark's Gospel already sets Jesus' teaching on divorce in a wider
context of teaching on household-related matters relevant to
members of Jesus' eschatological family (Mark 10.1–31). Matthew
follows Mark closely in this (19.1–30). But Matthew's interest in this
theme goes further: for in his version, the teaching on divorce
follows on from the fourth major discourse, which has to do with
instruction on life together in the brotherhood of the church (17.22–
18.35).[231] This is significant for the interpretation of chapter 19. It
implies that the scrupulous care for one's 'brothers' in the believing
fellowship, advocated in the discourse, is being advocated likewise
with respect to the related matters of divorce, the reception of
children, and attitudes to property and household ties which come
next. More specifically, it implies that this scrupulous care is to be
extended to those referred to in 19.12: those 'who have made
themselves eunuchs for the sake of the kingdom of heaven'.[232]

The link between the discourse and 19.1–12 is not just conceptual:
it is literary also. The characteristically Matthean ending of the
discourse (19.1a, corresponding precisely with the conclusion of the
first discourse, in 7.28) is simultaneously part of Matthew's introduction to the controversy dialogue following (diff. Mark 10.1). The
other interesting modification of Mark's introduction is that
whereas, in Mark, crowds come together to Jesus and he teaches
them (Mark 10.2), in Matthew, the crowds are πολλοί, they are
represented as 'following' Jesus (the redactional use of ἀκολουθεῖν
indicating that the teaching they receive in 19.3ff. is relevant to
disciples of Jesus), and Jesus heals them instead of teaching them
(19.2).

We need not examine in detail Matthew's modifications of the

---

[231] See the comprehensive redactional and compositional analysis by Thompson,
Advice.
[232] See Gundry, *Matthew*, 383: '[Matthew's] purpose is to urge full acceptance of
such men in the Christian brotherhood.'

controversy dialogue itself (19.3–9 par. Mark 10.2–12), except to note that Matthew is more hostile towards the Pharisees. He juxta-poses Φαρισαῖοι and πειράζοντες αὐτόν (v. 3a; diff. Mark 10.2b). He also turns the controversy into a debate about the interpretation of the divorce law – hence Matthew's κατὰ πᾶσαν αἰτίαν (v. 3b), and μὴ ἐπὶ πορνείᾳ (v. 9) – between rival teachers,[233] with a con-clusion, reminiscent of the 'antitheses' of the Sermon on the Mount (cf. 5.22, 28, 32, 34, 39, 44), which shows Jesus as upholder both of Moses and of a righteousness greater than that of the Pharisees (cf. 5.17–20).[234]

Matthew 19.10–12 is unique to the gospel. Vv. 10–11 are almost certainly Matthean redaction, whose important function is to link the strange logion in v. 12 to the teaching on divorce in vv. 3–9.[235] Matthew has made the Marcan saying prohibiting divorce and remarriage (Mark 10.11) the climax of Jesus' reply to the Pharisees (v. 9).[236] That the teaching of Jesus on divorce and remarriage is in effect no less strict in Matthew than in Mark is evident from the comment of the disciples in v. 10, where their response to Jesus' demanding prohibition shows – characteristically for Matthew – that they (partially?) understand (cf. 13.51):[237] 'If such is the case of a man with his wife, it is not expedient to marry.' Jesus' teaching prohibiting divorce and subsequent remarriage is rigorous: and the disciples recognize it to be so. In v. 11, Jesus goes on to indicate that this demanding teaching on divorce is appropriate only for dis-ciples: 'not all men can receive this saying (τὸν λόγον τοῦτον), but only those to whom it is given' (cf. 13.11). The λόγος to which he is referring is almost certainly the teaching leading up to and including the climactic saying prohibiting divorce μὴ ἐπὶ πορνείᾳ and remar-

[233] Note 19.4a, where Jesus replies to the Pharisees, οὐκ ἀνέγνωτε ὅτι ... (Matthew only). Also, in Matthew's re-presentation, it is Jesus who is the first to quote the torah (diff. Mark).

[234] See Gundry, *Matthew*, 376–81; also, Moloney, 'Matthew 19, 3–12', 43–4. Note that 19.9a shares with 5.32a the 'antithetical' formula, λέγω δὲ ὑμῖν ὅτι .... Note also that the climactic saying in v. 9 is addressed, in Matthew's version, to the Pharisees, not to the disciples in the house, as in Mark (10.10–11).

[235] So too, Brooks, *Community*, 107; Moloney, 'Matthew 19, 3–12', 45; Gundry, *Matthew*, 381–2; Quesnell, 'Eunuchs', 341–7.

[236] Matthew also omits the saying about a woman divorcing her husband (Mark 10.12), presumably because the Mosaic law does not give women the right to divorce their husbands, and Matthew is conforming to that, in the spirit of 5.17–19.

[237] See Gundry, *Matthew*, 381; Wilkins, *Disciple*, 136–7.

riage, in vv. 4–9.[238] If that is so,[239] then the saying in v. 12c identifies those to whom the λόγος of v. 9 particularly applies. In other words, those who 'have made themselves eunuchs for the sake of the kingdom of heaven' are men who have divorced their wives because of πορνεία and have not remarried, but have remained single and celibate instead. Within the wider context of the teaching of humility and brotherly love in chapter 18, the teaching in 19.10–12 reads then as an encouragement to the members of the Christian group to support such 'eunuchs' within its midst.

Can we be more precise about the issue which is the only legitimate grounds for divorce, according to a gospel whose general opposition to divorce is strong enough to include Jesus-tradition on the subject from both Q (Matt. 5.32 par. Luke 16.18) and Mark (10.1–12)? Unfortunately, it is impossible to be sure about the meaning of the redactional phrase, μὴ ἐπὶ πορνείᾳ (cf. 5.32, παρεκτὸς λόγου πορνείας – Matthew only), in v. 9. In context, it is hardly a liberalization of the teaching of Jesus: for Jesus' opposition to divorce and remarriage is quite stringent, both here (v. 10) and in the Sermon on the Mount, where it comes as part of his teaching of a 'greater righteousness' obedience to which makes the disciple τέλειος (5.48). Rather than signifying a liberalization, therefore, Matthew's editorial modification must be intended to deal with an important exception.

Some have argued that the important exception arises out of a situation in Matthew's church where certain Gentiles, already

---

[238] So too, Brooks, *Community*, 107; Moloney, 'Matthew 19, 3–12', 46 (citing the pattern of dialogue between Jesus and the disciples in 19.23–6 as a useful parallel). Likewise, Gundry, *Matthew*, 383: 'Therefore, "this saying" refers to Jesus' teaching against divorce with remarriage; and the ability to accept the saying does not distinguish higher disciples from lower disciples, but characterizes true disciples as those to whom God gives ability to accept even this high standard, over against nondisciples and false disciples, who do not have such ability.'

[239] It is the weakness of Wolff's interpretation, in 'Humility', 150–4, that even though he sees 19.10–12 as an expansion of 19.3–9, with vv. 10–11 as a redactional bridge to the dominical logion of v. 12, he fails to see that the subject of vv. 10–12 is the same as the subject of vv. 3–9: i.e. the prohibition of divorce and remarriage. Instead, Wolff interprets vv. 10–12 as dealing with 'the state of the unmarried within the context of instruction about marriage and divorce' (p. 152). This then allows him to posit a link of a material (*sachlich*) – though not a verbal – kind with the eschatological celibacy of the unmarried apostle Paul (1 Cor. 7.7). It must be significant, though, that where Paul can appeal to a word of the Lord, he does – as in the case of divorce (1 Cor. 7.10–11); but that, in the case of the 'unmarried' (παρθένοι) (1 Cor. 7.25ff.), he does not. See Quesnell, 'Eunuchs', 341.

married within the Levitical laws of prohibited degree (see Lev. 18.6–18), have become members.[240] Because their marital state contravenes Levitical law, their presence in the church is a cause of scandal and an affront to the claim that the teaching of Jesus accords with the teaching of the torah. To meet this problem, summed up in the word πορνεία (understood here as an incestuous union – as, apparently, in Acts 15.20, 29), Matthew modifies Jesus' prohibition of divorce (at 5.32 and 19.9) in such a way as to allow Gentiles married within the prohibited degrees to divorce. The additional teaching in 19.10–12 is intended, on this reading, to provide – in the form of a dominical saying – legitimation for Gentile disciples who have taken this step to remain single: they do so 'for the sake of the kingdom of heaven'. The strengths of this hypothesis are: first, that it posits a plausible *Sitz im Leben der Kirche* in order to explain Matthew's consistent redaction of the double tradition prohibiting divorce; second, that the hypothesis is consistent with the undoubted stringency of the ethical teaching of the Matthean Jesus in general, along with the Matthean concern not to depart from the torah; and third, that it allows sense to be made of 19.3–12 as a whole, such that vv. 10–12 are seen as a further development of the subject opened up already in vv. 3–9.

However, the hypothesis is not fully convincing, in my view. First, the meaning of πορνεία is notoriously slippery and varies widely in the New Testament, being used 'of every kind of unlawful sexual intercourse'.[241] So we should be wary of giving it such a particular sense as that proposed above for 5.32 and 19.9,[242] especially when the only other occurrence of πορνεία in Matthew (at 15.19) is not used in this sense. Second, the hypothesis makes the meaning of the text dependent upon the prior acceptance of an elaborate hypothetical reconstruction of a possible historical context, independent evidence for which is fairly meagre. To parody the approach, it is a matter, with respect to the presence of Gentiles (and their peculiar problems) in the Matthean church, of, 'Now you see them, now you

---

[240] So, Moloney, 'Matthew 19, 3–12', esp. pp. 44–5, 47–9, and those cited at n. 14; also, Fitzmyer, 'Divorce Texts', 205–11, followed by Stock, 'Divorce Texts', 25–9. The view goes back at least to Baltensweiler, 'Die Ehebruchklauseln'.

[241] Bauer–Arndt–Gingrich, *Lexicon*, 699. See further the useful survey by Jensen: 'Fornication?', *passim*.

[242] Gnilka, *Matthäusevangelium I*, 168, makes the point that the immediate context – the second 'antithesis', with its teaching about adultery (μοιχεία), in 5.27–30 – goes against interpreting πορνεία in 5.32 in a completely different sense as marriage within the law of prohibited degrees.

don't.' To put the same point in another way, such an approach is difficult to accommodate to what might be regarded as the plain meaning of the text. A third problem has to do with the plausibility of the hypothesis. It is doubtful that Gentiles married within the law of prohibited degrees would be required to divorce their wives as a condition of church membership, and then – to add insult to injury! – be expected to remain single. Significantly, we encounter no such teaching in the letters of Paul. On the contrary, in 1 Cor. 7.12ff., the believer is urged *not* to divorce his/her unbelieving partner if that partner is willing to remain married to the believer. Paul does deal with a case of πορνεία in 1 Cor. 5, where the issue is the fornication arising out of a man living with his 'father's wife' (stepmother?).[243] But the problem there is Christian libertinism, not the conversion of a partner already married within the prohibited degrees. A fourth problem is that the hypothesis makes the dialogue less intelligible as a dialogue between Jesus and the Pharisees in the pre-Easter period. Instead, we are asked to read the text as a subtle allegory of the time of Matthew. This does an injustice to Matthew's conservatism with regard to the Jesus tradition, and also to his fundamental concern to root the life of his church in the life and teaching of the earthly Jesus. None of these objections is insuperable, but they do leave the hypothesis open to doubt.

Less problematic is the more traditional view that the exceptive clause allows a man to divorce his wife if she is guilty of immorality by being unfaithful to her husband.[244] Behind this interpretation lies the commandment in the torah (at Deut. 24.1–4) according to which a man is entitled to divorce his wife if he finds in her a πρᾶγμα ἄσχημον (= *arwat dabar*, Deut. 24.1). As is well known,[245] the sense of this expression was a matter of debate among the rabbis, the school of Hillel interpreting it broadly as permission to divorce a woman for a wide range of possible offences, and the school of Shammai interpreting it narrowly as permission to divorce a woman on more limited grounds to do with sexual impropriety. The effect of Matthew's redaction of the Marcan tradition is to turn a controversy over the status of the Mosaic law itself (Mark 10.2) into a controversy analogous to the Pharisaic-rabbinic debate between

---

243 See Barrett, *First Corinthians*, 121.
244 So, e.g., Gnilka, *Matthäusevangelium I*, 168–9; Gundry, *Matthew*, 91, 381; Schweizer, *Matthew*, 124–5, 381; Banks, *Jesus*, 153ff.; Mohrlang, *Matthew*, 12; Strecker, *Sermon*, 73–6.
245 See Catchpole, 'Divorce', 93ff.; and the works cited in the previous note.

Hillelites and Shammaites – hence, the question of the Pharisees in 19:3, 'Is it lawful to divorce one's wife *for any cause* (κατὰ πᾶσαν αἰτίαν)?' On this reading, the answer of the Matthean Jesus is closer to, but also more rigorous than, the position of the 'conservative' Shammaites. He prohibits divorce and remarriage (vv. 4–6, 8): the only exception being the case of an unfaithful wife (v. 9). Further-more, the additional teaching in vv. 10–12 can be seen as an encour-agement to the man who has divorced his unfaithful wife to remain single and celibate, and not to remarry (cf. 1 Cor. 7.11).[246]

In sum, Matt. 19.1–12 is best interpreted, from a redactional viewpoint, as teaching from the Jesus tradition relevant to marital relations which Matthew has placed immediately after the discourse on the right ordering of the Christian brotherhood (17.22–18.35) as a development of the general theme of life together as the people of God. In taking over Marcan tradition, Matthew has adapted it in a direction which bears resemblance to rabbinical debates on legiti-mate grounds for divorce – although it is by no means necessary to infer from this that Matthew intentionally conforms the tradition to those debates.[247] At the same time, Matthew's position is distinct-ive. First, divorce is by no means taken for granted. Indeed, the fundamental position is one of opposition to divorce – a position consistent with Matthew's positive view of marriage elsewhere (cf. Matt. 10.37; diff. Luke 14.26; Matt. 22.5; diff. Luke 14.20),[248] and with his view of discipleship as demanding obedience to a more rigorous understanding of the will of God than that expressed in the torah (5.17–20). Second, legitimate grounds for divorce are limited severely: to unchastity on the part of the wife. Third, remarriage subsequent to divorcing one's wife is prohibited. The saying about 'eunuchs who have made themselves eunuchs for the sake of the kingdom of heaven' (19.12c), whatever its meaning(s) at an earlier stage in the history of the tradition, is joined by Matthew to this stringent teaching in order to support those among his audience in this position. The Christian brotherhood is to care diligently for those who have chosen the 'narrow way' of not remarrying but remaining single and celibate for the sake of the kingdom.

Taken in context, therefore, the 'eunuch saying' of Matt. 19.12 is not about the reception of eunuchs into the church, nor is it about

---

[246] So too, Quesnell, 'Eunuchs', defending the position taken in 1959 by Jacques Dupont.

[247] Dunn, *Unity*, 247, makes this assumption too quickly, in my view.

[248] See Quesnell, 'Eunuchs', 344–6.

celibacy *per se* as a way of expressing undivided devotion to God and his kingdom, nor is it about sexual asceticism out of considerations of ritual purity. Rather, it is a word for those who have accepted the discipline of Jesus' rigorous teaching prohibiting the disciple who has divorced his unchaste wife from remarrying.[249] The strengths of this interpretation are: first, that it does not require prior acceptance of an hypothesis about the presence of Gentile converts and their purported marriage irregularities;[250] second, that it makes sense of 19.1–12 as a whole; third, that it is plausible for the time of Jesus as well as for the time of the evangelist; and fourth, that it conforms with Matthew's understanding of the law, by adopting a position which represents a profound intensification of its demands (19.21). The primary significance of this text for our thesis is that it legitimates the transcending of normal marriage rules to the extent that the disciple who has divorced his wife on the ground of her unchastity is taught not to remarry but to remain single and celibate for the kingdom's sake.

When we turn to a literary-critical analysis of our text, there are several relatively brief points worth making. In relation to narrative sequence, we note how the subject of the fourth major discourse 'spills over' into the material immediately following. It is too simple merely to observe the standard (redactional) pattern of discourse followed by narrative. For here we find discourse followed by further teaching of Jesus, where the latter is best understood as building upon what goes before. Thus, the discourse on the life of the kingdom within the brotherhood of the church – with its demand for radical humility, for the exercise of discipline and pastoral care in order to avoid causes of 'stumbling' to the 'little ones', for measures to make possible reconciliation between 'brothers', and for unlimited forgiveness – is taken further in teaching of Jesus on household-related matters. The overall effect of this sequence is to reinforce the idea that believers in Jesus are members of a single family or brotherhood or household whose 'lord' (κύριος) is Jesus. With regard to the teaching in 19.3–12, in particular, the effect of the sequence is to imply that the prohibition of divorce and remarriage and the call to remain single once a divorce has taken place is a necessary corollary of what it means to be a member of that one family.

[249] So too, Gundry, *Matthew*, 382–3.
[250] *Contra* Moloney, 'Matthew 19, 3–12', 45, 47, 48.

The characterization conforms with what we have come to expect: it is relatively static. There are 'large crowds' who play their characteristic role of following Jesus and being ministered to by him.[251] It makes no difference that Jesus has left Galilee (19.1).[252] There are Pharisees, and they too play their characteristic role of opposition to Jesus and as a foil for Jesus and his teaching (19.3, 7). It is not coincidental that they come to Jesus 'testing (πειράζοντες) him', for this is the language typically used of the opposition to Jesus, not least of the devil himself (4.1, 3), but also of the Pharisees and Sadducees (16.1), the Pharisees and Herodians (22.18), and a 'lawyer' of the Pharisees (22.35).[253] Interestingly, σκληροκαρδία occurs only once in Matthew, in Jesus' reply to the Pharisees here (in v. 8). It is quite of a piece with what Freyne calls the language of vilification in the Matthean Jesus' treatment of his opponents, particularly with respect to the interpretation of the torah.[254] The disciples, once more, play the role of privileged recipients (vv. 11, 12d) of the teaching of Jesus (13.10–17, 36). It is they alone who receive the discourse on community (18.1): so it is not inappropriate that the special teaching on 'eunuchs for the sake of the kingdom' is imparted to them. In this episode, they function also as foils to the Pharisees, for it is only 'those to whom it is given' (v. 11) who are able to receive the 'hard saying' about the eunuchs. But it is Jesus who dominates the episode, as we have come to expect. It is Jesus who leads the way into Judaea: the crowds and disciples only follow. He it is who controverts the Pharisees on their own ground, scriptural interpretation (vv. 4–7), and then appeals above Moses to the will of God ἀπ' ἀρχῆς (v. 8b), and pronounces an authoritative ruling – λέγω δὲ ὑμῖν – which undercuts the Mosaic permission to divorce (v. 9). Finally, it is Jesus who imparts, in riddling language, the further teaching on divorce (vv. 10–12). So Jesus is depicted, over against the Jewish authorities represented in this instance by the Pharisees, as the one 'who is in complete accord with God's system of values';[255] and it is this divine authority which constitutes, in the wider narrative scheme, his power to 'save' and to bring the true family of God's people into being.

Given the 'eunuch saying' with which this episode ends (v. 12), it is the way Matthew communicates, the rhetoric, which also deserves

---

[251] See Minear, 'Disciples', 29–32; Wilkins, *Disciple*, 170–1.
[252] See Freyne, *Galilee*, 89.
[253] See Kingsbury, *Story*, 8, 21.   [254] Freyne, 'Vilifying', esp. pp. 132–7.
[255] Kingsbury, *Story*, 10.

attention. Focussing on this final saying,[256] we note immediately its
ordered, repetitive, three-part structure, the three principal clauses
each time beginning, εἰσὶν εὐνοῦχοι οἵτινες. There are three categories of 'eunuchs' listed. The first two are conventional, literal
categories, widely recognized: males who live as eunuchs because of
congenital incapacity, and males who have been castrated by
others.[257] The reader's expectation is that the third category will be
conventional also; and initially, the reader is not disappointed, for
reference follows to males who have castrated themselves. But then,
in the modifying adverbial phrase, comes the surprise: καὶ εἰσὶν
εὐνοῦχοι οἵτινες εὐνούχουσιν ἑαυτοὺς **διὰ τὴν βασιλείαν τῶν
οὐρανῶν**. The effect of this final phrase is to generate a radical shift
in the reader's comprehension, from the literal plane to the metaphorical. For a term (εὐνοῦχος) which ordinarily has extremely
negative connotations, particularly against the backdrop of
Matthew's first-century Jewish culture,[258] is given here an extremely
positive connotation. This creates a semantic tension, a tension
which can be resolved only by interpreting this third statement
metaphorically. The negative emotive power attached to a term of
obloquy and a category of taboo is transformed into positive
emotive power by the inversion of the category.[259] That this very
striking, even extreme, metaphor should be addressed to the disciples (and to readers who identify with them) emphasizes how total
is the demand of the kingdom of heaven. Like the extreme quality of
the metaphor, the demands of the kingdom can force the disciple
onto the margins of existence, conventionally understood. In the
context of the teaching on divorce, it appears that Matthew's rhetorical intention is to surprise and shock the disciple who has
divorced his unchaste wife into imagining the possibility of a new
mode of existence: remaining single and celibate, and thereby transcending family ties, for the kingdom's sake.

---

256 See also Tannehill, *Sword*, 134–40.
257 The rabbis distinguished, for example, between males 'castrated by the sun'
(i.e. from birth) and those 'castrated by human beings'. See *Str–B*, I, 806–7,
cited in Wolff, 'Humility', 152.
258 The evidence is collected usefully in Schneider, 'εὐνοῦχος'. See also Wolff,
'Humility', 152–3; Moloney, 'Matthew 19, 3–12', 50–1.
259 See Tannehill, *Sword*, 138: 'The reply would contribute no new facts or
arguments about Jesus, but it would challenge the fixed pattern of meaning
into which previously known facts had been arranged, setting free imaginative
thought so that a new pattern might emerge.'

202 Discipleship and family ties in Matthew

Is it possible to draw sociological inferences from Matthew's representation of the controversy over divorce in 19.1–12? Several possibilities are plausible, at least. As is the case with the issues dealt with in the 'community discourse' of chapter 18, questions to do with the regulation of marriage and divorce are fundamental to processes of community formation and maintenance in any society. The anthropological literature makes this quite clear,[260] as do studies of the New Testament *Haustafeln*.[261] Seen in this light, the teaching of the Matthean Jesus in 19.3–12 is interpreted plausibly as intended to contribute to the formation and maintenance of a distinctive, Christian community. In this community, the ordering of marriage and divorce follows the teaching of the founder, Jesus the Son of God, according to which marriage is highly regarded and divorce is prohibited. In the exceptional case where a man's wife is guilty of sexual immorality (πορνεία), divorce is permitted the offended husband: however, remarriage after divorce is prohibited, on the grounds that 'they are no longer two but one flesh' (v. 6a).

The distinctiveness of the community is reflected in the distinctiveness of its marriage rules:[262] that is the point, sociologically-speaking, of the disciples' comment in v. 10, and of Jesus' riddling reply in vv. 11–12, with its provocative and teasing conclusion, ὁ δυνάμενος χωρεῖν χωρείτω. By adopting a marital ethic of such rigour, in the context of a contemporary Judaism where the right of the man (in particular) to divorce and remarry is taken for granted,[263] the Matthean community can be seen as marking itself off as different. Here, it is not a matter of siding with a 'liberal' (Hillelite) interpretation of the torah, or of siding with a 'conservative' (Shammaite) interpretation. Nor is it a matter of separating out the community of the elect altogether from amongst the 'lawless' by

---

[260] See Fox, *Kinship*; also, Leach, *Anthropology*, ch. 6; Malina, *World*, ch. 5.

[261] E.g. Balch, *Wives*; Verner, *Household*; Yarbrough, *Gentiles*.

[262] For Judaism, this is well illustrated in Yarbrough, *Gentiles*, 7–29.

[263] See Josephus, *Antiquities* IV.253 (on Deut. 24.1): 'He who desires to be divorced from the wife who is living with him for whatever cause – and with mortals many such may arise – must certify in writing that he will have no further intercourse with her.' Also, in his comment on the initiative taken by Salome (the sister of Herod the Great) to divorce Costobarus, Josephus says: '[This] was not in accordance with Jewish law. For it is (only) the man who is permitted by us to do this, and not even a divorced woman may marry again on her own initiative unless her former husband consents' (*Antiquities* XV.259). The references come from Fitzmyer, 'Divorce', 214. In general, see further, Safrai, 'Home', 790–1. On the Ancient Near Eastern background, see Mendelsohn, 'Family', esp. pp. 25–36; also, Bardis, 'Family', 178–9.

withdrawing from marital ties and the company of women, as is the case with (at least some in) the sectarian community of Qumran.[264] Rather, it is a matter of following the more demanding command-ments of Jesus,[265] whose teaching of the will of God ἀπ' ἀρχῆς 'fulfils' the torah and makes it possible to become 'perfect', even in the midst of the mundane relations of marriage and family life. So the marriage rules are likely to have been of considerable sig-nificance in establishing the identity of Matthew's ἐκκλησία over against other groups and movements in contemporary Judaism (and beyond). It would be quite consistent with this to interpret the 'eunuch saying' as intended, in part at least, to provoke outsiders in Judaism, using a terminology of obloquy and abuse to emphasize how radical is the demand of the kingdom of heaven in relation to human relations generally and to marital relations in particular.[266]

But the sociological significance of the Matthean marriage rules will have gone further than their contribution to the identity of the group in relation to outsiders. They are even more likely to have been of significance for their contribution to the maintenance of the group's identity, self-understanding and common life 'from within'. A concern about the solidarity of the brotherhood – the need for humility, how to avoid apostasy, the imperative of pastoral care, the need for an orderly disciplinary procedure, and so on – comes to the surface unmistakably in the immediately preceding discourse. It would be surprising, therefore, if the teaching on divorce were not intended also to contribute to the solidarity of the brotherhood. It does so in at least three ways. First, awareness by members of the distinctiveness of their (founder's) teaching reinforces their sense of a common identity not shared with outsiders. Second, the practice of prohibiting divorce contributes (ideally) to the stability of the group by fostering the integrity and continuity of the marital relationships of its members.[267] Third, at the symbolic level, and in

---

[264] See Thiering, 'Asceticism', 429–30.

[265] See Keck, 'Ethics', 43: 'By Matthew's decade ... both the Jewish and the Christian community were defining themselves over against each other. From the Christian side, this meant appealing to Jesus as the warrant for its own ethos.'

[266] See Brooks, *Community*, 109: 'It may be a case of adopting language to describe celibacy that is calculated to be an affront to Jewish sensibilities, thereby setting the Christian adherent apart from Jewish views.'

[267] See Malina, *World*, 110 for an excellent analysis of the 'defensive marriage strategy' adopted by the Jews of the post-exilic period. Refering to Mal. 2.16 ('For I hate divorce, says the Lord the God of Israel ...'), Malina says: 'In the

line with the work of Mary Douglas on 'natural symbols', the integrity of the group is expressed and confirmed in the integrity of its members' marital ties, the 'one flesh' of the marriage bond embodying in microcosm the unity of the group as a whole.[268] Seen from this perspective of community maintenance and symbolic representation, it may be the case that the 'eunuch saying' is insider language (vv. 11, 12d), intended, by virtue of its paradoxical quality, to reinforce group members' sense of belonging to a different order of things. The (symbolically) marginal location of the eunuch for the sake of the kingdom of heaven expresses the marginal location of Matthew's group in relation to contemporary Judaism.[269] But it is this very marginality – confirmed again and again, no doubt, by experiences of hostility from kinsfolk and ostracism from 'their' synagogues – which reinforces the group's sense of being at the centre of God's new order, of being the vanguard of the true Israel.

7 Discipleship and family ties (Matt. 19.27–30 par. Mark 10.28–31)

The next piece of relevant material comes soon after 19.1–12, in the sayings of Jesus which follow Peter's affirmation, 'Lo, we have left everything and followed you' (19.27ff.). As pointed out above, Matthew follows Mark closely in the series of sayings related to household ethics (i.e. Matt. 19.1–30 par. Mark 10.1–31) which comes to an end at this point. Like Mark, Matthew understands this material as teaching about the meaning of the passion of the Son of Man for the life of the disciple (cf. Matt. 17.22–3 par. Mark 9.30–2) in relation, specifically, to marriage rules, attitudes to children, and attitudes to property and household ties. Having analysed the section on marriage rules, we turn here to the section on property and household ties. It is unnecessary to repeat the form-critical

circumstances addressed by Malachi, what God hates is the divorce of Jew and Jew; there is silence about the divorce of Jew and non-Jew.'
[268] Douglas, *Symbols*, noting her summary statement on p. 93: 'The social body constrains the way the physical body is perceived. The physical experience of the body, always modified by the social categories through which it is known, sustains a particular view of society. There is a continual exchange of meanings between the two kinds of bodily experience so that each reinforces the categories of the other.'
[269] See Stanton, 'Judaism', 282, where the Matthean community is characterized as a 'beleaguered sect' in relation to the wider Jewish and Gentile world.

comments made on this material in the chapter on Mark, so we begin with a discussion of Matthean redaction of Mark.

Matthew follows Mark in setting the exchange between Jesus and Peter (and the disciples) prior to the final passion prediction on the journey to Jerusalem (cf. Matt. 20.17–19 par. Mark 10.32–4) and as the climax of the episode of the rich young man (Matt. 19.16–30 par. Mark 10.17–31). The principal Matthean modifications of Mark are as follows.

Matthew redacts the story of the rich young man in a consistently 'ethicizing' direction. Thus, the question the man asks Jesus is about the 'good thing' he must do – τί ἀγαθὸν ποιήσω – to have eternal life (19.16b; diff. Mark 10.17b). Jesus' counter-question is also περὶ τοῦ ἀγαθοῦ (19.17a); and, in a clear expansion of Mark 10.19a, the Jesus of Matthew says, 'If you would enter life, keep the commandments (τήρει τὰς ἐντολάς)' (19.17b; diff. Mark 10.19a).[270] Furthermore, in order to cast Jesus in the role of teacher of the commandments, the interlocutor asks, 'Which [commandments]?'; and in Matthew's version of Jesus' reply, which uses the imperatival future with οὐ, the list of commandments is brought closer to the verbal form of the Hebrew and Septuagintal texts of the decalogue (Exod. 20.13–16: Deut. 5.17–20).[271] The characteristic Matthean emphasis on the love commandment then comes to the fore when this commandment is included as the climax of the list (19.9b, Matthew only; cf. 5.43–7; 22.34–40).

Subsequently, to highlight further the stress on total commitment through the doing of the commandments, Matthew depicts Jesus' interlocutor as a νεανίσκος (19.20a; cf. Mark 10.20b – ἐκ νεότητός μου), a 'young man' to whom Jesus shows the need to become mature and complete in his devotion to God: hence, εἰ θέλεις τέλειος εἶναι (19.21a, Matthew only; cf. 5.48).[272] The severity of the demand is maximized by Matthew's omission of the Marcan statement that Jesus looked upon the man and 'loved him' (Mark 10.21a). The teaching of the commandments by Jesus is what is important for Matthew: so potential distractions are removed. This is seen again in the teaching which follows, where Matthew abbre-

---

[270] For the idea of 'entering into life' in Matthew, see 7.14; 18.8b, 9b; 25.46.

[271] See Gundry, *Matthew*, 386.

[272] No 'double ethic' is implied by the term τέλειος. Rather, Jesus is speaking of what is required of all disciples. See further, Guelich, *Sermon*, 234–6; Schmidt, *Hostility*, 132.

viates Mark in order to have Jesus repeat singlemindedly his teaching on the difficulty for the rich to enter the kingdom: ἀμὴν λέγω
ὑμῖν ... πάλιν δὲ λέγω ὑμῖν ... (19.23–4; diff. Mark 10.23–25).
Finally, whereas in Mark, the disciples say πρὸς ἑαυτούς, 'Who
then can be saved?' (Mark 10.26), in Matthew, their question is not
kept to themselves: the πρὸς ἑαυτούς is omitted, and the question
becomes a question of disciples under tutelage to their teacher, Jesus
(19.25), who replies with a succinct statement (in typical Matthean
parallelism) about the sovereignty of God (19.26; diff. Mark 10.27).
According to the Matthean redaction, then, Jesus is the authoritative teacher of the severe will of God who demands of all disciples
detachment from possessions as a condition of entry into the
kingdom (6.2–4, 19–21, 24, 25–33, etc.).

This brings us to Matt. 19.27–30 par. Mark 10.28–31. Here, there
are a number of significant redactional modifications. First, Peter is
cast more clearly as a representative of the disciples, seeking more
teaching from Jesus. Thus, his question, τί ἄρα ἔσται ἡμῖν; (19.27c,
Matthew only), parallels the disciples' earlier question in 19.25b, τίς
ἄρα δύναται σωθῆναι;[273] His question is about the reward due to
the disciples for having left everything (unlike the νεανίσκος) and
followed Jesus, an understandable question in view of the promise
of Jesus earlier to the young man that, if he sells his possessions and
gives to the poor, he will have 'treasure in heaven' (19.21). Second,
Jesus' reply to Peter is clearly teaching for the disciples, for Matthew
adds both αὐτοῖς and ὑμεῖς οἱ ἀκολουθήσαντές μοι (19.28a, b;
diff. Mark 10.29a). Third, Matthew expands significantly Jesus'
reply to Peter. He does this in two ways. On the one hand, he makes
Jesus' reply double-barrelled, dealing first with the reward of the
twelve, via the inclusion of Q tradition (Matt. 19.28 par. Luke
22.28–30), and then with the reward of 'everyone' who has left
household ties for his sake (19.29–30). On the other hand, to take
the teaching on reward further, and to illustrate the idea that God
does not reward in a way commensurate with ordinary human
custom and expectation – an idea reiterated in 19.30 and 20.16 –
Matthew adds the Parable of the Labourers in the Vineyard
(20.1–16, Matthew only).

But more needs to be said on this much-expanded reply of Jesus
on the theme of reward. Drawing upon Q tradition, Matthew has

---

[273] See the previous, formally similar question of the disciples, in 18.1b: τίς ἄρα
μείζων ἐστὶν ἐν τῇ βασιλείᾳ τῶν οὐρανῶν;

Jesus promise his disciples that, 'in the new world, when the Son of man shall sit on his glorious throne, you who have followed me will also sit on twelve thrones, judging the twelve tribes of Israel' (19.28 par. Luke 22.30b). Several comments are pertinent. i. The identification of the addressees as ὑμεῖς οἱ ἀκολουθήσαντές μοι is probably an editorial way of smoothing over the dislocation caused by introducing non-Marcan tradition. The phrase serves to link the Q material with Peter's statement, ἠκολουθήσαμέν σοι, in 19.27.[274] The ἀκολουθεῖν terminology is a Matthean preference associated with the idea of discipleship, as we have seen on numerous occasions already. ii. The temporal phrase, ἐν τῇ παλιγγενεσίᾳ (Matthew only), puts the reward firmly into the future (lit. 'in the regeneration').[275] The eschatological setting of the reward, both of the twelve thrones and of the hundredfold households, contrasts somewhat with Mark, which speaks of reward νῦν ἐν τῷ καιρῷ τούτῳ (Mark 10.30a, omitted by Matthew). Presumably, Matthew does not wish to encourage the covetousness which had been the downfall of the rich man, so all reward is promised for the future (5.3–12; 6.1–4, 5–6, 19–21, etc.).[276] iii. The future is cast in terms of traditional Jewish apocalyptic so beloved of this evangelist.[277] It is, of course, not coincidental that judgment by the (Danielic) Son of Man sitting on his glorious throne is precisely the scenario in the Parable of the Sheep and the Goats (at 25.31; cf. Dan. 7.9–27). In the latter, κληρονομεῖν occurs also (25.34; cf. 19.29b, diff. Mark 10.30b), and ζωὴ αἰώνιος is promised, as here (25.46; cf. 19.29b par. Mark 10.30b).[278] iv. Because Luke's version of the tradition is so different and assimilation to the Last Supper setting of Luke 22.28–30 is highly likely, the history of the tradition is difficult to establish.[279] Nevertheless, it is clear that Matthew has inserted the saying into the teaching on rewards, and has modified it to fit both that discussion and his overall apocalyptic eschatology. Most importantly, the twelve disciples are distinguished as the future rulers of the tribes of Israel. As

---

[274] See Lindars, *Son of Man*, 125.

[275] On παλιγγενεσία, which occurs only here in the gospels, and at Titus 3.5 (referring to baptism), see Bauer–Arndt–Gingrich, *Lexicon, ad loc.*; and Beare, *Matthew*, 398.

[276] So too, Schmidt, *Hostility*, 133.

[277] See Stanton, 'Judaism', 278–81. On the idea of the righteous sitting on thrones, see Rev. 3.21; 1 Enoch 108.12; etc., cited in Tödt, *Son of Man*, 62.

[278] See Lindars, *Son of Man*, 125.

[279] See further, Bultmann, *Tradition*, 158–9; Tödt, *Son of Man*, 62–4; Lindars, *Son of Man*, 124–6.

a reward for leaving behind mundane personal and material ties to follow Jesus, they are promised a share in the sovereignty of the coming Son of Man. So whereas Mark has Jesus give only a general promise (οὐδείς ἐστιν ὃς ἀφῆκεν . . ., Mark 10.29), Matthew's Jesus promises the twelve specifically future sovereignty over a renewed Israel.[280]

The special reward promised to the twelve is followed by the promise to true disciples generally of a manifold recompense of the household and family ties they have left behind or given up for the sake of Jesus' name (19.29). Matthew differs from Mark here in three main ways. First, as already noted, both the manifold recompense and the reward of 'eternal life' are promised for the future, in the kingdom of heaven (5.5; 6.33). Second, Matthew omits the repetition of the household list (in Mark 10.30a), presumably for stylistic reasons, but perhaps also because he wishes to discourage possibly materialistic considerations in the motivation of his readers. This would be quite consistent with the standard set in the teaching of the Sermon on the Mount, at 6.19–21, for example. Third, so strong is his concern that eschatological reward should not become a preoccupation of the disciple, that he not only follows Mark in appending the free-floating logion, 'many that are first will be last, and the last first' (19.30 par. Mark 10.31): he also adds the parable of 20.1–16, which culminates, likewise, with the same logion of reversal (at 20.16).

The implications of these redaction-critical observations on 19.16–30 may be summed up thus. Overall, the material presupposes that leaving everything – including possessions and, as a special instance of this, household and family ties – for the sake of the name of Jesus is the sacrifice demanded of the disciple who would be τέλειος, and that becoming τέλειος is demanded of every disciple (5.48), since that is what brings the reward of eternal life (19.29b). This is none other than the ethic of the 'narrow gate' and the 'hard way' of the Sermon on the Mount (7.13–14), where Jesus likewise teaches his disciples (and the crowds from which disciples come) 'the way which leads to life' (7.14). But this is not a 'go-it-alone' ethic.

---

[280] See Gundry, *Matthew*, 393: 'In Daniel the saints who receive dominion are Israel, their subjects the Gentiles. Jesus promises dominion to the twelve and makes Israel their subjects. Matthew's use of "regeneration" agrees with Jesus' promise by making the governing of Israel harmonize with Israel's renewal in a messianic kingdom on earth. Thus, Matthew does not regard God's rejection of Israel (21:43) as permanent.'

Theologically, it is grounded in Jesus' teaching of the sovereignty of the fatherly God, with whom 'all things are possible' (19.26b). Christologically, it is grounded in the sacrificial example (4.1–11) and continuing presence of Jesus the Son of God, whom the disciple 'follows'. Ecclesiologically, it is grounded in the immediately preceding teaching of Christian brotherliness (17.22–18.35), as well as in the promise of belonging to the many households of the true family of Jesus as the reward for leaving one's own household behind (19.29).

If the sacrifice of possessions and household ties is one major focus of this material, the other, complementary focus is the theme of reward, which is the subject with which the teaching ends. To the young man, Jesus promises 'treasure in heaven' (19.21); to the twelve, he promises the twelve thrones (19.28); and to all disciples, the reward of manifold households, and eternal life (19.29), with the important proviso that God rewards his servants in surprising and incalculable ways (19.30–20.16). This interest in a doctrine of reward (and punishment) is quite characteristic of Matthew:[281] witness the parables which come in sequence at the end of the final, 'eschatological discourse', in 24.45–25.46. We may interpret it fairly, not just as a standard element of the apocalyptic world-view generally,[282] but also as Matthew's way of expressing a teleology of sacrifice.[283] Radical renunciation for Jesus' sake is neither arbitrary nor meaningless: it is an integral part of 'following' Jesus prior to the coming in glory of the Son of Man to judge the nations (25.31–46).

How is our appreciation of the meaning of this episode sharpened by approaching it as a text in its own right, independent of its historical–literary indebtedness to Mark and without reference solely to the (putative) intention of its author? Beginning with narrative sequence, we need not repeat the observations made above with respect to 19.1–10, to do with the common thematic thread of discipleship and household-related matters which unites the teach-

---

[281] See further, Mohrlang, *Matthew*, ch. 2 (on 'Reward and Punishment'), esp. pp. 48–57.

[282] See Russell, *Method*, 379–85.

[283] See Keck, 'Ethics', 48: 'In other words, Matthew's ethics is teleological, not in the sense of human needs and goals but of the telos, the goal and end of God's work – restoration of creation'; also, Schmidt, *Hostility*, 122, who speaks of Matthew's retention of the 'teleological devaluation' of wealth found in Mark; and Mohrlang, *Matthew*, 71.

ing in 19.1–30, and the way this follows easily from the discourse on
Christian brotherhood in 17.22–18.35. Here we may add that, just as
the teaching on the imperative of becoming 'like children', in 18.1–4,
gives rise immediately to 'case studies' which show what this
involves (18.5–9, 10–14, 15–20, 21–35),[284] so too, the teaching that
the kingdom of heaven belongs to 'such [children]', in 19.13–15,
prepares the way for the story of the νεανίσκος, who shows by his
refusal to renounce his possessions – and with superb irony – that he
is too immature to become a child of the kingdom. So he, who is to
all appearances one who is 'first', becomes 'last' and receives no
reward, whereas the disciples who have renounced everything, so
making themselves 'last', are the ones who will be made 'first' and
receive an eschatological reward. Once again, close attention to the
sequence and structure of the text provides important clues to its
meaning. It is by no means coincidental that the closing parable,
framed as it is by the proverbial statement (at 19.30 and 20.16),[285] is
a parable about the payment given by a householder (οἰκοδεσπότης) (20.1, 11). The theme of discipleship as belonging to a
'household' can be said to run right through from the fourth
discourse. The parable is a fitting reminder that the οἰκοδεσπότης is
like none other (10.25b; 13.27; 21.33).[286]

The structure of the episode deserves comment. Broadly, it is in
two equal parts: the exchange between the young man and Jesus
(19.16–22), and the exchange between Jesus and the disciples/Peter
(19.23–30). In this, it is strikingly similar to the two-part structure of
the episode in 19.1–12: an exchange between Jesus and the Pharisees
(vv. 3–9), followed by further teaching addressed to the disciples
(vv. 10–12). The effect of this structure is to allow the first part to
serve as a foil for the second; and, conversely, to allow the second
part to function as authoritative commentary upon, and elaboration
of, the issues raised in the first. Significant, in the latter respect, is
the fact that, whereas in 19.10 it is the disciples who initiate the
further teaching, in 19.23–4 it is Jesus who takes the initiative, so
important is the issue of possessions and household ties to true
discipleship.

The characterization plays an important role also. In Matthew,
the inquirer is depicted as a 'young man', as we have seen (19.20,
22). He comes to Jesus the teacher (v. 16b) and, with all the enthusi-

---

[284] See further, Thompson, *Advice*.   [285] See Bauer, *Structure*, 18.
[286] On Jesus as οἰκοδεσπότης in Matthew, see also Crosby, *House*, 66–7.

asm, naïvety and unselfconsciousness of youth, asks, first, about the 'good thing' he must do to have eternal life, and subsequently, about what yet remains to be done since he has kept the commandments already. He is, however, not ready for the demands of the greater righteousness laid upon him by Jesus (v. 21). The narrator's comment which concludes this exchange gives the reader explicitly the implied author's point of view: 'When the young man heard this he went away sorrowful; for he had great possessions' (v. 22). Although he claimed to have kept the commandments (v. 20), his inability to sell his possessions and give to the poor reveals the superficiality of his observance, especially of the last-mentioned command, to 'love your neighbour as yourself' (v. 19b). He is too young, too immature in the life of faith, to become a child, a 'little one'.

The disciples, once more, are depicted as privileged recipients of the teaching of Jesus. Their role is summed up in v. 23a: Ὁ δὲ Ἰησοῦς εἶπεν τοῖς μαθηταῖς αὐτοῦ ... (vv. 26a, 28a). In one sense, nothing distinguishes them from the young man. They ask questions, as he does; and they share his presupposition that wealth is no hindrance to membership of the kingdom of heaven (v. 25). The crucial difference is that, unlike the young man, they have 'left everything' and followed Jesus: and that is what matters. Peter is the only disciple to be singled out by name – as earlier, in 17.24, 25, and 18.21, for example. As in those cases, so here also, he is a representative of the disciples and their spokesman.[287] The statement placed on his lips in v. 27b is especially appropriate, because he is one of the four whose leaving all and following is narrated at the outset (4.18–22).

But the centre-stage of Matthew's narrative drama is kept, yet again, for Jesus. He is the διδάσκαλος (v. 16b) who is not reticent to teach the way to life. It is his words, his replies, which dominate the two sets of exchanges; and only he begins with an ἀμὴν λέγω ὑμῖν (vv. 23b, 28a). He, it is implied, is the one who is 'good' (v. 17b; cf. 20.15b).[288] He has the prescience to recognize precisely what is preventing the young man from becoming 'perfect'. And in the exchange with the disciples and Peter, Jesus speaks authoritatively the will of God in proverb (for example v. 24) and prophecy (vv. 28ff.).

Finally, a comment on the rhetoric of the passage. It consists

---

[287] So too, Brown, *Peter*, 77–8.   [288] See Gundry, *Matthew*, 385.

primarily of a question-and-answer pattern. Noticeable is the fact that the young man's mode of speech is almost entirely the inter-rogative (at vv. 16, 18a, 20b): likewise, that of the disciples and Peter (vv. 25b, 27c). Jesus, by contrast, asks but one question, in v. 17 (which he immediately answers himself! – showing that the question was rhetorical only), and otherwise speaks in the indicative and the imperative, stating with authority what is or will be the case and how to live in consequence. The narrator intrudes only once: at the crux in the story constituted by Jesus' summons to the young man, 'If you would be perfect, go, sell what you possess and give to the poor, ... and come, follow me' (v. 21). Here, he reliably informs the implied reader of the young man's response and its motivation (v. 22), information which paves the way for the subsequent teaching of Jesus to the disciples in vv. 23–30. Otherwise, the story is allowed to speak for itself. Above all, Jesus is allowed to speak for himself.

One other point about the rhetoric of the passage deserves mention: namely the reminiscence of the story of the call of the disciples, at v. 27 (4.18–22; 9.9). Here, Peter testifies in words used in the narrative of the call by the narrator himself: ἰδοὺ ἡμεῖς **ἀφή-καμεν** πάντα καὶ **ἠκολουθήσαμέν** σοι (4.20, 22 – οἱ δὲ εὐθέως **ἀφέντες** τὰ δίκτυα **ἠκολούθησαν** αὐτῷ ... οἱ δὲ εὐθέως **ἀφέντες** τὸ πλοῖον καὶ τὸν πατέρα αὐτῶν **ἠκολούθησαν** αὐτῷ). This implies that Peter is a reliable witness, for he confirms what the narrator has said already. It indicates also that what Peter bears witness to is impor-tant: the willingness to leave household and family ties is of the essence of discipleship.

From literary-critical considerations we turn to sociological analysis of the material, in order to take further what was said above in this respect about the teaching on marriage and divorce (in 19.1–12). There we saw in particular that the stringency of the marriage rules in Matthew may have been intended to contribute to the ordering of an alternative (Christian) social world, not only by distinguishing the group which adhered to this teaching from other groups in contemporary Judaism and beyond, but also by reinforcing commit-ment and familial solidarity within the group itself.

The material on the renunciation of possessions and household ties and the reward which comes to those willing to renounce them, in 19.16–30, points in the same direction. In particular, there is the strong emphasis on stringent demand. Keeping the commandments is commendable, but something more is required. The true disciple must become τέλειος. For Matthew, this means the practice of a wholehearted commitment to the will of God which acknowledges no other lordship, especially not that of mammon: 'No one can serve two masters; for either he will hate the one and love the other, or he will be devoted to the one and despise the other. You cannot serve God and mammon' (6.24; cf. 4.8–10).[289] The story of Jesus and the rich young man epitomizes this teaching; and, since it comes in the context of Jesus' threefold passion prediction and of the journey towards the events of the passion in Jerusalem (16.21ff.), it is an integral part of Matthew's understanding of what it means to follow Jesus.

Sociologically speaking, this recurring demand for total commitment is important on two fronts. In terms of community formation, it makes the cost of membership sufficiently high to provoke decision for or against. The decision to join will not be made lightly ('he went away sorrowful': v. 22a), but once made will probably be kept: for the sacrifice and renunciation are likely to generate loyalty and perseverance (v. 27b). Put differently, Matthew's is not a 'lowest common denominator' approach to membership of the people of God. It is not a matter, in antinomian fashion, of 'cheap grace' whereby anyone is welcome on any terms. On the contrary, precisely because of the possible threat of antinomian tendencies in earliest (including Pauline) Christianity (7.15–20, 21–3; 24.10–12),[290] and of the likely obloquy from within formative Judaism on that score, the emphasis in Matthew is on the practice of a quality of obedience to the divine will unparalleled elsewhere (5.20).

In terms of community maintenance, the polarized, either/or form of the demand symbolizes the polarization between Matthew's group and those outside. 'God' and 'mammon' are theological symbols for two opposed communities, two sets of allegiances, two ways of life: and it is impossible to belong with integrity to both. Those who attempt to do so are likely to become targets of social censure by means of the language of vilification: 'Woe to you, scribes and Pharisees, hypocrites (ὑποκριταί)!' (23.13, 15, 23, 25,

---

[289] See further, Gerhardsson, *Ethos*, 38–48.

[290] See Schweizer, 'Observance', 218: 'Matthew is struggling with the same problem as Paul and Luke, and in some sense also John. It is the enthusiastic life of a faith which is living by the experience of the risen and exalted Lord and the present activity of the Holy Spirit, but, at the same time, threatens to become more and more remote from the teaching of the earthly Jesus and the standard of his conduct.'

27, 29; see also 15.7; 22.18).[291] More constructively, the challenge to renounce one's possessions and give to the poor signifies the challenge to belong to a different order of things: what the Jesus of Matthew calls 'the kingdom of heaven'. The ability to act in this way then functions as a concrete, material measure of spiritual commitment and social adherence. In this way, renunciation of possessions and household ties is of a piece with other teaching in Matthew which advocates areas of life where a high level of self-control, and even asceticism, is expected – cases in point including verbal and emotional control (5.21–26, 33–7), sexual control (5.27–30), a detachment from wealth which issues in almsgiving (5.42; 6.2–4, 19–21), a piety practised in private, not just in public (6.1ff.), fasting (6.16–18), the avoidance of τὰ σκάνδαλα for the sake of 'the little ones' (18.5–9), and a willingness (in the realm of marriage rules) to become a 'eunuch for the sake of the kingdom of heaven' (19.12). Each of these is a discrete aspect of life where the sacrifice and self-control of the individual member is able to manifest itself in a way which both validates that member's spiritual commitment and reinforces the convictions, identity and solidarity of the group as a whole.[292]

The material in 19.16–30 sets forth, in essence, Matthew's doctrine of the 'two ways'. The rich young man is prevented by his attachment to mammon from becoming a follower: Peter, on behalf of the disciples, can testify to having left everything and followed Jesus. The one receives no reward, only his own sorrow: the twelve receive the eschatological promise of positions of authority over the tribes of Israel, while disciples in general are promised households one hundredfold in compensation for those they have given up. So renunciation of possessions and household ties is not presented as an end in itself, as if Matthew's is an anti-social ethic. Rather, it is

---

[291] See Freyne, 'Vilifying', esp. pp. 132–40, where language used to discredit opponents is shown also to function as a warning to members of one's own community. The issue of 'hypocrisy' is discussed specifically on pp. 133–4.

[292] See Fraade, 'Ascetical Aspects', 276, for the following astute comment: 'Late biblical and postbiblical Judaisms, by increasing the ethical, pietistic and legal expectations placed on the individual, had to find ways of dealing with the psychic and social pressures thereby created. Ideals of perfection are one thing; dealing with an individual's and a religious society's continuing failure to realize them is another. One of the ways in which asceticism deals with this problem is by defining discrete areas of self-control in which the individual's (and society's) will can be exercised successfully in fulfilment of transcendent purposes.' Fraade does not discuss the case of early Christianity, but in my view, the evidence of Matthew fits well with this generalization.

part of the idiom of wholehearted commitment to the kingdom of heaven, and the means of integration into a different kind of society, whose κύριος and οἰκοδεσπότης is Jesus (cf. 10.24–5). The sociological implications of 19.16–30 are therefore quite of a piece with the teaching on the practice of humble brotherhood in chapter 18, on marriage and divorce in 19.1–12; and on the reception of children in 19.13–15. For what Matthew has in mind is the reordering of all social relations – pre-eminent among which are the material and household relations between men, women and children[293] – according to the will of God as revealed to Israel by Jesus.

8 Conclusion

The detailed analysis of the main texts from Matthew relevant to the theme of discipleship and family ties is now complete.[294] It is appropriate, therefore, to draw together the threads of the analysis,

---

[293] On the kinship basis of economic relations in ancient Mediterranean society, see Malina, 'Wealth', *passim*.

[294] Several other texts could have been included in the analysis, but have been omitted, primarily because of the relatively tangential nature of the material for the purposes of this investigation. I cite two instances. The first is the controversy story over the resurrection (Matt. 22.23–33 par. Mark 12.18–27), where Jesus says to his Sadducean interrogators, 'For in the resurrection, they neither marry nor are given in marriage, but are like angels in heaven' (22.30). There is no evidence that this saying is of more interest to Matthew than it is to Mark, or that it has any effect on his understanding of marital ties. On the latter score, in fact, the evidence is quite to the contrary (5.31–2; 19.1–12). The point at issue with the Sadducees is resurrection belief itself, not the subordination of marital and family ties; and what Jesus says has to do with the eschatological future: ἐν τῇ ἀναστάσει.

The second text is 23.8–10 (Matthew only). Here, at the beginning of the fifth major discourse of Matthew 23–5, Jesus instructs the crowds and the disciples about status and honorific titles in the community of the true Israel: 'But you are not to be called rabbi, for you have one teacher, and you are all brethren. And call no man your father on earth, for you have one Father, who is in heaven.' In context, this teaching has nothing to do with ties of natural kinship, and can hardly be taken as an attack on patriarchy *per se* (*contra* Fiorenza, 'Father', 317). Rather, it is part of an extended impeachment of the scribes and Pharisees in their claim to be the authoritative teachers of the law, in the course of which christological and ecclesiological implications for the community which acknowledges only Christ as διδάσκαλος and καθηγητής, and only God as πατήρ, are made explicit. In other words, it is not household authority which is at issue, but *teaching* authority. Nevertheless, in so far as the church is like a household, it is significant that its authority relations are defined in more 'egalitarian' kinship terms: those of a brotherhood (23.8b). This is consistent with what we have seen elsewhere in Matthew (4.18–22; 5.22–4, 47; 12.48–50; 18.15, 21, 35; 25.40; 28.10). For a helpful analysis, see Garland, *Intention*, esp. pp. 34–63.

and to compare the findings for Matthew with those for Mark from the previous chapter. At the risk of oversimplifying, the results of the analysis may be summarized in the following points.

1. As in our reading of Mark, the attempt to interpret the pertinent Matthean texts in a more holistic way has shown itself to be not at all impossible or incongruous. On the contrary, by adopting a certain pluralism of approach, using methods of a literary-historical kind, a literary-critical kind, and a sociological kind, we have been able to understand the text of Matthew at a number of different levels. We have seen it as the heir to a (biblical and gospel) literary tradition which the evangelist has taken over and modified for his own kerygmatic and pastoral purposes; as a literary work in its own right which invites the reader to enter its narrative world and engage in the creative task of reading with understanding; and as the product of a particular social world, written both out of and to an audience of followers of Jesus in the time of formative Judaism and of the parting of the ways between 'Rebecca's children'.[295] I would claim, therefore, that this methodological pluralism is worth while and that it needs to be developed further, principally because it makes less likely an interpretative reductionism of one kind or another. The meaning of the text is less likely to be understood solely in terms of the intention of the author. Again, the meaning of the text in its final form is less likely to be seen just as a matter of reconstructing the prehistory of the text. Finally, the significance of a *leitmotif* such as discipleship and family ties is less likely to be interpreted solely in terms of the potentially disembodied notion of 'important ideas'.

2. The Gospel of Matthew shows no diminution of interest, by comparison with Mark, in the implications for household and family ties of discipleship of Jesus. On the contrary, not only does Matthew take over and modify all the relevant Marcan material, but he also includes non-Marcan tradition pertinent to the subject. Thus, not only do we find re-presentations in Matthew of the Marcan story of the call of the fishermen and of Levi (who becomes the apostle, Matthew), but we have also the radical summons to follow issued to the scribe and to the 'other disciple', taken over from Q (in 8.18–22). Not only does Matthew take over the biographical material about Jesus' mother and brothers and about

---

[295] I am using here the title of Alan Segal's recent book of that name, published in 1986. See Segal, *Children*.

Jesus' rejection in Nazareth, but he also includes, along with the material from Mark 13 warning of kinship enmity in the Last Days, sayings from Q which speak in hyperbolic fashion of the division within families which is precipitated by Jesus' coming and by following him (in 10.34–6, 37–8). Yet again, not only does Matthew take over the 'household code' from Mark 10.1–31 with Peter's testimony to having left everything for Jesus' sake, but he also appends to the teaching on divorce the saying about the 'eunuchs' (in 19.10–12). In addition, and as a major development of the kinship motif, only the beginnings of which are to be found in Mark, there is in Matthew a powerful thrust of the kinship idea in the direction of ecclesiology, via the notion of followers of Jesus as a brotherhood.

3. As in Mark, normally legitimate ties of household and kinship are strongly relativized by the demands of discipleship of Jesus. Only marital ties are left unscrutinized in this regard. This is due, no doubt, to the stringent teaching of Jesus forbidding divorce, in 19.3–9. Otherwise, Matthew places very heavy weight on the priority to be accorded following Jesus in response to the breaking in of the kingdom of heaven, a priority which is to take absolute precedence. Indeed, so high is the precedence given to following Jesus that only so fundamental an issue as family, household and occupational ties is adequate to make the point. This is why it recurs again and again in Matthew in the context of stories and sayings to do with the call to discipleship and the cost of discipleship. No other subject functions in relation to discipleship in quite this way.[296] But this is not to say that the thrust of Matthew's Gospel is anti-family. That would make nonsense of the genealogies and the birth and infancy narratives at the beginning of the gospel, with Matthew's high regard for Joseph and Mary, as well as of the prohibition of divorce (5.31–2; 19.3–9) and the approval of the fifth commandment (15.1–9; 19.19a) in the teaching of Jesus. It would also make inexplicable the use of the terminology of kinship to describe both Jesus' relationship with God as Son to Father and Jesus' relation-

---

[296] A useful analogy, however, is Matthew's attitude to wealth, of which the story of the rich young man (in 19.16–22) is a prime example. Schmidt's useful study of this theme in Matthew (*Hostility*, 121–34) comes to similar conclusions to the present study on family ties. But given the household basis of economic relations in antiquity, this similarity is precisely what we would expect. It is not coincidental that the young man's refusal to sell his possessions is contrasted in the story with Peter's testimony to having left all (including house, family and fields) for Jesus' sake (see 19.27–9).

ship with his followers as together belonging to the family of those who do the will of God. Rather, the thrust of the gospel is better described as being suprafamilial. The kingdom of heaven, the fatherhood of God and belonging to the 'spiritual' family over which Jesus is the 'lord' and 'householder' are what is of supreme importance: and every earthly and mundane tie is subordinate to that new, eschatological reality.

4. On this reading, therefore, Matthew is in substantial accord with his predecessor Mark on the implications of discipleship for family ties. Matthew shares with Mark the same fundamental theological, christological and eschatological beliefs on the basis of which mundane social obligations and quotidian social and economic values appear no longer in the same light. Instead, following Jesus involves participation in mission to all nations to proclaim the in-breaking of the kingdom of heaven and the soon-coming of the Son of Man. It involves also participation in the new covenant community inaugurated by Jesus. On both scores, family and household ties are relativized strongly. Likewise, and not surprisingly, resistance and hostility from members' own hometown and kinship groups is to be expected. Like Mark, Matthew's Gospel bears clear marks of the effects of church members' experiences of persecution and mortal enmity from their own families. Like Mark, Matthew uses stories about Jesus, such as the rejection in his *patris*, and vivid sayings of Jesus about, for instance, the 'sword' which will divide one family member from another, in order to legitimate the subordination of household ties and to provide a theodicy for suffering as a result of kinship-sponsored persecution. Matthew's fundamental unanimity with Mark on this score is a matter, not just of his 'conservatism' as a preserver and interpreter of the Jesus-tradition (although that may be a partial explanation): it is a matter also of basic lines of continuity between the ethos and lifestyle of their respective audiences, and of basic similarities in the kinds of resistance and persecution they encountered. In other words, it is likely that Matthew preserved and augmented the traditions which encourage the relativization of family ties because the Matthean community (like the Marcan) nurtured a radical social ethos oriented on itinerant missionary activity in accordance with the teaching and examples of Jesus and the first disciples, and because the Matthean community was beleaguered, ostracized and persecuted.

5. But if there are basic similarities, there are subtle differences as well. First, there is in Matthew a more explicit communal – in

doctrinal terms, ecclesiological – dimension to the material on family ties. The idea of Jesus' followers as his true family is augmented by the idea that the followers are related to Jesus and to one another as 'brothers', an idea intended to reinforce an ethic of humility and mutual acceptance and to overcome serious centrifugal tendencies of the kind hinted at in 7.15–23 and 24.10–12.

Second, there is a more clear-sighted focus on missionary activity in this time of eschatological crisis (cf. 9.35–11.1; 28.18–20), with consequently greater attention given to both the cost of such activity in respect of family and occupational ties and the reward stored up for those willing to pay the cost. The fact that no fewer than three of the sayings we examined above come in the instructions on mission, in 9.35–11.1, bears this out.

Third, the sense of threat from the evangelist's compatriots in Judaism, and especially from the scribes and Pharisees, is greater than in Mark. This corresponds with the greater sense of a growing separation between church and synagogue in Matthew's Gospel. It is not at all surprising that the pain and hostility of this separation are reflected directly in Matthew's 'hard sayings' about leaving the dead to bury their dead, and the like. Nor is it surprising that, in their efforts at group self-definition over against comparable groups in formative Judaism after 70, the issue of marriage rules should appear on the agenda, or that Matthew should encourage the more rigorous line represented so provocatively by the saying about 'eunuchs'.

The mention of communal self-definition provides the fourth and final difference: namely, that Matthew's Gospel is more self-conscious and deliberate in this area, more 'scribal' perhaps, in its evident concern to present, not just Jesus as the new source of authority (as in Mark), but also the content of Jesus' new authoritative teaching, especially in relation to the torah. The results of this are that Matthew includes more sayings tradition pertinent to issues of family ties (and to much else), and that the relativization of family ties arises out of the reinterpretation of life according to the torah in terms of the 'messianic biography'[297] of Jesus the Son of God which Matthew sets forth in such a 'scholarly' way. We have, then, not a new torah, but a person to be followed and obeyed, allegiance to whom transcends every prior allegiance, even one's own blood ties.

[297] So, Meeks, *Moral World*, 136–43.

5

CONCLUSION

It is appropriate now to summarize briefly the findings of the preceding chapters and to draw together the threads of the study as a whole. In general, it may fairly be claimed that the theme of the subordination of family and household ties for the sake of discipleship of Jesus has not been given sufficient attention in studies of Christian origins and of the gospels. The present study of the relevant sayings and stories from the Gospels of Mark and Matthew has attempted to begin to fill that gap.

Having in the Introduction surveyed evidence from the first two centuries of the Common Era which illustrates an awareness, on the part of both outsiders and insiders, of the intrafamilial tensions generated by conversion to Christ, we saw in Chapter 2 that such tensions were by no means unprecedented in both the religious traditions of Judaism and in the philosophical traditions of the Greco-Roman world. The Jewish sources – in particular, Philo, Josephus, and the Qumran documents – show repeatedly that allegiance to God and obedience to the will and call of God transcend allegiances of a more mundane kind, including and especially ties of natural kinship. This is not only a basic presupposition of Jewish monotheistic piety, reinforced by the absolute prohibition of idolatry; it finds expression also in what Philo says about proselytes to Judaism, in the portrayals by both Philo and Josephus of heroes of the past like Abraham, Moses, Phineas and Mattathias, and in the renunciation of marriage and household ties practised by the Therapeutae and the Qumran Covenanters. On the Greco-Roman side, the evidence of and about the Cynics shows that here too there existed a strong tradition of the subordination of conjugal and consanguineous ties for the sake of a higher good – namely conversion to philosophy. In a much more muted form, Stoicism also placed conversion to philosophy above family ties and filial piety.

Such precedents and analogies are important. They enable us to see that the gospels' summons to discipleship of Christ even at the cost of family ties is neither irrational nor arbitrary. Rather, it has a logic of its own which is thoroughly intelligible against the backdrop of the religious and philosophical traditions surveyed. Thus, it is fair to assume that followers of Christ both before and after Easter were able to make sense of the radical demand to subordinate family ties because they recognized the precedents and analogies which it evoked. It is difficult to say, and it has not been my purpose to show, precisely which precedents and analogies will have been evoked by Jesus' radical demand. Indeed, it is likely that for some in earliest Christianity, the connections with the precedents in the Bible and in Judaism will have been strongest, while for others, the Cynic analogies will have had the most powerful resonance. Such a diversity is evident, certainly, in the interpretation of these 'hard sayings' of Jesus today, whether they are seen in the terms set out by an Otto Betz or a Martin Hengel as the sayings of a Jewish eschatological prophet, on the one hand, or in the terms set out by a Gerd Theissen or a Gerald Downing as the sayings of a vagabond Cynic figure, on the other. If this is so today, it is not unlikely to have been the case from the beginning. The more important point, however, is to establish that the call to follow Jesus at the cost of family ties is best interpreted in the context of traditions in Judaism and the Greco-Roman world which legitimated the subordination of family ties for the sake of a higher good.

In Chapters 3 and 4, we saw that the Gospels of Mark and Matthew both give a surprising degree of attention to the implications of discipleship of Jesus for family and household ties. It is unnecessary to repeat the specific conclusions drawn at the end of each of those chapters. There are, however, several general points worth comment.

First, the prominence of the theme of the subordination of family ties in Mark and Matthew is due, in part at least, to the fundamental question of allegiance and identity posed by Jesus himself and by the evangelists after him. For in the 'follow me' of the gospels, there is an invitation to a new and transcendent allegiance which, on christological and eschatological grounds, relativizes other ties and offers the possibility of a personal identity defined no longer only in terms of what is ascribed according to blood and marriage but also in terms of what is achieved by association with Jesus the Christ.[1] It

---

[1] Interestingly, Nisbet, 'Kinship', 268–9, makes this same distinction between ascribed status and achieved status in his comparison of kinship societies and military societies in ancient Rome.

is because personal identity and status in antiquity – but not only then – were determined so much according to conjugal and con-sanguineous ties that discipleship of Jesus and the call to mission for the sake of the kingdom of God repeatedly pose a challenge to what is otherwise taken for granted. Not that Mark and Matthew, and the Jesus they portray, adopt an anti-social and anti-familial stance, after the Cynic fashion, for example; for filial piety and the bond of marriage still have their place. Rather, the call to follow Jesus places such ties and obligations in a new or different light. Now, identity is a matter of becoming 'like a child' (cf. Mark 10.15 par. Matt. 18.3) in order to enter the kingdom of God; it is a matter also of giving one's primary allegiance to a new solidarity which consists of the eschatological family of Jesus.

Second, the witness of Mark and Matthew to the intra-familial hostility and kin-group-sponsored persecution generated by dis-cipleship of Christ is an important clue to the counter-cultural aspect of early Christian discipleship.[2] To put it in the terms of a growing area of debate and investigation, the 'parting of the ways' between Judaism and Christianity was a parting that began at the most mundane level, that of domestic relations and household ties. It is at this level that the effect of conversion would be felt first, a probability expressed with great rhetorical force in the reply of Jesus to the man who would fulfil first his filial responsibilities: 'Follow me, and leave the dead to bury their own dead' (Matt. 8.22 par. Luke 9.60). It is at this domestic level also that the effect of conversion would be felt most keenly, as a disloyalty and betrayal justifying the most severe retaliation: 'brother will deliver up brother to death, and the father his child, and children will rise against parents and have them put to death' (Mark 13.12 par. Matt. 10.21). This is unlikely to be a mere apocalyptic commonplace. Rather, traditions like this bear witness to the intensity of feelings of hostility within households divided over allegiance to Christ. Of course, none of this is to deny the impact of factors like the conversion of Gentiles; the controversies over circumcision, law and temple; the fall of Jerusalem; and subsequent developments such as the ban on the 'heretics' (*minim*) from the synagogues. It is instead to add a significant domestic dimension to current explanations of the parting of the ways in formative Judaism. In this connection, it is worth recalling that in Mark's story of Jesus, the rejection of Jesus

---

[2] See Grace Jantzen's compelling essay, 'Spirituality'.

by the people as a whole in the second half of the story is anticipated in the first half by his own family's hostility and his rejection in his hometown.

Third, the anxiety about ties of natural kinship to which Mark and Matthew testify is not confined to these two gospels. In the Gospel of Luke, there is unquestionably an amelioration in the portrayal of Jesus' mother and brothers.[3] But there is also a very strong emphasis on missionary discipleship and on the cost of discipleship in relation to ties of family and property (cf. Luke 9.57–62; 12.51–3; 14.12–14, 15–24, 25–33; 18.18–30). Noteworthy, for instance, is the fact that only Luke of the Synoptists includes 'wife' in the list of household members left behind for the kingdom's sake, and that he does so twice (Luke 14.26 diff. Matt. 10.37; Luke 18.29 diff. Mark 10.29). In the Fourth Gospel also, the mother of Jesus is interpreted in a positive light (John 2.1–11; 19.26–7),[4] but there is at the same time a concern to deal with the adverse implications of discipleship for family ties. It is likely, for example, that the story of the man born blind in John 9 expresses something of the cost of discipleship in John's own day: expulsion from the synagogue and rifts between parents and their children (9.18–23).[5] This parallels Jesus' relations with his brothers. Not only are they distinguished from the disciples (2.11–12), but the final editorial comment on them in the gospel is that 'his brothers did not believe in him'

---

[3] The continuity of salvation history, linking Israel, Jesus and the church, is reflected in the positive portrayal of Jesus' family in Luke–Acts. This is quite at odds with the picture in Mark especially (so, too, Brown, *Mary*, 162–77; Fitzmyer, *Theologian*, ch. 3). Mary, for example, is more prominent in Luke than in any other New Testament writing. At the beginning of the gospel, she is the specially favoured woman in Israel chosen by God to give birth to his Son; and at the beginning of the Acts, she is present in the upper room (Acts 1.14). Her presence and witness are a guarantee of the salvific continuity between Israel and the church. It is noteworthy that the brothers of Jesus are in the upper room too. Unlike the Fourth Gospel (see John 7.5), Luke does not depict them as unbelievers. More clearly than in Mark and Matthew, Jesus' mother and brothers are affirmed as 'those who hear the word of God and do it' (see Luke 8.19–21 and parallels); nor are they included among those of Jesus' own *patris* who refuse to acknowledge him (see Luke 4.24 and parallels). Luke wants to present Jesus' brothers, James especially, as worthy leaders of the Jerusalem church and as reliable witnesses, after his ascension, to the truth about him.

[4] See further, Barton, 'Women', 50–1; also, Brown, *Community*, 192–8, noting especially the comment on p. 197: 'If the Beloved Disciple was the ideal of discipleship, intimately involved with that Disciple on an equal plane as part of Jesus' true family was a woman. A woman and a man stood at the foot of the cross as models for Jesus' "own", his true family of disciples.'

[5] See Martyn, *History*.

(7.5). Their unbelief is representative of the unbelief of 'the Jews' and of Jerusalem and Judaea as a whole. The prologue puts it in a nutshell: 'He came to his own home (εἰς τὰ ἴδια), and his own people (οἱ ἴδιοι) received him not' (1.11). Significantly, the children of God according to the Fourth Gospel are those who have been born spiritually 'from above' (ἄνωθεν) (3.3, 7), and the true descendants of 'our father Abraham' are redefined, not as his descendants by blood, but as those who believe in Jesus (8.31–59). Such material as this from Luke and from the Fourth Gospel is directly relevant to further exploration of the theme of discipleship and family ties beyond the scope of the present study.[6]

Finally, it is worth pondering why the concentration in the gospel material on the intra-familial conflict generated by conversion and the subordination of family ties demanded of disciples finds so few echoes in the rest of the New Testament. Certainly, for many readers, the main impression left by the New Testament as a whole is that, far from being disruptive of family ties, the Christian way is socially conservative and strongly supportive of the household order. The evidence for this is strong. For example, there is the teaching of Jesus prohibiting divorce (teaching repeated by Paul, in 1 Cor. 7.10–11); the stories of conversion by household in the Acts of the Apostles; the tendency of Paul to appear radical in his theology but generally pragmatic and conservative in, say, his teaching on women and slaves; the recurrent inclusion of traditional (and hierarchical) Hellenistic *Haustafeln* in the paraenetic sections of the epistolary material of the New Testament; the worries which surface in the Pastorals about the potential threat to patriarchal authority and household stability posed by 'busybody' widows; and the teaching there that women play no part in the public ministry of the word.

Among the possible resolutions of this intriguing 'dislocation' in the New Testament,[7] I would offer the following. First, and most important, because they bear witness to the Jesus of history in a way unparalleled by the other predominantly epistolary material, it is not surprising that the gospels preserve, and are shaped by, traditions which express the eschatological urgency of Jesus' mission and the counter-cultural impact of his summons to discipleship. The demand to subordinate family and household ties for the sake of following Jesus is an integral part of this tradition, as we have seen.

---

[6] See further, Barton, 'Family'.
[7] Schmidt, *Hostility*, 165–7, poses a similar problem in relation to traditions to do with hostility to wealth in the New Testament.

Second, the 'dislocation' is not as clear-cut as may appear at first sight. To put it another way, the move from the gospels to the epistles, from the 'hard sayings' of Jesus to the patriarchal household morality of the Pauline and especially post-Pauline traditions, is not just a matter of charisma and its routinization, or the 'delay' of the parousia, or the socio-ecological transfer from a ministry in rural Palestine to a ministry in Greco-Roman cities and their house-churches. These latter considerations may be important, although it is possible to make too much of them – as if, for example, it were only a choice between charismatic origins and a subsequent 'slide' into routinization, or as if the idea of a 'delay' in the return of the Son of Man could not have been present from the beginning, or as if Palestine were not itself also an area of urbanized Hellenistic civilization. Nor is it appropriate necessarily to bemoan the process of routinization or the transfer to the Hellenistic cities of Asia Minor and the West. Arguably, such developments were responsible for the very preservation and expansion of the Christian movement. Nevertheless, the point needs to be made that, if the gospels contain material which legitimates the subordination of family ties, as we have seen, they contain also material supportive of marital and family ties. Likewise, if the epistles appear in their practical admonition to be predominantly conservative of the social status quo, they also bear witness to ideas and practices subversive of it and in protest against it – whether the liminal apostolic lifestyle of Paul and his co-workers (both male and female); the women who pray and prophesy in the Corinthian house-churches; the practice of household table-fellowship shared between Jews and Gentiles; the prominent 'widows' of the Pastorals; the 'hundred and forty-four thousand' holy warriors who 'have not defiled themselves with women' of the Book of Revelation (14.4); and so on.

So there is a variety of stances on (what might be called) the relation of faith and social structure right across the New Testament corpus. It is not appropriate to polarize the gospels on the one hand and the epistles (and the Apocalypse) on the other. That being said, this study has shown that, in the Gospels of Mark and Matthew at least, the social structure of the household is by no means taken for granted in relation to discipleship of Jesus. On the contrary, discipleship is understood as a priority of the kingdom of God which relativizes all other ties of allegiance and makes possible access to a new solidarity, the eschatological family of 'brothers, sisters and mothers' who do the will of God.

BIBLIOGRAPHY

Achtemeier, 'Reflections' = P. J. Achtemeier, '"He Taught them Many Things": Reflections on Marcan Christology', *CBQ*, 42 (1980), 465–81

'Resources' = P. J. Achtemeier, 'Resources for Pastoral Ministry in the Synoptic Gospels', in E. E. Shelp and R. Sutherland, eds., *A Biblical Basis for Ministry*, Philadelphia, Westminster, 1981, pp. 145–85

Anderson, *Mark* = H. Anderson, *The Gospel of Mark*, London, Oliphants, 1976

Armstrong, *Philosophy* = A. H. Armstrong, *An Introduction to Ancient Philosophy*, 3rd edn, London, Methuen, 1957

Baer, *Male and Female* = R. A. Baer, *Philo's Use of the Categories Male and Female*, Leiden, Brill, 1970

Bailey, 'Matriarchs' = J. L. Bailey, 'Josephus' Portrayal of the Matriarchs', in L. H. Feldman and G. Hata, eds., *Josephus, Judaism, and Christianity*, Leiden, Brill, 1987, pp. 154–79

Balch, *Wives* = D. L. Balch, *Let Wives be Submissive: The Domestic Code in I Peter*, Atlanta, Scholars Press, 1981

'Debates' = D. L. Balch, 'I Cor. 7: 32–35 and Stoic Debates about Marriage, Anxiety and Distraction', *JBL*, 102 (1983), 429–39

'Codes' = D. L. Balch, 'Household Codes', in D. E. Aune, ed., *Greco-Roman Literature and the New Testament*, Atlanta, Scholars Press, 1988, pp. 25–50

Baldry, *Unity* = H. C. Baldry, *The Unity of Mankind in Greek Thought*, Cambridge, Cambridge University Press, 1965

Baltensweiler, 'Die Ehebruchklauseln' = H. Baltensweiler, 'Die Ehebruchklauseln bei Matthäus', *TZ*, 15 (1959), 340–56

Banks, 'Understanding' = R. J. Banks, 'Matthew's Understanding of the Law: Authenticity and Interpretation in Matthew 5:17–20', *JBL*, 93 (1974), 243–62

Jesus = R. J. Banks, *Jesus and the Law in the Synoptic Tradition*, Cambridge, Cambridge University Press, 1975

Community = R. J. Banks, *Paul's Idea of Community*, Sydney, Anzea Books, 1979

Bardis, 'Family' = P. D. Bardis, 'Main Features of the Ancient Hebrew Family', *Social Science*, 38 (1963), 168–83

Barr, 'Language' = J. Barr, 'Biblical Language and Exegesis – How Far does Structuralism Help us?', *KTR*, 7 (1984), 48–52

Barrett, *Background* = C. K. Barrett, *The New Testament Background: Selected Documents*, London, SPCK, 1956

'Eschatology' = C. K. Barrett, 'The Eschatology of the Epistle to the Hebrews', in W. D. Davies and D. Daube, eds., *The Background of the New Testament and its Eschatology*, Cambridge, Cambridge University Press, 1956, pp. 363–93

First Corinthians = C. K. Barrett, *The First Epistle to the Corinthians*, 2nd edn, London, A. & C. Black, 1971

Barth, 'Law' = G. Barth, 'Matthew's Understanding of the Law', in Bornkamm *et al.*, *Tradition*, pp. 58–164

Barton, 'Accommodation' = S. C. Barton, '"All Things to All Men" (1 Corinthians 9:22): The Principle of Accommodation in the Mission of Paul' (BA Honours Dissertation, Macquarie University, 1975)

'Cross' = S. C. Barton, 'Paul and the Cross: A Sociological Approach', *Theology*, 85 (1982), 13–19

'Resurrection' = S. C. Barton, 'Paul and the Resurrection: A Sociological Approach', *Religion*, 14 (1984), 67–75

'Place' = S. C. Barton, 'Paul's Sense of Place: An Anthropological Approach to Community Formation in Corinth', *NTS*, 32 (1986), 225–46

'Paul' = 'Paul, Religion and Society', in J. Obelkevich *et al.*, eds., *Disciplines of Faith: Religion, Patriarchy and Politics*, London, Routledge & Kegan Paul, 1987, pp. 167–77

'Community' = S. C. Barton, 'Community', in R. J. Coggins and J. L. Houlden, eds., *Dictionary of Biblical Interpretation*, London, SCM, 1990, pp. 134–8

'Ethos' = S. C. Barton, 'Ethos', in R. J. Coggins and J. L. Houlden, eds., *Dictionary of Biblical Interpretation*, London, SCM, 1990, pp. 210–12

'Mark' = S. C. Barton, 'Mark as Narrative: The Story of the Anointing Woman (Mk 14:3–9)', *Exp Tim*, 102/8 (1991), 230–4

'Women' = S. C. Barton, 'Women, Jesus and the Gospels', in R. Holloway, *Who Needs Feminism? Men Respond to Sexism in the Church*, London, SPCK, 1991, pp. 32–58

'Child' = S. C. Barton, article on 'Child/Children', in J. Green and S. McKnight, eds., *Dictionary of Jesus and the Gospels*, Downers Grove, Ill., IVP, 1992, pp. 100–4

'Communal Dimension' = S. C. Barton, 'The Communal Dimension of Earliest Christianity', *JTS*, 43/2 (1992), 399–427

'Family' = S. C. Barton, article on 'Family', in J. Green and S. McKnight, eds., *Dictionary of Jesus and the Gospels*, Downers Grove, Ill., IVP, 1992, pp. 226–9

Spirituality = S. C. Barton, *The Spirituality of the Gospels*, London, SPCK, 1992

'Sect' = S. C. Barton, 'Early Christianity and the Sociology of the Sect', in F. Watson, ed., *The Open Text*, London, SCM, 1993, pp. 140–62

Bauer, *Structure* = D. R. Bauer, *The Structure of Matthew's Gospel. A Study in Literary Design*, Sheffield, Almond Press, 1988

Bauer–Arndt–Gingrich, *Lexicon* = W. Bauer, W. F. Arndt, F. W. Gingrich, *A Greek–English Lexicon of the New Testament*, Chicago, University of Chicago Press, 1957

Beare, *Records* = F. W. Beare, *The Earliest Records of Jesus*, Oxford, Blackwell, 1962

'Mission' = F. W. Beare, 'The Mission of the Disciples and the Mission Charge: Matthew 10 and Parallels', *JBL*, 89 (1970), 1–13

Matthew = F. W. Beare, *The Gospel According to Matthew*, New York, Harper & Row, 1981

Beckford, 'Typology' = J. A. Beckford, 'A Typology of Family Responses to a New Religious Movement', *Marriage and Family Review*, 4 (1981), 41–55

Berger, *Amen-Worte* = K. Berger, *Die Amen-Worte Jesu*, Berlin, de Gruyter, 1970

Best, *Temptation* = E. Best, *The Temptation and the Passion: The Markan Soteriology*, Cambridge, Cambridge University Press, 1965

'Mark III' = E. Best, 'Mark III.20, 21, 31–35', *NTS*, 22 (1976), 309–19

'Sayings Collection' = E. Best, 'An Early Sayings Collection', *Nov T*, 18 (1976), 1–16

'Role' = E. Best, 'The Role of the Disciples in Mark', *NTS*, 23 (1976–7), 377–401

'Mark's Use' = E. Best, 'Mark's Use of the Twelve', *ZNW*, 69 (1978), 11–35

Jesus = E. Best, *Following Jesus: Discipleship in the Gospel of Mark*, Sheffield, JSOT, 1981

Mark = E. Best, *Mark: The Gospel as Story*, Edinburgh, T. & T. Clark, 1983

Betz, 'Freedom' = H. D. Betz, 'Paul's Concept of Freedom in the Context of Hellenistic Discussions about Possibilities of Human Freedom', in W. Wuellner, ed., *Colloquy 26 of the Center for Hermeneutical Studies in Hellenistic and Modern Culture*, Berkeley, 1977, pp. 1–13

Betz, 'Krieg' = O. Betz, 'Jesu Heiliger Krieg', *Nov T*, 2 (1957–8), 116–37

'Sinai-Tradition' = O. Betz, 'The Eschatological Interpretation of the Sinai-Tradition in Qumran and in the New Testament', *RQ*, 6 (1967), 89–107

'Jesus in Nazareth' = O. Betz, 'Jesus in Nazareth: Bemerkungen zu Markus 6, 1–6', in G. Müller, ed., *Israel hat dennoch Gott zum Trost*, Trier, Paulinus Verlag, 1978, pp. 44–60

Beyer, 'βλασφημέω' = H. W. Beyer, 'βλασφημέω κτλ', *TDNT*, 1 (1964), 621–5

Black, *Scrolls* = M. Black, *The Scrolls and Christian Origins*, London, Thomas Nelson, 1961

'Violent Word' = M. Black, 'Uncomfortable Words III: The Violent Word', *Exp Tim*, 81 (1970), 115–18

Bornkamm, 'End-Expectation' = G. Bornkamm, 'End-Expectation and Church in Matthew', in Bornkamm *et al.*, *Tradition*, pp. 15–51

'Stilling' = G. Bornkamm, 'The Stilling of the Storm in Matthew', in Bornkamm *et al.*, *Tradition*, pp. 52–7

Bornkamm *et al.*, *Tradition* = G. Bornkamm *et al.*, *Tradition and Interpretation in Matthew*, ET, London, SCM, 1963

Brett, 'Texts' = M. G. Brett, 'Four or Five Things to do with Texts. A Taxonomy of Interpretative Interests', in D. J. A. Clines *et al.*, eds., *The Bible in Three Dimensions*, Sheffield, JSOT Press, 1990, pp. 357–77

Brooks, *Community* = S. H. Brooks, *Matthew's Community: The Evidence of his Special Sayings Material*, Sheffield, JSOT Press, 1987

Brown, *Peter* = R. E. Brown *et al.*, *Peter in the New Testament*, Minneapolis, Augsburg, 1973

  Birth = R. E. Brown, *The Birth of the Messiah*, London, Geoffrey Chapman, 1977

  Mary = R. E. Brown *et al.*, *Mary in the New Testament*, Philadelphia, Fortress, 1978

  Community = R. E. Brown, *The Community of the Beloved Disciple*, London, Geoffrey Chapman, 1979

Brown, 'Representation' = S. Brown, 'The Two-Fold Representation of the Mission in Matthew's Gospel', *ST*, 31 (1977), 21–32

  'Mission' = S. Brown, 'The Mission to Israel in Matthew's Central Section (Mt 9.35–11.1)', *ZNW*, 69 (1978), 73–90

Bultmann, *Tradition* = R. Bultmann, *The History of the Synoptic Tradition*, 2nd edn, ET, Oxford, Blackwell, 1968

Burkill, *New Light* = T. A. Burkill, *New Light on the Earliest Gospel*, Ithaca, Cornell University Press, 1972

  'Blasphemy' = T. A. Burkill, 'Blasphemy: St. Mark's Gospel as Damnation History', in J. Neusner, ed., *Christianity, Judaism and Other Greco-Roman Cults* vol. I, Leiden, Brill, 1975, pp. 51–74

Cameron, 'Male' = A. Cameron, '"Neither Male nor Female"', *Greece and Rome*, Second Series, 27 (1980), 60–8

Campenhausen and Chadwick, *Jerusalem* = H. von Campenhausen and H. Chadwick, *Jerusalem and Rome: The Problem of Authority in the Early Church*, Philadelphia, Fortress, 1966

Casey, 'Jackals' = M. Casey, 'The Jackals and the Son of Man (Matt. 8.20//Luke 9.58)', *JSNT*, 23 (1985), 3–22

Catchpole, 'Divorce' = D. R. Catchpole, 'The Synoptic Divorce Material as a Traditio-historical Problem', *BJRL*, 57 (1974), 92–127

  'Silence' = D. R. Catchpole, 'The Fearful Silence of the Women at the Tomb', *JTSA*, 18 (1977), 3–10

Chadwick, '"All Things"' = H. Chadwick, '"All Things to All Men" (1 Cor. ix.22)', *NTS*, 1 (1954–5), 261–75

  Origen = H. Chadwick, *Origen: Contra Celsum*, Cambridge, Cambridge University Press, 1965

Cohen, 'Boundary' = S. J. D. Cohen, 'Crossing the Boundary and Becoming a Jew', *HTR*, 82 (1989), 13–33

Collins, 'Figures – I' = R. F. Collins, 'The Representative Figures of the Fourth Gospel – I', *Downside Review*, 94 (1976), 26–46

  'Figures – II' = R. F. Collins, 'The Representative Figures of the Fourth Gospel – II', *Downside Review*, 94 (1976), 118–32

Coppens, 'Le Célibat' = J. Coppens, 'Le Célibat essénien', in M. Delcor, ed., *Qumran: Sa piété, sa théologie et son milieu*, Leuven, University Press, 1978, pp. 295–303

Countryman, *Dirt* = L. W. Countryman, *Dirt, Greed and Sex*, London, SCM, 1989

Cousar, 'Eschatology' = C. B. Cousar, 'Eschatology and Mark's *Theologia Crucis*: A Critical Analysis of Mark 13', *Interpretation*, 24 (1970), 321–35

Crosby, *House* = M. H. Crosby, *House of Disciples: Church, Economics and Justice in Matthew*, New York, Orbis, 1988

Crossan, 'Mark' = J. D. Crossan, 'Mark and the Relatives of Jesus', *Nov T*, 15 (1973), 81–113

Culpepper, *Anatomy* = R. A. Culpepper, *The Anatomy of the Fourth Gospel*, Philadelphia, Fortress, 1983

'Story' = R. A. Culpepper, 'Story and History in the Gospels', *Rev Exp*, 81 (1984), 467–78

Davies and Allison, *Matthew I* = W. D. Davies and D. C. Allison, *The Gospel According to Saint Matthew*, vol. I, Edinburgh, T. & T. Clark, 1988

Derrett, 'Teaching' = J. D. M. Derrett, 'The Teaching of Jesus on Marriage and Divorce', in Derrett, *Law in the New Testament*, London, DLT, 1970, pp. 363–88

'Cursing Jesus' = J. D. M. Derrett, 'Cursing Jesus (I Cor. XII. 3): The Jews as Religious "Persecutors"', *NTS*, 21 (1975), 544–54

Dewey, *Debate* = J. Dewey, *Markan Public Debate: Literary Technique, Concentric Structure, and Theology in Mark 2:1–3:6*, Chico, Scholars Press, 1980

Dobschütz, 'Erzählerkunst' = E. von Dobschütz, 'Zur Erzählerkunst des Markus', *ZNW*, 27 (1928), 193–8

'Matthew' = E. von Dobschütz, 'Matthew as Rabbi and Catechist', in Stanton, ed., *Interpretation*, pp. 19–29

Donahue, *Are You the Christ?* = J. R. Donahue, *Are You the Christ? The Trial Narrative in the Gospel of Mark*, Missoula, SBL, 1973

'Neglected Factor' = J. R. Donahue, 'A Neglected Factor in the Theology of Mark', *JBL*, 101 (1982), 563–94

Donaldson, *Mountain* = T. L. Donaldson, *Jesus on the Mountain. A Study in Matthean Theology*, Sheffield, JSOT Press, 1985

Douglas, 'Liminality' = R. C. Douglas, 'Liminality and Conversion in Joseph and Asenath', *JSP*, 3 (1988), 31–42

Douglas, *Symbols* = M. Douglas, *Natural Symbols*, 2nd edn, London, Barrie & Jenkins, 1973

Downing, 'Cynics' = F. G. Downing, 'Cynics and Christians', *NTS*, 30 (1984), 584–93

Jesus = F. G. Downing, *Jesus and the Threat of Freedom*, London, SCM, 1987

Droge, 'Call Stories' = A. J. Droge, 'Call Stories in Greek Biography and the Gospels', in K. H. Richards, ed., *SBL 1983 Seminar Papers*, Chico, Scholars Press, 1983, pp. 245–57

Drury, 'Mark 1' = J. Drury, 'Mark 1.1–15: An Interpretation', in A. E. Harvey, ed., *Alternative Approaches to New Testament Study*, London, SPCK, 1985, pp. 25–36

Dungan, *Sayings* = D. L. Dungan, *The Sayings of Jesus in the Churches of Paul*, Oxford, Blackwell, 1971

Dunn, *Unity* = J. D. G. Dunn, *Unity and Diversity in the New Testament*, London, SCM, 1977

Eagleton, *Theory* = T. Eagleton, *Literary Theory. An Introduction*, Oxford, Blackwell, 1983

Edwards, *Story* = R. A. Edwards, *Matthew's Story of Jesus*, Philadelphia, Fortress, 1985

 'Uncertain Faith' = R. A. Edwards, 'Uncertain Faith: Matthew's Portrait of the Disciples', in F. F. Segovia, ed., *Discipleship in the New Testament*, Philadelphia, Fortress, 1985, pp. 47–61

Elliott, *Home* = J. H. Elliott, *A Home for the Homeless: A Sociological Exegesis of I Peter, Its Situation and Strategy*, London, SCM, 1982

Ellis, 'Jesus' = I. Ellis, 'Jesus and the Subversive Family', *SJT*, 38 (1985), 173–88

Ellis, *Matthew* = P. F. Ellis, *Matthew: his Mind and his Message*, Collegeville, Liturgical Press, 1974

Esler, *Community* = P. F. Esler, *Community and Gospel in Luke–Acts: The Social and Political Motivations of Lucan Theology*, Cambridge, Cambridge University Press, 1987

Feldman, 'Binding' = L. H. Feldman, 'Josephus' Version of the Binding of Isaac', in K. H. Richards, ed., *SBL 1982 Seminar Papers*, Chico, Scholars Press, 1982, pp. 113–28

Fenton, 'Mother' = J. Fenton, 'The Mother of Jesus in Mark's Gospel and its Revisions', *Theology*, 86 (1983), 433–7

Filson, 'Churches' = F. V. Filson, 'The Significance of the Early House Churches', *JBL*, 58 (1939), 105–12

Fiorenza, 'Father' = E. S. Fiorenza, '"You are Not to be Called Father": Early Christian History in Feminist Perspective', *Cross Currents*, 39 (1979), 301–23

 Memory = E. S. Fiorenza, *In Memory of Her*, London, SCM, 1983

Fitzmyer, 'Priority' = J. A. Fitzmeyer, 'The Priority of Mark and the "Q" Source in Luke', in D. G. Miller *et al.*, *Jesus and Man's Hope*, vol. I, Pittsburgh, Pickwick, 1970, pp. 131–70

 'Divorce Texts' = J. A. Fitzmyer, 'The Matthean Divorce Texts and Some New Palestinian Evidence', *TS*, 37 (1976), 197–226

 Luke I–IX = J. A. Fitzmyer, *The Gospel According to Luke I–IX*, New York, Doubleday, 1981

 Luke X–XXIV = J. A. Fitzmyer, *The Gospel According to Luke X–XXIV*, New York, Doubleday, 1985

 Theologian = J. A. Fitzmyer, *Luke the Theologian*, London, Geoffrey Chapman, 1989

Fleddermann, 'Flight' = H. Fleddermann, 'The Flight of a Naked Young Man (Mark 14:51–52)', *CBQ*, 41 (1979), 412–18

Fowler, *Loaves* = R. M. Fowler, *Loaves and Fishes: The Function of the Feeding Stories in the Gospel of Mark*, Chico, Scholars Press, 1981

Fox, *Kinship* = R. Fox, *Kinship and Marriage*, Harmondsworth, Penguin, 1967

Fraade, 'Ascetical Aspects' = S. D. Fraade, 'Ascetical Aspects of Ancient Judaism', in A. Green, ed., *Jewish Spirituality from the Bible through the Middle Ages*, London, SCM, 1989, pp. 253–88

France, 'Teaching' = R. T. France, 'Mark and the Teaching of Jesus', in R. T. France and D. Wenham, eds., *Gospel Perspectives*, vol. I, Sheffield, JSOT, 1980, pp. 101–36

Frankemölle, *Jahwe-Bund* = H. Frankemölle, *Jahwe-Bund und Kirche Christi*, 2nd edn, Münster, Aschendorff, 1974
Freyne, 'Disciples' = S. Freyne, 'The Disciples in Mark and the *Maskilim* in Daniel: A Comparison', *JSNT*, 16 (1982), 7–23
'Preoccupation' = S. Freyne, 'Our Preoccupation with History: Problems and Prospects', *PIBA*, 9 (1985), 1–18
'Vilifying' = S. Freyne, 'Vilifying the Other and Defining the Self: Matthew's and John's Anti-Jewish Polemic in Focus', in J. Neusner and E. S. Frerichs, eds., *'To See Ourselves as Others See us': Christians, Jews, 'Others' in Late Antiquity*, Chico, Scholars Press, 1985, pp. 117–44
Galilee = S. Freyne, *Galilee, Jesus and the Gospels*, Dublin, Gill and Macmillan, 1988
Gager, *Kingdom* = J. G. Gager, *Kingdom and Community. The Social World of Early Christianity*, Englewood Cliffs, N.J., Prentice-Hall, 1975
Gardner and Wiedemann, *Household* = J. F. Gardner and T. Wiedemann, *The Roman Household. A Sourcebook*, London, Routledge, 1991
Garland, *Intention* = D. E. Garland, *The Intention of Matthew 23*, Leiden, Brill, 1979
Garnsey and Saller, *Empire* = P. Garnsey and R. Saller, *The Roman Empire: Economy, Society and Culture*, London, Duckworth, 1987
Geertz, *Interpretation* = C. Geertz, *The Interpretation of Cultures*, New York, Basic Books, 1973
'Centers' = C. Geertz, 'Centers, Kings, and Charisma: Reflections on the Symbolics of Power', in J. Ben-David and T. N. Clark, eds., *Culture and its Creators*, Chicago, University of Chicago Press, 1977, pp. 150–71
Gerhardsson, *Ethos* = B. Gerhardsson, *The Ethos of the Bible*, ET, London, DLT, 1982
Gnilka, *Markus I* = J. Gnilka, *Das Evangelium nach Markus I*, Zurich, Benziger, 1978
Markus II = J. Gnilka, *Das Evangelium nach Markus II*, Zurich, Benziger, 1979
Matthäusevangelium I = J. Gnilka, *Das Matthäusevangelium I*, Freiburg, Herder, 1986
Matthäusevangelium II = J. Gnilka, *Das Matthäusevangelium II*, Freiburg, Herder, 1988
Goulder, *Midrash* = M. Goulder, *Midrash and Lection in Matthew*, London, SPCK, 1974
Graham, 'Prediction' = H. Graham, 'A Passion Prediction for Mark's Community: Mark 13:9–13', *BTB*, 16 (1986), 18–22
Grässer, 'Nazareth' = E. Grässer, 'Jesus in Nazareth', *NTS*, 16 (1969–70), 1–23
Grayston, 'Mark XIII' = K. Grayston, 'The Study of Mark XIII', *BJRL*, 56 (1973–4), 371–87
Guelich, *Sermon* = R. A. Guelich, *The Sermon on the Mount*, Waco, Word Books, 1982
Mark 1 = R. A. Guelich, *Mark 1–8:26*, Waco, Word Books, 1989
Gundry, *Matthew* = R. H. Gundry, *Matthew: A Commentary on his Literary and Theological Art*, Grand Rapids, Eerdmans, 1982

Hadas, *Tacitus* = M. Hadas, ed., *Complete Works of Tacitus*, New York, Random House, 1942

Hammerton-Kelly, 'Attitudes' = R. Hammerton-Kelly, 'Attitudes to the Law in Matthew's Gospel: A Discussion of Matthew 5:18', *BR*, 17 (1972), 19–32

Harder, 'Life Style' = M. W. Harder *et al.*, 'Life Style: Courtship, Marriage and Family in a Changing Jesus Movement Organization', *International Review of Modern Sociology*, 6 (1976), 155–72

Hare, *Persecution* = D. R. A. Hare, *The Theme of Jewish Persecution of Christians in the Gospel According to Matthew*, Cambridge, Cambridge University Press, 1967

Hare and Harrington, 'Disciples' = D. R. A. Hare and D. J. Harrington, '"Make Disciples of all the Gentiles" (Mt. 28. 19)', *CBQ*, 37 (1975), 359–69

Harnack, *Mission* = A. von Harnack, *The Mission and Expansion of Christianity in the First Three Centuries*, vol. I, ET, London, Williams and Norgate, 1908

Harrington, 'Exegesis' = D. J. Harrington, 'Second Testament Exegesis and the Social Sciences: A Bibliography', *BTB*, 18 (1988), 77–85

Hartman, *Prophecy* = L. Hartman, *Prophecy Interpreted. The Formation of Some Jewish Apocalyptic Texts and of the Eschatological Discourse Mark 13 par.*, Lund, Gleerup, 1966

Harvey, 'Forty Strokes' = A. E. Harvey, 'Forty Strokes Save One: Social Aspects of Judaizing and Apostasy', in Harvey, ed., *Alternative Approaches to New Testament Study*, London, SPCK, 1985, pp. 79–96

   Commands = A. E. Harvey, *Strenuous Commands: The Ethic of Jesus*, London, SCM, 1990

Hauck/Kasch, 'πλοῦτος, κτλ' = F. Hauck and W. Kasch, 'πλοῦτος, κτλ', *TDNT*, 6 (1968), 318–32

Held, 'Matthew' = H. J. Held, 'Matthew as Interpreter of the Miracle Stories', in Bornkamm *et al.*, *Tradition*, pp. 165–229

Hengel, *Leader* = M. Hengel, *The Charismatic Leader and his Followers*, ET, Edinburgh, T. & T. Clark, 1981

Hennecke/Schneemelcher, *NT Apocrypha* = E. Hennecke and W. Schneemelcher, eds., *New Testament Apocrypha*, vols. I and II, ET, London, SCM, 1974

Hill, *Matthew* = D. Hill, *The Gospel of Matthew*, London, Oliphants, 1972

Hoehner, *Herod* = H. W. Hoehner, *Herod Antipas*, Cambridge, Cambridge University Press, 1972

Holmberg, *Sociology* = B. Holmberg, *Sociology and the New Testament*, Minneapolis, Fortress, 1990

Hooker, 'Trial' = M. Hooker, 'Trial and Tribulation in Mark XIII', *BJRL*, 65 (1982–3), 78–99

   Message = M. Hooker, *The Message of Mark*, London, Epworth, 1983

Houlden, *Ethics* = J. L. Houlden, *Ethics and the New Testament*, London, Mowbray, 1973

Howell, *Story* = D. B. Howell, *Matthew's Inclusive Story. A Study in the Narrative Rhetoric of the First Gospel*, Sheffield, JSOT Press, 1990

Iersel, 'Community' = B. M. F. van Iersel, 'The Gospel According to St. Mark – Written for a Persecuted Community?', *NTT*, 34 (1980), 15–36
    Mark = B. van Iersel, *Reading Mark*, ET, Edinburgh, T. & T. Clark, 1989
Iersel and Linmans, 'Storm' = B. M. F. van Iersel and A. J. M. Linmans, 'The Storm on the Lake', in T. Baarda *et al.*, eds., *Miscellanea Neotestamentica, 2* (Leiden, Brill, 1978), pp. 17–48
Isenberg, 'Millenarism' = S. R. Isenberg, 'Millenarism in Greco-Roman Palestine', *Religion*, 3 (1975), 26–46
    'Power' = S. R. Isenberg, 'Power through Temple and Torah in Greco-Roman Palestine', in J. Neusner, ed., *Christianity, Judaism and Other Greco-Roman Cults*, part 2, Leiden, Brill, 1975, pp. 24–52
Jantzen, 'Spirituality' = G. M. Jantzen, 'Spirituality and the Status Quo', *KTR*, 13 (1990), 6–10
Jensen, 'Fornication?' = J. Jensen, 'Does *Porneia* Mean Fornication? A Critique of Bruce Malina', *Nov T*, 20 (1978), 161–84
Jeremias, *Theology I* = J. Jeremias, *New Testament Theology* vol. I, ET, London, SCM, 1971
Jonge, 'Jewish Expectations' = M. de Jonge, 'Jewish Expectations about the "Messiah" According to the Fourth Gospel', *NTS*, 19 (1972–3), 246–70
Judge, *Pattern* = E. A. Judge, *The Social Pattern of Christian Groups in the First Century*, London, Tyndale Press, 1960
Keck, 'Ethos' = L. E. Keck, 'Ethos and Ethics in the New Testament', in J. Gaffney, ed., *Essays in Morality and Ethics*, New York: Paulist, 1980, pp. 29–49
    'Ethics' = L. E. Keck, 'Ethics in the Gospel According to Matthew', *Illif Review*, 40/4 (1984), 39–56
Kee, *Community* = H. C. Kee, *Community of the New Age: Studies in Mark's Gospel*, London, SCM, 1977
    'Joseph' = H. C. Kee, 'The Socio-Cultural Setting of Joseph and Asenath', *NTS*, 29 (1983), 394–413
    'Setting' = H. C. Kee, 'The Social Setting of Mark: An Apocalyptic Community', in K. H. Richards, ed., *SBL 1984 Seminar Papers*, Chico, Scholars Press, 1984, pp. 245–55
    'Transformation' = H. C. Kee, 'The Transformation of the Synagogue after 70 C.E.: Its Import for Early Christianity', *NTS*, 36 (1990), 1–24
Kelber, *Kingdom* = W. H. Kelber, *The Kingdom in Mark: A New Place and a New Time*, Philadelphia, Fortress, 1974
    Mark's Story = W. H. Kelber, *Mark's Story of Jesus*, Philadelphia, Fortress, 1979
Kermode, *Ending* = F. Kermode, *The Sense of an Ending*, London, Oxford University Press, 1966
Kilbourne and Richardson, 'Cults' = B. K. Kilbourne and J. T. Richardson, 'Cults Versus Families: A Case of Misattribution of Cause?', *Marriage and Family Review*, 5 (1982), 81–100
Kilpatrick, 'Jesus' = G. D. Kilpatrick, 'Jesus, his Family and his Disciples', *JSNT*, 15 (1982), 3–19

Kingsbury, *Parables* = J. D. Kingsbury, *The Parables of Jesus in Matthew 13*, London, SPCK, 1969
   Structure = J. D. Kingsbury, *Matthew: Structure, Christology, Kingdom*, London, SPCK, 1975
   Matthew = J. D. Kingsbury, *Matthew*, Philadelphia, Fortress, 1977
   'Verb' = J. D. Kingsbury, 'The Verb *Akolouthein* ('To Follow') as an Index of Matthew's View of his Community', *JBL*, 97 (1978), 56–73
   'Peter' = J. D. Kingsbury, 'The Figure of Peter in Matthew's Gospel as a Theological Problem', *JBL*, 98 (1979), 67–83
   'Research' = J. D. Kingsbury, 'The Gospel of Mark in Current Research', *RSR*, 5 (1979), 101–7
   Story = J. D. Kingsbury, *Matthew as Story*, Philadelphia, Fortress, 1986
   'On Following' = J. D. Kingsbury, 'On Following Jesus: The "Eager" Scribe and the "Reluctant" Disciple (Matthew 8. 18–22)', *NTS*, 34 (1988), 45–59
Klassen, 'Musonius' = W. Klassen, 'Musonius Rufus, Jesus, and Paul: Three First-Century Feminists', in P. Richardson and J. Hurd, eds., *From Jesus to Paul*, Ontario, Wilfrid Laurier University Press, 1984, pp. 185–206
Klauck, *Hausgemeinde* = H. J. Klauck, *Hausgemeinde und Hauskirche im Frühen Christentum*, Stuttgart, Katholisches Bibelwerk, 1981
Koenig, *Hospitality* = J. Koenig, *New Testament Hospitality*, Philadelphia, Fortress, 1985
Kraemer, 'Conversion' = R. S. Kraemer, 'The Conversion of Women to Ascetic Forms of Christianity', *Signs*, 6 (1980), 298–307
Lambrecht, *Redaktion* = J. Lambrecht, *Die Redaktion der Markus-Apokalypse*, Rome, Pontifical Biblical Institute, 1967
   'Relatives' = J. Lambrecht, 'The Relatives of Jesus in Mark', *Nov T*, 16 (1974), 241–58
Lampe, 'Discipline' = G. W. H. Lampe, 'Church Discipline and the Interpretation of the Epistles to the Corinthians', in W. R. Farmer, ed., *Christian History and Interpretation*, Cambridge, Cambridge University Press, 1967, pp. 337–61
   'Denial' = G. W. H. Lampe, 'St. Peter's Denial', *BJRL*, 55 (1972–3), 346–68
Lane, *Mark* = W. L. Lane, *The Gospel of Mark*, London, Oliphants, 1974
Leach, *Anthropology* = E. Leach, *Social Anthropology*, London, Fontana, 1982
Lightfoot, *History* = R. H. Lightfoot, *History and Interpretation in the Gospels*, London, Hodder and Stoughton, 1935
   Message = R. H. Lightfoot, *The Gospel Message of Mark*, Oxford, Oxford University Press, 1950
Lincoln, 'Matthew' = A. T. Lincoln, 'Matthew – A Story for Teachers?', in D. J. A. Clines *et al.*, eds., *The Bible in Three Dimensions*, Sheffield, JSOT Press, 1990, pp. 103–26
Lindars, *Son of Man* = B. Lindars, *Jesus Son of Man*, London, SPCK, 1983
Lutz, 'Musonius Rufus' = C. Lutz, 'Musonius Rufus "The Roman Socrates"', *Yale Classical Studies*, 10 (1947), 3–147

Luz, 'Disciples' = U. Luz, 'The Disciples in the Gospel According to Matthew', in Stanton, ed., *Interpretation*, pp. 98–128

Matthew 1–7 = U. Luz, *Matthew 1–7: A Commentary*, Minneapolis, Augsburg, 1989

Matthäus II = U. Luz, *Das Evangelium nach Matthäus (Mt 8–17)*, Zurich, Benziger Verlag, 1990

McArthur, '"Son of Mary"' = H. K. McArthur, '"Son of Mary"', *Nov T*, 15 (1973), 35–58

MacDonald, 'Women' = M. Y. MacDonald, 'Early Christian Women Married to Unbelievers', *SR*, 19 (1990), 221–34

Malbon, 'Fallible Followers' = E. S. Malbon, 'Fallible Followers: Women and Men in the Gospel of Mark', *SEMEIA*, 28 (1983), 29–48

'Jesus' = E. S. Malbon, 'The Jesus of Mark and the Sea of Galilee', *JBL*, 103 (1984), 363–77

'Mark 2:15' = E. S. Malbon, 'TH OIKIA AUTOU: Mark 2:15 in Context', *NTS*, 31 (1985), 282–92

'Disciples' = E. S. Malbon, 'Disciples/Crowds/Whoever: Markan Characters and Readers', *Nov T*, 28 (1986), 104–30

Space = E. S. Malbon, *Narrative Space and Mythic Meaning in Mark*, San Francisco, Harper & Row, 1986

Malherbe, ed., *Epistles* = A. J. Malherbe, ed., *The Cynic Epistles: A Study Edition*, Missoula: Scholars Press, 1977

'Self-Definition' = A. J. Malherbe, 'Self-Definition among Epicureans and Cynics', in B. F. Meyer and E. P. Sanders, eds., *Jewish and Christian Self-Definition*, vol III, London, SCM, 1982, pp. 46–59

Aspects = A. J. Malherbe, *Social Aspects of Early Christianity*, 2nd edn, Philadelphia, Fortress, 1983

Malina, *World* = B. J. Malina, *The New Testament World: Insights from Cultural Anthropology*, London, SCM, 1983

Origins = B. J. Malina, *Christian Origins and Cultural Anthropology: Practical Models for Biblical Interpretation*, Atlanta, John Knox, 1986

'Wealth' = B. J. Malina, 'Wealth and Poverty in the New Testament and its World', *Interpretation*, 41 (1987), 354–67

Manson, *Sayings* = T. W. Manson, *The Sayings of Jesus*, London, SCM, 1957

Teaching = T. W. Manson, *The Teaching of Jesus*, Cambridge, Cambridge University Press, 1963

Marcus, 'Epistemology' = J. Marcus, 'Mark 4:10–12 and Marcan Epistemology', *JBL*, 103 (1984), 557–74

Mystery = J. Marcus, *The Mystery of the Kingdom of God*, Atlanta, Scholars Press, 1986

Marshall, *Luke* = I. H. Marshall, *The Gospel of Luke*, Exeter, Paternoster, 1978

Martin, *Mark* = R. P. Martin, *Mark: Evangelist and Theologian*, Exeter, Paternoster, 1972

Martyn, *History* = J. L. Martyn, *History and Theology in the Fourth Gospel*, 2nd edn, Nashville, Abingdon, 1979

Marxsen, *Mark* = W. Marxsen, *Mark the Evangelist*, Nashville, Abingdon, 1969

May, 'Shame/Honor' = D. M. May, 'Mark 3:20–35 from the Perspective of Shame/Honor', *BTB*, 17 (1987), 83–7

Mays, *Gospels* = J. L. Mays, ed., *Interpreting the Gospels*, Philadelphia, Fortress, 1981

Mealand, *Poverty* = D. L. Mealand, *Poverty and Expectation in the Gospels*, London, SPCK, 1980

Meeks, 'Sectarianism' = W. A. Meeks, 'The Man from Heaven in Johannine Sectarianism', *JBL* 91 (1972), 44–72

   'Androgyne' = W. A. Meeks, 'The Image of the Androgyne: Some Uses of a Symbol in Earliest Christianity', *HR*, 13 (1974), 165–208

   Christians = W. A. Meeks, *The First Urban Christians*, New Haven, Yale University Press, 1983

   Moral World = W. A. Meeks, *The Moral World of the First Christians*, London, SPCK, 1987

Mendelsohn, 'Family' = I. Mendelsohn, 'The Family in the Ancient Near East', *BA*, 11 (1948), 24–40

Metzger, *Commentary* = B. M. Metzger, *A Textual Commentary on the Greek New Testament*, London, United Bible Societies, 1971

Meye, 'Secret' = R. P. Meye, 'Messianic Secret and Messianic Didache in Mark's Gospel', in F. Christ, ed., *Oikonomia*, Hamburg, Herbert Reich, 1967, pp. 57–68

   Jesus = R. P. Meye, *Jesus and the Twelve*, Grand Rapids, Zondervan, 1968

Meyer, 'Challenges' = B. F. Meyer, 'The Challenges of Text and Reader to the Historical-Critical Method', *Concilium*, 1991/1, 3–12

Minear, 'Disciples' = P. S. Minear, 'The Disciples and the Crowds in the Gospel of Matthew', *ATR*, Supplementary Series, no. 3 (1974), 28–44

   Teacher's Gospel = P. S. Minear, *Matthew the Teacher's Gospel*, London, DLT, 1984

Moehring, 'Josephus' = H. R. Moehring, 'Josephus on the Marriage Customs of the Essenes', in A. Wikgren, ed., *Early Christian Origins, in honour of H. R. Willoughby*, Chicago, Chicago University Press, 1961, pp. 120–7

Mohrlang, *Matthew* = R. Mohrlang, *Matthew and Paul: A Comparison of Ethical Perspectives*, Cambridge, Cambridge University Press, 1984

Moloney, 'Matthew 19, 3–12' = F. J. Moloney, 'Matthew 19, 3–12 and Celibacy. A Redactional and Form Critical Study', *JSNT*, 2 (1979), 42–60

Moore, *Criticism* = S. D. Moore, *Literary Criticism and the Gospels*, New Haven, Yale University Press, 1989

Morgan, *Interpretation* = R. Morgan with J. Barton, *Biblical Interpretation*, Oxford, Oxford University Press, 1988

Morgenthaler, *Statistik* = R. Morgenthaler, *Statistik des Neutestamentlichen Wortschatzes*, Zurich, Gotthelf Verlag, 1958

Morosco, 'Matthew 10' = R. E. Morosco, 'Redaction Criticism and the Evangelical: Matthew 10, a Test Case', *JETS*, 22 (1979), 323–31

Moule, *Birth* = C. F. D. Moule, *The Birth of the New Testament*, 3rd edn, New York, Harper & Row, 1982

Neusner, *Politics* = J. Neusner, *From Politics to Piety*, Englewood Cliffs, Prentice-Hall, 1973
   Formative Judaism = J. Neusner, *Formative Judaism. Religious, Historical, and Literary Studies*, Chico, Scholars Press, 1982
   'Two Pictures' = J. Neusner, 'Two Pictures of the Pharisees: Philosophical Circle or Eating Club', *ATR*, 64 (1982), 525–38
   Trends = J. Neusner, *Major Trends in Formative Judaism*, Chico, Scholars Press, 1983
   Judaism = J. Neusner, *Judaism in the Beginning of Christianity*, London, SPCK, 1984
Neyrey, 'Purity' = J. H. Neyrey, 'The Idea of Purity in Mark's Gospel', *SEMEIA*, 35 (1986), 91–128
Nisbet, 'Kinship' = R. A. Nisbet, 'Kinship and Political Power in First Century Rome', in W. J. Cahnman and A. Boskoff, eds., *Sociology and History: Theory and Research*, New York, Free Press, 1964, pp. 257–71
Nock, *Conversion* = A. D. Nock, *Conversion*, Oxford, Oxford University Press, 1961
Orton, *Scribe* = D. E. Orton, *The Understanding Scribe*, Sheffield, Sheffield Academic Press, 1989
Overman, *Gospel* = J. A. Overman, *Matthew's Gospel and Formative Judaism*, Minneapolis, Fortress, 1990
Patte, *Exegesis* = D. Patte, *What is Structural Exegesis?*, Philadelphia, Fortress, 1976
Perrin, *Criticism* = N. Perrin, *What is Redaction Criticism?*, London, SPCK, 1970
   'Use' = N. Perrin, 'The Use of (παρα)διδόναι in Connection with the Passion of Jesus in the New Testament', in E. Lohse, ed., *Der Ruf Jesu und Die Antwort der Gemeinde*, Göttingen, Vandenhoeck and Ruprecht, 1970, pp. 204–12
   'Interpretation' = N. Perrin, 'The Interpretation of the Gospel of Mark', *Interpretation*, 30 (1976), 115–24
Pesch, *Markusevangelium I* = R. Pesch, *Das Markusevangelium I*, Freiburg, Herder, 1977
   Markusevangelium II = R. Pesch, *Das Markusevangelium II*, Freiburg, Herder, 1977
Petersen, *Criticism* = N. R. Petersen, *Literary Criticism for New Testament Critics*, Philadelphia, Fortress, 1978
Pitt-Rivers, *Shechem* = J. Pitt-Rivers, *The Fate of Shechem, or the Politics of Sex*, Cambridge, Cambridge University Press, 1977
Pryke, 'IΔE' = E. J. Pryke, 'IΔE and IΔOY', *NTS*, 14 (1967–8), 418–24
   Style = E. J. Pryke, *Redactional Style in the Markan Gospel*, Cambridge, Cambridge University Press, 1978
Przybylski, *Righteousness* = B. Przybylski, *Righteousness in Matthew and his World of Thought*, Cambridge, Cambridge University Press, 1980
Quesnell, 'Eunuchs' = Q. Quesnell, '"Made Themselves Eunuchs for the Sake of the Kingdom of Heaven" (MT 19, 12)', *CBQ*, 30 (1968), 335–58
Räisänen, *Parabeltheorie* = H. Räisänen, *Die Parabeltheorie im Markusevangelium*, Helsinki, Lansi-Suomi, 1973

Reicke, 'Test' = B. Reicke, 'A Test of Synoptic Relationships: Matthew 10:17–23 and 24:9–14 with Parallels', in W. R. Farmer, ed., *New Synoptic Studies*, Macon, Mercer University Press, 1983, pp. 209–29

Rhoads and Michie, *Mark* = D. Rhoads and D. Michie, *Mark as Story*, Philadelphia, Fortress, 1982

Riches, 'Sociology' = J. Riches, 'The Sociology of Matthew: Some Basic Questions Concerning its Relation to the Theology of the New Testament', in K. H. Richards, ed., *SBL 1983 Seminar Papers*, Chico, Scholars Press, 1983, pp. 259–71

Robinson, *Problem* = J. M. Robinson, *The Problem of History in Mark*, London, SCM, 1957

Russell, *Method* = D. S. Russell, *The Method and Message of Jewish Apocalyptic*, London, SCM, 1964

Safrai, 'Home' = S. Safrai, 'Home and Family', in S. Safrai and M. Stern, eds., *The Jewish People in the First Century*, vol. II, Assen/Amsterdam, Van Gorcum, 1976, pp. 728–92

Sanders, *Jesus* = E. P. Sanders, *Jesus and Judaism*, London, SCM, 1985

Sandmel, *Place* = S. Sandmel, *Philo's Place in Judaism*, New York, KTAV, 1971

  Philo = S. Sandmel, *Philo of Alexandria*, New York, Oxford University Press, 1979

Schmeller, *Brechungen* = T. Schmeller, *Brechungen: Urchristliche Wandercharismatiker im Prisma soziologisch orientierter Exegese*, Stuttgart, Katholisches Bibelwerk, 1989

Schmidt, *Hostility* = T. E. Schmidt, *Hostility to Wealth in the Synoptic Gospels*, Sheffield, JSOT, 1987

Schneider, 'εὐνοῦχος' = J. Schneider, 'εὐνοῦχος', *TDNT*, 2 (1964), 765–8

Schroeder, *Eltern* = H. H. Schroeder, *Eltern und Kinder in der Verkündigung Jesu*, Hamburg, Herbert Reich, 1972

Schürer, *History* = E. Schürer, *The History of the Jewish People in the Age of Jesus Christ (175 B.C.–A.D. 135)*, revised edn edited by G. Vermes, F. Millar, M. Black; Edinburgh, T. & T. Clark, 1973ff.

Schweizer, *Lordship* = E. Schweizer, *Lordship and Discipleship*, ET, London, SCM, 1960

  'Anmerkungen' = E. Schweizer, 'Anmerkungen zur Theologie des Markus', in W. C. van Unnik, ed., *Neotestamentica et Patristica*, Leiden, Brill, 1962, pp. 35–46

  'Observance' = E. Schweizer, 'Observance of the Law and Charismatic Activity in Matthew', *NTS*, 16 (1969–70), 213–30

  Mark = E. Schweizer, *The Good News According to Mark*, ET, London, SPCK, 1971

  'υἱός', = E. Schweizer, 'υἱός κτλ', *TDNT*, 8 (1972), 363–92

  Matthew = E. Schweizer, *The Good News According to Matthew*, ET, London, SPCK, 1976

  'Portrayal' = E. Schweizer, 'The Portrayal of the Life of Faith in the Gospel of Mark', in Mays, ed., *Gospels*, pp. 168–82

  'Church' = E. Schweizer, 'Matthew's Church', in Stanton, ed., *Interpretation*, pp. 129–35

Segal, *Children* = A. F. Segal, *Rebecca's Children: Judaism and Christianity in the Roman World*, Cambridge, Mass., Harvard University Press, 1986

Segovia, *Discipleship* = F. F. Segovia, ed., *Discipleship in the New Testament*, Philadelphia, Fortress, 1985

Senior, *Invitation* = D. Senior, *Invitation to Matthew*, New York, Doubleday, 1977

   Matthew = D. Senior, *What are they Saying about Matthew?*, New York, Paulist, 1983

Smith, *Magician* = M. Smith, *Jesus the Magician*, London, Gollancz, 1978

Sparks, 'Fatherhood' = H. F. D. Sparks, 'The Doctrine of the Divine Fatherhood in the Gospels', in D. E. Nineham, ed., *Studies in the Gospels*, Oxford, Blackwell, 1955, pp. 241–62

Stählin, 'σκάνδαλον' = G. Stählin, 'σκάνδαλον κτλ', *TDNT*, 7 (1971), 339–58

Stanton, *Interpretation* = G. N. Stanton, ed., *The Interpretation of Matthew*, London, SPCK, 1983

   'Judaism' = G. N. Stanton, 'The Gospel of Matthew and Judaism', *BJRL*, 66 (1984), 264–84

   'Origin and Purpose' = G. N. Stanton, 'The Origin and Purpose of Matthew's Gospel: Matthean Scholarship from 1945 to 1980', *ANRW*, 2.25. 3 (1985), 1889–1951

   Gospels = G. N. Stanton, *The Gospels and Jesus*, Oxford, Oxford University Press, 1989

   'Damascus Document' = G. N. Stanton, 'Matthew's Gospel and the Damascus Document in Sociological Perspective', in Stanton, *A Gospel for a New People: Studies in Matthew*, Edinburgh, T. & T. Clark, 1992, pp. 85–107

Stegemann, 'Radicalism?' = W. Stegemann, 'Vagabond Radicalism in Early Christianity? A Historical and Theological Discussion of a Thesis Proposed by Gerd Theissen', in W. Schottroff and W. Stegemann, eds., *God of the Lowly: Socio-Historical Interpretations of the Bible*, ET, New York, Orbis, 1984, pp. 148–68

Stein, 'Methodology' = R. H. Stein, 'The Proper Methodology for Ascertaining a Markan Redaction History', *Nov T*, 13 (1971), 181–98

Steiner, 'Essener' = A. Steiner, 'Warum lebten die Essener asketisch?', *BZ*, 15 (1971), 1–28

Stendahl, *School* = K. Stendahl, *The School of St. Matthew*, 2nd edn, Lund, Gleerup, 1967

   'Quis et Unde?' = K. Stendahl, *'Quis et Unde?* An Analysis of Matthew 1–2', in Stanton, *Interpretation*, pp. 56–66

Stock, 'Divorce Texts' = A. Stock, 'Matthean Divorce Texts', *BTB*, 8 (1978), 24–33

Strecker, *Sermon* = G. Strecker, *The Sermon on the Mount*, ET, Nashville, Abingdon, 1988

Suggs, *Wisdom* = M. J. Suggs, *Wisdom, Christology and Law in Matthew's Gospel*, Cambridge, Mass., Harvard University Press, 1970

Swartley, 'Function' = W. M. Swartley, 'The Structural Function of the Term "Way" (*Hodos*) in Mark's Gospel', in W. Klassen, ed., *The New Way of Jesus*, Kansas, Faith and Life Press, 1980, pp. 73–86

Tannehill, *Sword* = R. C. Tannehill, *The Sword of his Mouth: Forceful and Imaginative Language in Synoptic Sayings*, Philadelphia, Fortress, 1975
'Disciples' = R. C. Tannehill, 'The Disciples in Mark: The Function of a Narrative Role', in Telford, ed., *Interpretation*, pp. 134–57
Taylor, *Mark* = V. Taylor, *The Gospel According to St. Mark*, 2nd edn, London, Macmillan, 1966
Telford, *Barren Temple* = W. R. Telford, *The Barren Temple and the Withered Tree*, Sheffield, JSOT Press, 1980
Interpretation = W. Telford, ed., *The Interpretation of Mark*, London, SPCK, 1985
Theissen, 'Radicalism' = G. Theissen, 'Itinerant Radicalism: The Tradition of Jesus Sayings from the Perspective of the Sociology of Literature', *Radical Religion*, 2 (1975), 84–93 (ET of 'Wanderradikalismus. Literatursoziologische Aspekte der Überlieferung von Worten Jesu im Urchristentum', *ZThK*, 70 (1973), 245–71)
Followers = G. Theissen, *The First Followers of Jesus*, ET, London, SCM, 1978
Setting = G. Theissen, *The Social Setting of Pauline Christianity*, ET, Edinburgh, T. & T. Clark, 1982
Shadow = G. Theissen, *The Shadow of the Galilean*, ET, London, SCM, 1987
Thiering, 'Asceticism' = B. Thiering, 'The Biblical Source of Qumran Asceticism', *JBL*, 93 (1974), 429–44
'Suffering' = B. Thiering, 'Suffering and Asceticism at Qumran, as Illustrated in the Hodayot', *RQ*, 8 (1974), 393–405
Thiselton, 'Structuralism' = A. C. Thiselton, 'Structuralism and Biblical Studies: Method or Ideology?', *Exp Tim*, 89 (1978), 329–35
Thompson, *Advice* = W. G. Thompson, *Matthew's Advice to a Divided Community*, Rome, Biblical Institute Press, 1970
'Reflections' = W. G. Thompson, 'Reflections on the Composition of MT 8:1–9:34', *CBQ*, 33 (1971), 365–88
Tödt, *Son of Man* = H. E. Tödt, *The Son of Man in the Synoptic Tradition*, ET, London, SCM, 1965
Trilling, *Israel* = W. Trilling, *Das Wahre Israel*, 3rd edn, Munich, Kössel-Verlag, 1964
Trocmé, *Formation* = E. Trocmé, *The Formation of the Gospel According to Mark*, ET, London, SPCK, 1975
Tuckett, *Secret* = C. Tuckett, ed., *The Messianic Secret*, London, SPCK, 1983
Turner, 'Usage' = C. H. Turner, 'Marcan Usage: Notes, Critical and Exegetical, on the Second Gospel', *JTS*, 26 (1925), 145–56
Tyson, 'Blindness' = J. B. Tyson, 'The Blindness of the Disciples in Mark', *JBL*, 80 (1961), 261–8
Verhey, *Reversal* = A. Verhey, *The Great Reversal: Ethics and the New Testament*, Grand Rapids, Eerdmans, 1984
Vermes, *Jesus* = G. Vermes, *Jesus the Jew: A Historian's Reading of the Gospels*, London, Collins, 1973
DSSE = G. Vermes, *The Dead Sea Scrolls in English*, 2nd edn, Harmondsworth, Penguin, 1975

Scrolls = G. Vermes, *The Dead Sea Scrolls: Qumran in Perspective*, London, Collins, 1977

Vermes and Goodman, *Essenes* = G. Vermes and M. D. Goodman, *The Essenes According to the Classical Sources*, Sheffield, JSOT Press, 1989

Verner, *Household* = D. C. Verner, *The Household of God: The Social World of the Pastoral Epistles*, Chico, Scholars Press, 1983

Via, *Ethics* = D. O. Via Jr, *The Ethics of Mark's Gospel – In the Middle of Time*, Philadelphia, Fortress, 1985

Wallis, *Salvation* = R. Wallis, *Salvation and Protest*, London: Frances Pinter, 1979

Wansbrough, 'Mark III.21' = H. Wansbrough, 'Mark III.21 – Was Jesus Out of his Mind?', *NTS*, 18 (1972), 295–300

Watson, 'Secrecy' = F. Watson, 'The Social Function of Mark's Secrecy Theme', *JSNT*, 24 (1985), 49–69

Weaver, *Discourse* = D. J. Weaver, *Matthew's Missionary Discourse: A Literary Critical Analysis*, Sheffield, JSOT Press, 1990

Weber, *Jesus* = H. R. Weber, *Jesus and the Children*, Geneva, WCC, 1979

Weber, *Theory* = M. Weber, *The Theory of Social and Economic Organization*, ET, New York, Free Press, 1964

Weeden, *Mark* = T. J. Weeden, *Mark – Traditions in Conflict*, Philadelphia, Fortress, 1971

Wenham, 'Meaning' = D. Wenham, 'The Meaning of Mark III.21', *NTS*, 21 (1975), 295–300

'Structure' = D. Wenham, 'The Structure of Matthew XIII', *NTS*, 25 (1979), 516–22

White, 'Grid and Group' = L. J. White, 'Grid and Group in Matthew's Community: The Righteousness/Honor Code in the Sermon on the Mount', *SEMEIA*, 35 (1986), 61–90

Wiedemann, *Adults* = T. Wiedemann, *Adults and Children in the Roman Empire*, London, Routledge, 1989

Wilken, *Christians* = R. L. Wilken, *The Christians as the Romans Saw Them*, New Haven, Yale University Press, 1984

Wilkins, *Disciple* = M. J. Wilkins, *The Concept of Disciple in Matthew's Gospel*, Leiden, Brill, 1988

Wolff, 'Humility' = C. Wolff, 'Humility and Self-Denial in Jesus' Life and Message and in the Apostolic Existence of Paul', in A. J. M. Wedderburn, ed., *Paul and Jesus: Collected Essays*, Sheffield, JSOT Press, 1989, pp. 145–60

Yarbrough, *Gentiles* = O. L. Yarbrough, *Not Like the Gentiles: Marriage Rules in the Letters of Paul*, Atlanta, Scholars Press, 1985

INDEX OF PASSAGES

243

2.41–51, 67
4.16ff., 89
4.22, 88
4.23, 90n
4.24, 86, 90, 223n
4.25ff., 91
5.1ff., 14n
6.40, 168
6.43–5, 79
8.19–20, 79
8.19–21, 78n, 79, 223n
8.20, 79
8.21,79
9.6, 159
9.10, 159
9.51, 141
9.51–19.46, 141
9.57, 141
9.57–60, 125, 140, 155n
9.57–62, 141, 223
9.58, 146
9.59, 145n, 148
9.59–60, 12
9.59–62, 61
9.60, 41, 148, 222
9.61–2, 140, 141
10.1–16, 142
10.2, 156
10.12, 156
10.17, 159
11.14, 74
11.14–23, 79
11.14–28, 76n
11.15, 74
11.24–6, 79, 181
11.27–8, 71
11.28, 73
11.29–32, 79, 181
11.49, 146
12.2–9, 156
12.10, 76, 76n, 77n
12.49, 166, 167
12.49ff.,
12.49–50, 166n
12.49–56, 167
12.50, 166
12.51, 167
12.51–3, 125, 156, 162, 166, 223
12.52–3, 112n, 168
12.53, 168
13.30, 97
14.12–14, 223
14.15–24, 223
14.20, 198
14.25–33, 223

14.26, 169, 170, 198, 223
14.26–7, 47, 125, 156, 162, 166, 168
14.27, 170
16.18, 195
18.18–30, 223
18.29, 99, 107, 170, 223
22.28–30, 206, 207
22.30, 207
John
1.11, 92, 224
1.45–6, 88n
2.1–11, 223
2.11–12, 223
3.3, 224
3.7, 224
4.44, 86, 90
6.42, 88
7.5, 223n, 223–4
7.15, 88n
7.25–31, 88n
7.40–4, 88n
8.13–20, 88n
8.31–59, 224
9, 223
9.18–23, 223
9.24–34, 88n
13–17, 117n
16.2, 160
19.25–7, 67
19.26–7, 223
Acts
1.14, 223n
1.15–26, 139
4.36–7, 8n, 106
8.9–24, 8n
8.26–40, 8n, 192
9.1–19, 8n
10.1–48, 8n
10.36, 175
13.6–12, 8n
15.20, 196
15.29, 196
16.12–15, 8n
16.25–34, 8n
17.12, 8n
17.34, 8n
20, 117n
22.4–16, 8n
26.9–18, 8n

Romans
11.20, 92n
1 Corinthians
5, 197
7, 5

INDEX OF AUTHORS